*Using Aspect-Oriented
Programming for
Trustworthy Software
Development*

Using *Aspect-Oriented Programming for Trustworthy Software Development*

VLADIMIR O. SAFONOV

WILEY-
INTERSCIENCE

A JOHN WILEY & SONS, INC., PUBLICATION

Library of Congress Cataloging-in-Publication Data:

Safonov, V. O. (Vladimir Olegovich)
   Using aspect-oriented programming for trustworthy software development / Vladimir O. Safonov.
       p. cm.
   Includes bibliographical references and index.
   ISBN 978-0-470-13817-5 (cloth)
   1. Aspect-oriented programming. 2. Computer software—Development.
3. Computer software—Reliability. I. Title.
   QA76. 64. S253 2008
   005. 1—dc22

                                                                    2007041615

10 9 8 7 6 5 4 3 2 1

Contents

Preface

This book is devoted to the basic concepts and generic relationships of two new software engineering and computer science areas: trustworthy computing (TWC) and aspect-oriented programming (AOP).

These two disciplines are now so popular, even "fashionable," that many software students and experts are looking for more information about them. Both TWC and AOP and, in particular, their relationship, have not yet been described sufficiently in the scientific literature up to now, and this gap needs to be filled. The reason for the current status lies in the fact that both AOP and TWC are still quite novel even though their foundations were laid long ago, and the worldwide software engineering community has not yet acquired enough experience in these areas. The book should be very helpful in this regard.

The main principle behind the book is that AOP, used properly, can be beneficial in trustworthy software development, due to the fact that the two are related generically. To analyze, demonstrate, and teach using AOP for TWC, I take typical TWC tasks, such as security checks, in and out conditions, and multithreaded safety and show how they can be implemented using AOP, since I believe that in terms of AOP, most TWC tasks are *cross-cutting concerns* and, consequently, can and should be implemented as *aspects*. In the text I describe my team's latest results, analyzing my 30 years' experience in research, development, and university teaching in the areas of software engineering and computer science, and my 15 years' experience collaborating with leading global software companies: Microsoft Research, Sun Microsystems, and others.

In particular, I describe the results of two research and educational projects supported by Microsoft Research:

- *Aspect.NET* [1–6]: an AOP framework for the Microsoft.NET platform based on Microsoft Phoenix [7] and Microsoft Visual Studio.NET 2005. Aspect.NET is based on our approach to AOP as well as our AOP framework. Aspect.NET already has a number of users in 16 countries, including the United States, Canada, and other countries in the Americas, Europe, Asia, and the C.I.S. We hope the book will contribute to extending the Aspect.NET user community.
- *TrustSPBU.NET* [8]: a set of educational materials on advanced secure software engineering and trustworthy computing, Microsoft.NET and C#, compilers, software engineering and compiler development, and my related project, SPBU.NET [9], used as the foundation for TrustSPBU. NET. The curriculum materials of these two projects, available on Microsoft Developer's Network Academic Alliance Curriculum Repository Web site, have already attracted the attention of both students and software experts.

For all examples of trustworthy software design and code included in the book, I use our Aspect.NET framework. I consider the basics of Aspect.NET architecture, its advantages compared to other AOP tools, its functionality, and examples of trustworthy application development using Aspect.NET. The book is not limited to Microsoft technologies, although we do appreciate using such advanced toolkits as Visual Studio.NET and Phoenix. We consider general principles and other software technologies and tools applicable to using AOP for trustworthy software development, such as Java and AspectJ [10], based on Java, currently the most widely used AOP instrument.

Chapter 5 is devoted to teaching, but actually, the style used to present all the material in the book is based on the ERATO teaching paradigm [9], on which I have based my university teaching for many years. ERATO is an acronym for *experience, retrospective, analysis, theory, oncoming perspectives.* Erato is the name of the muse of romantic poetry in ancient Greek mythology. The ERATO teaching paradigm can be summarized as follows:

- *Experience:* describing my long-term commercial and research software project experience in my courses. In particular, in 1992–2002 I led St. Petersburg Sun projects in the compiler development and Java technology areas. In 2002 I started working with Microsoft Research on the Aspect.NET project, in 2003 on the Phoenix compiler development tool, in 2004 on SPBU.NET, and in 2006 on TrustSPBU.NET educational projects. Such types of things are of deep interest to students since they can judge how closely coupled academic learning and teaching activity can be to advanced research and tools and working with leading companies, so it helps to better illustrate concepts and principles to be taught. They can participate personally in our projects to get their own experience.

- *Retrospective:* considering the historical background of each topic being taught since its early origin, for deeper understanding of fundamental concepts by the students. For example, I consider the concepts of *concurrency* and *multithreading* since Dijkstra's 1960s pioneering work on semaphores; *generics* since Liskov's CLU language *parametrized types* in early 1970s (rather than since 2004–2005, when generics were implemented in Java 1.5 and C# 2.0).

- *Analysis:* making critical and comparative analysis of the most important related and mutually influenced concepts and technologies when teaching them. For example, I analyze the Microsoft.NET platform, compared to the competitive Java platform, and explain the fundamental reasons why .NET is more general and open-style. On the other hand, I show to students that .NET technologies have a backward influence on Java. I believe that in this way students can better understand the dialectic nature of software engineering.

- *Theory:* formulating and explaining the essence of theoretical definitions, justifications, known theorems, and issues relevant to the topic being taught. In particular, when teaching the concept of data type, I make a review of the techniques of formal specifications of abstract data types: Hoare's theoretical papers on data types published in the 1960s and 1970s; papers by Scott on type theory; and pioneering papers on initial and final algebra semantics of abstract data types by the ADJ group (1970s), resulting in algebraic data type specification languages OBJ and SDL.

- *Oncoming perspectives:* explaining the vision of future progress in the topic being taught by a variety of software experts.

The book is targeted primarily at undergraduate and graduate students who would like to study TWC and AOP, but it will also be useful for software managers, computer scientists, software engineers, and university teachers in the area, especially those working with and teaching Microsoft.NET. For readers who want to learn the basics of trustworthy computing and its application to modern software development platforms such as .NET and Java, Chapter 2 will be appropriate. Chapter 3 focuses on readers interested primarily in aspect-oriented programming and Aspect.NET. Those specifically interested in applying AOP to develop trustworthy software are directed to Chapter 4. Chapter 5 will be of most interest to those who wish to teach TWC and AOP and related areas of software engineering.

For more information, the reader is directed to the book and to the Aspect. NET Web site: www.aspectdotnet.org. The site contains all the examples used in the book, other material selected from the book, the Aspect.NET framework with documentation, and data on other publications related to Aspect.NET.

Please send your questions, remarks, suggestions, and proposals regarding Aspect.NET or my book directly to my e-mail address: *v_o_safonov@mail.ru.*

ACKNOWLEDGMENTS

First, I would like to thank my colleagues from Microsoft: Igor Agamirzian, Marco Combetto, Peter Drayton, Van Eden, Kang Su Gatlin, Alexander Gavrilov, Alexander Gil (who was my doctoral student), John Larcheveque, John Lefor, Mark Lewin, Vassily Lutsarev, Shahrokh Mortazavi, John Spencer, Andrey Terekhov, Damien Watkins, Yan Xu, Romualds Zdebskis, and many others. They have provided a lot of support to me and my team.

Thanks also to my teachers from a variety of universities and companies whose ideas, papers, education, and attention have had a great influence on my work, results, professional views, and interests: Professors Alfred Aho (Columbia University), Igor Bratchikov, Boris Martynenko and Joseph Romanovsky (St. Petersburg University), Gregory Tseytin (St. Petersburg University, now with IBM), and Niklaus Wirth (ETH Zürich).

Special thanks to Professor Gregor Kiczales, the inventor of AOP, for fruitful e-mail discussions that helped me to understand the essence of his approach more deeply.

I would like to memorialize two people whose papers inspired my professional work: corresponding member of the Russian Academy of Sciences Professor Svyatoslav Lavrov, my scientific advisor, the developer of the first ALGOL compiler in the Soviet Union in the early 1960s, and the author of many books and projects well known in our country; and Professor Adolph Fouxman of Rostov University, the author of the vertical cut technology (1979), predecessor of aspect-oriented programming, and initiator of pioneering projects on automated program synthesis, whose software engineering papers of 1970s look quite contemporary.

Finally, I would like to thank deeply my Aspect.NET implementation team: my doctoral students Dmitry Grigoryev, the developer of the Aspect.NET weaver using Microsoft Phoenix [7]; Mikhail Gratchev, the developer of the Aspect.NET framework and its integration in Visual Studio.NET 2005 and Aspect.NET installer; and Alexander Maslennikov, the developer of the Aspect.NET.ML metalanguage converter to C#. They have not only developed several releases of Aspect.NET but have also proposed and implemented a lot of their own bright ideas to improve and enhance Aspect.NET architecture and functionality. The results of their work should be considered an inherent part of my book. Also, thanks to my graduate students Oleg Romashin and Ruslan Mukhanov, who helped me to develop AspectRotor, a version of Aspect.NET for SSCLI (Rotor), and to Anna Kogay, who developed a number of useful aspect examples of using Aspect.NET for the design-by-contract technology used in the book.

Last but not least, my thanks to all Aspect.NET users and supporters.

1

Introduction

In this introductory chapter we explain why aspect-oriented programming is so closely related to trustworthy software development, and review the organization of the book in detail.

1.1 THE ROLE OF ASPECT-ORIENTED PROGRAMMING IN TRUSTWORTHINESS

Each software product is expected by its users to be trustworthy. But the concept of software trustworthiness consists of many parts and aspects, as we'll see later. Intuitively, this concept has evolved since the early days of programming. Thanks to Microsoft's announcement in 2002 to follow and support the *trustworthy computing initiative*, software experts are paying much more attention to the task of making trustworthy computing a more systematic discipline.

It is very important to understand that viewing particular software as trustworthy or nontrustworthy generally evolves over time and may also depend on the environment and the target platform. Software considered to be trustworthy at one moment or in one environment may demonstrate nontrustworthy behavior at another moment or after porting to another platform or environment. Let's consider a real example that occurred in the 1980s with

Using Aspect-Oriented Programming for Trustworthy Software Development,
By Vladimir O. Safonov
Copyright © 2008 John Wiley & Sons, Inc.

one of our university's mathematical packages written in FORTRAN that we were porting from IBM 360 mainframes to Soviet Elbrus [11] computers with tagged architecture. The package seemed to work fine and to deliver trustworthy results for a few years while running on an IBM 360. During the first run of the package on Elbrus, an interrupt occurred and a runtime error ("invalid operand") was detected by hardware. It appeared that some noninitialized variable was used in the package. It is intriguing that the package worked reasonably on an IBM 360, but porting to a new, more secure hardware architecture obviously contributed to making the software more trustworthy, by detecting and fixing the bug immediately.

As another example, let's consider a library, part of a legacy code that works well and is trustworthy in a single-threaded environment but needs to be updated to become multithreaded (MT) safe. The library may contain static variables and other implementation specifics that can preclude its trustworthiness in a multithreaded environment, so to achieve MT safety, its code needs to be updated systematically by, at a minimum, adding calls to synchronization primitives (semaphores, mutexes, etc.) before and after the operations that retrieve or update global resources shared by the library's functions.

There are many more other situations in which the existing code should be updated to become more trustworthy. Due to the evolving nature of hardware and software platforms, networking and operating system (OS) environments, and the tasks to be solved by software, most software products cannot be developed to be trustworthy "once and for all." So a typical task in modern software development is to update software to improve its trustworthiness in some sense or in some relation. Such a software update should be made safely and systematically, according to an explicit and consistent plan, using special tools adequate to such a task, preferably with the help of formal methods such as specification and verification.

It is very important to realize that the task of updating software to attain more trustworthiness generically has a "cross-cutting" nature. For example, to insert synchronizing actions into library code modules, it is necessary to locate in its code the scattered fragments responsible for updating or retrieving global shared resources, and then insert synchronizing actions before and after them. In other words, what is needed is to cross-cut the existing code for the purpose of adding tangled (but logically related) fragments responsible for synchronization.

All of the above can be achieved using aspect-oriented programming (AOP) [12]. AOP is a new discipline targeted to systematic software updates using a new type of modular units: *aspects*, whose code fragments are *woven* into the target application according to explicit *weaving rules* provided in the aspect definition. The main goal of AOP is to handle *cross-cutting concerns* [13]: ideas, considerations, or algorithms whose implementation, inherently, by its nature, cannot be implemented by a generalized procedure: a new function, class, method, or hierarchy of such related entities. Implementing a cross-cutting concern requires weaving (injecting) tangled code fragments into existing code modules. Typical cross-cutting concerns formulated by the classicists of AOP are *security, synchronization*, and *logging*—all related to trustworthy computing. So, generally speaking, we can state that typical cross-cutting concerns are related to trustworthy software development. In this book you'll find practical confirmation of this important principle, and practical recipes for how to use AOP for trustworthy software development, based on many examples. More precise definitions of trustworthy computing (TWC) are provided in Chapter 2, and of AOP, in Chapter 3.

1.2 HISTORICAL BACKGROUND AND PERSONAL EXPERIENCE

The foundation of trustworthy software development was laid out in the 1960s and 1970s, when programming became a systematic discipline, due to pioneering work by the classicists of *structured programming* (C. Boehm, J. Jacopini, E. Dijkstra, N. Wirth), *modular programming* (D. Parnas, G. Myers), and *abstract data types* (C. A. R. Hoare, F. Morris, D. Scott, J. Goguen, et al.).

In the late 1960s, the problem of "bowl-of-spaghetti" programs was investigated [14,15]. The criticism of such programs was that the code "overpatched" with *goto* statements—added quickly to patch existing code. As a result, programs became nontrustworthy and even unreadable. To correct this situation, the discipline of *structured programming* [16,17] was proposed. Structured programming is based on using a limited set of syntactically and semantically clean constructs: a succession of statements, *if* and *while* statements, without the use of *goto*, can therefore be considered the first attempt to make the code and the process of its development more trustworthy. An inherent part of structured programming is *stepwise refinement*: an incremental top-down software design and implementation technique using Pascal-like *pseudocode* to design each node of the program structure tree. Structured programming and stepwise refinement have played a historical role and are still being used in many projects, especially for rapid prototyping. Structured programming has many advantages: It provides a comfortable way to develop a software prototype quickly; it makes it possible to design and implement parts of the code in parallel; it enables clear control structure in the resulting code (which, in this sense, appears to get more trustworthy). However, structured programming has some limitations and shortcomings: It is suitable for statements (executable constructs of the code) but unsuitable for use in designing and developing definitions and declarations; it is not comfortable to use to make changes in a program; it is not well suited to error and exception handling; and it may cause the development of low-quality code since it can target highly skilled developers to design high-level pseudocode and have nonexperienced programmers make all implementations (i.e., actually produce the resulting code for the software product).

Modular programming [18,19] is another important step in trustworthy software development. It is intended for structural decomposition of a program into logically independent parts: *modules*. It is very important to understand that from a modular programming viewpoint, parts of the module interface are not only its name, arguments, and result types, but also a list of possible *exceptional conditions* of its possible abnormal termination. What is especially important for TWC is that trustworthy checks and exceptional conditions can be tied to modules. In terms of modular programming, TWC principles can be formulated as follows: *Each module and all module relationships should be trustworthy*. For that purpose, the module should self-check its pre- and post conditions, handle all internal exceptions, and explicitly export its public exceptions to be processed by its users. Ideally although it has not yet been achieved in most software projects), the trustworthiness of the module should be proved by its formal verification, based on some form of its formal specification. The main shortcoming of classical modular programming [19] is lack of support for *cross-cutting concerns*. In traditional meaning, a module is visible and accessible from the rest of the application via its interface only. Implementation of the module is hidden, and it is not possible to change it from the outside in any way: in particular, to inject any new code into its implementation. However, as we have seen, the tasks of trustworthy software development require injecting new code (e.g., for synchronization or for security checks) into the implementation of existing modules. From a conventional modular programming viewpoint, it may be considered as a violation of modular programming principles. But since support for systematic code injections is a practical need of trustworthy software development, the concepts and views of modular programming have been augmented to justify systematic ways to inject or change tangled code. AOP is one approach to achieving this goal.

Abstract data types (ADTs) [20,21] represent the third classical approach to making software development more trustworthy, based on defining a set of operations on some data structure or collection (tree, list, graph, stack, etc.) as a new abstract data type whose implementation is *encapsulated* (hidden) inside the ADT definition. From the most general viewpoint, an inherent part of an ADT is its *formal specification*, which allows us formally to *verify* the correctness of its implementation (i.e., to prove that the implementation of the ADT corresponds to its formal specifications). Unfortunately, most existing languages, tools, and environments that include ADT mechanisms do not support formal specification and verification, which makes applying the discipline and concepts of ADT less trustworthy than expected. However, two very important ideas that the concept of ADT has brought to trustworthy software development are encapsulation of the concrete representation of the data type and exclusive use of *abstract operations* (implemented via methods, functions, macros, etc.) to handle objects of the data type without "intrusion" into its representation by straightforward use of its concrete elements.

So, to summarize, the concepts of structured programming, modular programming, and abstract data types, together with the related formal methods, contributed a lot to trustworthy software development of executable parts of programs: statements (structured programming), program architecture by its decomposition into modules (modular programming), and operations on complicated data types and structures (abstract date types). But all of these approaches lack the support of cross-cutting concerns—hence the important role of AOP, which provides such support.

As for object-oriented programming (OOP), it has been playing an outstanding role in the rapid development of software, but its key principles and mechanisms, inheritance and class hierarchy, are not always trustworthy. As shown in analytical and critical papers on OOP, it has many pitfalls [22]. The most serious of them is *conceptual explosion*, an immediate consequence of implementation inheritance. By inheriting an exponentially growing number of classes and methods, an OOP programmer is likely to develop nontrustworthy and unreadable code, since it uses hundreds of implicitly inherited features implemented by other programmers, whose semantics is often unclear and not well documented. Nevertheless, OOP constructs are comfortable for tying various features to classes and methods: in particular, security checks and other TWC support code.

As for security and information protection, one of the earliest papers on this subject seems to be that if Saltzer and Schroeder [23], dating back over 30 years, which considers basic concepts and principles related to information protection and access rights to information. Trustworthy computing issues related to sharing and scheduling common resources were studied in the 1960s and 1970s, primarily in relation to operating systems. New types of security issues arose later, due to evolution of networking, the Internet, and the Web.

My own experience of trustworthy software development began in the 1970s. It happened that the first hardware and OS platform I used for developing research and commercial software projects was not IBM or PDP, but Elbrus [11], a Soviet family of computers whose architecture was inspired by the ideas of Iliffe's paper [24] and Burroughs 5000/5500/6700/7700 hardware architecture. Elbrus software, including the operating system, compilers, and application packages, was developed from scratch by thousands of highly skilled Soviet software engineers in a specialized high-level language. I was the project lead of the St. Petersburg University team, which in a few years developed Pascal, CLU, Modula-2 compilers, and FORTH-83, SNOBOL-4, and REFAL [25] interpreters for Elbrus. These projects became my first school of trustworthy computing. Elbrus architecture was based on *tags*, hardware-supported runtime data-type information attached to every word of memory. Another important principle of Elbrus was its support of basic features of high-level languages and their implementation in hardware. There was no assembler language in Elbrus in the traditional meaning of the term. Instead, all its system software, including the OS and compilers, was developed in EL-76 [26], a dynamically typed high-level language whose syntax was close to that of ALGOL 68. It is interesting now, from a modern TWC viewpoint and with our .NET experience, to analyze Elbrus architecture. At first, what was helpful for TWC was its tagged architecture, a kind of dynamic typing. An example of how it helps has already been given. Hardware-supported dynamic typing helps to detect the use of noninitialized variables, due to the special *empty* tag representing noninitialized data detected by each instruction (e.g., arithmetic operation) and causing an interrupt. A tagging mechanism prevents the spread of nontrustworthy results over the program execution data flow. It also helps to protect memory: a special *descriptor* tag marks each address word that points to an array, and contains its initial address and size. So no violation of array bounds, no buffer overrun [27] security flaws, and no C-like address arithmetic operations (which often cause TWC issues) are possible with tagged architecture. So such architecture looks more trustworthy and more secure than the traditional ×86 architecture. However, tagged architecture requires substantial overhead for analyzing the tags of the operands by hardware during execution of each instruction. For that reason it is not often used in modern hardware.

When I switched from Elbrus to using an IBM PC with MS-DOS and Turbo Pascal in the late 1980s, I was enjoying a very comfortable and trustworthy integrated development environment (IDE). I was surprised, however, that the IDE did not, by default, detect bugs such as array indexing out of bounds, which is especially dangerous since it may cause buffer overrun flaws. To detect indexing out of bounds, the user needed explicitly to switch on a special code generation option that generated much less efficient code, whereas tagged architecture would catch indexing out of bounds at once. So, in a sense, a new IDE working on a traditional hardware platform appeared to be less trustworthy than "good old" tagged architecture. For me, that was a useful lesson in trustworthy computing.

Much later, in the mid-1990s, due to my work with Sun, I became acquainted with Java, and in the early 2000s, due to collaboration with Microsoft Research, started working with Microsoft.NET. I was pleasantly surprised to discover in those new software technologies a "new incarnation" of the ideas of dynamic typing that became the basis of Java and .NET trustworthiness, in the form of managed code execution using metadata. Dynamic typing in Java and .NET provide a basis for security checks, runtime type checking, array bounds checking, and a lot of other elements of trustworthy code execution. It would not be realistic to use hardware-supported tags for TWC purposes in modern computing, due to modern software requirements of scalability, flexibility, cross-platform nature, and network- and Web-awareness. Instead, the two related technologies—common intermediate code (Java bytecode and MSIL) based on postfix notation, and efficient just-in-time compilation of that intermediate code to native code—are used in Java and .NET to support type-safe execution.

I became acquainted with the principles and concepts of AOP in 2001 through an article by Elrad et al. [28]. Reading the article made me realize that like many other experienced software developers I had intuitively used and developed principles similar to AOP throughout my professional life, although without explicit use of AOP terminology or adequate tools. For example, a typical everyday software engineering task is to correct or extend some functionality in an existing application: either your own or that of other developers (which can be much more difficult). To do that you should first locate the implementation of the functionality being considered within the application code and then modify and enhance it. Typically, implementation of some functionality consists of a related group of modules (class hierarchies, libraries of functions, etc.) and a set of scattered code fragments (i.e., definitions and calls of modules) in different parts of the application code. It may be very tricky and time consuming to locate and identify all of them unless the original developers of the application have used some technologies and software processes to enable quick search of any functionality implemented in the code. In terms of AOP, this task is referred to as *aspect mining* [29], extracting aspects from non-aspect-oriented programs. If there are no adequate tools and technologies to help software developers locate some functionality in existing applications, software engineers responsible for code maintenance have to explore the code "by hand" (or using simple text-searching tools such as *grep*) and often fail to perform the task completely (e.g., forget to find some of the scattered code fragments implementing the functionality). This causes more bugs and security flaws in the new version of the application. This is just one example of why AOP can be so helpful, since it supports aspect mining. In terms of AOP, the task of updating the scattered functionality can be considered as modifying the aspect and its join points within the target application. In AOP terms, adding functionality is considered as weaving the aspect that implements it.

In the 1980s, before the advent of AOP tools, my team used *TIP technology* [11], an enhancement of modular programming and abstract data types, to make the process of developing, self-documenting, and updating the code more systematic. Speaking in modern terms, TIP technology was based on a set of design and code templates using a predefined scheme of *abstraction levels* and *vertical cuts* (groups of operations). The application (e.g., a compiler) was designed as a related set of *technological instrumental packages* (TIPs), each responsible for implementing a set of abstract operations on a data structure (e.g., a table of definitions in the compiler). Each TIP was designed and implemented according to its predefined and recommended design template, typically (for compiler development projects) consisting of three abstract layers (in bottom-up order): *representation level, definition level*, and *concept level*; and four vertical cuts: *creation/deletion interface, access interface, update interface*, and *output interface*. Although for any other area (e.g., operating systems) the set of TIPs and their layers would be different, the principles of using the predefined "two-dimensional" horizontal layering and vertical operation grouping scheme would be the same. The users of TIPs (any other modules of the application) were granted access only to the TIP upper abstract (concept) layer, which supported adequate high-level abstract operations such as iterators and associative search. The code of each TIP was self-documented and self-explanatory, so that our colleagues from other institutions working on related compiler projects used the code of our TIP interfaces as working documentation. Each operation of each TIP had a comfortable mnemonic name that helped quickly to locate all its uses by ordinary text-searching tools such as *grep*. This discipline of programming helped us not only to develop trustworthy and bug-free code, but also to update or enhance it quickly and trustworthily, since due to use of such technology, each code modification could be represented as a simple sequence of steps to update each abstract layer and each vertical cut. Much more detail on the TIP technology is provided in my book on Elbrus [11]. To summarize, our TIP technology was an important step leading to AOP and an understanding of its importance to trustworthy code development. Compared to AOP, what was *not* specified in a TIP (but what *is* specified in aspect specifications in modern AOP) is an explicit set of *weaving rules* on how to apply a TIP's operations and where to insert its calls. Although we provided clear comments to the code, we didn't use specific weaving tools and we inserted or modified the operations' calls by hand. Nevertheless, our TIP technology experience was another school of trustworthy software development. Our latest experiences and results with AOP are described in this book.

1.3 ORGANIZATION OF THE BOOK

The structure of the book is very simple. The chapters are not strongly interdependent, so any chapter can be read or studied separately.

In this chapter, our primary goal has been to activate the readers' interest and draw their attention to the problems considered in the book, to provide an initial understanding of them, and to illustrate them by examples and the results of my team's long experience with software development.

In Chapter 2 we explain the history, essence, and modern aspects of trustworthy computing as a discipline. We see how TWC concepts originated, developed, and were brought to the attention of academia and industry by Microsoft. Microsoft's TWC initiative and its four pillars—*security, privacy, reliability*, and *business integrity*—are explained and analyzed. Finally, we consider the implementation of TWC ideas and principles in the two latest software development platforms, Java and .NET.

Chapter 3 is devoted to aspect-oriented programming in whole and as related to our AOP framework for .NET, Aspect.NET in particular. We consider the history and basics of AOP, review both existing approaches to it and AOP tools, prevent the reader from being caught by some AOP "pitfalls," and in the main focus of the chapter, consider in detail the principles of our approach to AOP and its implementation for .NET, our Aspect.NET framework, together with its advantages, features, use and perspectives.

Chapter 3 should be read before Chapter 4, since the latter describes principles and uses of AOP for trustworthy software development using Aspect. NET. A number of typical TWC-related tasks—such as synchronization, security checks, and design-by-contract checks—are considered in Chapter 4, and recipes and examples are given on how to implement solutions to those tasks using AOP and our Aspect.NET framework. Following the traditions of the Wiley series of which this book is a part, a discussion of the use of quantitative analysis to improve productivity and efficiency is a primary focus. Applying AOP for TWC, we prove that solutions using Aspect.NET are as runtime efficient as those developed by hand, using performance tests. We provide a self-assessment of Aspect.NET using SQFD and ICED-T models. AOP and its roles are compared to some other popular approaches, such as agile software development. The main conclusion in Chapter 4 is that AOP with Aspect. NET is an adequate and efficient instrument for trustworthy software development. More examples of aspect definitions using Aspect.NET are provided in the Appendix.

Chapter 5 is for university teachers and students. In this chapter I summarize my teaching experience in the areas of TWC, AOP, and related domains. I describe my *ERATO* teaching paradigm, my principles of teaching TWC and AOP, and the contents of my courses and seminars related to them. Actually, all the university courses that I teach—secure software engineering, operating systems, compilers, .NET, and Java—appear to be closely related to TWC and penetrated by TWC ideas. My secure software engineering course contains a special chapter on AOP. All my courses are available at Microsoft Developer's Network Academic Alliance Curriculum Repository (MSDNAA CR) Web site, so readers can download and use them for both teaching and self-training.

In Chapter 6 we outline perspectives on AOP and TWC: in particular, their relation to knowledge management, and some ideas on how to implement them.

The Appendix contains a self-documented code of aspect definitions to be used with Aspect.NET and the target applications to weave the aspects. The Appendix plays the role of practical addition to Chapter 4. The code of all samples is available at the Web site related to the book, www.aspectdotnet. org, and to the Aspect.NET project.

2

Trustworthy Computing, Software Engineering, and Computer Science

In this chapter we consider the concept of trustworthy computing (TWC) in detail: its historical roots, the growing need for TWC, its contemporary status and perspectives, and Microsoft's TWC initiative and its four pillars: security, privacy, reliability, and business integrity. Two modern software development platforms, .NET and Java, are considered from a TWC viewpoint.

2.1 HISTORY OF AND GROWING NEED FOR TWC

As defined in a classic book on trustworthy computing [30]: "Trustworthiness is assurance that a system deserves to be trusted—that it will perform as expected despite environmental disruptions, human and operator error, hostile attacks, and design and implementation errors. Trustworthy systems reinforce the belief that they will continue to produce expected behavior and will not be susceptible to subversion."

As emphasized by many authors, the concept of trustworthy computing is multidimensional and contains a lot of scientific, engineering, business, and

Using Aspect-Oriented Programming for Trustworthy Software Development,
By Vladimir O. Safonov
Copyright © 2008 John Wiley & Sons, Inc.

human factors. This book is devoted to only a part of this concept but one of the most important ones: trustworthy software development.

In my opinion, trustworthy computing issues arose with the appearance of the first computers, in the 1940s and early 1950s. Programs for those early computers and their data had to be input by the single user in person, using punched tapes, decks of punched cards, or an operator's control panel. Any bug (e.g., hardware fault when reading the program or its data, an extra hole in a punched card, incorrectly set trigger on the control panel) could cause overall failure of program use, hanging up or halting the system without clear information regarding what happened. In addition, the use of explicit binary codes and concrete absolute addresses in programs made the process of coding and debugging critically unreliable. Early computers were untrustworthy because of their unreliable and poor user interface, ever when used by a single programmer to solve a single task. Their trustworthiness depended, first, on the trustworthiness, attention, and responsible behavior of the people who used them. Computer gurus of those times remembered by heart the right addresses to input programs into memory and the appropriate combinations of control panel triggers. The reason the computer stopped should have been guessed by solving the puzzle of LED combinations on the control panel. We'll refer to all of these as *primary TWC issues*.

Some of the primary TWC issues were solved partially by using checksums of the input programs and data; others were resolved by using assembler and high-level languages. But *software reliability TWC issues* (e.g., buggy or malicious addressing of another task's memory or accessing a resource already belonging to some other user or task) have been experienced up to now, even at a much higher level of application development than before.

Some papers on trustworthy computing say that trustworthy computing issues arose in the 1960s, when multiuser and multitasking computer systems appeared. For example [31], one of the first attempts to classify the goals and needs of trustworthy computing was undertaken in the mid-1960s, about 40 years before Microsoft's TWC initiative, by the Allen-Babcock company, whose business was related to time-sharing computers. This is quite logical, since in any computer system consumed by several users and tasks simultaneously, common resource-sharing issues and related security, privacy, and reliability problems may arise at any moment, even without using LANs or the Internet. We'll refer to the issues of TWC related to sharing computer resources by several users or tasks as *sharing TWC issues*.

For example, because of an unchecked bug in address arithmetic operation such as $p++$ in C, an application could easily intrude on some other application's memory area, or mistakenly access some other array of its own memory that differs from the one addressed by the p pointer. In another example, because of a bug in the operating system, a race condition could occur for any types of resources common to different users or tasks: memory, hard disks, or CPU cycles.

Allen-Babcock's approach to trustworthy computing [31] was based on the following principles, very similar to the four pillars of Microsoft's trustworthy computing approach formulated in 2002 [32]:

- "An ironclad operating system [reliability]
- Use of trustworthy personnel [business integrity]
- Effective access control [security]
- User requested optional privacy [privacy]"

One of the major issues for most users in that "batch jobs and time-sharing era" was how to speed-up processing a job and thus maximize the number of turnarounds per day—starting with its input by the operator (or activating it from a terminal), until getting a listing with results. One of the widely used (but surely not correct) ways to do that was to negotiate with the operator, penetrate the computer room where the shared mainframe was working, use the operator's console, increase the priority of your job while temporarily blocking others, and cut your listing from the printer and get away. From a contemporary TWC viewpoint, such types of behavior can be regarded as a "manual" attack that makes nontrustworthy use of the mainframe by others (regarded as your competitors), since they are unpleasantly surprised by what's happening with their jobs and have to waste their working time. In the regular mode, all users shared the single mainframe computer (not networked to any others) and could, at most, start their jobs from their terminals, interact with them (input the job's data and attach the debugger to the job), watch the remaining time the job was allowed to run in batch mode, and learn the job priority assigned by the OS according to the maximal time and memory resources claimed in the "passport" of the job at its start.

So in those batch times, one of the main security issues was to keep physical security in the computer room. Another was to keep the operator's login and password away from users. In general, access control issues could arise when the user somehow phished another user's or operator's login and password and therefore could spoof the other user's identity and consume or update resources or privileges to which he or she did not have access. Then came the era of networking, e-mails, the Internet, and the Web. Computing history says that regional networks such as ARPANET were created in the 1960s; e-mail came into wide use in the late 1970s; TCP/IP protocols, the basis of communications via the Internet, were developed in the 1970s; regional and global networks were integrated into the Internet in the late 1980s; HTML and the Web were invented in the early 1990s. In addition, the process of personalization of using computers (minicomputers in the 1970s and personal computers in the 1980s) connected into networks made possible many more TWC issues. Among them are spreading viruses, worms, and Trojan programs over the network; escalating hackers' attacks, such as distributed denial of service (DDoS), to cause servers to crash; breaking the security of electronic control systems of banks, military bases, and enterprises; corrupting Web sites of high importance; *phishing* users' logins and passwords and account and credit cards numbers; and *pharming* users to malicious Web sites to steal their private information. Fifteen years ago one could hardly imagine that double-clicking an e-mail attachment to open it in your e-mail client application could be dangerous and might lead to infection of your computer and everything else in your LAN by an Internet worm. Dozens of spam e-mails intrude on each machine every day, despite spam filters, which sometimes filter out important e-mails from commercial companies or colleagues instead of spamlike advertisements. All of the issues described briefly here should be categorized as *TWC networking issues*.

In general, the *primary, sharing, networking*, and *software reliability issues* of trustworthy computing considered belong to major categories of TWC issues. Surprising as it may seem, all of them, except of course primary issues, have grown more and more, beginning from the early days of computing. The reason is as follows: The more complicated a system is, the more ways that can be used to break the system by an attack, and the higher the risk that it can be done. Hence, there is a growing need in systematic approaches to TWC, combining theory, methods, software development platforms, and tools. Although a lot of work has been done and a lot of progress has been achieved in the areas of TWC, these problems are still far from having a complete solution.

2.2 MICROSOFT'S TWC INITIATIVE

In January 2002, Bill Gates sent a historic e-mail [33] to all Microsoft employees, announcing the beginning of the trustworthy computing initiative. The essence of all aspects of the TWC initiative was explained in more detail in Craig Mundie's white paper [32]. Another important foundation document on the TWC initiative is the second Bill Gates' TWC e-mail [34], dated July 2002.

Although some authors [31] are still skeptical about the TWC initiative and regard it as a kind of justification of Microsoft's security patches to Windows, Outlook, and other Microsoft's products mostly subject to security attacks, I consider the TWC initiative from a more general viewpoint and think that this initiative plays a very important role, since it really stimulated many software engineering researchers, teachers, developers, and companies to more active joint efforts toward secure and reliable software. What is regrettable is that Microsoft didn't announce the TWC initiative before—say, ten years ago. Otherwise, we'd now already have in use comfortable TWC frameworks and environments, and contemporary computing would already be much more trustworthy than it is now.

The four pillars of Microsoft's trustworthy computing initiative are *security, privacy, reliability*, and *business integrity*. Their brief definitions, as the main goals of TWC, in terms of software product customer's expectations, are given by Mundie et al. [32]:

- *Security.* "The customer can expect that systems are resilient to attack, and that the confidentiality, integrity, and availability of the system and its data are protected."
- *Privacy.* "The customer is able to control data about themselves, and those using such data adhere to fair information principles."
- *Reliability.* "The customer can depend on the product to fulfill its functions when required to do so."
- *Business integrity.* "The vendor of a product behaves in a responsive and responsible manner."

Note that according to these definitions, the treatment of TWC by Microsoft is not limited to software and hardware issues. It is much wider: It includes business, legal, and social issues, emphasizes the role of computing in everyday life and work, and notes the issues to be resolved in this relation.

When participating in Microsoft academic days on trustworthy computing in April 2006 in Redmond [35], I appreciated the spirit and the principles of such a wide and general approach to TWC. As a software engineering expert, I was very interested to listen to the presentations on .NET security, Windows security, and writing secure code. But what pleasantly surprised me as an expert in knowledge management were the talks on intelligent software tools like those to help companies to keep their business legal, advising on the appropriate laws from the knowledge base. I agree with Microsoft that such tools are also part of contemporary TWC, in addition to principles of trustworthy software development.

It should also be emphasized that despite skeptics' opinions [31], Microsoft has, due to its TWC initiative, not only promptly reorganized its software product development and testing business to make the products more trustworthy, but is also demonstrating a positive example and appealing to other software companies to act similarly and participate in the TWC initiative. The reason that Microsoft's software products (and Microsoft itself) are so subject to attack is clear: Microsoft's operating systems, office applications, and software development tools have been among the most widely used all around the world for over 30 years.

Of the four TWC pillars formulated by Microsoft, security and reliability are the most traditional. For many people, the motto of TWC is associated first with *security*: encrypting programs and data, struggling with viruses and worms, mitigating network attacks, and so on. *Reliability* is an equally important area for TWC, since nonreliable software is vulnerable to attack based on its known bugs and other problems, and may cause insecure and unsafe situations.

The remaining two TWC pillars, *privacy* and *business integrity*, are dependent primarily on people's activity and behavior, since they not only require people to keep the software business correct and legal (as to private and confidential information), but must also recommend following software process disciplines aimed at making software products trustworthy. So the human factors remain an important part of TWC. What software technologies can do to make the human factors more trustworthy is to implement and offer appropriate suggestions and software process disciplines to users.

Implementation of intelligent advice related to changing situation, generally speaking, requires *knowledge management technologies* and *tools* that use an extensible domain-specific *knowledge base*. So I think, in the near perspective, that knowledge management should become an inherent part of TWC tools. As one present opportunity to represent and use knowledge for TWC purposes and to implement intelligent TWC solutions, software developers working for the Microsoft.NET platform can use our knowledge management tool, Knowledge.NET [36], which makes it possible to combine knowledge management and traditional .NET software engineering techniques and features, using our extension of C# by ontologies, frames, and rule sets while working in a Visual Studio.NET development environment, with Knowledge.NET integrated as an add-in. Detailed consideration of Knowledge.NET is beyond the scope of this book.

In my opinion, all four pillars of TWC are very important, but I think a fifth one equally important should be added: *usability—ease of use and a user-friendly interface.* When assessing whether or not a product is trustworthy, this quality of any software product is so important from the user's viewpoint that he or she will not use the product if it is not attractive for some reason and its appearance and operating interface are awkward and uncomfortable. I noted earlier the nontrustworthy interface of early computers, based on triggers and LEDs on the control panel. That "growth shortcoming" was overcome long ago. But from time to time, software products appear that force users to perform a number of redundant actions. They impose on users some nonflexible disciplines of operation which most users do not agree with but are unable to customize. Their output consists of incomplete, unclear, or silly messages. Therefore, users waste their time and, as a result, are pushed away not only from using these products, but also from using computing technologies, for a long time. No usability—no trust; so I think that usability features are as important as security, reliability, and privacy from a TWC viewpoint. In the TWC white paper [32], *usability* is defined as one *means* to achieve the four main goals, but in my opinion, it should be one of the TWC pillars, as it is a crucial for product quality.

2.3 THE FOUR PILLARS OF TWC

2.3.1 Security

Definitions of *security* differ, both in the general meaning of the word and as related to computers. Here are two of them which I think explain best the essence of this very important concept:

- "Security is the condition of being protected against danger or loss ... that originate[s] from outside" [37].
- As applicable to computing, "computer security is a field of *computer science* concerned with the control of *risks* related to computer use" [38].

There are three parties to the security paradigm: the *system* to be secured; the *user*, who is eager that the system be secure; and the *attackers*, who are trying to break into the system. The most important focus in any definition of computer security is on *explicit systematic measures* to be taken to keep a system secure. These security measures are aimed, first, at guarding the system from attack, and second, at keeping its functionality comfortable for use, despite security actions implemented in the product. The user of the system should understand the alternatives and grades regarding how he or she can protect the system, what types of security checks will be performed at each security level, and how his or her activity will or should reasonably be restricted at each security level to achieve the desired level of security.

The following major tasks can be formulated in relation to computer security:

1. *Classification and analysis* of systems and their types of security, categories of users (from a security and allowable actions viewpoint), known and imaginable types of attacks and attackers, and possible security measures to be taken. There is a lot of very interesting literature in this area: in particular, the book by Howard and LeBlanc [27], the best one I know.

2. Finding ways to use *quantitative assessment* of security. This task is one of the most complicated—an intellectual challenge to be solved. As far as I can judge, we are now only starting on our path to solving it. Using mathematical formulas in terms of probability theory and statistics would be too simplified an approach, due to the polymorphic and complicated nature of security and a lot of human factors that participate. But clearly, any scientific approach to such a complicated problem as computer security should include its quantitative evaluation.

3. More practical and traditional for software engineering up to now has been developing *security technologies and tools*. A lot of progress has been made in this direction. Actually, each operating system and software development platform pays a lot of attention to the security technologies involved, and this tendency is growing stronger.

This book deals primarily with solving the third task, although in Chapter 4 we touch on the second.

In a more practical and ubiquitous sense, for *home users*, security involves primarily everyday struggles with viruses and worms: from flash memory devices you are using to port information from outside computers or from the Internet (mostly by e-mail). Such attacks may crush a system or at least are likely to make the user waste a lot of time cleaning up after viruses. Another important aspect is your understanding of how to configure security on your computer: for example, when using an Internet browser whose new, more secure versions may require that you explicitly select and set up a suitable layer of security.

For *office users*, there are a lot of security aspects to be remembered and used every day, such as protection of confidential information from malicious actions or from curious colleagues, securing local and wide area networks (LANs and WANs), and installing and using security patches developed for operating systems and software tools in everyday use. Some of these actions can be delegated to the system administrator of your company, but the basic concepts and principles should be understood by each user.

For *software developers*, security should be an inherent part of the software process and discipline. A developer should think about the security of the product every day, at every milestone and stage of project development. At the product maintenance stage, *security patches* should be issued when needed to protect the product and its users from newly invented attacks and malicious software.

Security activity by software users and developers should follow the *STRIDE* (spoofing, tampering, repudiation, information disclosure, denial of service, elevation of privilege) threat categorization scheme and DREAD (damage, reproducibility, exploitability, affected users, discoverability) threat-assessing paradigm, whose detailed descriptions may be found in the book by Howard and LeBlanc [27].

In its TWC white paper [32], Microsoft formulated an integrated approach to the *means* of achieving security goals: the *security development life cycle* (*SDL*) software process scheme. Its main principles are summarized as SD^3+C: secure by design, secure by default, secure in deployment, and communication.

The *secure by design* principle means that beginning at the early stages, the software product should be designed to enable it to protect itself and its data from attack. In particular, it may use a data encryption algorithm and may support extra checks for data integrity, especially when data are received via Internet or intranet. The software product should be intelligent enough to recognize typical attacks and to "learn" how to mitigate more and more of them. The latter quality means that in the ideal case, *knowledge bases, data mining*, and *machine learning* techniques should be used by products to process network traffic (e.g., firewalls) and large data streams. Especially important is the *least privilege* design principle: Secure software should run correctly when launched by an ordinary user without an administrator's permission. When developing and testing software, developer engineers often log into their workstations under login names with an administrator's privileges, so they are likely to miss the fact that the software may not run when an ordinary user launches it.

Secure by default means that the security checks should be turned on by default when using the product, according to the heuristic that the other software in general is assumed to be insecure by default. For example, when using the latest Internet Explorer versions, users may be surprised that unlike in previous versions, the default security level requires that a user explicitly select a set of trusted Web sites. However, this security functionality is quite reasonable and easy to use to avoid malicious redirections. To investigate whether or not your .NET application is secure by default pass it to Microsoft *FxCop* utility [39] for checking against its security rules. You might be surprised how many security violations FxCop detects. In more allegoric terms, such software quality as security by default may be compared to a mystic battlefield, with troops of knights and dragons struggling against each other in such a way that every knight puts his helmet on and holds his sword by default, since he assumes that a dragon can attack at any moment. Although in some cases that will not be quite comfortable for the knight, he can save his life and health by pursuing this security principle. Whether to carry a heavy helmet and sword, or die of an occasional dragon's attack, is up to each knight to decide.

Secure in deployment means that the product and its documentation should help ordinary users and system administrators to use it securely, and to easily install and deploy security updates of the product. For example, on booting the latest versions of Windows, a number of security alerts are issued: for example, a warning that antivirus software is not installed, or is off, if so. Also, as well known, Windows notifies its users as to any security updates, and downloads and installs them automatically, unless the user has explicitly refused to do that.

In the context of the security formula above, *communication* means that the developers of the product should be responsive to end users' and system administrators' requests as to product vulnerabilities discovered and on help needed by users on appropriate security settings for the product. Developers should make patches promptly to fix new security vulnerabilities and make them available for download, installation, and use. Microsoft demonstrates pursuing this policy every day; security patches for all Microsoft products appear promptly on their Web sites.

The *security development life cycle* (SDL) [40] is a method of organizing the software process that enables the design and development of secure software, based on the SD^3+C principles cited above. Actually, SDL is an enhancement of a traditional software life-cycle scheme, the *waterfall* software development process, whose major phases are *requirements, design, implementation, verification, release, support*, and *servicing*. The scheme of the security life cycle [40], tied to the stages of the traditional waterfall life cycle, is shown in Figure 2.1.

Implementation of the SDL scheme should enable three facets of developing secure software pointed out by Microsoft: *repeatable process, engineers' education*, and *metrics and accountability*. The value of a repeatable process has been pursued by Microsoft for over five years. It includes regular

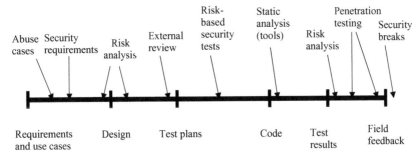

Figure 2.1 *Secure software development life cycle.*

engineering education performed by special security experts such as Michael Howard. As to metrics, even the latest publications on this subject [41,42] recommend using sets of metrics that *post-assert* the security qualities of the product version already developed, whereas the most valuable approach might be to develop and use *predictive security metrics* that could be helpful in making an assessment of the efforts required to secure software development—but the latter task is much more complicated.

Next, let's review the phases of the SDL and related security measures according to Microsoft's scheme. To manage and control the development of a secure software product and to educate engineers regarding security, a *central security team*, consisting of high-level security professionals, is created at the developer company. In my opinion, the task of creating a separate highly skilled security team is only realistic for large companies. For small companies, at least a *security expert* should be hired—permanently or temporarily. This is especially important for managers of small companies, who, experience shows, sometimes neglect human and budget resources for quality assurance and are likely to repeat the same mistake regarding security experts.

In the *requirements* phase, the product team interacts with the central security team, which assigns a staff member as a *product security advisor*. The product team works with the security advisor to develop security plans, integrate them into the product schedule, and clarify security requirements based on user recommendations, previous experience, and industry standards.

The *design* phase should be targeted for security. The main principle that should be followed is to use a *trusted computing base*. Microsoft recommends using secure design techniques such as *layering* and *strong typing*. We can add to this set the principles of *modularity* and *abstract data types* (*encapsulating data representation*). All these design principles have proved their practical applicability and importance since the 1970s, long before the "TWC era." In addition, Microsoft formulates three closely related security design principles: minimal attack surface, least privilege, and threat modeling. *Minimal attack surface* means that the default configuration of the software should minimize chances of a successful security attack, since the software is supposed to be used in a nonsecure environment. The *least privilege* principle recommends designing, developing, and testing software under the assumption that it will be launched and used by an ordinary nonprivileged user rather than by a system administrator, in case system administrator privileges are really not necessary for running the software—this is the case for most software products. It helps to avoid granting extra privileges and their malicious use by attackers. *Threat modeling* [43] should be performed, starting at the software design stage, to determine possible types of attacks and the ability of the software to resist them. Microsoft also emphasizes the importance of defining *supplemental (security-related) shipping criteria* at the design stage: in particular, criteria for the product to be free of externally reported security vulnerabilities before shipping its new version. This principle concurs with that of minimizing an attack surface, since when products are shipped with a list of known security bugs (or probably some others not yet discovered) rather than fixing these bugs prior to release, it may widen the attack surface for hackers.

The *implementation* stage is the most decisive from a security viewpoint, since the developer's team should avoid security vulnerabilities in the product code resulting from this phase. The following principles are recommended by Microsoft as part of SDL at the implementation stage:

- Apply coding and testing standards.
- Apply security testing tools, including fuzzing tools.
- Apply static analysis code-scanning tools.
- Conduct code reviews.

Coding standards should include security recommendations: how to avoid typical security flaws such as buffer overrun, and to insert proper security checks into the code.

In addition to coding standards, good secure coding practice would also use *secure coding templates* provided by an integrated development environment or by special security coding tools developed and integrated into the IDE. Without coding templates such as suggestions to call *EndInvoke* at some point after a call of *BeginInvoke* in asynchronous call implementation, there is a high risk of introducing bugs nondetectable by the compiler and difficult to detect by static code checkers. To be more concrete in relation to .NET, security coding templates should also recommend annotating the code by appropriate security attributes, to avoid situations when the code is insecure by default—the latter can be observed very clearly using *FxCop* utility. Secure coding templates are just one area where AOP, and in particular, the Aspect.NET tool, can help (see Chapters 3 and 4 for more details).

Another way to make code more secure and to find security bugs is *security testing*, including *fuzz testing* (or *fuzzing*) [44]. Fuzzing is a technique for automated boundary value testing using "semicorrect" data. For example, using this approach, all the input data for the test are taken to be correct, except for an integer input value taken as 1 less than the minimal correct value, or as 1 more than the maximal correct value. The boundary value testing principle was formulated by G. Myers in the 1970s [45], but now, in the TWC era, the principle has become especially important. The fuzzing technique is applicable not only to integer input data but also to IP addresses when testing network protocol implementations, which is of great importance since it is well known that generating sequential IP addresses is a popular technique used by hackers to find a security breach, and the networking software products should be resistant to such attacks.

Tools for either source or binary code static analysis are powerful instruments for improving code quality: in particular, code security. The most famous, the UNIX classic static code checker, is *lint* [46], initially designed and developed for C, but with newer variations for C++, Java, JavaScript, C#, and others. Lint makes it possible to find bugs or potential bugs in the source code not detected by most compilers. For example, typical lint-style checking and warning are related to "fall-through": Detection and diagnostics of a *break* statement, which should have terminated an alternative in a C switch statement. Such a bug may lead to security flaws, so lint's help in detecting such bugs is invaluable. Novel tools that are more specialized for security are PREfix and PREfast [47], developed by Microsoft Research and used within Microsoft for years. PREfix is a tool for interprocedural analysis of C and C++ code. It is used primarily to analyze Windows code: kernel, drivers, and services. PREfast is a tool for intraprocedural analysis. As mentioned on Microsoft's security Web pages, software developers would like such tools as PREfast to be integrated with future releases of Visual Studio.NET. Now, PREfast is integrated into the Visual Studio 2005 Team System for Software Developers as the "Code Analysis" option for C++ applications. More widely used beyond Microsoft is FxCop [39], a tool that performs a wide spectrum of .NET assembly binary code analysis, including security checks. Each FxCop checking rule can be turned on or off by the user. In some .NET software development companies, FxCop use to analyze product code is mandatory, which is good practice.

Code reviews are also an important part of the implementation stage of the SDL. They contribute a lot to improving code security. In my opinion, code reviews conducted "by hand" by experienced developers are invaluable but are too expensive. The effort necessary for detailed review of the code is comparable to that of implementing the code, or even more time consuming, given the fact that the reviewer may not be totally familiar with the specifics and semantics of the code under review. So I think the optimal decision in most cases could be detailed self-review of the code (guided by security books such as that of Howard and LeBlanc [27]), in combination with a selective code review by security experts (guided by a priori heuristic suggestions on typical security bugs).

The *verification* phase is the stage of verifying a functionally complete product. At this stage, Microsoft recommends a *security push*, which consists of additional security code reviews and focused security testing. Security code review and security testing are recommended during the period of beta testing of the product. Microsoft's practice [27,39] since 2002 of using a security push during the verification phase has confirmed improvement in product quality.

During the *release* phase, the product is subject to a *final security review* (FSR) organized by the product security advisor and performed by the central security team. The goal of the FSR is to determine the overall security picture of the product, to determine the underlying causes of the security vulnerabilities detected and to provide recommendations to the product team. As a consequence of the FSR, the product team may have to return to earlier stages of the product life cycle and implement appropriate corrections to make the product more secure. The FSR may also result in additional security training of the product team.

Finally, at the *support and servicing* phase, the product maintenance team analyzes reports on the security vulnerabilities found and provides prompt response and product security patches if necessary. However, the impact of the response phase should be deeper; the team learns from the errors found and improves the software process so as to avoid such security flaws afterward. The security team may also update the code scanning tools used in code reviews to take into account newly found security vulnerabilities.

To summarize the security development life-cycle scheme, it should be mentioned that it can be organized by large software companies. Small ones may just not have enough resources to do so, but they should at least delegate an experienced software engineer to be responsible full time for security of the company's software products. It is also very important to teach SDL at universities as part of software engineering and software security courses so that security-oriented software development style will be acquired by young software experts and later brought by them to the software companies they join upon graduation. We discuss educational issues in more detail in Chapter 5.

It is very important to realize at which stages and in which ways aspect-oriented programming can help to implement the security development life-cycle scheme. In general, AOP is most useful at every stage of the SDL when systematic software updates are required. At the design stage, AOP may be useful to design aspects that implement security code patterns. At the implementation stage, AOP can be used to define aspects that convert the product code according to security coding standards: for example, to inject security checks at appropriate points in the product code. AOP can also help to strengthen the product code through logging, tracing, coloring, and so on, and therefore help to automate the resource-consuming process of detailed code review. In addition, aspects can help to make systematic updates not only to the product itself but also to code-scanning tools, since those tools may require enhancements related to the security vulnerabilities found. A possible way to use AOP for TWC code-injecting purposes would be to take Visual Studio.NET with the Aspect.NET framework integrated, take the existing legacy code, choose and weave into the target legacy code the appropriate TWC aspects, and get a more secure and reliable code. This is a very brief and preliminary overview of how AOP can help; details and examples are provided in Chapter 4.

2.3.2 Privacy

According to one of its common use definitions [48], "privacy is the ability of an individual or group to keep their lives and personal affairs out of public view, or to control the flow of information about themselves." The current level of information technology (IT) development and its influence on people's everyday private lives and business makes privacy another equally important pillar of the TWC initiative. For example, imagine that a compact disk (CD) with a computer database of full names, addresses, and contact phones of the people living in some country or city is on sale publicly in the subway or at newstands. This would pose a serious threat not only to people's information security and privacy but also to their lives, safety, and health, since this information could be used by criminals for kidnapping and blackmail purposes. Probably the best way to cope with this would be through appropriate laws and an obligation for people to obey them. Punishment for their violation should be not only for malicious use of such CDs but also for their sales. This is just one example to demonstrate that using only IT methods and tools, even only at a very high level, is not enough to maintain privacy. What also matters is law enforcement and an evolving personal consciousness. Everyone should work to ensure that everything is being done to prevent improper use.

Another common example is an attempt at *phishing*: experienced by almost everyone when using e-mail. Imagine getting an e-mail stating that your Citibank account is in danger and you need just click a Web link and *enter your name and bank account number* to make the account secure. This is a typical attempt to steal your private data with an obvious goal. Clicking on the Web link will *pharm* you to a malicious Web site set up by a criminal group. They may even use in their "bait" e-mail design and colors that resemble those used at your bank's site. You defend against this by placing your mouse cursor on the Web reference and reading the URL (universal resource locator) in the pop-up window without clicking on it. You will probably find that the reference is *not* to the Citibank Web site. Looking at this situation from a more general viewpoint, let's try to analyze how to struggle with all such situations. Using ordinary spam filters does not avoid the problem completely, as we've already noted. Spam filters often filter out important e-mails, leaving all the "baits" in your inbox. Microsoft's new *SmartScreen* [49,50] technology, built into the latest Microsoft Outlook, combats spam by using probability-based weighting to analyze an e-mail messages and to find and close Web beacons that can be used by spammers to determine active e-mail addresses. In some cases, the *human interface proofs* (HIP) [49] technique is helpful in preventing automated registration and creating new Web and e-mail accounts by spammer malware (rather than by humans). The idea of the HIP technique is to use exotic text labels readable and understandable by humans but nonrecognizable by spammer programs. Special laws and social measures are necessary to struggle with spam and phishing, and these have already been undertaken in many countries.

Equally important, if a software product you use occasionally asks you to enter any kind of private information, either for activation purposes, for registration, or during everyday use, you should determine how this private information will be used by the product. This is a very important privacy principle followed by Microsoft [49] in the latest versions of all of its software products. The same principle is followed if a Microsoft software product is collecting private information during use. Keeping users fully informed as to the private data collected by the software and the purpose of such collection helps greatly to retain the users' trust.

To enhance privacy and security features, Microsoft has implemented the *Windows XP Service Pack 2* [49], which includes:

- The *Internet Explorer InfoBar*, to prevent malicious "pop-under" dialogue screens
- A built-in pop-up blocker turned on by default, which is especially valuable in getting rid of lots of advertisements imposed on a user while browsing and opening an unfamiliar Web page
- A download blocker to suppress unsolicited downloads
- A redesigned version of an *AuthentiCode* [51]*-based dialogue box* to double-check the identity and integrity of downloaded code before its installation
- The *Never Install* option, which allows the user to avoid unsolicited and undesirable downloaded code installations

All of the new functionality is easy to use and intended to guard the user against a variety of common attempts to bring malicious code to the user's machine, and install it. Although the process of solicited downloading now takes a little longer because of the need to explicitly handle new, related GUI (graphical user interface), it is quite justified. Although pop-up advertisements do not violate normal functioning of a system, they may lead to a waste of the user's time struggling with them, so the XP Service Pack 2 provides several advantages.

An important part of privacy is *encryption* of data, programs, e-mails, instant messages, banking information, and other types of information used when communicating via the Internet. This topic has already been investigated thoroughly and discussed widely in the scientific literature. In particular, e-mail encryption is a common practice in many IT companies that are trying to keep their technical information private and confidential. There are also new types of file systems with automatic data encryption, such as the ZFS in Sun's Solaris 10. Although encryption is a favorite topic of students, we do not consider it further.

How can AOP help to implement privacy? The same way that it helps to implement security. Many useful aspects can be woven into appropriate target application checks (e.g., checks for permission to handle sensitive information) and data conversions (e.g., encryption and decryption) to enable privacy. We discuss these in more detail in Chapter 4.

2.3.3 Reliability

According to the IEEE's definition [52], reliability is "the ability of a system or component to perform its required functions under stated conditions for a specified period of time." Reliability theory estimates the reliability of any technical system in terms of *mean time between failures* (MTBF) [53], the average time between system failures. Also, to measure software reliability, software *complexity* metrics are often used, such as the number of source code lines, or Halstead's metrics (i.e., the number of operands and operators in a program), or cyclomatic complexity (McCabe's metrics—the number of control branches in a program) [54]. The latter approach is based on the heuristic suggestion that the more complicated a system is, the less reliable it is likely to be, which is surely not always true. Even the authors of a paper on thorough software reliability measurement [54] recognize that measuring software, and software reliability in particular, is actually in its infancy. So, as applicable to software, practitioners, including Microsoft's experts, understand reliability more intuitively [32], close to the IEEE definition: *Reliable software* is software that customers can rely on, in the sense that when required, it fulfills its expected functions.

It is a very complicated task to develop an appropriate, precise, and complete quantitative theoretical estimate of software reliability, for the following reasons:

- Each software module requires a separate reliability assessment, and the ways in which modules communicate also require a reliability assessment.
- Software is evolving much more rapidly than hardware, due to bug fixes and functionality enhancements in the course of software maintenance.
- The environment in which software runs must also be taken in account, and that environment may vary for different machines. Each update of the environment setting can change the reliability of a software system; for example, a manual update of the Windows registry by the *regedit* utility may cause the failure of some software tools considered 100% reliable, since the tools work based on the fact that some information is located in the registry.

Under these circumstances, a simple quantitative assessment such as one MTBF or one cyclomatic complexity number throughout the entire system is not appropriate but is somewhat helpful, since it can reflect statistics on system use or provide general understanding as to whether the system taken as a whole can be considered reliable. A more general theoretical quantitative assessment model of reliability, taking into account the environment, all software components, and any software updates, is likely to be hardly usable because of its complexity. So in this book I use the term *reliability* in the intuitive sense of the IEEE definition.

Currently, the following techniques are used to improve software reliability:

1. *Reliable design and implementation methods:* modularity, abstract data types, structured programming, object-oriented analysis and design, design by contract, aspect-oriented programming, and others. The goal of all those technological approaches is to decompose software into reliable components easy to specify, design, integrate, reuse, test, document, and maintain. According to Myers [19], to improve the reliability of a software module, the module should check that its input information (arguments) is consistent and complete, and if any precondition is violated, should terminate with a clear notification of the abnormal condition detected ("throw an exception," speaking in modern terms).

2. *Software testing:* unit testing, system testing, black box testing, white box testing, measuring and increasing test coverage, boundary value testing, equivalence class partitioning, fuzzing, and so on. Testing techniques and tools are numerous. Most valuable, from a reliability viewpoint, are tools to measure the completeness of testing and to recommend to the user how to make the process of testing more and more complete.

3. *Formal specification and verification methods:* Floyd–Hoare program calculus (Hoare's triples), algebraic specification (particularly, using the SDL or OBJ specification languages), set-theoretic specification (in particular, Z notation), denotational semantics, and so on. Formal methods seem to produce "100% reliable" code, since they prove formally that the code corresponds to the given set of specifications. But it should be noted that the software specifications and software correctness proofs themselves can be buggy. In addition, formal methods may be difficult for practitioners to apply, for the simple reason that software developers can just forget mathematics after years of hard work on commercial software projects. A deeper reason was formulated by Tseytin [55]: The paradigm of thinking and the basic concepts of computer science are fundamentally different from those of mathematics, the basis of formal methods. In particular, in computer science a variable is treated as a changeable "cell," whereas in mathematics, a variable (say, x) usually denotes some magnitude whose value is supposed to be *constant* during some module of mathematical reasoning: in particular, in a theorem proof. That contradicts the dynamic nature of programming and may cause difficulties in attempts to

describe the changeable behavior of a program using mathematical concepts. However, it seems clear that suitable formal methods will be worked out that will be really helpful to software reliability improvement. Two positive examples are: SDL, the algebraic specification language used as a de facto standard in telecommunication software development; and Spec#, an extension of C# and Visual Studio.NET through formal specification and verification features designed and implemented by Microsoft Research.

All of those techniques of reliable software development have proven their practical importance in 60-odd years of computer programming. However, software is getting more and more complicated, so these techniques need to continue to evolve.

As for the use of aspect-oriented programming to make software more reliable, it is certainly one of the soundest technologies for this purpose. Aspects can be defined to weave a variety of reliability checks or settings into target applications, particularly checks for consistency of the input arguments and the results of the methods selected, which is characteristic of the design-by-contract approach. However, it should be mentioned that applying AOP inappropriately can worsen software reliability. We discuss this in more detail in Chapters 3 and 4.

2.3.4 Business Integrity

The business integrity pillar of TWC is more closely related to human, social, and law factors than the other three and is less subject to scientific analysis. Business integrity [32] means that a software developer company must react promptly to any customer report, especially one related to security, privacy, or reliability. Any security vulnerability should be fixed promptly, and the patched version of the product should be made available to customers as soon as possible. Any customer question should be answered quickly, and detailed recommendations on product settings should be provided. The customer should feel the developer's attention and strong desire to keep the customer's trust. Otherwise, the customer is likely to switch to another product by other developer company.

Recognizing Microsoft's current efforts to maintain business integrity, I would like to share my personal experience of software customer communications. I acquired a lot of software product maintenance experience in the 1990s when I was the project leader of the Sun Pascal compiler. I soon realized that quick response by a software maintenance team was extremely important for customers. Due to our maintenance work on Sun Pascal in 1992–1993, when we fixed several hundred open "legacy" bugs (inherited from the previous maintenance team) and issued two bug fix releases (3.0.2 and 3.0.3) in one year, Sun Microsystems succeeded in keeping such a big customer as Siemens, whose 400 software engineers used intensively the compiler for which I was responsible. Our work received press notice in newspapers and journals [56].

Siemens was a kind of "P1" customer, in the sense that each bug or request for enhancement they submitted was priority 1 or 2 (extremely urgent). When you are the project leader you must forget about other work and days off until you fix the bug. A special case was a customer from Germany who tested our compiler very scrupulously against the Pascal ISO standard (which we were grateful for, although we did use a test suite for Pascal standard compatibility testing). Some customers persisted in not switching to the new version 4.0, whose front end we refurbished to speed it up two- to fourfold over the preceding version. But some customers were scared that their Pascal applications would stop working on the new compiler version, and it took a lot of convincing to get them to use the new version.

To sum up my Sun Pascal maintenance experience, I formulate the following recommendations to software maintenance teams on how to organize their work to enable business integrity:

1. *Learn the source code of the product by heart.* I am quite serious. Thorough knowledge of the product sources and design (even though you are not the person who developed that code originally) is the basis for successful maintenance and, accordingly, for business integrity. I used to teach my students to print out the sources of the product they maintain, to make it their desktop book, and to read it every night instead of their favorite novel before going to sleep, in order to learn the sources and feel their behavior as if it were their own creation (although, actually, the product can be a result of the efforts of many years of work by several companies, with different design and coding styles applied). This takes time but is time well spent.

2. *The project leader should be the person who answers any customer's question or evaluates any bug without spending days or weeks of digging into the sources and documentation* (it should be done within 5 minutes to a few hours). This example of business integrity should be based on deep knowledge of product sources.

3. *Take special care of bug duplicates.* One or two months after a product is shipped, the product development and maintenance team commonly receives a bunch of e-mails from customers with bug reports. Actually, the same bug or a similar bug is generally found simultaneously by different people in different countries, different environments, and different locales, using different customer applications (some of them may be proprietary), reported by different bug identifiers. The task of the project leader is to recognize duplications of complaints, to answer customers promptly, to fix the bug if it hasn't yet been done, to indicate explicitly which bug is actually being referred to in the duplicates reported for the same bug, and to issue a product patch promptly, with the bug fixed. The task of recognizing bug duplicates cannot be accomplished by any software tool or technology, and its rapid, successful solution must rely on the project leader's experience and deep knowledge of the product design and source.

4. *Never "close" a bug report as "will not fix."* Customer trust weakens if they receive an update on a bug report, with the bug closed because the product manager decided not to spend human resources to fix it (the official explanation is "no resources"). A customer's bug report should always be given top priority. The customer should feel "the breath" of the maintenance team working on the bug and should soon receive the results (the bug evaluation) and in a few days the product patch with the bug fix rather than the refusal of the product team to fix the bug—there's nothing worse. A similar situation to be avoided is the common practice of decreasing the priority of the bug before the new product release, the goal being to avoid fixing it within a reasonable time. This can also undermine customer trust and business integrity principles.

5. *Don't rush to fix the bug and test the fix; check the fix very carefully.* Many software engineers, especially young ones, are too anxious to fix a bug very quickly, report the fix to their boss, and then report very promptly to customers. They think they are right and are very proud of how fast they managed to solve a complicated problem. But instead, they are likely to create new problems for the product team, their management, and their customers because of integrating a fix that was not tested properly. Developing new tests complete enough to test a new bug fix, and running all the existing test suites against the patched version of the product, takes time, and intuitively and emotionally speaking, the maintenance engineer is sometimes reluctant to do everything to ensure that the fix is correct. This is a common software process mistake to be avoided. There should be (and actually there is) a systematic software process discipline used to test any new bug fix. The customer can wait a few days to receive a correct and complete fix but may stop trusting you if from time to time he or she receives untested and/or erroneous bug fixes.

6. *Don't zero out the product bug count in the bug tracking database to leave the product alive.* This principle may sound funny and paradoxical. Nevertheless, it does make sense, as our Sun Pascal practice shows. When we fixed *all* the Sun Pascal bugs and zeroed out the product bug count, Sun management soon decided to classify Sun Pascal as being "end of life" and put it into a purely maintenance mode. It has not been supported for more than 10 years; and it is well known that when a software product is not supported by the developer company, it dies.

To stay closer to the subject of the book—how can AOP help business integrity? The answer should be clear now that we have considered software maintenance experience and principles—the basis for business integrity. Evaluating any bug, an everyday ubiquitous task of any software engineer who maintains a software product, can be formulated in terms of AOP as *aspect mining*. To fix a bug, the software engineer is to locate implementation of the functionality to be fixed in the product source code. Often, the implementation of the feature to be fixed is scattered inside many different modules of code in the form of stand-alone declarations, definitions, statements (e.g., method calls), and definitions of modules: classes, methods, procedures, or macros. Logically, all these scattered fragments should form the complete and consistent implementation of some feature, but "physically" they are spread around the code of the product. If the product design, coding, and code self-documenting style is not perfect and not systematic (which is often true), and if the software maintenance engineer does not know the product source well, the task of locating the implementation of the functionality scattered in the code turns into a detective story and risky adventure. New bugs are likely to be introduced into the code by nonsmart, erroneous, and incomplete bug fixes. AOP can help improve the situation in two respects: using *aspect mining techniques and tools* to locate all the scattered fragments of the functionality implementation to be patched, and *designing new functionality* in a proper way—*as a new aspect or aspect library,* easy to locate in the code later, and easy to weave into the target application using AOP techniques.

2.4 SOFTWARE ENGINEERING TECHNOLOGIES AND TOOLS FOR TWC

By now, many approaches, software tools, technologies, and platforms have been designed, implemented, and used to make software more trustworthy. AOP is just one new prospective approach that can be helpful in solving this complicated problem, although the goals of AOP are much wider than those of TWC. At present we cannot say that there exists a universal technology to develop 100% trustworthy software. Each approach described or overviewed in this book, including the latest .NET and Java platforms and AOP technologies and tools, if used properly, can be very helpful for TWC purposes, but their use does not guarantee trustworthiness of the result. The reason for that should be clearer from our previous analysis: TWC is so multifactored, multi-aspected, and dynamically changing a discipline that it is not possible to take into account in one ready-to-use technology all factors that constitute our understanding of TWC: software engineering and computer science, economics and business, law, human (vendor's and user's) psychology, and so on.

Currently, there are two software development platforms, .NET and Java, to provide state-of-the-art technologies designed to assist in trustworthy software development. We should caution from the very beginning the need to avoid a common mistake often made by people who study or teach Java or .NET—an attempt to consider each of these platforms as isolated from the others and to claim that only in Java or .NET is a unique approach to TWC achieved. Instead, Java and .NET should be considered and can best be understood in a historical retrospective and comparative analysis: by comparing them to each other and to older platforms and tools. Java and .NET can be compared to the "tops of icebergs" or, perhaps more appropriate, to the finalizing components (beautifully decorated cupolas, columns, and naves) of magnificent cathedrals, whose (theoretical and technological) foundations have been carefully designed and constructed during the previous 50-odd years of software development, with the contributions of many prominent people and companies integrated (more about that in Chapter 5).

.NET is more general than Java and more open, since it is targeted to the use of an extensible collection of programming languages, and Java technology is a priori more limited, due to the initial intent by the authors of Java to have software developers use the Java language only, or mostly, as a dominant language, without using "Java assemblers," in combination with the use of C/C++ in native methods. Nevertheless, TWC models and technologies used in .NET and Java are very similar and mutually influential. We consider them in more detail in Sections 2.5 and 2.6.

2.5   TWC AND .NET

2.5.1   .NET Overview

.NET is definitely most secure and most TWC-oriented software development platform right now, so we start our overview of TWC technologies with this platform. It should be emphasized that unlike Java, whose specifications are still proprietary documents of Sun Microsystems, .NET was created in 2000 as a set of international ECMA standards [57,58] developed by an international committee, with participation of representatives of the world's leading software development companies. So the first thing to learn about .NET is that it is *not* just a Microsoft product, but a set of international standards specifying all main parts of .NET: *common language infrastructure* (CLI) and *C# language*. The CLI standard includes the specification of *common type system* (CTS), a unified base set of types to which the types of each .NET programming language should be mapped, and *common language specification* (CLS), a set of requirements to implementations of programming languages such that full compliance to this set enables interoperability in one application of modules compiled from various languages. The main goals of .NET can be formulated as *multilanguage interoperability, type safety*, and *security*.

In addition to *Microsoft.NET* [59], the commercial version of .NET wide spread throughout the world, there are two other worldwide implementations of .NET standards: *shared-source common language infrastructure* (SSCLI), also known as *Rotor* [60], launched by Microsoft in 2002 and then used and enhanced by academics for research and teaching, and *Mono* [61], an open-source implementation of .NET compatible with the international standard, sponsored initially by Novell, now developed intensively by hundreds of remote developers from the Mono community. Potentially, anybody or any company can develop "its own .NET," a software product compatible to .NET standards, without purchasing a license to permit them to do so, unlike the common practice with Java.

Again as opposed to Java technology approach, the C# language [57] is *not* considered the only or mandatory .NET language, but it is definitely the most powerful and comfortable of the languages available on the .NET platform. The entire set of .NET languages available at present includes those implemented by Microsoft: *C#.NET, Visual Basic.NET (VB.NET), Managed C++. NET, J#.NET* (a language similar to Java, derived from old Java dialect), and *JScript.NET. Microsoft's Intermediate Language* also belongs to this set and is considered a peer-to-peer .NET programming language. There are also a lot of third-party language implementations for .NET: *Eiffel.NET* [62], *Active Oberon (Zonnon).NET* [63], and a variety of others: both old languages such as FORTRAN and COBOL and newer ones such as Perl, Python, and Ruby. The number of .NET languages is being increased extensively. Moreover, the bright start of .NET in the new millennium stimulated an incredible growth in compiler development projects, much wider than the "boom" of programming languages and compilers that we experienced in the 1970s.

According to the .NET approach, any compiler from a .NET language compiles its source code into *Common Intermediate Language* (CIL), binary code based on postfix notation of operations. *Microsoft Intermediate Language* (MSIL) can be considered Microsoft's implementation of CIL. At runtime, CIL code is processed by *Common Language Runtime* (CLR), a common execution time support for all .NET languages. Part of CLR is a *just-in-time* (JIT) *compiler* (more exactly, there are several JIT compilers in CLR) that compiles CIL code dynamically to native code of the target platform, method by method, when the CIL method is first called. The next call of the method will execute its native code. So, based on this principle, CIL code is the platform-independent binary representation of any program to be executed in an .NET environment.

Another key principle of .NET is *metadata*, a language-agnostic representation of the types defined and used in a .NET program module, referred to as *assembly*. Metadata are generated by any .NET compiler for each assembly, along with the assembly's CIL code. A .NET assembly consists of CIL code, metadata, and a *manifest*, an inventory list of the assembly. An assembly can consist physically of one or more *portable executable* (PE) *files* and *resources*, typically multimedia files, used by the assembly. Metadata are used by all components of .NET as unified information on all types to be processed by any .NET tool. Metadata are available at runtime to CLR and to the JIT compiler in particular. Due to that fact, .NET enables *type checking* and *security checks*, fundamental elements of TWC. .NET code enhanced by metadata is referred to as *managed code*, and its execution by CLR, with type and security checking, is referred to as *managed execution*. Such reliable and safe execution of managed code is possible because CLR knows the type of each object via its *managed pointer*, a pointer not only to data but also to *metadata* (i.e., to the type of data being processed). In a sense, the idea of using metadata at runtime resurrects the old idea of tagged architecture, but it is much more flexible because the metadata structure is not "frozen" in hardware.

As a very important part, metadata contain *attributes*, annotations that can be added to any .NET named entity: assembly itself, a class, its method, or a field. Attributes can be *predefined* (in particular, they can be used for security purposes), or *custom*, user defined. Attributes are a powerful program annotation and extension mechanism. Actually, *metadata and attributes are the foundation of .NET trustworthiness*. In particular, custom attributes can be used to represent aspects in AOP. The Aspect.NET toolkit is one of the first AOP tools to use custom attributes in that way.

Metadata also help CLR to "understand" the types that come from different languages. One of the most difficult tasks of implementing a language for .NET is *to map the language types to the types of common type system* (CTS), a part of CLI. To be able to use assemblies compiled from two different languages in one application, both language compilers should comply with the requirements of the *common language specification* (CLS), expressed in the form of a set of rules (in .NET 2.0, there are 48 CLS rules). For example, one rule states that no field in a class should have the same name as a method in the same class. Actually, CLS, as well as metadata, *is one of the keystones of .NET trustworthiness*; it enables safe and secure *interoperability* in one application of modules written in different languages. The set of .NET multilanguage interoperability features includes *multilanguage inheritance*. It is quite possible, for example, to define a class in C#, its "son" in VB.NET, and its "grandson" in managed C++.NET. Interoperability also means *multilanguage exception handling*; for example, on .NET you can throw an exception from C# code and catch it in C++ code.

Yet another part of the .NET trustworthiness foundation is its *assembly naming and versioning system*. Each assembly typically has a *version number* of the following structure: *major.minor.build.revision*. For example, the number *1.0.2664.20445* is the version number of the *AspectDotNet.dll* library, part of Aspect.NET 2.1 binary code. Each assembly can use another assembly, and should refer to the latter explicitly, using its version number. This is the basis of reliable execution of applications, so in .NET it is no longer possible, unlike the earlier model of Windows or UNIX operating systems, to "break" a workable application because of installing a new release of dynamically linked library that will not work with the current version of the application relying on the previous version of the same DLL. The problem described is often referred to as *DLL hell* and has been overcome in .NET. The version number is part of the *strong name* of a .NET assembly, which also includes its *symbolic (string) name, public key token*, and *culture (locale)*. Strong names enable the integrity of .NET assemblies. Strongly named assemblies on each machine are placed to the *global assembly cache* (GAC), a system subdirectory, which helps to find and check them easily.

.NET has an enhanced and flexible *security system*, described in more detail in Section 2.5.2. .NET provides a variety of features, powerful and reliable ways to define and use *Windows Forms* and *Web Forms; ActiveX Data Objects.NET (ADO.NET)*—API to handle relational databases; and flexible technology to develop *XML-based Web services* to be published, discovered, and consumed. Configuration files and data exchange mechanisms in .NET are based on XML, which provides an easily readable and checkable text format, the de facto standard of contemporary programming.

All in all, *.NET is a software development platform targeted to TWC.* Nevertheless, it should be understood that even .NET with its TWC features doesn't automatically guarantee complete trustworthiness of user applications. To ensure that a .NET application is trustworthy, .NET should be used properly. For example, if you relax just one security restriction by using a module of *unmanaged code* (e.g., an ordinary *.exe* file in "old Windows style") in your application, you may create a security hole and widen the attack service of your program. It is enough to maliciously alter a security configuration file in some directory to create a chance for hackers to elevate their privileges. This threat is realistic, due to the fact that the configuration file is in XML format, which is easily understandable.

2.5.2 .NET Security

The .NET security model is illustrated in Figure 2.2. It is based on the following cornerstones: *code access security, role-based security, evidence-based security*, and *configurable security policies.* The main .NET security principle is as follows: Unlike earlier security models (e.g., UNIX), which bind security features and permissions to the *user* and *user group*, .NET ties security permissions to the *code* (*assembly*) and the *user executing the code.* Actually, The .NET security approach combines and enhances former security approaches: code- and user-centric. The code-centric approach is based on the concepts of *code access security* and *evidence-based security.* The user-centric approach

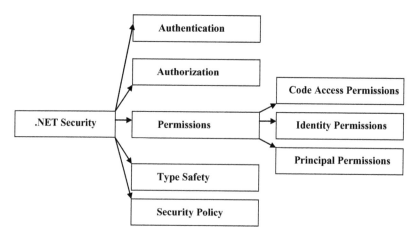

Figure 2.2 *.NET security architecture.*

relies on the concept of *role-based security*, which is a generalization of the UNIX-style user group model.

During code execution, .NET CLR loads each assembly "by need" the first time the assembly is called. During assembly load, CLR collects *evidence* (information) about the assembly that helps CLR to determine whether or not the assembly is trusted and secure, and what type of security permission it should be granted. The following types of evidences are collected: information on the *location from which the assembly code is loaded* (*site, URL, zone,* and *application directory*), information on the *code developer* (*strong name* and *publisher*), and the *hash* value of the assembly.

Evidence of the assembly is checked by CLR against the *security policy*, which can be defined at different levels: for *user, machine, enterprise*, and *application domain*. Security policies should be configured by system administrators and are typically specified in special XML configuration files. Based on the assembly's evidence, CLR checks whether the security policy permits the assembly to be executed.

Generally speaking, at runtime, .NET security checks are possible, due to .NET's *managed, type-safe execution mode*. The metadata (types) of any assembly are available to CLR, so it can check at runtime any security-related type or attribute of the code. If it were not for managed code and metadata, it would not be possible to make all necessary runtime security checks.

Code access security can be expressed in terms of *permissions* granted to a code. This set can be described either in *declarative style*, by *security attributes* annotating the pieces of code, as shown in Figure 2.3, or in *imperative style*, by *objects and API calls* representing the security permissions and their demands by the code, as depicted in Figure 2.4. The semantics of both C# code fragments is the same. Note the use of the *sealed* class; .NET security guideline documents recommend minimizing the attack surface of the application. The difference between those styles is as follows. Security attributes are activated once, at *assembly load time*, so using a declarative approach is more efficient, secure, and reliable, since the CLR is guaranteed to check the security permissions expressed by attributes, and code-checking utilities can easily detect them. However, an attribute-based approach does not provide an opportunity

```
using System.Net;
using System.Security.Permissions;

public sealed class Utilities {
  [
    DnsPermission(SecurityAction.Demand,
                  Unrestricted=true)
  ]
  public static IPAddress GetHost(string h) {
    return Dns.GetHostByName(h).AddressList[0];
  }
}
```

Figure 2.3 *Declarative style of representing permissions in .NET.*

```
using System.Net;
using System.Security.Permissions;

public sealed class Utilities {
  public static IPAddress GetHost(string hostName) {
    DnsPermission p
      = new DnsPermission(PermissionState.Unrestricted);
    p.Demand();
    return Dns.GetHostByName(hostName).AddressList[0];
  }
}
```

Figure 2.4 *Imperative style of representing permissions in .NET.*

for exception handling. The other approach, the imperative style of checking permissions, is more flexible but less secure and reliable. The code can check for a permission (e.g., whether it is possible to write to a file) when actually needed, handle any possible security exceptions, and issue appropriate messages to the user when necessary. However, without using attributes that "stick" security permissions to the code, there is a risk of forgetting to make imperative security checks, and as a result, the code terminates with the security exception.

A very important mechanism used in .NET security is the *security stack walk*. To enforce CLR to check if security permission is granted, the method currently running calls the *Demand* method of the corresponding security permission object. Then the CLR performs a security stack walk: It checks whether *each* method on the stack is granted the same permission. If not, *SecurityException* is thrown. Although, obviously, this mechanism is expensive, it guarantees that a partially trusted malicious assembly cannot call a fully trusted assembly's method of elevating privileges and performing an action that it is not allowed to perform.

From an AOP viewpoint, both approaches to injecting security checks—declarative and imperative—can be supported by AOP, as we show in Chapter 4. With Aspect.NET, the code developer can create and use aspects that inject security attributes marking appropriate points of the target code, thus making the code more secure. Also, the user can develop aspects to inject security API calls before a code that needs some security permissions: for example, a call of *Demand*, as described above.

User-centric security in .NET is based on concepts of role-based security that enhance the traditional framework of users and user groups. The user in .NET is described by the concept of *principal*—in the more common sense of this term, the person most responsible for making the business decisions related to the application. A principal can have one or more *roles*: similar to the old UNIX approach, where a user can belong to one or more user groups. Examples of roles are *sysadmin, manager*, and *engineer*. The set of roles expressed by strings is user-defined. The *IsInRole* method of the *IPrincipal* interface allows us to determine if a given principal belongs to a given role. The *PrincipalPermission* object ties a principal to his or her role. An example

```
String id1 = "John";
String role1 = "Manager";
PrincipalPermission p1 =
  new PrincipalPermission(id1, role1);

String id2 = "Mary";
String role2 = "Sysadmin";
PrincipalPermission p2 =
  new PrincipalPermission(id2, role2);

(p1.Union(p2)).Demand();
```

Figure 2.5 *Role-based security in .NET.*

of the use of role-based security is shown in Figure 2.5. Reference to the current principal can be extracted from the current Web request; it reflects the Web-aware nature of .NET. The principal object contains a reference to its *identity*: the *user name, authentication type*, and the flag designating whether the principal has been authenticated. One possible authentication type is *Windows authentication*, based on a traditional Windows login name and password. The other authentication type is *passport authentication*, based on *.NET Passport*. There are some other types of authentication, such as *Kerberos authentication*.

In general, the concepts of user-centric security—principal and identity—in .NET are flexible enough, although they don't bring anything novel to the security field: They are based on similar concepts in earlier versions of Windows and in UNIX. From an AOP viewpoint, a lot of opportunities arise to control user-centric security. For example, *authentication aspects* can be developed for different types of authentication and can be woven into appropriate join points of target applications to authenticate users. Also, security aspects can be developed that check whether a principal belongs to some roles.

The common teaching issue about .NET security [8] is that it appears a bit complicated for students and users. However, it is quite logical, and its complicated nature reflects real needs for different types of security settings and checks: *assembly evidences*: checking the a priori trustworthiness of the assembly code and its developer; *security permissions*: checking or demanding the rights of the code to perform different types of actions; *authentication and roles*: checking the user and the set of his or her permissions; and *security policy*: settings performed by system administrators to configure security on a machine, domain, or zone. The combination of the above is the resulting security discipline in .NET. As we have seen and will see again in Chapter 4, AOP can help to make security settings and checks more explicit, systematically organized, and clear.

2.5.3 .NET and Reliability

.NET is designed for developing reliable software. The following core features of .NET support reliable programming: *managed execution, attributes, proper-*

ties, exception handling, and *reflection*. Due to these features, which work for single- or multilanguage applications, .NET enables much more reliability than do traditional programming languages and systems with weaker typing models, especially C and C++.

The *managed execution mode* guarantees that the actual type for each object *p* can be determined at runtime using metadata. In the managed execution mode, for each operation *A op B*, CLR checks that the types of *A* and *B* operands comply to the operation *op*; otherwise, an exception is thrown. In particular, especially important for reliability as well as for security, is the fact that in the managed execution mode, address arithmetic (adding an integer to a pointer) or arbitrary casts of a pointer to any type are not allowed, and attempts to take such actions cause immediate exceptions as well as an attempt to address via a null pointer. The managed execution mode eliminates a lot of bugs and security threats and ensures that no array limits are exceeded by any index (otherwise, an exception is generated by CLR). In this relation, .NET's managed execution mode resembles the old principles of tagged architecture, first formulated and implemented in the 1960s (see Chapter 1), although managed execution is implemented programmatically via metadata and runtime type checking performed when the native code is executed. Surely such a dynamic typing approach requires substantial overhead, but it is much more reliable than ignoring actual data types at runtime.

Attributes in .NET are the way to annotate any named entity (class, method, field, etc.) by any useful information that can help to preserve and make available at runtime any specification and design decisions in the code: formal specification, input and output conditions, contracts, aspects that the code defines, and so on. At runtime, CLR and any utilities that process the code of the assembly (debuggers, verifiers, profilers, etc.) can check its attributes via a *reflection* mechanism to control the runtime behavior of the code, check it for correctness (compliance to the specifications by which the code is annotated), and transform and enhance it (e.g., weave some aspects into the code). So if used properly, attributes are very helpful in increasing software reliability.

Property is a concept that makes it possible to define a "virtual" information item in a class, with two basic operations: *get*, used to access (or calculate) the value of an item, and *set*, used to assign a new value to an item. In C#, "syntactic sugar" is provided, so that the programmer can write *p.X = V*, where *p* is an object and *X* is its property name. Actually, the concept of property in .NET is another incarnation of the idea of *procedural data representation*, which originated in the 1970s. Instead of defining the data (by a field), operations (methods) to access it and to assign it are provided. Implementations of *get* and *set* may contain arbitrary code. If used properly, this technique may improve code reliability, since any type of value, environment, or security (permission) check can be added to *get* or *set*. .NET security guideline books and documents recommend using, in any class, *public* properties (with necessary checks included) but *private* fields.

Although not invented by .NET authors, *exception handling* became an inherent part of the .NET execution model and contributes to software reliability. A typical example is related to checking the arguments by a method. Suppose that there is a condition (contract) expressed by a predicate $P(x)$ that should hold for argument x of method m. The method's code should check it, and if the contract does not hold, generate an exception. The exception should be specified in the method's header and can be caught and processed by any caller method. There are hundreds of predefined exception types, such as *NullReferenceException*, to identify typical bugs in the code. The advantage of .NET compared to all previous programming platforms with built-in exceptions is that the exception thrown from a module written in one language can be caught by another module written in another .NET language if the implementations of both languages are CLS compliant.

Reflection is a way to determine and analyze at runtime the type of any object and its components. It is very important to implement any type of runtime type checks and analysis in addition to those made by CLR. Reflection also provides access to attributes whose role has been considered above. Used properly, reflection can enable any kind of type checking not performed by .NET compilers and the CLR. Unfortunately, used improperly (or maliciously), reflection enables us to work around the access restrictions provided by *private* and *protected* access modifiers.

How can AOP help increase software reliability in .NET? It can do this by designing and implementing aspects that incorporate many types of checks that increase the reliability of the target code: design-by-contract checks and others (details in Chapter 4).

2.5.4 .NET TWC Tools FxCop and Spec#

The type-safe, reflective, and self-descriptive nature of .NET stimulates the development of various checking and verification TWC tools. Since the assembly binaries in .NET are accompanied by metadata—full information on the types defined and used in the assembly—it is quite possible to analyze any .NET code using its assembly only, without retrieving the sources. On the other hand, at the source code layer, it is quite possible to annotate the code by custom attributes that contain specifications of the code and to use the attributes at all stages of code processing: from code specification and design to debugging and profiling.

Many research and development projects and tools for .NET are based on these ideas. The best known of them are *FxCop* [39], a Microsoft software product, and *Spec#* [64], an experimental project by Microsoft Research. Both tools are reviewed in this section. *FxCop* is a tool to analyze .NET assemblies and check them against an extensible list of rules and recommendations that may concern design, security, and performance. There are versions of FxCop available for .NET 1.1 and .NET 2.0. The latest available version at the moment of writing this book is FxCop 1.35. In some software companies it is mandatory to check their software products using FxCop. Especially effective are FxCop's security checks. To make an experiment, you can write a simple "Hello world" console application in Visual Studio.NET, build it, and then pass the resulting assembly to FxCop, as a "target for analysis." Then press the "Analyze" button, and you will see four messages: warnings and recommendations. Surprising as it may seem, it appears that the simplest console application has one violation marked by FxCop as *breaking*: FxCop highly recommends explicit specification of *security permissions* for the code (see Section 2.5.2). This does not seem quite comfortable for .NET programmers: Everyone prefers that when writing some simple code, he or she should not "pay" for security that is unnecessary for the goals sought (e.g., training, getting some computational results quickly). However, for security reasons, in serious commercial software projects, following this FxCop's recommendation is highly recommended. The remaining three recommendations of FxCop are classified as "nonbreaking": assigning a strong name to the assembly, explicitly marking the code as CLS compliant, and removing the unused parameter of the *Main* method. So, as seen clearly by the style of its recommendations, FxCop is targeted to checking commercial software products intended for long-term use, in combination with applications and modules written in different languages, and designed with special attention to security and performance. So FxCop is a comfortable tool for software companies and engineers who are developing commercial code. As for software newbies, FxCop helps them learn the necessary elements and principles of secure and efficient code development.

Spec# is an extension of C# by design-by-contract specification and implementation features. It seems to be the first programming system to implement Hoare's idea of a verifying compiler [65], a compiler that not only checks language compatibility but also checks program *correctness*: its compliance to specifications of the source code is annotated with (i.e., performs) *formal verification* of C# programs. The word *formal* here is used to distinguish between program verification checks that Spec# performs, and the present common meaning of the term *verification* in the .NET realm; the latter means checking by CLR of a newly loaded assembly, which is far from the meaning of program verification introduced by Hoare in the 1960s. Formal methods are still considered by many software practitioners to fail in making real software products more trustworthy. But due to Meyer's papers on design by contract [66] and the Eiffel language [67], and currently, due to Spec# implementation, we now have a practical working approach and tools to use formal specification and verification methods in combination with traditional programming languages. Spec# is implemented as an add-in to Visual Studio (using the same integration technique as our Aspect.NET). It means that the user can create and manage Spec# language projects.

The Spec# language, in addition to C# features, has the following extensions: *nonnull types, pre- and postconditions (parts or contracts)*, and *object invariants*. Nonnull types are useful to check whether any object reference is always nonnull: For example, when declaring *T! p* in Spec#, we can be sure that the *p* reference to objects of type T will always be assigned nonnull values only. The Spec# compiler will generate code to perform a runtime check for nonnull values for each assignment to *p*. Using nonnull types is comfortable, reliable, and rigorous, since software developers often forget to make an explicit check for null values. As for pre- and postconditions and invariants, they have all been part of formal specification and verification mechanisms since the 1960s. The Spec# compiler generates code to check at runtime that the pre- and postconditions and the invariant hold. The user can specify in Spec# language, by means of an *otherwise* clause, what type of exception to throw if any of those conditions are violated. All these features make the code more trustworthy. From a design-by-contract viewpoint, Spec# can be considered a language and tool to specify contracts adequately and to check rigorously that they hold, instead of formulating contracts in natural language as part of program documentation, as in most languages and APIs now; verbal specifications are impossible to check formally.

The architecture of the entire Spec# system is as follows. The Spec# system has its own compiler of Spec# language to MSIL code. The specification part of Spec# code is translated into BoogiePL specification language. This form is used as an input to the Simplify theorem prover. Both BoogiePL and Simplify have been developed by HP Research [67]. The theorem prover typically works in automatic mode and generates the "correct" answer, or a list of errors. It is also possible to work with the theorem prover in interactive mode, which is more suitable for logic and specification gurus. As a result, due to using Spec# instead of C#, the code becomes more trustworthy in two respects: first, it is statically verified by the theorem prover; second, all the specification conditions, if necessary, are checked at runtime. These are the benefits of this system.

The shortcomings of Spec# are as follows. According to the approach taken by the developers, all the extensions are introduced into Spec# as the elements of the source language itself (rather than as annotations). So users who develop code in Spec# have to compile it by a specific Spec# compiler. The user cannot just take C# code and annotate it by specifications (say, using custom attributes). As a result, the Spec# system is somewhat limited by its own compiler. When switching to new versions of Visual Studio.NET, C# users willing to use Spec# extensions have to wait until a new version of the Spec# compiler and the entire Spec# system (add-in) is developed for this new version of Visual Studio.NET.

By contrast, the Aspect.NET approach to implementing aspects is based on using custom attributes. Users can simply annotate the C# code using the AOP annotations understandable by Aspect.NET and not prevent the code from processing by ordinary C# compiler from Visual Studio.NET. Moreover, by using aspects in Aspect.NET, it is quite possible to implement all necessary design-by-contract runtime checks without "freezing" AOP features in a specific extension of C# without the need to develop a special C# extension compiler for it. Design-by-contract checks can be injected into the target code by weaving the appropriate design-by-contract aspects (details in Chapter 4).

To conclude this I recommend a set of recommendations paper by Meier et al. [68] for .NET 2.0 secure coding, which is beyond the scope of this book. This is also true for .NET 3.0 [69], shipped in late 2006, which contains a lot of new components and technologies, such as Windows Communication Foundation, Windows Presentation Foundation, Windows Workflow Foundation, Windows CardSpace, and new ways of developing secure applications and their integration with XML. Applying AOP to .NET 3.0 is a task for the near future.

As we've seen in this section, AOP can be applied productively to enhance the trustworthiness of .NET applications. There is a very good basis for that: managed execution, metadata, and custom attributes. Chapters 3 and 4 are devoted to more detailed descriptions of how to implement and apply AOP for .NET.

2.6   TWC AND JAVA

2.6.1   Java Overview

This book is devoted primarily to applying AOP in a .NET environment. Nevertheless, being an expert in Java technology and working with Sun on enhancement and use of Java since 1996, I decided to include a section on Java and TWC. I am using my Java experience in teaching Java. My Java book [70] is widely used in Russian universities as an officially recommended basic textbook on Java technology.

Of modern software platforms, Java was the first (five years before .NET) to resurrect and implement the principles of dynamic typing and what is now called managed execution, whose principles are especially important for trustworthy programming (see Section 2.5). Java was the first Internet-aware object-oriented software platform shipped for free download (in 1995). Many aspects and features of modern software development are well designed in Java technology: object orientation, typing, modularization, reflection, persistence, component-oriented programming (JavaBeans and Enterprise Java-Beans), runtime class loading, networking features, applets and servlets, security, and many others. Java has several editions targeted for use in various applications and on various hardware devices: the *Standard Edition, Enterprise Edition*, and *Micro Edition*. Unique Java API has been developed not only by its creators, Sun Microsystems, but by millions of third-party commercial and research programmers. The community of Java users is now one of the largest in the world and is comparable to that of C++ programmers. This is due to Java's relative simplicity (compared to its predecessors, especially C++), combined with power and flexibility. Java basics can be taught or learned in five or six lectures (which cannot be said about .NET, although both platforms deserve high praise). Java's role is outstanding in open- and shared-source project development; for example, the widely used Java NetBeans has been developing as an open-source project. Many new research projects and software engineering approaches, such as AOP, were implemented first in Java since it was easier to do than in most other languages, and in addition, guaranteed platform independence for project implementation. The Java compiler translates Java source into *bytecode*, a platform-independent postfix notation used as an intermediate binary form of the program, stored in a *class file*. Class files also contain full information on types defined and used by a Java compilation unit, similar to .NET metadata, although Java doesn't use this term and does not structure typing information as systematically as .NET does. In Java, all types are stored in the *constant pool* of the class file, together with string constants. The *Java Virtual Machine* (JVM) uses a just-in-time compiler to translate the bytecode to native code, method by method. JVM has full access to typing information (Java "metadata") from class files. In this relation, Java and .NET are very similar. Java was the first to adopt the principle of just-in-time compilation.

Nevertheless, Java technology has its limitations. First, Java technology is limited by the Java language. Adding to a Java application some modules of legacy code or newly developed modules written in other languages is not easy. The set of languages to be used in addition to Java in one application is limited to C and C++. For those languages, Java provides Java native interface (JNI), an API to enable access to Java objects, classes, and methods. Software developers who would like to create a multilanguage application are limited to the only opportunity: to mark the headers of certain methods of the Java application as *native* (actually, in Java context, that means "C or C++ implemented") and to implement them in C or C++ using JNI. So Java plays the role of the "master" language, and the "native" methods and languages play the role of "slaves," which is not a desirable situation. In addition, JNI is not 100% safe and secure; neither is it available with JME. Such an approach (compared to .NET, with its multilanguage interoperability support) looks limited. In addition, unlike .NET, there is no "legal" Java assembler, a symbolic representation of bytecode that could be used as one of the full-fledged programming languages in Java technology approved by Sun. As a consequence, there are many third-party research projects targeted to creating their own Java assemblers. Compare this to the role of MSIL in .NET (see Section 2.5).

Despite its limitations, Java technology is used worldwide and supported by such major companies as IBM, Nokia, Motorola, Panasonic, and many others which have their own Java implementations and use them for developing mobile phone software and enterprise solutions. Java and .NET are mutually influential: Features have been transposted from Java to .NET. As noted above, there is also a "backward" inheritance—from .NET to Java. Examples are *boxing* and *unboxing, attributes* in .NET and *annotations* in Java, and *properties.* Let's consider them in more detail since they are closely related to trustworthy software development.

Boxing in .NET is an implicit conversion of a value (say, an integer) to object form, and unboxing is an inverse operation. This mechanism is reliable and secure, since type information is stored when boxing a value and checked when unboxing it (unlike C/C++, with their "conversions of pointers to any type"). In Java before version 1.5, similar features were implemented explicitly but a little bit awkwardly, by *wrapper classes* (e.g., *Integer*) used as object wrappers to simple values. In Java 1.5, however, the Java developers made a decision to implement implicit boxing and unboxing in .NET style, since it is easier to use and makes the code more compact.

The multipurpose importance and role of *attributes* in .NET is discussed in Section 2.5.1. In Java, before version 1.5, there were no analogs. As a result, Java developers had to use empty *marker interfaces* (e.g., *Serializable*) to mark a class as having some important quality or property. I've always thought of these marker interfaces as looking awkward. However, in Java 1.5, *annotations* were implemented: an interface-based analog of attributes. So in the latest versions of Java since Java 1.5 (as well as in .NET) it is possible to annotate the code by any useful information, moreover, Java 1.6 allows users to implement their own annotation processors.

Property is a useful concept of reliable data processing in .NET (Section 2.5.3). As for Java, before the JavaBeans technology was introduced in 1996, one year later than Java 1.0, there had been no properties. In JavaBeans, however, the concept of property was introduced not as a Java language feature but as a code design and implementation pattern—as a pair of getX/ setX methods. Such a situation has been taking place in Java up to now. However, when Sun releases Java 1.7, they intend to introduce properties into the Java language similar to those in C# at the language syntax and semantics levels.

2.6.2   Java Security

Security issues have been around since the early release of Java (JDK 1.0 shipped in 1995) because part of the Java model of Internet client–server application are *applets*—client Java applications related to HTML Web pages, loaded together with them, and invoked in HTML rendering by the browser. Although the new opportunity to animate Web pages by applets was very attractive, some users worried about possible harm that malicious applets loaded to their machines could cause. When I started working on Java for Sun in 1996, my university colleagues asked about the applets reported by the browser to start on a computer without the user's will: "Are new types of viruses being developed by Sun?"

To exclude any possibility of developing malicious applets that could harm client computers, Sun introduced in Java 1.0 a restrictive *sandbox model* for applet security. According to this model, an applet cannot read or update local files on a client machine, cannot get any information on the client host configuration and environment, can only use resources that it "brings" from the same Web server from which the applet is loaded, and can establish network connections to its "parent" Web server only. An applet gets its parameters from its parent HTML file and can only communicate with other applets bound to the same HTML page. Such restrictions guarantee that it is not possible to develop an "applet virus" or "applet worm." But from the viewpoint of developing distributed client–server solutions with intensive use of applets (e.g., a solution that controls business processes in a company), the Java applet sandbox model is too restrictive.

Another key element of the early Java security model is *SecurityManager*. It is a class to be implemented by the Java developer or by the Java-enabled Web browser. The security manager contains methods to check various security permissions, speaking in .NET terms, in "imperative style" (e.g., *canRead* or *canWrite*). There was no way in that model to specify security permissions in declarative style. In practice, Java security managers implemented in different browsers differed: For example, in the Netscape (Mozilla) browser the security manager was more restrictive than the security manager implemented in Sun's HotJava browser.

Starting with Java 1.1, the restrictive sandbox security model was relaxed. An opportunity appeared to implement digitally signed applets, which if their signatures are checked, gain the rights of trusted code (i.e., executed in the JVM like an ordinary local Java application). By default, an applet or a Java Web Start application is still put into a sandbox, and a local Java application is not. The current Java security model [71] has much in common with a .NET security model. Similar class names, such as *Permission*, are used to represent basic security concepts on both platforms. Nevertheless, the notion of security manager was preserved in Java. To check permissions, it is necessary, first, to get the security manager from the system, as in: *smgr = System.getSecurity-Manager*() call, and next, check the security permission perm against the security manager: *smgr.checkPermission (myPermission)*. If there is no permission, as well as in .NET, a *SecurityException* is thrown.

Similar to .NET, the concept of *security policy* was added to Java, specified by the *java.security.Policy* class. Although, unlike .NET, in Java any given invocation of Java runtime uses only one security policy, an object of the *Policy* class. Checking for a security permission is performed in Java quite similar to a .NET security stack walk. The default *SecurityManager* uses *java.security. AccessController*, which walks along the current call stack and checks the required permission against the current security policy, first for the current method, then for its caller, and next for any method in the "dynamic chain" of methods called on the stack. If any method in the dynamic chain is not granted permission, an exception is thrown.

Java security API pays a lot of attention to cryptography (*Java Cryptography Extension*), in particular public key–based cryptography (*Public Key Infrastructure*), authentication (*Kerberos authentication, smart card authentication, username/password authentication*), and secure communication (SSL/TLS,

SASL). In general, security services in Java are enabled via one or more *security providers*, objects of the *java.security.Provider* class. There can be more than one security provider, and a Java application may request an implementation of some security service (e.g., the implementation of some authentication mechanism) from any of the security providers available by specifying the name of the provider and the name of the service. By default, Sun's security providers are taken, but any third-party implementation can implement its own set of security providers. This is an interesting idea that gives Java security somewhat more flexibility than even in .NET security.

Unlike .NET, there is no explicit concept of evidence in Java security. Nevertheless, when loading a class file, the Java class loader (which can be taken by default or defined by the user) checks where the code is loaded from, who signed the code, and what default permissions should be granted to the code. This mechanism can be regarded as an analog of evidence in some limited form.

To tie this section to the main subject of the book, for the Java platform it is quite possible to implement an AOP framework that helps to improve the security of Java applications. In my opinion, such implementations of AOP should use annotations similar to the use of custom attributes for representing aspects in our Aspect.NET. As for the current status of this issue, common-use AOP frameworks for Java (e.g., AspectJ) don't use annotations and require full switching to AspectJ Java extension and its specific compiler (more exactly, in AspectJ, an alternative annotation form of defining aspects is possible, due to integration of AspectJ with AspectWerkz). It is not possible to take an *existing* Java application and make it more secure with the help of AspectJ aspects, staying within the "classical" Java language, without switching completely to an AspectJ compiler and development environment (more about that in Chapter 4). I don't yet know any AOP framework for Java that uses the advantages of Java annotations. I do think that the use of annotations is the future of Java AOP.

2.6.3 Java and Reliability

Most of what I've said about .NET and reliability (see Section 2.5.3) is also applicable to Java, since the two platforms are very similar. Strong typing of the language, combined with runtime type checking by the JVM using type information from class files, enables reliable type-safe execution (in analogy to .NET, "Java-managed execution"). In Java as well as in .NET, software developers can use annotations (since Java 1.5), properties (since Java 1.7), exception handling, and reflection to make Java applications more reliable.

Specific issues of reliability arise when using Java API for multithreading. It is very easy to develop a multithreaded Java application that causes a *deadlock*. For example, the *t.stop*() and *t.suspend*() methods introduced in Java for the purpose of stopping a thread *t* or suspending it appeared to be so unreliable that since Java 1.1 they have been claimed *deprecated*, that is, not recommended and to be replaced by newly implemented methods. The reason is rooted in the basics of multithreading and multiprocessing. Concurrent threads typically use some common resources, and code to handle these resources is referred to as *critical sections*. Execution of critical sections related to the same shared resources should obey a *mutual exclusion* discipline. So, just imagine that the thread *t* has entered such a critical section, and occasionally, another thread calls the *stop* or *suspend* method of thread *t*. As a result, *t* "hangs" within its critical section, so it is likely to keep some shared resource needed by other concurrent threads waiting for it. This is a typical example of a deadlock. So Java needs more reliable ways to control threads. The way to resolve this issue recommended by the authors of Java [70], based on using loops and the *wait/notify* pair of methods, does not appear to be clear and self-explanatory.

How could AOP help to solve such reliability problems? It is quite possible to develop an aspect that handles the thread *t* with more care than *stop* or *suspend*, that uses some checks of the status of the thread *t* prior to stopping it, that uses extra mutexes or semaphores, and so on. Those aspect's actions (or advices, speaking in terms of AspectJ) could be woven before, after, or instead of the calls *stop* and *suspend* of deprecated methods.

In my Java development experience, although it may sound surprising, reliability issues in Java were detected in the simplest and common-use constructs: arithmetic. When I started writing Java code a decade ago, in testing the results of integer arithmetic operations, I happened to use *try/catch* blocks, in the hope of handling *ArithmeticException* as an overflow in operations such as + or *. I was surprised to learn that integer overflow is not detected in Java. In this respect, .NET and C# provide much more reliability, since it is possible in C# to use *checked/unchecked* blocks to switch the control of arithmetic overflow on or off.

Another not-quite-reliable element of Java arithmetic is lack of *unsigned* types. Since the appearance of C in the early 1970s, software developers have been using *unsigned* arithmetic, which was also adopted in .NET. In Java, to model *unsigned* arithmetic operations, programmers have to use lower-level constructs such as logical *and* with appropriate masks to extract one, two, or four bytes from an integer number. This is not reliable at all, since it is very easy to forget using the logical *and* operation, and there is no way to catch it, except for code inspection.

Yet another reliability issue in Java is related to floating-point arithmetic. It's fine that floating point in Java is implemented according to the IEEE 754 standard. But most programmers are not quite accustomed to make explicit checks for specific values such as *positive infinity, negative infinity*, and *not a number* (NaN) in modules related to floating-point arithmetic, although in Java they really need to do that. It is surprising that the result of an equals operation such as $x == y$ can be *false* if x and y have the *same* value but that value is a *Double.NaN*! When implementing intensive floating-point calculations in one of my Java projects, I had to write a special method to compare two floating-point numbers, with explicit checks for cases of positive and negative infinities and NaNs.

A reliability pitfall in Java is also related to the *String* type. Almost every Java beginner is initially trying to compare two strings, $s1$ and $s2$, using an ordinary equality operator: $s1 == s2$. However, this is a bug; the correct version is $s1.equals$ ($s2$). This bug is not detected by the Java compiler. I am quite sure that there are many such undetected bugs in existing Java code.

Even AOP can hardly help to detect the Java arithmetic reliability issues considered in this section, since any software developer prefers to use the traditional infix-style form of arithmetic operations instead of defining special methods to implement more reliable versions of floating-point or unsigned arithmetic, but typical AOP tools can operate with and update method calls rather than analyze and update every or selected "+" operations in the source code. So that although Java is a contemporary, strongly typed language that enables development of reliable code, there are a number of typical bugs that require special TWC tools to detect: Java static source code analyzers or byte-code analyzers, considered in Section 2.6.4.

An interesting reliability issue in Java is related to trying to work around the lack of macro definitions support in the Java platform. Many programmers use C and C++ macros: *define*'s and their macro calls (extensions). In Java, there are no macro definitions, which is unfortunate. Often, programmers prefer to define simple macros (rather than methods whose execution is time consuming) to implement such operations as converting or comparing numbers, or extracting some fields of objects. Since in Java they cannot do that, they try to find a workaround. Some of them decide to use the C preprocessor *cpp* for that purpose. So instead of developing a pure Java code, they initially develop a mixed-style code consisting of Java code augmented by C-style *define* macro definitions and their calls. As a result, they think in terms of their mixed-style code, but after preprocessing, they get an unreadable Java code that can consist of very long lines and is actually nondebuggable and nonmaintainable because of its awkwardness.

2.6.4 Java TWC Tools

Java developers managed to make Java a more trustworthy programming language than the previous languages used worldwide. Moreover, the Java compiler *javac* itself helps to make Java applications more trustworthy and can itself be regarded as a Java TWC tool. For example, the compiler checks for the use of noninitialized local variables. To make the Java compiler quiet, Java programmers have to explicitly initialize all local variables. To compare this situation with C, ordinary C compilers don't perform such checks, and to detect such bugs, programmers have to use *lint*, a classical static code verifier for C.

In addition, we can find a lot of TWC tools and options built into common-use Java-integrated development environments: NetBeans, Eclipse, IDEA, and others. Most of them offer *refactoring* options suitable to make applications more trustworthy. A typical example of refactoring is to surround the selected statement by a *try/catch* block. It helps to automate coding for exception handling, one of the most important TWC features of modern languages. In general, refactoring is another code transformation technology which, in addition to AOP, can be used to convert any code to a more trustworthy version.

As for specific Java static code verifiers making subtle checks to improve the trustworthiness of Java applications, most notable of them is *Wasp for Java* [72], which analyzes Java source code. Wasp is helpful to statically detect typical runtime bugs and design and coding flaws such as the following:

- Various attempts to use noninitialized variables
- Method arguments with *null* values, and other cases of attempts to use *null* pointers
- Unreachable code in *if, try/catch*, and *switch/case* statements
- Integer arithmetic overflow (see Section 2.6.3 for more detailed analysis of this issue)
- Array index out of bounds
- Unused variables

Unfortunately, Wasp doesn't analyze multithreaded applications. In general, Java programmers lack a good multithreaded applications analyzer and deadlock detector. We have already given an example of how AOP can help in detecting possible deadlocks.

2.7 SUMMARY

This chapter is a brief overview of the origins of TWC and progress achieved in developing TWC technologies and tools in modern software platforms. I quite understand that many complicated TWC issues, interesting ideas, and technologies are mentioned only briefly or not mentioned at all. But in each section, I tried to find and emphasize the possible role of AOP and suggest how it can help in solving TWC issues. In the next two chapters we show how such use of AOP to improve the trustworthiness of code can be implemented in a .NET environment using the Aspect.NET tool.

Further progress in TWC technologies should probably be based on reasonable combinations of formal methods and practical tools and development environments. The Aspect.NET project and framework should be beneficial for that.

3

Aspect-Oriented Programming and Aspect.NET

In this chapter we describe aspect-oriented programming (AOP), one of the most prospective paradigms and technologies of software development. The history of AOP, the work of predecessors, and AOP basics, principles, and tools are considered. The Aspect.NET [1–6] AOP framework for Microsoft.NET is described: its prerequisites, principles of architectural design, comparison to other approaches to AOP and to other AOP tools, Aspect.NET features, use and advantages, and AOP and Aspect.NET perspectives.

3.1 HISTORY OF AOP

The history of AOP started long ago, in the 1970s, although modern authors tend to date AOP to the mid-1990, with the pioneering work of Kiczales and his team [13] on AOP and AspectJ [10] at Xerox PARC and, later, at the University of British Columbia. The importance of those papers is invaluable; the term *AOP* itself and all the basic concepts of AOP were formulated by this world-leading school.

But long before, in the 1970s, computer scientists tried to resolve complicated software architectural issues originating from the everyday needs of reusing and maintaining software. In 1968, while working on the THE operat-

Using Aspect-Oriented Programming for Trustworthy Software Development,
By Vladimir O. Safonov
Copyright © 2008 John Wiley & Sons, Inc.

ing system, Dijkstra [73] introduced the concept of *abstraction level*, which he used to make operating system code design easier. Abstraction level k ($k > 0$) is an element of hierarchy of a complicated software system that consists of a group of modules whose implementation uses (calls) modules of level $k - 1$ only. Abstraction level 0 is considered to be the set of either hardware instructions, or the constructs and concepts of the implementation programming language, depending on the problem domain. Thus, according to this approach, a complicated software system should be designed and implemented bottom-up, from abstraction level 0 to abstraction level n, where n is the maximal depth of this hierarchy.

The role of the abstraction-level concept in the history of programming technologies is fundamental. Generally speaking, all the software is developed and evolved according to this principle, and each software developer now starts from a high-enough abstraction level rather than from abstraction level 0 ("from scratch," as it was in the 1950s or 1960s). Nevertheless, it is interesting to note that very few of the present programming languages and development environments explicitly support the concept of abstraction level. From well-known languages supporting it, I can only mention the compiler design language CDL/2 [74] by Koster.

It should be mentioned, however, that since the architecture of software systems is evolving and becoming more and more complicated, in a large software system it is not always possible to determine exactly to which abstraction layer a given module M belongs, since the architecture of the system may not be adequately described as a "pyramid" of abstraction layers. The architecture of a complicated software system can be modeled by a forest of trees, or, sometimes, as a semantic net (graph) with nonhierarchical relationships of modules. In other words, what is important is not the abstraction level of the module M, but the module's relations to other modules, which should be easily located and updated as needed.

On the other hand, Parnas [18] and Myers [19] in the early 1970s formulated another fundamental concept of software decomposition: a *module*. A module is a program unit that has an explicit syntactic definition and an explicit method of activation (call), is semantically independent, performs a definite subtask in a software system, and has some definite (ideally, minimal) set of "contact points" with the rest of the program, in both data flow (arguments, global variables, etc.) and control flow (calls by the module from other modules in the program). The implementation of a module should not be known to its user. What should be known about the module is its *interface*: the module *name*, the number and types of its *arguments* and its *results*, a set of possible *exceptions* (or abnormal situations the module's call may cause), the *side effect*—a set of the global variables and objects modified by the module, and yet the most difficult to formalize, the *semantics* (*functionality*) of the module. Note that in classical modular programming, no user other than the developer responsible for module design and implementation should "break" implementation of the module, trying to change it or to add new code.

The most famous Russian expert in software modularity was Gregory Tseytin, who considered a software module to be a *unit of programming knowledge* (or implementation of an *independent idea*), and implemented a prototype of a modular programming system based on a *semantic net of modules* [75] such that it became possible to synthesize the program "of independent ideas" using Tseytin's modular semantic net toolkit.

So, in simple cases, a software system can be designed and implemented as a set of modules organized according to the abstraction-level hierarchy scheme. However, it was realized early that such basic architectural mechanisms are not enough. There are a lot of *concerns* e.g., considerations, tasks, subtasks, ideas) that cannot be implemented in software just as module hierarchy. Programmers often need to "cross-cut" the current module hierarchy to implement new features or to modify existing ones. As an example, let's consider a compiler from some language (say, C# 1.0), organized according to a classical scheme: lexical analyzer, parser, semantic analyzer and intermediate code generator, and object code generator and optimizer. As the source language evolves, a typical task is to enhance the compiler by implementation of a new feature (say, generics or a new kind of statement). To do that, it is not enough just to add modules to the existing compiler's module hierarchy. It is necessary to implement new sets (hierarchies) of modules that support the new feature's implementation in different parts of the compiler, and then (and probably most difficult) to add at appropriate *join points* within the existing compiler code the calls of the new modules and the new definitions and declarations related to using the new modules. It appears that each part of the compiler should be updated: lexical analyzer, to implement new keywords of the source language; parser, to parse the syntax of the new constructs; semantic analyzer, to make appropriate semantic checks and generate intermediate code related to the new constructs; object code generator, to generate object code implementing new constructs; and others. The implementation of the new feature appears to be *pervasive*; it cross-cuts all the code of the compiler by nontrivial code injections *scattered* or *tangled* in the compiler code. We came to the concept of *cross-cutting concern* [13] introduced by modern classicists of AOP, *a concern that cannot be implemented by one generalized procedure* (*related set of modules*). A simpler example in more common use is *logging*, implementation of the "verbose" mode of software system execution such that each module (procedure, method) outputs the tracks of its start and finish in a global system log. Other common-use examples are *MT safety*, adding to the existing code (e.g., a library) tangled fragments (e.g., resource synchronization calls) to make the code multithreaded safe; and *security*, adding to the existing code a number of tangled security checks: permission requests and authentication calls (see Section 2.5.2).

Now back to AOP history. In the 1970s, experts in programming technologies realized that in addition to the *horizontal, one-dimensional* scheme of abstraction layers, it is often helpful to design and implement a software system and to think of the system in another dimension: the *vertical*. In 1979, a professor at Rostov University, Adolph Fouxman, published a pioneering monograph [76] that can be considered as a predecessor paper of AOP, although, unfortunately, it does not yet appear to be known in the United States or Western Europe. Hopefully, this will change and people will begin to pay attention to this very deep paper, which has a lot of interesting ideas that sound quite contemporary. Fouxman introduced the term *vertical cut*: a set of *tangled actions*, tangled (scattered) code fragments in a software system that implement some independent functionality (*extending function*, as he called it). He suggested implementing a toolkit to support his *vertical cut technology*, a set of operations on vertical cuts: to find and visualize a vertical cut, to modify it, and to add new vertical cuts to the software system. Unfortunately, Fouxman's ideas were not implemented in a commercial software product, but Fouxman's vertical cuts of the 1970s and modern aspects in AOP in the 1990s are very close to each other. The architecture of a software system, considered in a "two-dimensional" view as a hierarchy of abstract levels and a set of vertical cuts, is shown in Figure 3.1.

Thus, due to the use of abstraction levels and vertical cuts as elements of software architecture, we can assign to each module M its "horizontal coordinate," the name and the number of the abstraction level to which it belongs, and its "vertical coordinate," the name (and the number, if applicable) of its vertical cut, a functionality whose part the module implements. Such a systematic view is very helpful for the purpose of program modification and to improve program reliability. If we need to update the system (change or add a functionality), we can express those actions as a set of simple operations that we need to perform on parts of vertical cuts and abstraction levels.

However, there are three main issues in this scheme: *oversimplification, reuse*, and *semantics*. A real software system may be so complicated that it is difficult to locate a module using its horizontal and vertical coordinates only, since the module can be reused in more than one subsystem. In addition, what if we decide to reuse module M in another system? Which coordinates should its "clone" be assigned in another application with probably quite a different context and application domain? Also, the *semantics* of abstract levels and vertical cuts should be taken into account. In the *TIP technology* [11] used by

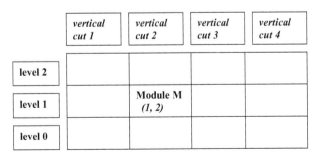

Figure 3.1 *Abstraction layers and vertical cuts in a software system.*

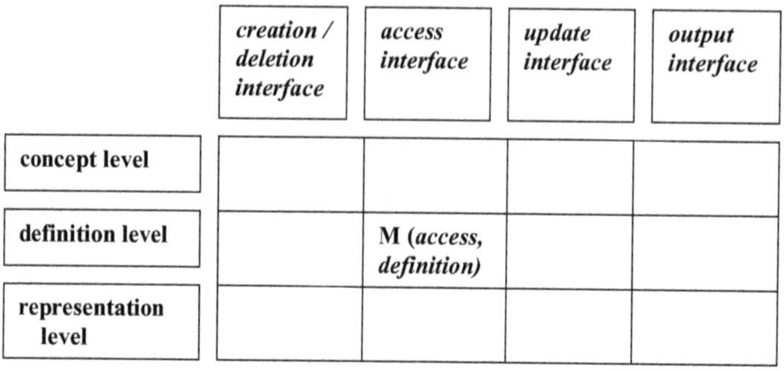

	creation / deletion interface	access interface	update interface	output interface
concept level				
definition level		M (access, definition)		
representation level				

Figure 3.2   *Abstraction layers and vertical cuts in TIP technology.*

our team for compiler development in the 1980s, I tried to resolve the issue of semantics of abstraction levels and vertical cuts by using the following predefined sets of abstraction layers and vertical cuts with some definite semantics suitable for the problem domain: abstraction levels, *representation level, and definition level, concept level*; and vertical cuts, *creation/deletion interface, access interface, update interface, and output interface* (see Figure 3.2; more details on TIP technology are provided in Section 1.2 and in the book [11]). Although this predefined two-dimensional design scheme was very simple, it appeared to be sufficient for our projects in the problem domain of compiler development. By using TIP technology to develop a family of compilers for one hardware platform [11], we solved the problem of reusability; about 20 to 30% of modules developed for one compiler project appeared to be reusable in another. However, we didn't consider the goal of automated code injection (weaving) based on some conditions, as in AOP. We did all code modifications by hand, following the principles of TIP technology. Nevertheless, this TIP discipline of programming helped us to make our software more readable, reliable, and reusable.

3.2   AOP BASICS

Aspect-oriented programming (AOP) [13] is a new programming paradigm developed to support software component reuse, modification, and enhancement, based on defining and applying (weaving) aspects that implement crosscutting concerns. Parts of AOP are *aspect-oriented analysis, design*, and *implementation*. The goal of aspect-oriented programming is to design and develop programs by, first, *separation of concerns* in terms of *aspects*, and second, constructing the resulting applications by *weaving* the aspects to the basic modules that implement the skeleton of the application. Each application can be regarded as a collection of implementations of *concerns*: ideas, considerations, principles, disciplines, restrictions, algorithms, and so on.

Following AOP classicists [13], let's use the term *core concerns* for the main concerns that implement the business logic of the application. Typically, each can be implemented as *modular concern*, a programming module (in classical sense) or a related collection of modules.

Another type of concern is referred to as a *cross-cutting concern*. These are the basic elements of AOP. They cannot be implemented simply by a related set of modules, but for their implementation also require activating (injecting) a set of tangled program fragments [usually, executable statements or definitions (declarations)] to the modules, implementing other concerns. Examples of cross-cutting concerns are given in Section 3.1. An important question related to cross-cutting concerns occurs immediately: From the viewpoint of classical modular programming of the 1970s (in Myers' style [19]) it is not possible to penetrate implementation of a module by adding new code or modifying existing code. Nevertheless, the developer of a cross-cutting concern and an aspect *has to do that*, since he or she has to inject tangled code fragments into the code of modules implementing other concerns, developed by other engineers, modules with which the developer of the aspect is typically not very familiar. So in some respects, AOP can be regarded as a software technology that helps to break modules written by other developers; hence, it should be used with a lot of care. The question arises: Is AOP really modular? A good way to think about that might be as follows: Someone drives though a red traffic light. Other people object that the driver's behavior is a violation of the traffic rules. He replies: *No, this is a new traffic rule.* When I posed the modularity to the originator of AOP, initially it seemed to look quite similar: Yes, AOP is modular since aspect is an extended type of module. But actually the situation with AOP is quite different from the situation with traffic rules. To meet the real needs of complicated modern software architecture and the real needs of implementing cross-cutting concerns, we have to extend the concept of a module when using AOP. Aspect is a module whose scope, unlike that of classical Myers-style modules, is not limited by its definition. The aspect's scope is extended to all of its weavings into one or more applications. In particular, an aspect can weave a new variable definition into a "foreign" module, but that definition will be visible only by the aspect, not by the target module.

Modern AOP originated in the 1990s during the age of intensive commercial use of the object-oriented approach. This is not occasional: The more OOP is used, the more its limitations and pitfalls become clear [22]. Similar to using classical modules and abstraction layers, by operating class hierarchies only it is not possible to solve modern tasks that require implementations of cross-cutting concerns. A group at Xerox PARC supervised by Gregor Kiczales introduced the notions of *cross-cutting concern* and *aspect*. Kiczales's group developed the world's first (AOP) tool, AspectJ [10], based on Java. Another early Java-based AOP project is IBM's HyperJ [77]. The AOP Web site [12] contains many other references. We overview the existing AOP tools in Sections 3.3, 3.5, and 3.6.

According to the classical AOP terminology [13,78], *aspect* is part of a program that cross-cuts its *core concerns*, the primary architectural components of the system implemented by modular concerns. An aspect definition contains a set of *advices*, actions to be applied (or *woven*, in AOP terms) to the target application, at some *join points*, selected points in the control flow of the target program. By *weaving*, the advices are, in some sense, injected into the target application. Any part of aspect definition specifying how to weave some advice can be regarded as a construct of the type

*if Condition **then** Advice*

where *Condition* is a condition to hold during execution of the target program for the *Advice* to be activated. The real syntax of those constructs differs in different AOP tools. Let's use a simpler term, *weaving condition*, rather than the more complicated term, *pointcut designator*, used for similar AOP elements in AspectJ.

There can also be separate *definitions of named pointcuts*, sets of potential join point descriptions (the weaving conditions and related advices to be woven) isolated from a concrete aspect, to which several aspects can refer. The architecture of an aspect and the result of its weaving into an application are shown in Figure 3.3. Unlike a traditional module, whose call is located at some definite point in the program, the results of aspect weaving are scattered around the program and cross-cut many of its modules.

Actually, all programmers use aspects in their everyday work but generally in an implicit way. As a result, not enough attention is paid to make the task of *locating* and *updating* aspects easier. It makes program debugging and maintenance costly. One of the reasons is lack of AOP functionality in programming languages and tools. Before the advent of AOP languages and tools, we had to do it "by hand." When dealing with a complicated software system it is very

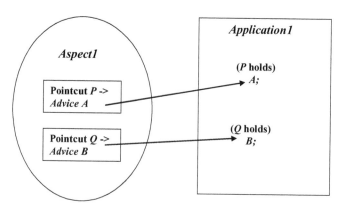

Figure 3.3 *Architecture of an aspect and the result of its weaving.*

difficult and risky to solve a typical task such as locating and modifying the tangled code fragments that implement some functionality or to add tangled code that implements a new functionality. We are likely to forget something. For example, suppose that we have to solve by hand the task of adding resource synchronization operations based on semaphore. Then we are likely to insert the call for closing semaphore operation before the code updating a common resource, but forget to insert the pairing call of the open semaphore operation after updating the resource. What will be the result of such a bug? (By the way, it will be very difficult to detect afterward.) It is very likely to cause a deadlock. But due to using AOP, we can avoid all such bugs. We can implement an appropriate synchronization aspect containing advices for both calls (opening and closing the semaphore, and specify weaving conditions in an appropriate way), weave the call of the close semaphore operation before updating the resource, and weave the call of the open semaphore operation after updating the resource. Thus, we will not have to check the correctness of each weaving of our synchronization aspect: AOP mechanisms will guarantee that both advices will be woven as appropriate. This is a real example of how AOP can improve the trustworthiness of an application. The architecture of the synchronization aspect and the result of its weaving are depicted in Figure 3.4. In Chapter 4 we define and weave a synchronization aspect using Aspect.NET.

A very important problem is that of the *reusability* of aspects. Not only modules in the classical sense, but also aspects may be useful in many programs or may be applied several times to parts of the same program. To make aspects reusable, it is necessary to define them in the most general form possible, applicable to many target programs, although the existing AOP languages and tools somewhat limit the development of general-purpose reusable aspects because the weaving conditions are expressed in terms of the lexical structure of target applications; for example: "Activate the advice below after the call of each method whose name starts with *Set*." A related problem is *reliability* and *conceptual clearance* of aspect weaving: What if we specify the synchroni-

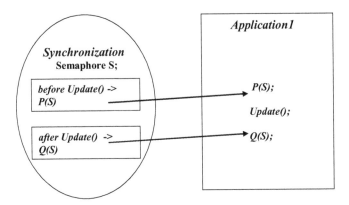

Figure 3.4 *Architecture of the synchronization aspect and the results of its weaving.*

zation aspect so that the advice with the semaphore closing operation will be activated before each call starting with *Set*, and the advice with the semaphore opening operation will be activated after each call starting with *Set*? If we have "blindly" woven such an aspect, a lot of obsolete weavings of semaphore operations are likely to be done: for example, before and after each call of the *SetColor* method, which just sets the foreground color in our GUI and has nothing to do with shared resources! This example shows that blind weaving of an aspect, without prior analysis of the join points in the target program actually subject to weaving, may worsen the reliability of the target application and may lead to unpredictable results. So a lot of issues still need to be solved in AOP tools before we can make aspects really reusable. In Aspect.NET we give users an opportunity to visualize the join points and to deselect some of them prior to weaving, in order to avoid absurd weavings such as that (before and after calls of *SetColor*) we considered in our example. AOP tools should provide an opportunity to formulate weaving conditions not at the lexical level as at present (in terms of class and method names), but in higher-order and more adequate terms of *program semantics*.

Another important problem in AOP is how to implement weaving. AOP approaches and tools differ a lot in this respect. Two different viewpoints on weaving are theoretically possible: *static* and *dynamic*. Consider again the general form of weaving condition and advice:

> **if** Condition **then** Advice

Static weaving means that the code of *Advice* is in some sense (possible options are described below) injected to all join points in the target application where the *Condition* in the target application holds: for example, before calls of all methods whose name starts with *Set*.

Dynamic weaving means that the AOP tool works somewhat similar to a debugger: At runtime, for each point in the target application, a check is made to see if the *Condition* holds. If so, the *Advice* code is executed at this join point (rather than being injected into the target application code).

Actually, the dynamic approach to weaving in AOP is very similar to settings and the use of breakpoints in debuggers—a traditional mechanism known for many years. Such a mechanism is very time consuming, since an AOP tool has to check *after each executable statement* whether or not each condition in the aspect(s) under consideration holds. This is highly justified and is comfortable for users when they are debugging an application, but is not acceptable when the efficiency of the application is critical.

Static weaving has its own advantages and shortcomings. It can be implemented very efficiently, but the application code resulting from weaving can be changed so substantially (as compared to its original familiar version) that the user can feel discomfort and confusion when seeing a lot of "instrumentation code" inserted into an application for the purpose of AOP. This instrumentation code can be very awkward from the user's viewpoint. In addition, a static approach to weaving (as for any other type of macro expansion) can lead to a dramatic increase in the size of the code, which is not always acceptable (especially if the resulting code is to be executed in a mobile device with serious memory limitations).

Most existing AOP tools use static weaving. Basically, static weaving can be done in the following ways:

1. *At the source code level.* The code of the woven advices and the related instrumentation code are inserted into the source of the target application. The updated source is stored in a temporary file which is passed to the compiler. The advantage of this method is that the user can visualize the resulting source code and better understand the result of weaving, can document the resulting source code, and can debug the updated application with full access to the updated source. But weaving at the source code level is impossible when the sources of the target application subject to weaving are not shipped (quite a common situation for commercial software products).

2. *At the intermediate code level.* The AOP tool transforms the code of the target application and the code of the aspect to be woven into the intermediate form most suitable for weaving operations: treelike representation or linked list. On weaving, the resulting code is typically transformed into object code. In some sense we use this form in Aspect.NET (more details in Section 3.8). Such an approach is more comfortable for implementation but has some important concerns: The AOP tool loses backward compatibility with the resulting source code. The updated source code actually does not exist, and the AOP tool has to reconstruct it for visualization and debugging purposes, especially important for users.

3. *At the object code level.* The AOP tool has access to the object code the target application and the aspect to be woven. Weaving is performed in terms of the object code. This method of weaving implementation is rarely used in AOP, since it is uncomfortable for both users and implementers of the AOP tool. But in most cases the AOP tool has to start with the object code of the application and the aspect (or with its standard portable intermediate binary code used in the underlying software platform: MSIL code for .NET or bytecode for Java). Pure binary code in linear form is not convenient for weaving operations, which require many code insertions and replacements. So, AOP tools often transform the binary object or standard intermediate code of the target application and the aspect into more suitable higher-level intermediate representation: trees or linked lists. Weaving is actually performed in terms of that higher-level representation, and the target application code is then transformed into standard binary object or lower-level intermediate code. The Aspect.NET weaver is based on this technique (see Section 3.8 for more details).

4. *At class loading time.* This method is used (as an alternative) in AspectJ (see Section 3.3.1). It typically requires redefining the class loader in the virtual

execution engine (in Java, JVM) to its enhanced "weaving-aware" version, which in loading a class performs all actual weavings related to it.

5. *During just-in-time compilation* (actually, at runtime). This method is applicable to Java or .NET or to another platform where JIT compilation is used. Instead of weaving at the source, or the intermediate binary code level, the AOP tool generates specific tables or files with the input information for weaving for a just-in-time compiler. Actual weaving is delayed until runtime. When translating a target application method to native binary code, the just-in-time compiler performs weaving in terms of that native code. This method may be helpful to avoid a dramatic increase in the size of the intermediate code, but it requires that the JIT compiler be "aspect-aware." For the latter reason, it is probably the most difficult to implement.

The initial, very important problem that arises when starting to implement an AOP tool is the *problem of choosing an aspect specification language and a way of representing aspects*. On this subject, different AOP researchers and developers have quite different viewpoints. In any case, as new notions lacking in traditional programming languages aspects and the other AOP concepts (i.e., advices, weaving conditions, join points, pointcuts), require some kind of *AOP specification language*. On the other hand, the resulting target application code after weaving should be represented in some *implementation language* of the underlying platform (Java, C#, or an earlier language). The question is: Should the AOP specification language be different from the aspect implementation language?

If so, we have to implement the AOP specification language separately: by an interpreter, by a compiler, or by a converter to the implementation language. Such an approach looks more complicated, since we have to implement yet another language for AOP purposes. But if we implement the AOP specification language as a converter to the implementation language, it will be more understandable for the user (if we make the process of conversion transparent and easily understandable). This is the method used in Aspect.NET: The AOP specification metalanguage is implemented as a converter to C# (more details in Sections 3.7 and 3.8).

If we did not introduce another language for AOP specifications, we should extend the implementation language by AOP concepts as the developers of AspectJ did [10]. This method is quite logical for research projects; let's add AOP to Java or C# to see how it helps. But we may encounter several dangers on the way. The first is *conceptual confusion*. Aspects are very generic concepts in programming that describe ways in which to transform target applications. So it would seem that they should not be mixed with the concepts of concrete programming languages: C++, Java, and C#. If we make a decision that the "aspect" construct becomes a new construct of the implementation language, a lot of questions arise at once. First, what should be the relationship between aspects and classes? Can aspects inherit from classes, or classes from aspects? And so on. For simplicity and reliability purposes, it seems clear that constructs and mechanisms of defining and weaving aspects should not be confused with mechanisms of ordinary class inheritance in OOP languages, to avoid conceptual confusions. AOP features should be "orthogonal" to OOP features, but the developers of AspectJ decided to mix them up. I am far from intending to criticize AspectJ, the most famous, widely used, and most powerful AOP tool. Due to AspectJ, many IT experts learned what AOP is. But after over a decade of successful development of AOP, it seems clear that AOP researchers and implementers should investigate other ways of implementing aspects and other viewpoints on AOP (more about that in Section 3.7).

The second danger in introducing AOP constructs and concepts directly into the implementation language is the dependence *on one's own specific tools for extended language support* (compiler, debugger, visualizer, etc.) and *difficult integration with common-use tools and IDE* worldwide used for the implementation language itself, without AOP extensions. If an AOP implementer developed his own compiler from extended Java or C#, isolated from the common-use compiler for the implementation language (*javac* for Java, *csc* built into .NET Framework and Visual Studio.NET for C#, etc.), he or she has to continue doing the same and enhancing his or her specific compiler as long as the implementer wants the AOP product to live. Even if a new version of the implementation language was implemented (e.g., a new version of the *csc* compiler appeared), not related to AOP, the AOP implementer has to update his or her own extended language compiler to support compatibility with the new version of the implementation language. However, the code generated by this extended language compiler will not be compatible to the common-use debugger, profiler, and other tools used by all customers in the IDE.

Another important AOP development problem: *What should the AOP specification language look like*? It should be very simple to learn and use, should be comfortable for users, and should be general enough to be suitable for a larger set of implementation languages. However, some AOP developers who are implementing their own AOP specification languages, to make their life easier, decide to use the XML format of the AOP specification language. An example is Weave.NET [79]. The only advantage of XML is that it is easy to parse and there are a lot of ready-to-use XML parsers that can be used to implement the XML-based AOP specification language. But XML code is not perfectly readable and learnable by users. It is uncomfortable to use XML as a programming language or a specification language. Aspect.NET users in our working e-mail communication emphasized as one of Aspect.NET's advantages that the AOP specification language is simple and is "not XML." We do use XML for internal implementation purposes: The weaver and the Aspect. NET framework communicate via an XML file containing a list of the join points. But that XML file is not visible to users.

As it should be possible with AOP to weave aspects, another "reverse engineering" task should be possible to solve with AOP: *aspect mining* [29], extraction of aspects from non-aspect-oriented programs. Aspect mining can be considered as one of the ways to achieve software reusability. Actually, aspect mining is a task that software developers have to solve "by hand" in their ubiquitous work—in software maintenance. When fixing a bug, the initial task is to locate inside the sources of your application the code responsible for implementing the functionality to be fixed. A similar situation arises if the software engineer needs to enhance some existing functionality in the application. The code of the functionality is typically scattered within the sources and can be considered as an aspect. But the problem is the lack of adequate tools. How is the software engineer to find *all* the tangled fragments of the cross-cutting concern in case the sources are not well written and not properly self-documented, and, in addition, the maintenance engineer is not sufficiently familiar with the sources (since he or she is not the author of the code)? The situation can be compared to "looking for a black cat in a dark room, especially if there is no cat." A common practical solution is to dig into a debugger and try to understand how the buggy application works. But the debugger can only help to track flow of control and to show how the values of the variables change rather than to suggest where the buggy code is located. So a quite common method that many programmers use to locate some specific code is a *text search tool*, such as the UNIX *grep*. For example, *grep* can help to find all calls of some method, or all uses or assignments to some variable. But the overall architecture of the sources remains unclear, since the tangled fragments of the code that implement different cross-cutting concerns are not properly marked (colored). In our practice, when using TIP technology [11] we used special types of mnemonic variable and function names, or some specific comments marking the lines of the source code, to distinguish (speaking in modern terms) between different cross-cutting concerns. But this is not enough. The most comfortable aspect mining tool should paint different aspects in different colors and help to browse them. An example of a working prototype of an aspect mining tool is AMT [29]. However, compared to the popularity of AOP tools such as AspectJ, aspect mining tools are not yet so wide spread. The reason for this is based on the special difficulty of the task of aspect mining. Some possible approaches to aspect mining have been formulated by Hannemann and Kiczales [29]: using *lexical structure* of the sources (i.e., *names of the entities*) or using the set of *types defined in the application* as the basis for locating potential aspect definitions and tangled code fragments, the potential results of their weaving. In Aspect.NET, for example, we are now only on our way to developing an adequate aspect mining tool. Nevertheless, it is quite clear that without comfortable and powerful aspect mining tools, AOP will be much less widely used than expected initially. The aspect mining problem could be solved much more easily if the code were developed "in proper style" from the very beginning. But most existing sources are legacy code whose quality is far from ideal. I think the task of aspect mining is still a real intellectual challenge for AOP developers.

   The scope of applying AOP is, I hope, wide enough, although AOP is not yet as ubiquitous as desired. As we've seen, the notion of cross-cutting concern is generic in nature. There is an everyday need to locate, update, and add cross-cutting concerns when developing and maintaining any application. AOP can be helpful in solving these tasks for any problem domain and for the purpose of satisfying any recommendations, requirements, and disciplines, such as trustworthy computing (considered in Chapter 2). AOP is just one of the *postobject-programming* [28] technologies developed because using OOP appeared not to be enough. Some other POP technologies are overviewed in Section 3.3.

Issues of AOP use and recipes for increasing its popularity are the same as for any other new approach to software engineering. AOP developers should train users in AOP more than they do now, present more AOP tutorials at international conferences, publish more practical books on AOP and its applications, and make AOP tools more and more comfortable. Nevertheless, it is well known that most users are reluctant to acquire new software technologies. They are accustomed to use their favorite programming language and a development environment sufficient for their tasks. They would probably start using AOP only if their, say, favorite FORTRAN dialect would have AOP extensions. In addition, users who are oriented primarily to rapid prototyping of software will hardly use AOP: The advantages of AOP are more evident for skilled software developers who have experience in software maintenance and code improvement rather than during the initial rapid prototyping. To make users less "scared" of AOP, its tools and languages should be made as simple as possible.

A serious danger is the possible use of AOP by hackers who are trying to inject nonsecure and malicious actions into the code. So we should seriously think about *secure AOP tools*, although as far as I can judge, even research work in this area is just starting. In addition, some very experienced software developers, including my Russian colleagues, are still skeptical about AOP, saying that "AOP is not efficient enough." It is really so, or may seem so, if an AOP tool generates a lot of "instrumentation code" which is difficult to understand and looks inefficient. However, based on experience with Aspect.NET, I think the efficiency issues can be overcome. To make a historical analogy, similar things were said about abstract data types (ADTs) in the 1970s and 1980s when they started to be used in the industry. But right now, ADT features have become an inherent part of modern software development platforms such as Java and .NET and have been implemented quite efficiently. So I hope that in a few years the same will happen with AOP. As for efficiency of Aspect.NET weaving, it is proved in Chapter 4.

Summary of Requirements for AOP Tools   We have considered basic concepts of AOP, its tasks, principles of AOP implementation, and AOP use directions and issues. To conclude this introductory section on AOP, we can summarize a set of requirements for AOP tools that follow from our considerations. They may seem too optimistic, since there are no AOP tools right now to satisfy all of them. But I think that such analysis can stimulate further development of AOP tools.

1. *Implementing basic features of specifying (defining) and weaving aspects.* Parts of aspect specification should be some forms of weaving conditions and related advices (actions) to be woven. Also, a kind of pointcut construct (a group of weaving conditions and related advices separate from the aspect definitions) should be provided. Implementation of AOP functionality can be done either by implementing an enhancement to existing implementation language, or by implementing a separate AOP specification language and a way to translate aspect specifications into their implementations

2. *Aspect-operating GUI to perform basic operations on aspects: visualization, coloring, modification, adding, and deleting.* It should be kept in mind that thinking of the application in terms of cross-cutting concerns and aspects may be too complicated for some users. The best way to help users is to implement GUI to visualize aspects and to browse them and their weavings. The code of each aspect and the results of its weavings should be colored differently from the other aspects.

3. *Integration to common-use IDE.* The users will be most likely to use aspect operating GUI integrated to the appropriate IDE (e.g., Eclipse and NetBeans for Java, and Visual Studio for .NET). All common-use IDEs support developing add-ins or plug-ins, driven by a GUI activated simultaneously by calling the IDE or by selecting a specific item of extendable menu of the IDE. Ideally, the users of an AOP tool would like to create special types of projects in the IDE: aspect specification projects, use of aspect code templates, use of the text editor integrated into the IDE to type and edit the code of aspects, and use all other features provided by the IDE (e.g., highlighting, code completion, debugger, profiler, test generation tool) for applications with woven aspects. Integration into a common IDE will not be possible or will be incomplete if the AOP tool is based on extending the implementation language by AOP features.

4. *Support of "manual" control of the weaving process by the user: Browse hypothetical aspect weaving results (join points), and prior to weaving itself, if needed, manually deselect some of the selected join points.* "Blind" weaving of an aspect into all possible join points that satisfy the weaving condition (e.g., before the calls of all methods whose names start with *Set*) can lead to absurd results and make the updated application nondebuggable and unreliable. To avoid this, the user of the AOP tool should have an opportunity, using the aspect-operating GUI, to find all possible aspect join points prior to weaving, to browse those join points, and to deselect those join points that don't make sense (such as weaving before calls of the *SetColor* method). We have implemented this technique in Aspect.NET (see Sections 3.7 and 3.8).

5. *Support of aspect reusability; using aspect libraries (repositories) for a variety of problem domains and programming paradigms.* As we noted, one of the main goals of AOP is to improve code reusability. Component programming platforms such as Java (with its JavaBeans and Enterprise JavaBeans)

and .NET support reusability of more traditional types of modules: interfaces and classes. Similarly, AOP should support reusability of aspects. For this purpose, aspect libraries (or repositories) should be developed to implement typical cross-cutting concerns of various problem domains and programming paradigms (e.g., design by contract and security). Large applications should be developed using not only basic class libraries as now (for implementing modular concerns), but also using aspect libraries (for implementing cross-cutting concerns).

6. *Support of debugging in terms of aspects.* Using AOP changes the accents at the debugging stage as well as at the design and implementation stages of the software life cycle. A user who has designed and implemented a set of aspects and has woven them into a target application is likely to continue to work with the application in terms of aspects. For example, when debugging an application after weaving the synchronization aspect, a debugger command *"stop in synchronization aspect"* would be more adequate than a similar command expressed in terms of the aspect implementation. Next, on stopping in some aspect, the user is likely to output some values of the aspect's data and visualize the source code fragment of the updated target application (with the aspect woven). The latter trick would not be possible if the AOP tool does not support backward compatibility between the resulting binary code after aspect weaving and its source code. However, AOP developers should recognize the user's right to see the debugged fragment of the target application in terms of its source code. Otherwise, if the user instead has to see a decompiled assembler form of the resulting binary when debugging it, the user is likely to stop using AOP.

7. *Support of aspect mining.* The ideal AOP tool should definitely support aspect mining. However, generally speaking, really "smart" aspect mining requires formalization and understanding of the *semantics* of the program rather than just operating class and method names, or even types defined in some modules. As the first step to aspect mining, the AOP tool should offer the user some type of interactive aspect mining process based on the lexical structure of the underlying program, on its types, or on both. The user can also be asked to enter (or to point to) aspect code templates to look for in an application under aspect mining analysis, to make the life of the aspect mining tool easier.

8. *Support of aspect modeling.* It is quite common to use software modeling languages and tools at early stages (requirements and specifications) of the software life cycle. For this purpose, UML and UML-based tools are in common use. UML fits object-oriented modeling ideally. Many systems are based on automated design, code, and even test base generation for an application. Moreover, many IDEs support such reverse engineering task as painting a UML class relationship diagram given the source code of an object-oriented application. It helps greatly to make the code easier to understand and to develop documentation. For AOP purposes, a kind of "aspect-oriented UML"

extension should be developed and used for aspect-oriented modeling, similar to the present process using UML for object-oriented systems.

Having formulated requirements for current and future AOP tools, in the next section we overview the existing AOP tools, and technologies similar to AOP, that can also be classified as *post-object programming*.

3.3 AOP AND RELATED TECHNOLOGIES AND TOOLS

3.3.1 AspectJ and AspectWerkz

AspectJ [10,80] is the most famous and widely used AOP tool, often referred to as the de facto standard of AOP, both as a set of basic AOP terms and as a set of AOP features. The first version of AspectJ was developed in 1995 by the AOP founder Gregor Kiczales and his team at Xerox PARC. It happened in the same year that Java 1.0 was announced and shipped. The version of AspectJ available at the time of writing this book is 1.5.4. Let's emphasize again that AspectJ is now over a decade old, as is Java. So a lot of experience has built up in teaching AspectJ and using it throughout the world. Aspect. NET is much younger; its principles were designed in 2003–2004, and the first working prototype appeared in 2005.

AspectJ is an AOP extension of Java, or "aspect-oriented Java." The latest version of AspectJ is now available as an Eclipse foundation open-source project. AspectJ is available as a stand-alone product and in forms integrated with Eclipse and with NetBeans, the most popular Java IDE. Using AspectJ integrated with Eclipse (*AspectJ Development Tools (AJDT)* [81]) is the most comfortable choice, due to the general advantages of Eclipse Java IDE (relatively quick IDE deployment and comfortable GUI) and to the well-crafted integration of AspectJ with Eclipse Java IDE by the AspectJ team. When the Eclipse IDE is installed, to add the AspectJ support plug-in, it's enough to download the AJDT archive, unpack it, and copy the contents of its *features* and *plug-in* directories to the corresponding directories of the Eclipse installation.

The main architectural components of AspectJ are:

- *ajc:* AspectJ compiler. Compiles AspectJ language source code (Java extended by AOP features) to Java bytecode "understandable" by the ordinary Java Virtual Machine (*java*). *ajc* is available both in command-line mode, with a rich set of options, and via the IDE.
- *ajdoc:* utility similar to Java JDK's *javadoc*, which generates HMTL hypertext javadoc-type documentation to the source code of an aspect-oriented application written in AspectJ. The documentation includes a description of the cross-cutting structure of the application.

- *ajbrowser:* AspectJ browser, a GUI to visualize aspects, their relationships, and the cross-cutting structure of the program. AspectJ Browser
  makes it possible to call the *ajc* compiler to compile AspectJ programs.
  However, functionality to select or deselect join points manually is lacking
  in AspectJ.
- *AspectJ ant tasks:* support of building tasks for a popular Java building
  tool, Apache *ant* [82], used in many Java environments including
  Eclipse.
- *AspectJ load-time weaver:* "weaving class loader" that performs deferred
  weaving when the JVM loads the appropriate class. It is possible to
  develop and add third-party *load-time weaving agents* to perform the
  same task. AspectJ also supports *compile-time* weaving (performed after
  the *ajc* compiler translates an AspectJ compilation unit) and *post-compile
  weaving* (when the ready binary class and jar files are used as input for
  weaving).

AspectJ language includes a variety of useful AOP features and is still used
as a criterion of completeness for many other AOP frameworks and tools that
appeared later (including Aspect.NET). The features are *aspect definitions,
named pointcut definitions*, and *intertype declarations*. Aspect definitions
contain *advice declarations*, which, in turn, can include *thisJoinPoint*—type
constructs to handle reflective information about the join points in the target
application.

Aspect definitions in AspectJ are a new type of modular unit that encapsulate and can expand (weave into target application) some type of cross-cutting
behavior, such as logging or security checks. Aspect can be defined as, for
example:

```
aspect Logging { // Aspect that Introduces logging
behavior
    pointcut AnyCall (): // Named pointcut
        call (void MyClass.*(..));
    before(): AnyCall () {
        System.out.println("Hello" + thisJoinPoint)
    }
    after(): AnyCall () {
        System.out.println("Bye" + thisJoinPoint)
    }
} // Logging
```

This aspect introduces logging behavior to the class *MyClass*. Before any
call of any method *M*, it executes the advice that outputs the message of the
type *Hello M*, and after any call of *M*—an advice to output similar *M* leaving
message: *Bye M*. For demonstration purposes, I included in the aspect the

definition of the named pointcut, *AnyCall*. In this simple aspect we could use an anonymous pointcut:

```
before(): call (void MyClass.*(..)){ ... }
```

In the bodies of advices, I used *thisJoinPoint* object, which binds the advice to the target join point. It provides a lot of useful features to work with the join point and its context. I used only the simplest of them: the implicit call of the method *thisJoinPoint.toString*(), which outputs the actual name of the target method captured by the pointcut. Pointcuts can also be parametrized, private, and abstract.

In general, aspects in AspectJ can inherit from other aspects or classes. It is "in the spirit of Java," although one can argue whether or not it is secure and modular and whether it can cause some kind of conceptual confusion. I prefer not to judge the "pioneers of AOP" on this decision.

Aspects can also introduce new declarations into other classes, *intertype declarations*:

```
aspect MyAspect {
    int MyClass.VisibleFromMyAspectOnly; ...
}
```

In this example, the aspect *MyAspect* adds a new field, *VisibleFromMyAspectOnly*, to the class *MyClass*. The field, according to its name, is visible from the aspect only, although it actually becomes part of the class *MyClass*. In Java, adding such functionality is really helpful. But for .NET, such features for incremental class development are already covered in .NET 2.0 by *partial classes*: If some class is lacking a field, the field can be added to the class definition "in incremental style" in a separate source file—no need to use aspects for that. In addition, this visibility discipline in AspectJ can be violated by reflection: Although the aspect "thinks" of itself as the owner of this field, the class can use reflection and detect it. Despite all that, let's emphasize again that intertype declarations are a useful feature.

Aspects can also be defined as *privileged*. In this case they get access to the private fields of the target classes. This is a correct decision, since cross-cutting functionality to be added or enhanced by the aspect can involve private information of the class. For example, private fields can encapsulate some common resource to be shared by concurrent threads, and the aspect can be intended to add MT safety to the class.

Advices in AspectJ, defined in aspects to be woven into target applications, can be applied *before, after,* or *around* (the latter actually means *instead* of) the *join point* in the target code captured by the pointcut accompanying the advice. In advices of the *after* type, the actual point at which to activate the advice can be clarified. For example, the code

```
after () returning (int result): call (int MyClass.M
()) { ... }
```

means that the advice is activated after each return from the call from method *M* in the class *MyClass*, and the result of the call is assigned implicitly to the argument *result* of the advice and can be analyzed in the advice body. In a similar way, it is possible to clarify activation of the advice when *throwing* an exception during a call, with an opportunity to handle the exception.

In their turn, pointcuts in AspectJ can be of many kinds and classify different types of join points in Java applications in a very subtle way: *call*, capture call of some method; *execution*, capture execution of some method body; *initialization*, capture initialization of some object; *staticinitialization*, capture initialization of static fields of some class; *set*, capture assignment to some field; *get*, capture retrieving the value of some field; *handler*, capture the moment of handling an exception of some class or its subclass; and so on. Keeping in mind that it is possible to use most types of pointcuts in combination with *after, before*, or *around* advices, the user gets a variety of opportunities to catch different moments in Java program execution and activate advices in those moments.

Since AspectJ 1.5, due to merging of AspectJ with another AOP project for Java, *AspectWerkz* [83], an alternative syntactic form of defining aspects and their parts is available using *annotations* implemented in Java 1.5. AspectWerkz itself is not an extension of the Java language by AOP; it is a toolkit that supports aspect definitions in the form of Java annotations. For example, in AspectWerkz syntax, an annotation of the kind

```
@aspect Logging . . .
```

has semantics similar to using the usual syntax of defining the aspect *Logging* in AspectJ language format, as explained above.

In this section we overview only the basic features of AspectJ, of which there are many more. The paper by Laddad [80] and AJDT documentation [81] describe them in more detail.

AspectJ is supported by some major software companies that support Java technology: IBM, Sun, and others. It really has a lot of influence to many Java programmers and AOP researchers and developers. Each major conference on AOP and software technologies offers an AspectJ tutorial. AspectJ has a promising future and is likely to be used by more and more Java developers. However, some features of AspectJ are much more difficult to learn and use properly, even by experienced software developers, than is core Java language. The main issues of learning and using AspectJ are very subtle clarifications of various types of join points (method call or execution, etc.), the great variety of implemented features not "orthogonal" to each other, and mixing up basic Java concepts and constructs and those of AOP. Many experienced software developers, primarily Java programmers, appreciate the power and the historical role of AspectJ, greatly respect its authors, and understand that AspectJ can be (and is) used successfully both in industry and in research. The invaluable importance of AspectJ is that it is the first *practically oriented and applicable approach to AOP*. But the subtle and tricky "cuisine" of defining and weaving aspects in AspectJ can still be considered too "magic" and too complicated for most software practitioners. I foresee two major groups of AspectJ users: very experienced Java developers who have come across some software design, development, or maintenance issues and believe that AOP and AspectJ will help them to solve it; and young enthusiasts, mostly under-graduate and doctoral students who like researching and experimenting and who are very interested in trying a new prospective programming paradigm of AOP.

3.3.2 Other AOP Tools and Approaches to Separation of Concerns

Separation of concerns [84] as one of the foundations of computer program-ming is a general idea formulated by Dijkstra in 1974. From this general viewpoint, all common programming paradigms and approaches—modular programming, object-oriented programming (OOP), abstract data types, aspect-oriented programming, and many others—can be regarded as different approaches to separate concerns in software development. For example, OOP is a way to separate concerns into hierarchies of classes; modular programming is a way to separate concerns as groups of modules; and AOP is a way to sepa-rate cross-cutting concerns as aspects.

There are a number of approaches similar to AOP using different terminol-ogy which also intend to separate cross-cutting concerns. The most general approach was probably offered by IBM researchers [85] based on the concepts of *hyperspace* and *multidimensional separation of concerns*. This approach became the basis of the second widely known (after AspectJ) AOP tool, *HyperJ* [86], now available through IBM's alphaWorks Web site. HyperJ is an AOP extension of Java, as well as of AspectJ, although HyperJ is much more difficult to use. In my experience, developing, updating, and understanding HyperJ's configuration files is an overcomplicated task. Such difficulties in practical use were probably the reason that the HyperJ project was canceled. However, the approach itself is very interesting to consider and analyze.

The authors define their main concept of multidimensional separation of concerns as "flexible and incremental separation, modularization, and integra-tion of software artifacts based on any number of concerns" [85]. As the main goals of their approach, they claim:

- "Encapsulation of *all* kinds of concerns in a software system, *simultaneously.*
- Overlapping and interacting concerns.
- On-demand *remodularization* ... to encapsulate new concerns at any time."

The main concept and construct for achieving multidimensional separation of concerns is *hyperspace*, a concern space that consists of *hypermodules*, modules based on concerns. The basic idea related to concerns is that they are grouped into *dimensions*. Each dimension is a set of concerns that have nothing in common (i.e., are disjoint). A *unit*, a point in hyperspace (the model of the architecture of the programming system in question), is projected into exactly one concern in each dimension. Hypermodules, in their turn, are basic building blocks of a software system. Each hypermodule consists of *hyperslices*, collections of units specified in terms of the concerns in the hyperspace, and a *composition rule* that specifies how to integrate the hyperslices. To change a functionality of the system, a new unit should be added, which can result in adding the new unit to existing hypermodules, or in creating a new hypermodule.

Even a brief description of this approach shows that it is based on complicated geometry-like structures. In Section 3.1 we considered some simpler approaches based on analogies from geometry: one-dimensional, abstraction levels (Dijkstra), and two-dimensional, based on abstraction levels and vertical cuts (Fouxman). In both of them, a software module has definite "coordinates" (one or two). From this viewpoint, IBM's multidimensional approach to modeling concerns in a software system can be regarded as a generalization of Dijkstra's and Fouxman's approaches. It is surely interesting from a theoretical viewpoint, but hasn't yet proved its practical applicability compared to AspectJ. Complicated geometry analogs are close to the way of thinking used by mathematicians doing theoretical research, but unfortunately, geometry is not so native for most other people, including software engineers. In my opinion, as already noted in Section 3.1, geometry analogs are not always suitable for describing software architectures. Graphs and trees are much more suitable for this purpose.

Multidimensional separation of concerns is based on another earlier approach to program composition, *subject-oriented programming* (SOP) [87]. A *subject* in that approach is a semantically related collection of classes and their fragments in an object-oriented system, implementing a separate concern. The object-oriented system should be constructed of different subjects, according to *composition rules* on how to integrate them. The approach is targeted to developing systems as sets of features where the code for each feature is kept separate. SOP support for C++ was implemented in the mid-1990s as an extension of IBM's VisualAge IDE.

Adaptive programming [88] is another widely known approach to separation of concerns proposed by Lieberherr and implemented by his team in the *DemeterJ* system, which supports adaptive programming for Java. Adaptive programming is a method to design and develop object-oriented software systems with changing class hierarchies and method relationships. The key ideas in adaptive programming are as follows. A method should not be hardwired to the details of class hierarchy; otherwise, a lot of changes will be required during any design or implementation update and should be implemented using minimum possible information. General *strategies of class hierarchy traversal* should be specified in a higher-order language (referred to as DEMETER, following Demeter's law, which states that one should communicate only with his close friends). For example [89], if a software system is intended to automate a higher education hierarchy and structure (department of education, university, faculty, teacher), it may include a method to answer a request of the type: How many teachers do we have at the universities? Instead of straightforward implementation of the query, with explicit visiting of all the levels in the hierarchy, the operation should be implemented in DEMETER in two parts: *traversal clause* (traverse the hierarchy from the department of education to the teacher) and *teacher wrapper* (when reaching a teacher node, increase the number of teachers by 1). So the traversal clause encapsulates details of the class hierarchy, and the wrapper implements "business logic" to calculate the number of teachers. These ideas are very close to the earlier abstract data type principles of Liskov and Guttag [20] of encapsulating representation details in *iterators*, higher-level operations to traverse complicated data structures that separate the structure implementation details from the business logic to handle the elements of the structure. The program in DEMETER should then be translated to Java or C++. Due to the principles described, object-oriented programs become more adaptable to changes and evolution.

Composition filters [90] is an approach to composing multiple cross-cutting concerns proposed by a group of authors from the University of Twente. The composition filters model is intended for object-based systems whose functionality relies on message passing between objects. The *interface* part, observable behavior of an object, is declared as a set of composition filters: *input and output filter sets*. The interface part is modular and independent of an implementation language. It is written in a simple declarative specification language (specifying *"what* but now *how"*). The *implementation* part, written in a concrete implementation language, (e.g., Java) defines two types of methods: regular methods and *conditions* (side-effect-free requests to analyze the state of an object). To specify cross-cutting concerns, a *superimposition clause* is used. The model was implemented for three languages: Smalltalk, C++, and Java.

An interesting practically oriented approach, referred to as *concern graphs* [91], was offered and implemented in the FEAT system by Robillard and Murphy. It considers program models as labeled directed graphs—a form which is much more suitable than multidimensional geometric structures to describing relationships in a software system. The FEAT system, as well as AspectJ, is implemented as a plug-in to the Eclipse IDE. FEAT allows us to visualize concerns and all their participants in an explicit way: for example, for each method, to see from what other method it was called and by what other method it was overridden. The system allows the user to build a complete *concern graph* of a software system, in terms of its *types, methods,* and *fields* and their relationships. Moreover, it allows us to detect several types of inconsistencies in the source code. All of that is very helpful for users to better understand a software system's functionality and to be able to modify it properly. Concern graphs and FEAT help users to solve one of the most complicated tasks of software development: understanding and updating existing source code.

Rather than viewing all the interesting approaches to separation of cross-cutting concerns whose goals are close to AOP, let's briefly mention only two of them:

- *Intentional programming* [92]: approach based on the idea of reflecting in the source code of a software system the original *intention* of the developer of the system, expressed precisely and at a proper level of abstraction.
- *Generative programming* [93]: approach based on "modeling and implementing system families in such a way that a given system can be automatically generated from a specification written in one or more textual or graphical domain-specific languages."

AOP support and tools are implemented for a lot of modern and older programming languages and platforms: Java, C, C++, JavaScript, C#.NET, VB.NET, COBOL, Perl, PHP, Lua, Python, Ruby, XML, and so on. The AOP Web page in Wikipedia [94] and the aspect-oriented software development Web site [12] provide hundreds of references to AOP approaches and tools.

3.4 PITFALLS OF AOP

In 1995, during the period of intensive use of OOP and its more and more comfortable tools, a very interesting book [22] on the "pitfalls" of OOP appeared. It, as well as other critical publications on OOP, prevented its users from feeling too much "euphoria." By the way, it appeared about 20 years after OOP was actually invented by the authors of the SIMULA language. In the same year, the first version of AspectJ was shipped, as an alternative to "pure OOP" and the first tool that supported the new approach of AOP that complements OOP in modularizing and handling cross-cutting concerns.

Now that more than a decade has passed since the real origin of AOP and the start of its practical use, it's time to formulate some pitfalls of AOP. Some of them are already explained by the authors of AspectJ in their documentation on AJDT [81] and by AOP experts, the authors of the Wikipedia article on AOP [94]. Let's continue this list and add some more analysis. Some of the topics discussed below were touched on in Section 3.2 and are considered here in more detail.

1. *Consequences of "blind weaving": poor reliability, difficulties in understanding, debugging, and maintenance.* Most existing AOP tools provide only

"lexical-level" filtering of join points. They use wild cards for capturing target class and method numbers. This is suitable for global text search routines such as *grep* but is not quite suitable for AOP tools. The user can expect that a AOP tool will "understand" the semantics of an application well enough. However, the AOP tool only navigates using lexical-level wild cards for program entity names rather than semantic specifications or annotations. As a result, redundant aspects' code fragments can be injected everywhere in the target code where they are not appropriate. A typical example of the use of method names starting with *Set* as the basis to seek join points was described in Section 3.2. There are many other types of prefixes and suffixes of method names in common use that are dangerous from this viewpoint: *Get, Send, Receive, Lock, Unlock, Stop, Suspend, Resume, Init, Begin, End,* and many others. When designing their aspects, the users cannot rely on the fact that a suitable prefix will always imply suitable semantics. AspectJ provides a way to limit the scope of applicability of pointcuts: For example, the *withincode* construct in a pointcut limits the scope to the code of a given class. But this is not enough; the risk of injecting the code into inappropriate join points is great because the lexical-level filters don't quite correspond to program semantics: *Get* is not necessarily the prefix of the method of getting the value of the shared resource to be synchronized; *Stop* is not necessarily the prefix of the method to stop a thread; and so on. As the result of such "blind weaving" based on wildcards in pointcuts, the behavior of the program may be updated in an unclear way that makes it difficult to understand, debug, and maintain. A general recipe for resolving this issue is *to make filtering join points semantically oriented*. But such an approach requires, as a minimum, annotating each logically independent code fragment (statement, method, class, etc.) of the target application by some kind of semantics (e.g., algebraic or design by contract) prior to "training" an AOP tool to understand the program semantics. So a simpler and more practical recipe is needed. We offer such a recipe in Aspect.NET: functionality for the user to browse potential join points and to deselect undesirable ones. Only the user can understand the semantics of his or her application appropriately (more details in Section 3.7).

2. *Tricky and complicated AOP specification language or extension.* In most AOP tools there is a tendency to make its AOP extension of the implementation language, or its separate AOP specification language, if any, more complicated and tricky. For many software practitioners, however, overcomplicated AOP language can be a serious reason not to use it any longer. If the process of program modification and enhancement using just the core implementation language and IDE (without AOP) appears to be simpler to understand than using an AOP extension or AOP specification language for this purpose, the AOP tool will not be used. So the AOP languages and extensions should be as simple as possible. Many users will probably be reluctant to use too-tricky join point filters, combinations of aspects and classes, or multidimensional geometric constructs as the basis for their program transformations.

3. *Conceptual confusion of AOP concepts with those of the implementation language: AOP/OOP conceptual explosion* (see Section 3.2). Users of AOP tools should not be confused about how AOP features and basic implementation language features interact: whether or not they are independent. The users should not think about inheriting aspects from classes, classes from aspects, or alternative ways to declare classes as parent and child using AOP extensions rather than basic OOP features (as the current version of AspectJ allows). New AOP features and tools should be easy to use and should not make even more difficult use of the existing object-oriented features of the basic implementation language. In addition, the author of a book on the pitfalls of OOP [22] warned about a *conceptual explosion* when using OOP: exponential growth of the number of concepts, classes, and methods with nonclear semantics and behavior at each deeper level of class hierarchy. This is easily applicable to systems such as AspectJ, where AOP and OOP features are mixed. The methods used to overcome it in future AOP tools will probably be to separate aspect specification language from the basic implementation language, and to make the AOP specification language as simple as possible. AOP features should not duplicate such typical OOP features as hierarchy and inheritance.

4. *Security issues.* At present, all AOP tools are "open" to all kinds of hacks and attacks. They make it easy to inject any type of code, insert handling of an exception, and so on, which may lead to malicious use of AOP by hackers. To prevent that, AOP security disciplines, policies, and features should be designed and implemented in new and existing AOP tools. Otherwise, they may appear to be too dangerous from a security viewpoint.

5. *Semantic gap between the sources and the application code after aspect weaving.* The only type of weaving (see Section 3.2) that guarantees that users will get updated source codes of their applications after weaving is static weaving at the source code level. But it is not always possible or efficient, so many AOP tools use bytecode-, MSIL code–, or object code–level weaving. As a result, users will get updated applications they will not be able to debug and analyze at the source code level. The way to solve this problem is to implement some way of reconstructing the updated application's source code for the purpose of debugging and visualization.

6. *Losing aspect configuration information, or its conflict with common-use tools.* This is an AOP implementation issue which may affect users. Now, in the "XML age," many types of tools, including some AOP tools, prefer to use XML to configure everything: in particular, to specify aspects or their configuration or composition rules. It is not comfortable for users—but we are now discussing another issue. Any other types of files, either text or binary, can be used for the same purpose: to store AOP configuration information. As a result, a user who is expecting to find in his or her binary code directory the only *.class* or *.jar* file (for Java), or the only *.exe, .dll* or *.so* binary file of the compiled aspect or the resulting application after weaving will also be

surprised to find one or more configuration files (*.xml, .txt,* or files with some unknown name extension) that will contain aspect configuration information vital for the AOP tool being used. The user can just forget to archive, copy, or move these extra configuration files, and the AOP tool will fail to work, reporting that some mysterious files were not found. The way to resolve this issue would be to use the opportunities supported by the implementation platform to keep the aspect configuration information in the *same* binary file as the aspect's or the application's code. But such an approach may hide another pitfall: The resulting extended binary code file, with the AOP configuration information occupying some of its sections, may not be understandable by common-use language tools of the target platform—debuggers, profilers, JIT compilers, and others. For the latter reason, some of the approaches to AOP force the runtime environment to be "aspect-aware." This is undesirable because modifying, say, JVM in Java or CLR in .NET for the single purpose of adapting some third-party AOP tool is not realistic. So designers and implementers of AOP tools should use "legal" ways of extension or enhancement of binary code files: for example, *annotations* in Java and *custom attributes* in .NET, understandable by their AOP tools but not breaking the normal work of common-use language tools such as debuggers or profilers. We used this idea in Aspect.NET (see Section 3.7).

To summarize this section, it seems clear that all the AOP pitfalls considered are resolvable during the development of existing and future AOP tools.

3.5 AOP FOR JAVA

For historical reasons, due to the development of AspectJ, Java became the first AOP implementation language. But AspectJ and AspectWerkz (now merged to AspectJ) considered in Section 3.3 are not the only AOP tools for Java. There are hundreds of other Java AOP tools: JBoss AOP [95], Seasar [96], CaesarJ [97], JAC [98], Dynaop [99], Javassist [100], LogicAJ [101], Reflex [102], JMangler [103], and Spring Framework [104], among many others. Java attracts AOP researchers and developers not only because of AspectJ tradition, but also as a modern field of experiments and as a powerful cross-platform language and environment for implementing their AOP tools. Let's consider the most popular and interesting of them in more detail.

JBoss AOP [95] is probably the most famous and most often utilized AOP framework for Java after AspectJ. It can be used either integrated to the popular JBoss application server or in any other Java programming environment. A characteristic feature of the JBoss AOP approach is that it does not introduce any new language syntax to Java for AOP purposes. It makes it possible to use the ordinary Java compiler for JBoss AOP applications. Aspects in JBoss are actually defined in Java, in combination with AOP configuration files written in XML format. It is also possible to define aspects in JBoss with the help of annotations. Implementation of aspects in JBoss AOP employs reflection. A special type of aspect in JBoss AOP is an *interceptor*, an aspect with only one advice, named *invoke*. The purpose of an interceptor is to wrap up the call of any method with some extra actions (e.g., profiling) performed before and after the call. Syntactically, an interceptor aspect in JBoss AOP is a class that implements the predefined interface *Interceptor*. JBoss AOP allows for other tricks, such as *introductions*. For example, suppose that you have a class *MyClass* which you are going to make serializable. To do that, instead of editing and recompiling your Java code for the class, you should add a simple *introduction XML file* to explain to the JBoss AOP environment that it should add inheritance from the *java.io.Serializable* interface to *MyClass* code. So, using pure Java (including annotations), a predefined library of AOP support, and simple aspect configuration files in XML format, authors of JBoss AOP managed to find elegant solutions to many problems involving Java code enhancement and maintenance. JBoss IDE is integrated with Eclipse. The main advantage of the JBoss AOP approach compared to AspectJ is its simplicity.

CaesarJ [97] has taken a lot from AspectJ but has added some important new ideas. CaesarJ uses the keyword *cclass* (CaesarJ class) instead of the keyword *aspect*. One of key points in CaesarJ is aspect deployment. Aspects can be declared as *deployed*, which means that a singleton instance of the aspect is deployed automatically. Another alternative of aspect deployment is to use an executable statement of the type *deploy A*, where *A* is the name of an aspect. There is also a statement with inverse semantics: *undeploy A*. More exactly, aspects in CaesarJ are considered as *objects* rather than classes (i.e., there can be several instances of the same aspect available in one application at a time). To integrate cross-cutting concerns, *virtual classes* and *wrapper classes* can be used. Especially important is the fact that CaesarJ allows us to integrate distributed components and call them using the Java remote method invocation. As compared to JBoss and even to AspectJ, the CaesarJ approach to aspects supports more AOP features (multiple instances of an aspect, distributed aspects, etc.), but it is more difficult to use. As all other Java AOP tools considered above, CaesarJ is integrated to Eclipse.

Javassist [100] is not specifically an AOP tool for Java, but a useful class library for editing Java bytecode. It provides two-level API to handle Java code: source level (knowledge of bytecode structure is not needed for using it) and bytecode level. In particular, this class library can be used for AOP purposes. Javassist was used as the basis for *Reflex* [102]: a kernel for multi-language AOP. Reflex has three-layered architecture: a *transformation layer* (based on *behaviorial reflection*), a *composition layer* (supports aspect composition and its automatic detection), and a *language layer* (based on the original approach to assimilation of domain-specific languages). Of all Java AOP tools, it provides the most general and flexible approach, making it possible to plug any language and use it for AOP purposes. Further practical adaptation should demonstrate the applicability of this approach.

JMangler [103] is a tool for generic interception and transformation of Java programs at load time. It does not require source code and is not dependent on a class loader. Such a tool can be used for AOP purposes.

JAC [98] is an aspect-based distributed dynamic framework intended to develop distributed aspect-oriented Java applications. Aspects in JAC can be defined as subclasses of the predefined class *AspectComponent*. JAC allows us to define *dynamic wrappers*, a kind of generic advice. A dynamic wrapper is an object that defines behaviors to extend the behavior of regular objects. JAC provides functionality for users to define their own domain-specific languages by declaring a set of configuration methods. For configuring aspects, JAC uses and parses textual configuration files (with an *.acc* extension). The mechanisms of JAC can be applied to distributed objects: A given cross-cut can modify the semantics of remote objects located on distributed hosts.

To summarize this section, let's formulate the common features of many AOP tools for Java:

- *Using terminology, elements of syntax, and semantics of AspectJ:* aspect, pointcut, advice, join point. Nevertheless, as we have seen from this brief review, approaches to implementing these basic elements of AOP may be quite different.

- *Supporting interceptors:* mechanism to wrap a method call with some actions to be executed before and after the call.

- *Supporting mix-ins:* classes that export some functionality to its sub-classes but are not used as stand-alone classes. Mix-ins allow subclasses to enrich their functionality by multiple inheritance from several mix-ins.

- *Supporting wrappers* for classes that allow us to enrich their behavior.

- *Providing several layers* of architecture, including the *layer of aspect composition* and the *language layer* to define the user's own *domain-specific language* to implement applications.

- *Using aspect configuration files in XML or other textual format* in addition to the aspect code.

- *Using Java annotations as the only or alternative form of aspect specification* if the tool was implemented after shipping Java 1.5 with annotations.

- *Implementing the AOP tools as plug-ins to Eclipse.*

Most of the common features noted above look quite positive, except for XML configuration files in addition to aspect definition code. We discussed the pros and contras of using XML in AOP tools in Section 3.2. Especially important and convenient for users is the fact that all authors of AOP Java tools make them available as Eclipse plug-ins.

3.6 AOP FOR .NET

The subject closest to me from those related to the main goals of the book is efficient and adequate implementation of AOP for .NET. Initially, when .NET appeared in 2000, some authors intended to implement AOP for .NET, following the success of AspectJ—simply took AspectJ syntax and semantics and tried to introduce them some way into C#, either as a language extension or as an addition to C# code in the form of XML. However, the nature and specifics of .NET have some inportant differences from Java (see Section 2.5.1). For readers to better understand these differences, most sensitive for AOP implementation, let's look at two important ideas that we used when designing and implementing Aspect.NET.

First, .NET is a multilanguage programming platform, more open in style than Java. For Java technology, the only way to implement a new programming paradigm such as AOP is either to extend the Java language or to develop Java API to support it. For .NET, the situation is different—it is a multi-language programming environment. So the first idea I proposed in 2002 when starting to do AOP for .NET was that *AOP for .NET should preferably be language-agnostic*. It would contradict the spirit of .NET and its principles of multilanguage interoperability if AOP features would enhance C# language only and would not be available, say, in Visual Basic.NET or in Managed C++.NET. However, further reasoning on this subject can lead to implementing too radical a solution: *Let's make .NET's Common Language Runtime*, the basis for multilanguage interoperability (or at least its shared-source version, Rotor), *"aspect-aware," to support AOP in the strongest way*. That was my initial intent. Later, I understood that the idea of "teaching" CLR to understand AOP was not right. Seven years have passed since the origin of .NET. Hundreds of AOP tools for .NET, discussed below in this section, were developed. A lot of attempts have been made to unify approaches to AOP for .NET and to implement within the CLR some common "AOP engine." The intent of the very interesting seminar "AOP goes .NET," organized at Microsoft in November 2005, was specifically to develop a common approach to AOP for .NET. But up to now, it has not been made. There are many reasons for that. I think the primary ones are: *a variety of different approaches to AOP*, and the *strategic importance of the CLR*, which is too important and critical to any changes to accept the risk of updating for the needs of a new programming paradigm. It would be too risky if some of the hundreds of approaches to AOP for .NET were selected and "frozen" in the CLR. What happens if a bright new idea comes to the minds of AOP developers for .NET but would not fit the AOP mechanism frozen in the CLR? So, in 2002 I came to the following version of "language-agnostic AOP for .NET": *Implementation of AOP for .NET should not be tied to any programming language* (say, C#). *It should be language-agnostic. But it should not prevent us from doing normal work by common-use .NET tools: CLR, debuggers, profilers, and so on*. In other words: Implement AOP for .NET using the extension mechanisms it provides, but don't require that common-use .NET tools be "AOP-aware."

This principle leads to the second idea I formulated in 2002 and described in early 2003 [1]. .NET has a general and comfortable extension mechanism: *custom attributes*. They ideally fit to implementing any type of annotation: formal specifications, comments on the code, and for *annotating some code as belonging to some aspect*. Annotations in the form of custom attributes are understandable by the appropriate specialized tools—formal verifier and theorem prover, aspect weaver, and so on—the tools those annotations are intended for. Other common-use .NET tools (CLR, debugger, etc.) just ignore those custom attributes. But as compared to any separate XML configuration file, .NET makes possible custom attributes that are an inherent part of the binary code and portable executable file, are traveling in the same file with the MSIL code, and cannot be "lost" when the code of the assembly is passed over the network. As far as I know, Aspect.NET was the first AOP tool for .NET that used custom attributes. A few years later, other AOP researchers arrived at similar beliefs and started using custom attributes to represent aspects for .NET.

Another key question that arises when implementing aspects for .NET is: At what level should the weaving process take place? The following answer looks evident: Since .NET is a multilanguage platform and all .NET languages are compiled into MSIL code, MSIL should become the basis for weaving. There are two issues in MSIL related to weaving. First, MSIL postfix-style code has a linear structure and is not comfortable for weaving: adding, inserting, or replacing pieces of code. So an MSIL-level weaver should first convert MSIL code of the aspect and the target application into a more suitable treelike or graphlike format, then perform the weaving and convert the resulting target code back into MSIL. Second [1], if the AOP tool uses custom attributes to mark aspects and the results of their weaving, the attributes can only mark the named entities in the code: assembly, class, method, and field definitions. They cannot mark executable statements of MSIL code (assignments, branches, calls, etc.). So after weaving some aspects into a target code, it will not be, in general, possible to "color" the fragments that relate to different aspects. However, if all aspect code injections contain calls of aspect methods or access to aspect fields, the aspect visualizer can use them to identify the code fragments related to weaving of each aspect.

Keeping the foregoing considerations in mind, let's overview and analyze the most popular AOP tools for .NET. AOP for .NET principles is discussed in more detail in Section 3.7. Names and references for some AOP-for-.NET tools follow: LOOM.NET [105], AspectDNG [106], Aspect# [107], PostSharp [108], DotSpect [109], Encase [110], Compose* [111], Weave.NET [79], Seasar.NET [112], Spring.NET Framework [113], Puzzle.NET NAspect [114], Wicca and Phx.Morph [115], among others.

LOOM.NET [105] implements both runtime weaving (by Rapier-LOOM.NET weaver) and static weaving (by Gripper-LOOM.NET weaver).

The ultimate goals of the project are to help in developing and enhancing *dynamically reconfigurable multithreaded software* that sometimes cannot be restarted for reconfiguration, for reliability reasons. The Rapier-LOOM.NET weaver is used to generate and weave dynamic proxies. Aspects in LOOM. NET are defined via *aspect classes*. LOOM.NET implements some AspectJ-like features for the commercial version of .NET and for Mono [61]. *Advice custom attributes* are used in aspect class definitions to mark aspect classes, their methods, and to explicitly specify the weaving conditions. The dynamic weaver uses its factory methods to generate interwoven objects. The important restriction on this dynamic weaving approach is as follows: The methods to be interwoven should be virtual or should be defined via interfaces. For purposes of the project, it is acceptable. However, for more general use of the system, this restriction looks serious. LOOM.NET is also used to implement design-by-contract aspects. The authors of the approach pay a lot of attention to performance and reliability.

AspectDNG [106] is a multilanguage aspect weaver that works at the MSIL level. It allows us to weave any .NET 1.1 or .NET 2.0 assemblies. The project was inspired by AspectJ and is implemented in C#. Due to the fact that the weaver works with MSIL code, the aspects and the target application can be written in any language compiled in MSIL. The weaver accepts two forms of join point languages. The first is XPath, the language widely used for navigation in XML namespaces. The second is the language of regular expressions. AspectDNG is definitely a helpful tool, but it cannot yet be regarded as a full-fledged AOP framework: It lacks a proper aspect specification language and an IDE. I don't think XPath is a proper language for AOP specification, but AspectDNG can be useful as part of a larger AOP development platform.

Aspect# [107] is an AOP tool for C#. It consists of a simple (non-XML) aspect configuration language and an aspect engine (weaver). The advices supported are limited to interceptors only. The aspect engine (specified by an instance as the AspectEngine class) is called from C# using its *Wrap* method, whose argument is the type to be extended by weaving interceptors. The list of interceptors is provided in the configuration file. The result of the *Wrap* method is the proxy to the extended type. Pointcuts are also limited to a primitive form of regular expressions. To identify the separately defined elements of the aspect (interceptors) in the aspect definition, string keys (like "*interceptor1*") are used. Aspect# has no IDE; neither is it integrated to Visual Studio or another existing IDE for .NET.

PostSharp [108] is a *postcompiler* for the .NET platform. It works as an MSIL code transformer and uses custom attributes. This tool can be useful for many purposes, including AOP. To illustrate the AOP capabilities of PostSharp, a high-level aspect weaver, *PostSharp Laos*, was developed on top of PostSharp. An aspect in PostSharp, intended for use with the PostSharp Laos weaver, should be defined as a special type of *custom attribute* which can be used with any class or method to extend its functionality (say, add some security checks on entry to this method). The project site contains the following example of such aspect that sheds more light on the AOP cuisine of PostSharp:

```
public sealed class RequiresRoleAttribute :
OnMethodBoundaryAspect
{
  string[] roles;
  public string[] Roles
  {
   get { return this.roles; }
   set { this.roles = value; }
  }
  public override void OnEntry(
  MethodExecutionEventArgs e )
  {
   ((ISecurable) e.Instance).RequireRoles( this.roles
   );
  }
}
```

This class defines an aspect as a custom attribute that adds security functionality of checking the user's roles on entry to some given methods (say, methods performing deletion of some information). The aspect can be applied to any assembly using the ordinary custom attribute definition in C#:

```
[assembly: RequiresRole( Roles=new string[] { "Delete"
}, TargetMethods="Delete*" )]
```

When processing the MSIL code of the application, the PostSharp Laos weaver understands this custom attribute as an instruction to weave into any method in the assembly whose name fits the *Delete** wildcard, an interceptor aspect injecting the security action on entry to the method. This type of approach is typical for many AOP tools for .NET: They don't provide a single conceptually clear AOP framework with its own aspect specification language and set of concepts (more difficult to implement), but instead, use the existing features (classes, methods, custom attributes) to specify aspects directly by means of the implementation language (C# in most cases). The smartest and most complicated part of such AOP tools is a weaver whose work and semantics are considered as some kind of tricky "magic." I can characterize such an approach to AOP as "experimental," which is normal for research projects.

Weave.NET [79] is a project and AOP tool targeted *to language-independent aspects*. This term is understood by the authors in the sense that I explained earlier in the section: *MSIL-level aspects*. The input for the weaver is a set of .NET assemblies and an XML file to specify weaving directives in the style and spirit of AspectJ. Weaving is performed at load time.

Wicca [115] is an AOP framework that implements various kinds of weaving strategies: both static and dynamic weaving, at the source code and MSIL code levels. In particular, MSIL-level weaving in Wicca is supported by Phx.Morph, which is based on Microsoft's Phoenix [7] back-end compiler infrastructure (as well as the weaver in Aspect.NET). Dynamic weaving in Wicca is implemented using another Microsoft technology and tool: the *Microsoft Managed Debugger (mdbg)* [116]. C# source code–level weaving in Wicca is implemented by *wcs*, a source code compiler and weaver. The *wcs* tool implements a small extension of C#: *statement annotations*. Here is an example from the Wicca Web site:

```
public SimpleDraw() {
    [Log(Sev.Info, "Creating a line")]
    Shape s = new Line(new Point(1, 9), new Point(9,
    1));
}
```

Such annotation before the assignment statement is converted by *wcs* into ordinary C# code like this (again, the example is from the Wicca Web site):

```
[Statement(19, "LogAttribute", Sev.Info, "Creating a
line")]
    public SimpleDraw() {
    Shape s = new Line(new Point(1, 9), new Point(9,
    1));
}
```

The latter code is compiled by common-use C# compiler. This is, I should say, an original decision of the problem of annotation lack for statements, although the issue is resolved at the C# source code level rather than at the MSIL code level. The only disadvantage of this technique is lack of readability. The user who thinks in terms of the extended C# may not understand what happened to his or her code, since in debugging the user will see the latter fragment of the source code (with the mysterious number 19) or its image in MSIL code.

As you can see from the examples, AOP implementation in Wicca is based on custom attributes. As for many other AOP projects for .NET, the goal of the project authors is to implement all functionality of AspectJ. This goal has not yet been achieved. Nevertheless, the project is notable by three advantages: a wide spectrum of weaving techniques is offered to users, an interesting method of statement annotations (applicable to Java as well as to C#) is utilized, and the latest Microsoft technologies and tools are used.

Here is a brief summary of the AOP tools for .NET. They contain a lot of original approaches to implementing AOP and share the "spirit of experimentation" with their users. Many of them use custom attributes. Some of them (e.g., LOOM.NET) have experience of use for real tasks. But the following shortcomings should be noted in the existing AOP tools for .NET:

1. *Lack of multilanguage interoperability; dependence on C# or MSIL.* Most AOP tools for .NET are tied to C# only, so they don't use properly one of the main features of .NET: multilanguage interoperability. The only approach used to achieving interoperability in some other AOP tools for .NET is dependence on MSIL (which is surely not a high-level language).

2. *Lack of proper aspect specification language.* Most projects prefer to use C#, MSIL, and .NET "as is," explicitly defining aspects as C# classes inherited from some specific "core aspect implementation classes" using custom attributes or "side-door" aspect configuration files not easy to understand. They just model AOP and AspectJ features in a lower-level implementation language. With such an approach, AOP for .NET becomes simply a kind of discipline, not quite reliable (since when explicitly defining complicated AOP custom attributes, it is easy to make a mistake), without any support at the aspect design stage. Note that for Java AOP tools (see Sections 3.3 and 3.5), unlike .NET AOP tools, I formulated as one of the shortcomings quite a different thing, too-complicated aspect specification languages. It looks as if most AOP researchers for .NET experience such a deep influence of AspectJ that they make one of their major goals modeling AspectJ features by C# classes and XML configuration files rather than discovering new, more general, and open-style AOP features that may be supported by .NET.

3. *Too much XML.* This shortcoming was discussed in Sections 3.2 and 3.5, so my viewpoint on this subject should be clear to readers.

4. *Lack of aspect manipulation and visualization GUI.* Since most AOP tools for .NET are still in an early stage of development, they only provide AOP supporting API and (some of them) AOP configuration files in XML, but they lack GUI to manipulate aspects, to visualize them, to debug them, and so on—everything we are accustomed to doing with "non-AOP" applications, due to modern integrated development environments.

5. *Lack of integration to Visual Studio.NET or other IDE for .NET.* It is widely appreciated that Microsoft Visual Studio.NET is the most convenient and powerful IDE for .NET. Millions of users are accustomed to its rich set of features: source code navigation, highlighting and refactoring, project templates, automatic code generation for the most complicated kinds of programs (such as Web services), multilanguage debugging at the source code level, profiling, automated unit test generation, teamwork, and so on. No code is developed from scratch. The user always has a skeleton (and a visual image, if appropriate) if his or her code is at the design stage. So when learning and assessing a new technology such as AOP, users are not going to lack any of

these features. They don't want to use command-line interface to start AOP tools. They don't want to suffer when typing complicated XML configuration files for an AOP tool in *notepad*, without the support of templates. They would like to see their aspects in proper images: what they look like, which join points they have with the target application, what results they should expect from weaving (in terms of the source code), and so on. Many AOP tools for Java (e.g., AspectJ) are integrated to Eclipse—one of the most popular Java IDEs, and offer the features just described. But unfortunately, most existing AOP tools for .NET are not yet integrated to Visual Studio.NET, although this IDE provides two integration methods: as an *add-in* and through *Visual Studio Integration Program API*.

But all the shortcomings noted probably represent simply growing pains. In a few years the quality and usability of AOP tools for .NET should improve.

3.7 Aspect.NET PRINCIPLES AND ARCHITECTURE

Our approach to AOP described in Section 3.7 and implemented in the Aspect. NET framework [1–6] is based not only on the ideas of classical AOP projects but also on my own 30 years of experience in developing compilers, software engineering tools, knowledge engineering, and Java technology at St. Petersburg University [11,70].

3.7.1 Motivation and Key Ideas

The following ideas and considerations regarding AOP are proposed, investigated, and implemented in Aspect.NET.

Ubiquity of AOP AOP is a refinement, generalization, and support by appropriate tools of everyday practical tasks and needs of software engineers (i.e., software enhancement, bug fixing, software reuse) related to cross-cutting concerns and their implementation. Millions of programmers attempt to carry out their tasks using nonappropriate tools for the purpose of separating and handling cross-cutting concerns. The life and work of any programmer can be made easier using AOP. So AOP should become a *ubiquitous technology* for every software developer since it is targeted to separation and implementation of cross-cutting concerns.

Generic Nature of AOP AOP is generic and language-independent in nature. General principles and concepts of AOP (cross-cutting concerns, aspects, pointcuts, advices, weaving) are independent of any programming language and software development platform. Moreover, AOP is "orthogonal" to any other common-use programming paradigms, such as modular programming, OOP, abstract data types, and functional or logic programming. The notion of aspect is as deep, general, and fundamental as the concepts of module, function, class, object, or abstract data type. The concept of aspect relates to programming methodology and software architecture in general rather than to concrete paradigms or languages. There is currently a tendency, first, to consider and implement any new approach to software engineering in its relation to OOP. But OOP is not a panacea, as stated long ago [22]. It is also quite clear that cross-cutting concerns arise and have to be implemented in program development using not only OOP languages (C#, Java, C++, or Smalltalk), but also when using FORTRAN, C, COBOL, ML, F#, PROLOG, or LISP. So it makes sense to consider and implement aspects for OOP, modular, procedural, functional, or logic programming languages. It means that AOP and aspects should, ideally, be specified in as general a form as possible, to be applicable to any language or platform. Tying aspects only to a concrete language, be it Java or COBOL, would be too narrow. So the basic concepts used in AOP implementation should not be expressed in OOP terms, as in most AOP tools now, so as not to lose generality. However, there can be particular implementations of AOP for concrete languages, which is also useful.

AOP and Knowledge Engineering   As a knowledge engineering expert, I try to understand AOP more deeply not only from a software engineering viewpoint but also from a knowledge engineering viewpoint. This is not just a theoretical speculation, but an intent to lay a more general foundation of AOP and to provide a more flexible and general use implementation for it. A knowledge engineering–based approach to AOP corresponds to modern trends of integrating software engineering and knowledge engineering techniques [117]. During all stages of the software life cycle, using any programming paradigm, software engineers use *domain-specific knowledge* of the problem area and general *knowledge on separation of concerns, program composition, transformation*, and *behavior*. This knowledge is typically used implicitly and is not formulated in a suitable specification language. It gets "frozen" in the resulting code of the software product. So, understanding the program semantics and finding proper ways to update the program based on its *meaning* (rather than its lexical and syntactical structure) disappears soon after the completion of code development. Therefore, we experience many problems when we update or enhance software. Why is AOP so helpful for the purpose of software update? Because an aspect can be considered a hybrid collection of *knowledge* on solving some task in the application domain, knowledge that is lacking, say, when a software engineer starts maintaining some unfamiliar and complicated legacy code. *Procedural knowledge* is used to implement the aspect's methods or functions; *conceptual* and *heuristic knowledge* are used to specify the application domain of the aspect. The weaving rules of the aspect (i.e., pointcuts and their paired advices) can be considered as *knowledge* on *how to apply the aspect to the target application*, or, in other words, *knowledge on program* *transformation.* The conceptual model of an aspect, which can be expressed as $Pointcut_1 \rightarrow Advice_1; \ldots ; Pointcut_n \rightarrow Advice_n$, is very close to the *rule set* (or *production system*) concept and construct used widely in such knowledge engineering languages as PROLOG. A group (library) of all known aspects in the problem domain can be considered a specialized aspect knowledge base. Weaving is the result of applying the knowledge base of aspects for program transformation to a concrete target application. Although I don't know of any research and papers using similar ideas, it does make sense to do research toward *aspect knowledge*, accumulating and applying *aspect knowledge bases* to enrich the functionality of the software.

.NET as a Platform for AOP   At present, the only software development platform that has appropriate mechanisms to implement AOP in the most general way possible is .NET. In .NET, regardless of how the aspects are expressed syntactically in concrete programming languages, they can be represented in the general form of MSIL (implementation of aspect's advices) and metadata (aspect structure and pointcuts). Even an advanced AOP system such as AspectJ, because of its tie to Java, looks somewhat limited. Trying to apply AspectJ aspects to native methods written in C or C++ will result in failure, as AspectJ and its aspects are isolated from other languages except for Java.

AOP Annotations and Requirements for AOP Specification Language   The importance of the AOP specification language should be adapted to the practical needs of programming. Most users (e.g., C# programmers) will not learn and use a new isolated and complicated specification language, even if they get interested in AOP. Instead, programmers should consider AOP not very complicated but useful and tightly integrated to the source code being developed and debugged. So the most practical approach is to implement the AOP specification language as a collection of *AOP annotations* for an aspect's implementation source code. The annotations should be simple to develop and understand. Using annotations for AOP is absolutely in the spirit of the annotation concept: "Let's write some source code and annotate it as belonging to an aspect, if appropriate." However, the language of AOP annotations should be a *separate high-level language-agnostic AOP specification language.* For AOP purposes, straightforward use of the mechanism to define annotations in the implementation languages ("@"-style annotations in Java, custom attributes in .NET) ties AOP specifications to a concrete implementation language (e.g., C# or Visual Basic). Don't forget that we would like to achieve language independence for AOP annotations. But they will be more understandable to users if we provide a standard clear way of *conversion* (or *projection*) of each AOP annotation to some construct of the implementation language: say, standard conversion of AOP annotations to definitions of customs attributes in C#. So for each implementation language used with AOP annotations, we should develop a converter of the AOP annotations to definition of custom attributes (annotations) in this language. There will be a separate AOP annotations converter for C# and another for VB.NET. The converter can easily be integrated into the common-use IDE, which is very important (no need to develop a special, much more complicated compiler such as *ajc* in AspectJ because of AOP extensions only). The users can, if they like, specify aspects either in higher-level AOP annotations metalanguage, or directly in terms of custom attributes in the implementation language. Another important consideration is also practical: What if the user would like to forget about AOP, deciding to use only the existing workable code and ignore the AOP annotations? The simplest decision would then be to comment out the source code lines with AOP annotations, or to delete those lines. So the structure of the united aspect code containing AOP annotations and the implementation code should allow us to do that (which is, by the way, *not* the case in AspectJ, where aspects are mixed with basic Java features). The user should be able to comment out or delete AOP annotation lines so that the resulting code remains a *syntactically and semantically correct and complete source code of a compilation unit in the implementation language.* The ideas described were used to design and implement Aspect.NET.ML, a metalanguage of AOP annotations for Aspect.NET whose structure is described below. Let's briefly summarize our requirements for an AOP metalanguage:

- Simplicity
- Conceptual economy
- Independence of concrete programming languages and paradigms
- Annotation style of AOP constructs

3.7.2   Basic Concepts of AOP

In our approach, an *aspect* is an implementation of some cross-cutting concern. An aspect is not associated with a class or a concrete construct of a concrete language. Aspect is a general metanotion of software development formulated in a special *AOP specification language.* Implementation of the aspect is written in an implementation language. Aspect specification should not depend on the implementation language. It should be possible to use the same aspect specification for its implementation in different languages (say, C#.NET and VB.NET). However, specification of the aspect for integration with implementation should be made in the form of *aspect-oriented annotations* to the implementation's source code. The integrated code of the aspect definition (AOP annotations plus implementation of the aspect) consists of the following parts:

- Aspect *name*
- Aspect *modules*
- Aspect *data*
- Aspect *rules*

A *module* of the aspect is a method, function, procedure, subroutine, co-routine, or other type of basic modular unit provided by the implementation language. This unit should be annotated in AOP metalanguage as a module of the aspect. For an object-oriented implementation language, any aspect module is implemented by a *method*. For a procedural programming language the module can be implemented by a procedure or function, for example (using the term *module* here in its classical meaning) [19].

The *data* of the aspect comprise any definitions or declarations provided by the implementation language. The aspect data encapsulate the information with which the aspect works. The data can be omitted. If they are present, they should be annotated as the aspect's data.

The *rules* of the aspect define its weaving functionality. Each weaving rule consists of the *condition* and the *action* to be activated in a *join point* matching the condition after weaving the aspect into the target application. Each action can be implemented by a basic module of the implementation language. It should be annotated as an action of the aspect and by its weaving condition. Use of the term *action* instead of the term *advice* used for similar functionality in AspectJ is intentional, as the term *action* better reflects the semantics of the aspect functionality. It appears that the term *advice* used in AspectJ was borrowed from artificial intelligence languages, following a historic tradition. For better understanding by users, we use the term (*weaving*) *condition* here instead of *pointcut*, and the term *rule* for the entire construct that unites the weaving condition and the action to be woven. Note that the terms and the aspect architecture used are very simple and do not depend on any concrete programming paradigm (e.g., OOP).

The syntax and semantics of AOP metalanguage are made as simple as possible. Each of its constructs (an AOP annotation) is written as separate lines of the source code and starts with a special keyword. All AOP keywords start with "%" to separate them easily from the rest of the source. If AOP annotations are deleted or commented out, the remaining source is a correct compilation unit of the implementation language. AOP metalanguage should be applicable equally to C#.NET and VB.NET.

A simple example is a semaphore-based *Synchronization* aspect. It can be implemented by a *module* (class) defining *P* and *V* operations, and by two *actions*: calls of *P* and *V* operations. The *rules* of weaving these actions are as follows: *P* operation is to be called *before* an update of the common resource; *V* operation is to be called *after* an update of the resource. Details of the syntax of AOP metalanguage are provided later. Figure 3.4 illustrates the architecture of the *Syhcnronization* aspect example given below.

Aspect Mining, or Aspectizing One of the most important tasks of AOP which has not yet received enough attention is *aspectizing*: transforming a non-aspect-oriented program into an aspect-oriented program, or extracting aspects from non-aspect-oriented programs. When discussing our Aspect.NET approach, we prefer to use the term *aspectizing* instead of the term *aspect mining* [29] used in some earlier research papers on this subject. Aspectizing is decomposition of a program into a collection of aspect definitions and weavings. The purpose of aspectizing, as of AOP in general, is to make analysis, maintenance, and reuse of software easier. An aspectizer can be based on a set of "starting" source file names of the aspect, a set of wild cards describing its identifiers, or a starting set of types defined in the aspect. Then the aspectizer will take into account all the modules called from an underlying source code suspected to belong to the aspect, and so on. Finally, the aspectizer should suggest to the user its version of decomposing the program into aspects. But users should be able to make the final decisions themselves and, if necessary, aspectize parts of the program by hand.

Requirements for the AOP Framework   Let's briefly summarize requirements of the AOP framework formulated in Section 3.2:

- Defining and weaving aspects
- Reusability of aspects
- Aspect visualization, modification, addition, and deletion GUI
- Option to check the results of aspect weaving and to perform it partially by hand
- Implementation of AOP metalanguage
- Support of aspectizing, automated or by hand

Generic Aspects   An appropriate technique to make aspects more general is *generics*, introduced into the CLU language [20] in the 1970s. *Generic aspects* should probably be part of the AOP metalanguage, although up to now, no AOP tools support generic aspects, and we haven't yet implemented them in Aspect.NET, although this is planned. For example, *Synchronization* aspect could be parametrized by synchronization conditions. By instantiation we get a more specific aspect of synchronization through a concrete resource or condition. Why generics? Because they are in the spirit of AOP: Aspects can be regarded as general transformation and enhancement schemes for existing code. Such schemes will lose their generality if they cannot be parametrized. The reader can argue that there are generics in C# and Java and there is no need to add generics to aspect specifications. However, generics in C# and Java are very limited to passing type parameters only, with static checking of the restrictions of the actual type parameters passed (i.e., checking that the actual type parameter implements the required set of interfaces). This is definitely not enough. To strengthen the argument, let's continue our example using the *Synchronization* aspect. The synchronization condition is not a type—it is a pointcut (speaking in AspectJ terms)—so C# generics cannot be used to implement such a generic aspect.

3.7.3 Example

The program example below is a generic *Synchronization* aspect definition. AOP annotations are shown in bold. Note that it will *not* work in Aspect.NET 2.1 [6]. We plan to implement generic aspects in future releases of Aspect.NET. Including this example in the conceptual part of the discussion demonstrates the original idea [1] and the elegance of generic aspects; there is no need to develop many almost identical aspects which differ only in their synchronization conditions. To make this work in the current version, the user should omit the *<ResourceUpdate>* formal parameter in the aspect header and to do instantiation by hand by replacing two applied occurrences of *ResourceUpdate* with a concrete synchronization condition from the application [say, the condition *%call MyClass.SetMyResource(..)*], all calls of *SetMyResource* method in the class *MyClass*.

```
%aspect Synchronization <ResourceUpdate>
public class Synchronization
{
%modules
    public class Semaphore {
      private boolean Open = true;
      public void P() {
        lock (Open) {
          Open = false;
          while (!Open) {
            System.Threading.Monitor.Wait(Open);
          }
        }
      } // P
      public void V() {
        lock (Open) {
          Open = true;
          System.Threading.Monitor.Pulse(Open);
        }
      } // V
    } // Semaphore
%data
    public static Semaphore s = new Semaphore();
%rules
    %before ResourceUpdate
    %action
     public static void lockAction() { s.P(); }
    %after ResourceUpdate
    %action
     public static void unlockAction() { s. V(); }
} // Synchronization
```

An example of weaving the aspect (typically, weaving is made via GUI provided by the Aspect.NET framework):

```
%to MyNameSpace %apply Synchronization <%assign Res.
buffer>
```

Weaving with another synchronization condition, an assignment to the field `Res.r1` or `Res.r2`, looks as follows:

```
%to MyNameSpace %apply Synchronization <%assign Res.r1,
Res.r2>
```

Defining aspects by AOP metalanguage should not be the only way to introduce a new aspect. In AOP tools all features should also be available via Aspect GUI.

3.7.4 Representing Aspects by Custom Attributes

AOP annotations in the example in Section 3.7.3 should be converted to definitions of AOP custom attributes. Due to .NET architecture, extra information on aspects represented as custom attributes will not prohibit normal functioning of CLR, compilers, and other .NET tools. Aspect metadata are used only by the AOP tool; the other tools can just ignore it. However, unlike metadata, it is not possible to attach custom attributes to MSIL instructions. No doubt such a feature could be useful not only for the purposes of AOP, but it could decrease the runtime performance of .NET.

So, while it is possible to keep AOP information for definitions, there is no straightforward way to indicate that a piece of MSIL belongs to an aspect. Neither is it possible to attach mnemonic labels or comments to the *binary* format of MSIL. The solution is as follows. MSIL code contains *metadata tokens*, references to named entities used in the code. An MSIL code manipulation tool such as Microsoft Phoenix should be used to analyze MSIL instructions and metadata, to extract metadata tokens from MSIL instructions, and to recognize from their custom attributes to which aspect the MSIL code belongs.

In general, any of the actions of an aspect may contain not only references to the aspect modules and data, but also references to other aspects, or to standard API such as `System.Console::WriteLine`. Require each statement of an aspect's actions to refer to *its* modules or data or to be represented as a separate method or function within the aspect compilation unit. Otherwise, aspect actions after weaving (e.g., an explicit `WriteLine` a call) will be "dissolved" within the MSIL code of the program without any information on the applied aspect. So if we are to implement, say, a `Logging` aspect with two actions, logging the start and end of a call, we should define two methods, `LogStart` and `LogFinish`, within the aspect compilation unit. Only in this way are we guaranteed that MSIL code of the aspect woven into any program will contain a metadata token for this local aspect's method, so the `Logging` aspect will be recognized as belonging to this MSIL code.

Another solution could be to use the *ilasm*, the "MSIL assembler," and *ilasm* source code as an intermediate representation of a program in an AOP tool. Unlike MSIL binaries, *ilasm* code contains mnemonic labels for each instruction and may contain comments. The usual format of the *ilasm* label is `IL_n`, where n is the instruction number. Replacing this label by a more mnemonic label that contains the name of the aspect and a unique id of this concrete weaving of the aspect will not crush *ilasm* utility. But as a result, *ilasm* will generate MSIL binaries *without* any tracks of the labels or comments above, with all references to MSIL instructions replaced by their offsets: signed integers.

Besides, using *ilasm/ildasm* and another intermediate form of the program can decrease the performance of AOP tools. In compiler terms, *ilasm* code would require several extra passes of the entire program, whose size may be very large. In addition, using *ilasm* code is not convenient for users who prefer to work in terms of the source code in C#, VB, or an other high-level language. However "assembler-level aspects" with AOP annotations in metalanguage and the implementation of aspects in *ilasm* code may themselves be useful.

A theoretically possible solution is to retain for each module the custom attribute `AppliedAspectActions`, the list of all weavings of all aspect actions within this module. But it does not correspond either to .NET architecture or to general principles of informational relationships: If the program is modified by a non-AOP tool, the values of `AppliedAspectActions` attribute may get out of date.

Keeping in mind all of the above, the following architecture of an AOP tool for Microsoft.NET appears to be the most adequate. Any named and typed entity in a program (class, field, method, etc.) must have an `AspectRef` custom attribute with the `Name` field, the name of the aspect to which the given entity belongs. Values of `AspectRef` attribute can be defined in the source code either by the "syntactic sugar" of AOP metalanguage or just by the common syntax of .NET attributes: by an expression in square brackets for C#.NET or in angular brackets for VB.NET.

An aspect definition in the form of a compilation unit plus AOP annotations discussed above is compiled into a PE assembly file containing aspect MSIL code and metadata. Compilation of AOP annotations can be done as a separate preprocessing (conversion) phase. For each of the items of the aspect definition, the `AspectDef` custom attribute is defined, with three main fields: `Name` of the aspect; `Role` of the item within the aspect (module, data, action); and `Value`, role-specific information (string). For an action, its `Value` is the weaving rule. For the main module the `Value` is the aspect's formal parameter list, if any. On processing the aspect its header items and weaving rules are transformed into values of the `AspectDef` attribute. The *actions* are transformed into *methods* in MSIL code, with custom attributes indicating the role of the method (as *action*) within the aspect and the *weaving rule* of the action. Applying an aspect is implemented as copying MSIL code and metadata of its actions into appropriate join points of an assembly file of the program using the aspect. For any MSIL instruction, its belonging to aspects should be determined by analyzing metadata tokens used in the MSIL instruction.

An important user interface issue is mapping the foregoing representation of aspects back to the program source. Users should not have to learn or handle aspects at the MSIL code level and should have an opportunity to work with aspects in terms of the source code of the language. Decompilation as the method of such mapping should be avoided. So two solutions are possible: relying on debugging information and the appropriate options of the compiler to generate it, or having a special custom attribute (say, Source) for each module to retain a reference to its source or a copy of its source. The former method looks appropriate to .NET architecture; the latter is unacceptable for the same reason as the AppliedAspectActions attribute is mentioned above. The task of *aspectizing* a program is considered as evaluating the AspectRef attribute for each of its named and typed entities, and identifying the aspect(s) for each of its CIL instructions (or source code constructs).

3.7.5 Example in Terms of Custom Attributes

Now reconsider the example in Section 3.7.3 written in "pure C#" in "AOP-preprocessed" form, with the AOP annotations replaced by C# attribute usage constructs. *AspectDotNet* is the AOP namespace provided by Aspect.NET.

```
using AspectDotNet;
[AspectDef
        (Name = "Synchronization",
        Role = "MainModule",
        Value ="Param:<resourceUpdate>")
]
public class Synchronization
{
        [AspectDef
                (Name = "Synchronization",
                Role = "Module"
                )
                ]
        public class Semaphore { ... }
        [AspectDef (Name = "Synchronization", Role =
        "Data")]
        public static Semaphore s = new Semaphore();
        [
                AspectDef
                        (Name = "Synchronization",
```

```
                     Role = "Action",
                     Value = "%before resourceUpdate"
                     )
     ]
     public static void lockAction() { ... }
     [
             AspectDef
                 (Name = "Synchronization",
                  Role = "Action",
                  Value = "%after resourceUpdate")
     ]
     public static void unlockAction() { ... }
} // Synchronization
```

3.7.6 Summary of Our Approach to AOP

Now let's summarize the key ideas behind our approach to AOP:

- *Static aspect weaving*: implementing aspect weaving as MSIL binary code injections
- *Language neutral AOP annotations*: AOP annotations and AOP meta-language independent of the programming language being used
- *Using custom attributes* to attach AOP annotations tightly to the code to which they relate
- *Cross-language aspects interoperability*: multilanguage aspects and MSIL-level aspects being used together
- *Aspect-oriented knowledge management*: treating and processing aspects as metaknowledge that consists of procedural knowledge: implementation of components that are parts of aspect definition; conceptual knowledge: domain-specific knowledge on the application domains (formal specifications); and heuristic knowledge: the weaving rules for aspect actions
- *Integration to latest Microsoft technologies and tools for software development*: Microsoft Visual Studio.NET 2005 and Microsoft Phoenix

Static Aspect Weaving Although many of the useful AOP features (e.g., error handling) are convenient to use with dynamic join points, there is a growing need to "color" aspects in existing and oncoming applications that adequately correspond to a "static" (weaving by binary code injections) AOP model. Due to this model, aspects can be clearly seen and updated by an AOP GUI-based tool. On the other hand, treating aspects as described below, our approach to AOP is open to a "dynamic" model of join points.

Language-Neutral AOP Annotations Most current AOP tools are based on their own specific languages, both to specify and define aspects and for their implementation. One of the goals of our Aspect.NET project, in the spirit of Microsoft.NET, is to make aspects really workable across languages. For this purpose, we offer a simple AOP "metalanguage" that can be used to specify aspects regardless of their implementation language (C#.NET, VB.NET, C++. NET, JScript.NET, J#.NET, etc.). AOP specifications defined in our AOP meta-language can be regarded as *AOP annotations* that don't really depend on the aspects' implementation language. In our AOP metalanguage we only use such self-evident and language-neutral notions as "compilation unit," "programming module," "data definition," and "generics."

Using Custom Attributes   As for implementing aspects for .NET compared to XML-based approaches (see Section 3.6), using *custom attributes* for this purpose appears more reliable and justifiable. Custom attributes are intended for any program annotations related to specific parts of applications (assemblies, classes, methods, etc.): in particular, to AOP annotations. Their advantages are, first, their clarity and self-evidence, and second, their close relation and adherence to the program parts to which they are tied. To compare custom attributes to XML schemas: Custom attributes are always tied to the program units and fragments to which they relate; XML schemas can very easily be lost or "forgotten" during program transformations. More clearly and concretely, due to their goal, custom attributes always accompany any kind of program transformation and are used only when appropriate (by AOP tools only, or by other kinds of tools "understanding" these attributes) and thus can be ignored by any common-use .NET tools (debuggers, garbage collectors, etc.).

Cross-Language Aspects Interoperability   This is one of the primary purposes of our approach to AOP. Currently, the only appropriate common language to use to express aspects for .NET is MSIL (plus metadata). It is quite suitable for system programmers who may define "MSIL-level" aspects, due to the OOP nature of CIL, but is not quite appropriate for a number of end users who are tied to their favorite languages (C#, VB, etc.). The decision is to allow for "MSIL/metadata level" aspects but to implement *conversion* or *transformation of "language-neutral" AOP "syntactic sugar"* (*AOP metalanguage*) *to language-specific custom attributes definitions* (e.g., the appropriate C# constructs in square brackets, or VB.NET constructs in angular brackets). The idea behind this approach is as follows: AOP custom attributes can be regarded as *language-neutral annotations* or even *comments* on the source of an application. If needed, we can forget about aspects, comment out the AOP annotations (which is easy to implement, due to their simplicity and their keywords starting with "%"), and use them for information only. On the other hand, software developers who use our approach to AOP can just ignore our "syntactic sugar" (suppose that they just don't like any kind of sugar) and implement aspects explicitly in their applications using AOP attribute definitions in a language-dependent form.

Aspect-Oriented Knowledge Management Let's forget that almost all existing AOP tools are based in Java. From a more general viewpoint, aspects can be regarded as *hybrid knowledge,* or even *metaknowledge,* because they contain information on how to apply them (in other words, the procedural knowledge implemented in their definitions) to existing applications (in our terminology, *weaving rules*; in classical terms, *pointcuts* and *join points*). Taking this viewpoint, aspects can be considered as a special type of module in our approach: compilation units of any implementation language used, accompanied by AOP annotations, whether expressed in syntactic sugar or in language-dependent form. We think such treatment of aspects can provide a basis for further research in what we call *aspect-oriented knowledge management*: research on using formal specifications as part of aspect definitions.

Integration to Latest Microsoft Technologies and Tools for Software Development: Phoenix This is one of the most important principles in our work on Aspect.NET. When we started the project, there was no suitable tool for handling .NET portable executable (PE) files; everybody who needed such a tool had to "reinvent the wheel." Then the Microsoft Phoenix version appeared, which could handle PE files and convert them into Phoenix high-level intermediate representation (Phoenix HIR) suitable for weaving implementation. In 2005 we implemented the first version of a weaver using Phoenix, and since then, four versions of Phoenix have been developed and its API has been changed substantially. By keeping track of all these changes, we could update our weaver accordingly. Rather than reinventing the wheel we used .NET PE file parser from Phoenix.

Integration with Microsoft Visual Studio.NET This is also a key point and one of the main advantages of Aspect.NET. We noted in Section 3.6 that current users of many AOP tools for .NET suffer from lack of a comfortable GUI and lack of integration to Visual Studio.NET, the most comfortable development environment for .NET. We managed to design and implement the *Aspect.NET framework,* a GUI integrated to Visual Studio.NET 2005, as an add-in. It is very comfortable for users to start their favorite Visual Studio and see Aspect.NET GUI also started and ready to use. Many users e-mail their appreciation of this feature.

3.7.7 Aspect.NET Architectural Principles

Based on the above, we have implemented the following features in Aspect. NET:

- Defining and weaving aspects
- *Supporting reusability of aspects*: in particular, the ability to apply aspects to a whole application, a selected class or namespace, and so on

- *GUI* for aspects visualization, modification, adding, weaving, and deletion
- *Checking the possible results of "automatic" aspect weaving,* to undo some of these modifications and to perform them by hand
- *Implementation of AOP metalanguage*: in the first release, as a preprocessor for C# that converts syntactic sugar AOP annotations to C#-dependent ones: constructs of defining and using appropriate custom attributes; in future releases, converters to other .NET languages (e.g., Visual Basic.NET)
- *In future releases: aspectizing* (automatic or partially by hand) with the appropriate GUI

Aspect GUI enables users, first, to check and manually control the results of aspect weaving by hand (to prevent "blind" weaving when using wild cards), and second, to initiate, check, and manually control the results of aspectizing, to enable an appropriate start with a reasonable set of types or regular expressions wild cards, and to prevent unclear and inappropriate results of "automated" aspectizing.

In Aspect.NET, an *aspect definition* is a *compilation unit* of the implementation language being used (C#, VB.NET, etc.): namespace, class, and so on, plus *AOP annotations* (in AOP *metalanguage*). *Aspect weaving* can be expressed by either a *construct of an AOP metalanguage*, or by means of *aspect GUI*. Semantically, aspect weaving consists of:

- The name of the underlying application or its module to which the aspect is applied
- The name of the aspect (definition) to weave
- (optional) The aspect *actual parameters*, corresponding to its formal parameters in the aspect definition, if any

In Aspect.NET, aspect definitions are treated as definitions of modules, actions, and the weaving rules for each of the actions that can be applied to any application or to its class, as a kind of *"tangled" MSIL code injection*, with the actual parameters (if any) substituted for an aspect's formal parameters. As a pointcut-like construct, we introduce *rule sets*. A rule set in Aspect.NET is a special kind of module (with AOP annotations only) for defining a set of join points that can be used for weaving *any aspect*.

Now let's briefly summarize our initial ideas regarding Aspect.NET architecture:

- *C# preprocessor*: converts AOP annotations into AOP attribute definitions. It works with C# source code. The current version of the preprocessor is implemented on the basis of C# regular expression-handling features.

- *Aspect weaver*: performs the command *"Weave aspect A [parametrized by <FP>] [with actual parameters <AP>]* into a program, class, method, ... P."* It works with PE files, including AOP attributes.
- *Aspect editor*: performs the operations *"locate an aspect"; "update an aspect"; "delete an aspect."* It works with PE files, including AOP attributes.
- *Aspect visualization GUI (Aspect.NET framework)*: provides an interactive user interface for the components above. Visualizes different aspects in different colors.

3.7.8 Syntax of AOP Metalanguage (Version 1.0)

Let's consider the initial version of the AOP metalanguage [1,2]. The version of the metalanguage (Aspect.NET.ML) actually implemented in Aspect.NET 2.1 is described in Section 3.8. In the EBNF specification below, the constructs of the aspect implementation language (in the first version, of C#) are shown in bold. These are: module definitions, data definitions, variable or field use, function or method definitions, statements, and compilation unit definitions. The metanotions *WeavingRule* and *Params* may appear in strings that denote the values of the attributes. In those cases, as well as in ordinary cases when they appear in regular EBNF, they should be replaced by the results of their inference in EBNF grammar. For example, the construct

```
"WeavingRule"
```

can be replaced by

```
"%before ResourceUpdate",
```

and the construct

```
"Param:<Params>"
```

can be replaced by

```
"Param:<ResourceUpdate>"
```

Here is the syntax of the first version of the Aspect.NET.ML metalanguage (a period denotes the end of a syntax rule):

> AOPMetaLanguageConstruct = AspectDef | AspectWeave | RuleSet .
> AspectDef   = AspectHdr AspectModules **[** AspectData **]**
>   AspectActions .
> AspectHdr   = **%aspect** AspectName **[** FormalParams **]** .

AspectName   = Id .
FormalParams   = < Id+ > .
AspectModules   = %module   **ModuleDefOfImplLanguage+** .
AspectData   = %data   **DataDefOfImplLanguage+** .
AspectActions   = ActionDef+ .
ActionDef   = %action WeavingRule %do Action .
WeavingRule   = WeavingCondition JoinPoint .
WeavingCondition = %before | %after | %instead .
JoinPoint   = Params | Patterns .
Params   = Param | Params , Param .
Param   = Id .
Patterns   = Pattern | Patterns , Pattern .
Pattern   = %assign   **VariableOrFieldOfImplLanguage** |
                       %use   **VariableOrFieldOfImplLanguage** |
                       %call   **FuncOrMethodOfImplLanguage**
                       %ruleset .
Action   = **StatementOfImplLanguage** |
                       FuncOrMethodCallOfImplLanguage .
RuleSet   = %ruleset RuleSetName WeavingRule+ .
RuleSetName   = Id .
AspectWeave   = [%to   **CompUnitIdOfImplLanguage**]
                       %apply AspectName
                       [Patterns | %ruleset RuleSetName] .

Metadata custom attributes to represent aspects are as follows:

1. **AspectDefAttribute**: metainformation on aspect definition. This attribute can be tied to an assembly, class, method, field, property, enumeration, or structure. Fields of *AspectDefAttribute*:
   - Name (string)   the name of the aspect/rule set being defined.
   - Role (string)   the role of the named item in the aspect definition. It can be as follows:
     - "mainModule"   the main module of the aspect.
     - "module"   a module of the aspect.
     - "data"   a data item of the aspect.
     - "action"   an action of the aspect.
     - "ruleset"   a rule set attached to some compilation unit via its custom attributes. A *rule set* is a named list of weaving rules to be applied when weaving any aspect to any compilation unit. The definition of a rule set is tied via custom attributes to some main com-

pilation unit (e.g., to a C# namespace). For a particular weaving, when a rule set is indicated, the list of the aspect's weaving rules is concatenated to the list of the rule set's weaving rules, and they apply jointly as if they were all in the aspect's definition.

- `Value (string)`   role-dependent extra information:
  - For *mainModule*   "(" if nongeneric
                        "Param:<Params>" if generic
                          (e.g., "Param:<ResourceUpdate>")
  - For *module*   not used
  - For *data*   not used
  - For *action*   "WeavingRule"
                          (e.g., "%before ResourceUpdate")
  - For *ruleset*   "WeavingRule ..."
                          list of weaving rules

2. **AspectRefAttribute**: metainformation on assigning a named entity to an aspect. It marks any fragment that is the result of weaving some aspect and helps to "color" the aspects. Field of *AspectRefAttribute*:
   - `Name (string)`   the name of the aspect woven.

3.7.9 Another Example

As another illustration of our approach, consider an example of the C# definition of a useful aspect that performs logging of some action in an application: a call of a given method, an assignment to a given field, and so on. Note that Aspect.NET features allow us to define that aspect in the most general form, as *parametrized* by the logging condition and the appropriate message to be issued. So there is no need to define a lot of specific logging aspects for more concrete logging conditions instead.

The definition of the aspect looks as follows (fragments of the AOP metalanguage are in bold):

```
%aspect Logging <LoggingCondition, LoggingMessage>
public class Logging
{
%modules
   public static void LogStart()
   (
        System.Console.WriteLine("Starting " +
        LoggingMessage);
   }
   public static void LogFinish()
   (
```

```
        System.Console.WriteLine("Finishing " +
        LoggingMessage);
    }
%rules
    %before LoggingCondition
    %action
        public static void logStartAction() {Logging.
        LogStart();}
    %after LoggingCondition
    %action
        public static void logFinishAction() {Logging.
        LogFinish();}
} // Logging
```

An example of weaving the Logging aspect:

```
%to MyClass %apply Logging <%call MyMethod, " MyMethod
call">
```

The effect of the AOP metalanguage construct above is as follows: Before
and after calling the given method, a logging message of starting and finishing
the call will be issued. Weaving the same Logging aspect with another logging
condition, an assignment to the given public static field named *MyField*, and
a related message is activated in AOP metalanguage in the following way:

```
%to MyClass %apply Logging
<%assign MyField, " MyField assign: value =" +
MyClass.MyField>
```

The effect of the AOP metalanguage construct above will be as follows:
Before and after each assignment to the given field, a logging message will be
issued containing the current value of the field.

3.8   FEATURES AND USE OF Aspect.NET

In this section we describe Aspect.NET "as is" now, in its latest version available at the moment of writing the book, Aspect.NET 2.1. The section can serve
as a user's guide to Aspect.NET. Emphasis is on existing features and their
use rather than on principles, since the principles were described in detail in
Section 3.7. The user's guide for Aspect.NET 2.1 is available for downloading
[6], as is Aspect.NET 2.1 itself. Note that the description in this section is only
a "snapshot" of the current status of Aspect.NET. The system is in a state of
evolution, so when using a newer version of Aspect.NET, consult the user's
guide bundled with that version.

3.8.1   Prerequisites for Using Aspect.NET 2.1

Aspect.NET 2.1 is intended for use in a.NET 2.0 environment on machines running under Windows XP with Service Pack 2. Note that Aspect.NET 2.1 has not yet been tried or tested under Windows Vista or under .NET 3.0. That will be done in future releases with the appropriate version of Phoenix.

The Aspect.NET framework, the aspect manipulation GUI that makes it possible to use all Aspect.NET functionality, is implemented as an *add-in* to Visual Studio.NET 2005. This means that the user can use Aspect.NET in combination with the integrated development environment provided by Visual Studio.NET and its numerous comfortable features for developing software applications: project types, code templates, refactoring, debugging, profiling, and so on.

In practice, it means that the user need not start Aspect.NET separately. It starts together with Visual Studio, and the GUI of Aspect.NET Framework can be considered as part of an extended GUI of Visual Studio.NET. To install and use Aspect.NET 2.1, you need to install the following software packages and tools:

- Windows XP Service Pack 2
- Visual Studio.NET 2005 (Whidbey) Release: either the Professional or Standard Edition
- Microsoft Platform Research Development Kit (RDK) Codenamed "Phoenix," March 2007 Release (the latest Phoenix release available) [7]
  Note: Before using the March 2007 version of Phoenix (which we use in Aspect.NET 2.1), add the following path to your PATH environment variable:

```
C:\Program Files\Microsoft Visual Studio 8\Common7\IDE
```

(or replace "C" by another logical partition letter in case Visual Studio is installed on that partition rather than on C:).

3.8.2   Previous Releases of Aspect.NET and the Compatibility Mode

Previous releases of Aspect.NET include:

- *Aspect.NET 1.0:* uploaded in September 2005; works with the version of Phoenix RDK dated February 2005, and with Visual Studio.NET 2005 beta 2. No longer recommended for use, since it uses obsolete versions of Phoenix and Visual Studio.NET.
- *Aspect.NET 1.1:* uploaded in March 2006; works with the version of Phoenix RDK dated November 2005 and with Visual Stutio.NET 2005 Release (Professional or Standard Edition). No longer recommended for use, since it uses an obsolete version of Phoenix.

- *Aspect.NET 2.0:* uploaded in September 2006; works with the version of Phoenix RDK dated May 2006 and with Visual Stutio.NET 2005 Release (Professional or Standard Edition). No longer recommended for use, since it uses an obsolete version of Phoenix. Aspects developed using an Aspect.NET 2.0 environment can be also used with Aspect.NET 2.1, except for those samples based on using Phoenix API (e.g., *MAddNop/ MAddNopCounter* in our bundle), since Phoenix API has been changed a lot since its May 2006 release.

The current version (Aspect.NET 2.1) provides many new features. The implementation of aspects in the current version differs from that in previous versions. For that reason we have implemented a specific mode for backward compatibility. In this mode, users can use Aspect.NET 2.1 with "old" (1.0 or 1.1) aspect definitions in Aspect.NET.ML metalanguage and in C# (with an *AspectDef* custom attribute), as described in Section 3.7. The backward-compatibility mode is turned off by default. It can be switched on using Visual Studio.NET GUI by clicking Tools/Options, selecting "Aspect.NET Framework," and checking the "AspectDef 1.0" radio button in the area labeled "Aspect.NET attributes version."

So, to port aspects from Aspect.NET 1.0 or 1.1 to Aspect.NET 2.1, one can use old aspects, either at the AOP metalanguage level or at the C# + custom attributes level, without changes, with the following exception: In Aspect.NET 1.0 / 1.1, a *temporary* scheme for communicating the aspect to the join point was implemented. It was based on a kind of "temporary ABI convention" between Aspect.NET and the author of an aspect: that the arguments of an aspect action, if any, were used to pass the name of the target method and the reference to the target object. This is not true in Aspect.NET 2.1. In the new version we use special Aspect.NET.ML constructs (e.g., *%TargetMemberInfo*) to refer explicitly to parts of join point's environment, and special types of constructs to explicitly capture target arguments. So, if you need to port your old aspects to Aspect.NET 2.1, you should not use old-style conventions on accessing join point's context via action arguments. Instead, use a new mechanism and constructs to access the context of join points described below.

Users should also keep in mind that they cannot use the "old-style" *MAddNop/MAddNopCounter* sample (from the Aspect.NET 1.0 [5] package), based on Phoenix, with Aspect.NET 2.1. This is because the Phoenix API has changed since its previous releases. Instead, an updated version of the *AddNop-Tool/MAddNopCounter* sample working with Aspect.NET 2.1 is provided with Aspect.NET 2.1 distribution on the MSDNAA CR Web site.

3.8.3 Aspect.NET Architecture

An *aspect* in Aspect.NET is defined as the source code of a class (more generally speaking, a compilation unit) in C# or other .NET language, annotated by the AOP metalanguage (referred to as Aspect.NET.ML) statements to highlight parts of the aspect definition. They are: *aspect header* (optional); *aspect data* (typically, private fields); *aspect modules* (methods); and *aspect weaving rules*, which consist of *weaving conditions* and *actions* (to be woven into a target assembly according to these rules). In Aspect.NET 2.1, only aspects defined in Aspect.NET.ML and C# are supported. The plan for future releases is also to support Visual Basic as aspect implementation language.

The aspect weaving rules determine the join points within a target application where the actions of the aspect are to be woven. The aspect actions provide the aspect's functionality. *The Aspect.NET preprocessor (converter)* converts AOP annotations to C# definitions of AOP custom attributes especially designed for Aspect.NET to mark classes and methods as parts of the aspect definition (see Figure 3.5). Next, the common-use .NET compiler available in Visual Studio.NET 2005 transforms the AOP custom attributes to the aspect assembly's metadata, stored together with the MSIL code.

Join points in Aspect.NET are determined by weaving rules that are part of the aspect definition or are defined in a separate rule set module. The weaving rules contain conditions of calling aspect actions (before, after, or instead of); the context of the action call [a call of some method, assignment to a variable (field), or use of some variable (field)]; and a wild card used to find the context of the aspect action's call. In Aspect.NET 2.1, only call join points are implemented. Other types of contexts will be implemented in future releases.

The process of *aspect weaving* consists of two phases: *scanning* (finding join points within the target application) and *weaving* the calls of the aspect actions into the join points found. The weaver is based on Microsoft Phoenix [7].

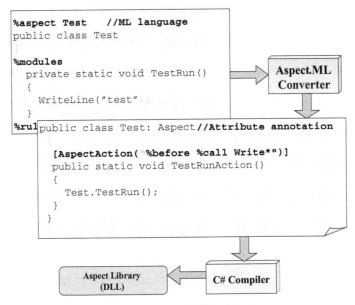

Figure 3.5 *Aspect.NET architecture.*

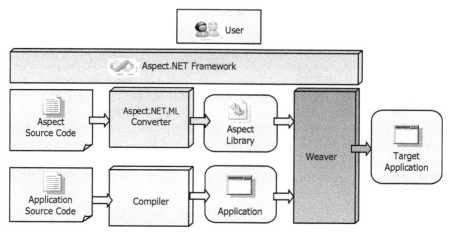

Figure 3.6 *Components of Aspect.NET.*

Unlike many other AOP tools, Aspect.NET allows the user to select or "unselect" any of the possible join points using Aspect.NET Framework GUI, to avoid "blind" weaving that could make the resulting code much less understandable and nondebuggable. It allows us to resolve "the Set* wild-card issue" described in Sections 3.2 and 3.4 with the help of the users, who only know the semantics of their applications and can determine whether a given potential join point found and suggested by the weaver does actually make sense.

The user can use either the Aspect.NET.ML form or the C# custom attributes form for defining aspects. In the Aspect.NET framework, both types of aspect definition projects are supported. For both sources—Aspect.NET.ML and C# using Aspect.NET's AOP attributes—special types of projects are built into Visual Studio.NET, with the corresponding code templates. The main components of Aspect.NET—*weaver* (designed and implemented by Dmitry Grigoryev), *metalanguage converter* (designed and implemented by Alexander Maslennikov), and *Aspect.NET framework* (designed and implemented by Mikhail Gratchev)—and their interaction are shown in Figure 3.6.

3.8.4 Case Study: Using the Aspect.NET Framework

In this section we describe the process of using Aspect.NET, based on a very simple example of target application and aspect definition to be woven in. Let's go through all steps of aspect definition, weaving the updated application with the help of Aspect.NET, and testing the updated application's functionality as compared to the original version. It should show readers how to use the Aspect.NET framework.

1. Here is the target C# console application:

```
using System;
using System.Collections.Generic;
using System.Text;
namespace ConsoleApplication1
{
    class Program
    {
        static void P()
        { Console.WriteLine("P"); }
        static void Main(string[] args)
        {
            Console.WriteLine("Main");
            P();
        }
    }
}
```

Suppose that we have created a solution named *Application1* using Visual Studio.NET 2005 for this console application. Let's create and build such a solution. The application's output to the console is as follows:

> *Main*
>
> *P*

2. On installing Aspect.NET over Visual Studio.NET 2005, let's now create an aspect to insert logging messages of the kind

> *Hello P*

and

> *Bye P*

before and after a call of each method *P* in a target application (more exactly, the name and header of the method will be logged). This aspect will, so to speak, help to make the target application "polite."

To create an aspect solution, invoke Visual Studio.NET 2005 and chose *File/New/Project*. Note that the Aspect.NET Framework window will appear as part of VS.NET GUI, as shown in Figure 3.7. Chose an "*Aspect.NET ML module*" type of project. This means that we'll create the specifications for our aspect using Aspect.NET.ML metalanguage.

Note that there is another kind of aspect project: the *Aspect.NET module*. You should use it if you decide to skip the phase of the Aspect.NET.ML definition and use AOP custom attributes in C# code directly.

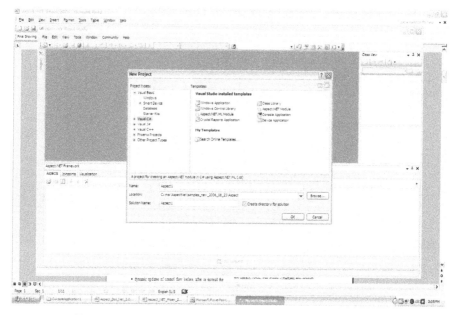

Figure 3.7   *Creating an aspect project in Visual Studio.NET 2005.*

Suppose that the project name is *Aspect1*, taken by default. You will see the following aspect definition file template generated by the Aspect.NET framework:

```
%aspect Aspect1
using System;
class Aspect1
{
    %modules
    %rules
}
```

named *Aspect.an.* ".*an*" (from "*Aspect.Net*") is the extension for the Aspect. NET AOP metalanguage (Aspect.NET.ML) files. We use such an extension following the tradition of AspectJ (where the extension *.aj* marks the source code in AspectJ).

Let's now complete the aspect definition code:

```
%aspect Aspect1
using System;
{
    %modules
        public static void Say (String s)
        { Console.WriteLine(s); }
```

```
%rules
   %before %call *
   %action
   public static void SayHello ()
   { Say ("Hello " + %TargetMemberInfo.ToString());
   }
   %after %call *
   %action
   public static void SayBye ()
   { Say ("Bye " + %TargetMemberInfo.ToString()); }
}
```

Our *Aspect1* aspect consists of:

- The aspect *header* %aspect Aspect1. The Aspect.NET converter will convert it to the header of the *class* named *Aspect1*. You can also use the *Aspect1* class header explicitly after the aspect header; in this case the class header will not be generated.
- The *modules* part, where you should specify the modules of the aspect, as public static methods.
- The *rules* part, where the aspect's weaving rules are specified. Each weaving rule consists of the *weaving condition (%before %call *, %after %call *)* and *action*. The condition is used to determine the set of *join points* in the target application subject to the aspect weaving (before or after the call of each method, accordingly). The set of the method names subject to weaving is specified by a wild card. The action shoud be defined as a *public static* method.

To log the actual name of the target method application at each join point, the *%TargetMemberInfo* Aspect.NET.ML construct is used. It is converted to a C# construct to access the target method name.

3. Now let's build the *Aspect1* solution. You will notice that the following new C# source file—*Aspect1.an.cs*—was added to the solution automatically by the converter, as the first step in building.

```
//----------------------------------------------
// <auto-generated>
//     This code was generated by a tool.
//     Runtime Version:2.0.50727.42
//
//     Changes to this file may cause incorrect behavior
//     and will be lost if the code is regenerated.
//</auto-generated>
```

```
//——————————————————————————————————————————————————
namespace Aspect1 {
    using System;
    using AspectDotNet;
    public class Aspect1 : Aspect {
            public static void Say (String s) {
  Console.WriteLine(s);
        }
        [AspectAction("%before %call *")]
            public static void SayHello () {
  Say ("Hello " + TargetMemberInfo.ToString());
        }
        [AspectAction("%after %call *")]
            public static void SayBye () {
  Say ("Bye " + TargetMemberInfo.ToString());
        }
    }
}
```

From this code you can notice that at the C# language layer, the aspect is represented as a C# class inheriting from the class *Aspect* predefined in our AspectDotNet namespace, and each action is marked by the *AspectAction* custom attribute that contains the weaving condition and is used by Aspect. NET. Note that by implementing aspects as classes in Aspect.NET, we don't violate any of the principles formulated in Section 3.7. The higher-level form of aspect specification in Aspect.NET.ML does *not* require explicit mention of the :*Aspect* inheritance. The user is not allowed to think about it. The Aspect. NET.ML converter inserts the :*Aspect* fragment automatically.

If you like, you can start creating an aspect from a C# source without using Aspect.NET.ML at all. In this case you should choose an "*Aspect.NET module*" kind of project and will start from the following C# code template generated by Aspect.NET:

```
using System;
using System.Collections.Generic;
using System.Text;
using AspectDotNet;
namespace Aspect1
{
    [AspectDescription("MyAspect description")]
    public class MyAspect : Aspect
    {
    }
}
```

Figure 3.8 *Opening the target application and the Aspect.NET window.*

4. To weave the *Aspect1* aspect into the *ConsoleApplication1* application open the *ConsoleApplication1* solution (see Figure 3.8). You will see the Aspect.NET framework window. Then choose the *Aspect1* aspect's assembly (DLL) by using the "Open" icon located on the "*Aspects*" tab. Typically, the aspect assembly is placed by Visual Studio.NET into the *bin\debug* subdirectory of the aspect solution.

You will see the open aspect's components (name and actions) visualized by the Aspect.NET framework (see Figure 3.9). Please note that each weaving rule is displayed by the header of the action and the corresponding weaving condition. There is also a brief form of displaying the aspect, without the weaving rules, displayable by clicking the minus sign on the left of the aspect name.

In general, you can open several aspects and watch all of them with their weaving rules. You can also "deselect" (delete from the *Aspects* tab) some of the aspects. Moreover, the Aspect.NET framework remembers all aspects you used last time with some solution and offers to open them next time. That feature is implemented using a special *.anf* configuration file.

After opening the aspect to be woven, you should invoke the weaver in the join points locating mode by pressing the *Find Joinpoints* button. You will see the weaver's output in the output console. Note that weaving in Aspect.NET is performed at the *.NET assembly* (MSIL code + metadata) level. In this respect, Aspect.NET differs from many other AOP tools. The resulting assembly, with Aspect.NET aspects woven, can be processed by any common-use

Figure 3.9 Displaying the open aspect.

.NET tool (e.g., *ildasm*) or a debugger. When the weaver works, you can watch the log of its working in the output window.

Back to our example: On finishing the weaver, you can use the *Joinpoints* tab to see the join points found (see Figure 3.10). At this stage, you can *manually select or unselect each of the join points*, to avoid blind weaving through all of the application. This Aspect.NET feature allows control of the weaving process by the user, to make it safer and smarter. Note that such a feature is lacking in other currently used (even widespread), AOP tools. Pay a lot of attention to this feature and use it if appropriate. Otherwise, you may get absurd or even dangerous results from weaving to some of the join points, especially if the source code of the target application is not quite familiar to you.

At this stage, you can also visualize each of the join points in the target application source by using the *Visualization* pane and clicking an appropriate red line in the schematic view of the application. Finally, to weave the aspect, you should invoke the weaver in the weaving mode by pressing the *Weave aspects* button. You will again see the weaver's output in the output console, and after weaving you'll be offered to run the updated application immediately by a button click. The path to the binary of the resulting assembly is displayed.

The updated application, with the aspect woven, is placed by the weaver into the same directory as the application's initial code. The resulting applica-

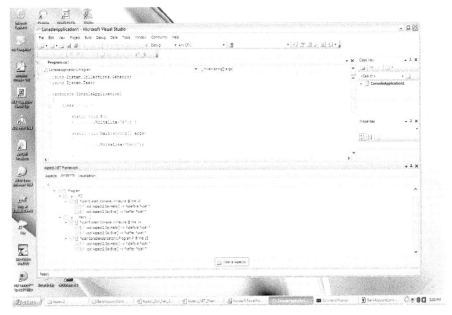

Figure 3.10   *Displaying the join points found by the weaver.*

tion's name is of the type *~TargetAppName:* in our example, *~ConsoleApplica-tion1.* Its output is much more verbose than that of the original version:

> *Hello Void WriteLine(System.String)*
> *Main*
> *Bye Void WriteLine(System.String)*
> *Hello Void P()*
> *Hello Void WriteLine(System.String)*
> *P*
> *Bye Void WriteLine(System.String)*
> *Bye Void P()*

Note that the standard *WriteLine* method calls are also made "polite" by this aspect. You can then remove the aspect's assembly, load another aspect's assembly, reload all the aspects' assemblies, and manipulate the list (queue) of the open aspects using the appropriate icons on the *Aspects* tab.

3.8.5 Aspect.NET Framework Options

You can set up Aspect.NET framework options by selecting *Tools/Options/ Aspect.NET Framework* (see Figure 3.11). As you see, by default, Aspect.NET

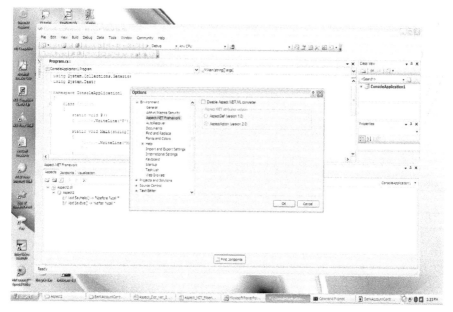

Figure 3.11   Aspect.NET options.

generates new (2.1) AOP custom attributes: *AspectDescription* (your comments to aspects or its parts) and *AspectAction* (used in Aspect.NET 2.1 to
mark an aspect's actions). If you like, for backward compatibility, you can use
the aspects you used with Aspect.NET 1.0 or 1.1. They should not use the old
limited temporary method of analyzing the context of the join point, which
was based on the action's arguments. If you check the *AspectDef (version 1.0)*
radio button, Aspect.NET (both the converter and the weaver) will work in
1.0 compatibility mode and generate and use the old-style *AspectDef* AOP
custom attribute. Finally, as one of the options, you can disable the Aspect.
NET.ML converter phase and use the C# with the custom attributes ("Aspect.
NET module") type of project for defining aspects.

3.8.6   Aspect.NET.ML Metalanguage

Following is a full definition of the syntax and semantics of Aspect.NET.ML
metalanguage constructs, as implemented in Aspect.NET 2.1. Note that it
differs from the version of the metalanguage described in Section 3.7; the latter's initial version includes generic aspects and other types of join points
besides call. In this section we look at an actual working version of Aspect.
NET.ML.

Syntax definition is given in EBNF; Aspect.NET.ML keywords (e.g.,
%aspect) are in bold. EBNF metacharacters such as:

$$[\ ]*|.$$

(the period denotes the end of the syntax rule) are also in bold.

Aspect Definition

Syntax

AspectDefinition =
  %aspect AspectName CSharpClassDefinitionWithModulesAndActions.
AspectName = Id.

Semantics The definition of an aspect starts with its header, the **%aspect** keyword followed by the aspect name. The body of the aspect definition can be any C# class definition source code. The name of the class should be the same as the name of the aspect. The header of the class (**class** *AspectName*) can be omitted. In this case the header of the class is generated by the Aspect. NET.ML converter.

The aspect definition class should contain definitions of the *modules* (preceded by the **%modules** keyword) and the *weaving rules* (preceded by the **%rules** keyword) of the aspect. The modules of the aspect (the *modules* section is optional) should typically be the aspect's class private methods (see the example above).

Note that our approach differs from that of AspectJ. We don't introduce a new type of construct into C# language itself, but instead, annotate C# code to explain to users and the Aspect.NET system that a given class code should be considered an aspect. We think such an approach is simpler, does not create confusions of aspects and classes at the language level, and in future, releases will allow us to implement similar Aspect.NET.ML annotations for other . NET languages (e.g., VB.NET).

Aspect Weaving Rules

Syntax

AspectWeavingRulesSection =
  %rules
  WeavingRule + .
WeavingRule =
  WeavingRuleCondition
  WeavingRuleAction .
WeavingRuleCondition =
  WeavingRuleConditionClause ['**||**' WeavingRuleConditionClause] * .

WeavingRuleConditionClause = WeavingContext JoinPointKind
MethodPattern

WeavingContext =
   %before | %after | %instead .

JoinPointKind =
   %call .

MethodPattern = MethodNameFilter **[** MethodArgumentTypes **]**
[Restrictions **]** .

MethodArgumentTypes = ' **(** ' **..**' | CLRType **[**'**,**' CLRType**]*** '**)** ' .

MethodNameFilter =
   [public | private | ***] [static]** [CLRType**|** *] MethodNameWildCard .

Restrictions = Restriction **[** '**&&**' Restriction **]** * .

Restriction =
   %args '**(**' arg'**[**' IntLiteral '**]**' **[** '**,**' arg'**[**' IntLiteral '**]**' **]** * '**)**' |
   %args '**(..)**' |
   %['!']within '**(**' TypeNameWildCard'**)**' |
   %['!']withincode '**(**' MethodNameWildCard '**)**' .

WeavingRuleAction =
   %action PublicStaticMethodDef .

Examples

```
%after %call *
%action
    public static void SayBye ()
    { System.Console.WriteLine("Bye"); }
```

This weaving rule enables the following functionality: After calls of each
method of the target application, a call of the *SayBye*() static method (action)
is injected which outputs "Bye" to the console. So, applying such a weaving
rule adds a kind of simplified logging functionality to the target application.

```
%instead %call *BankAccount.withdraw(float) && args(..)
%action
  public static float WithdrawWrapper(float amount)
  {
     BankAccount acc = (BankAccount)TargetObject;
     if (isLicenceValid(TargetMemberInfo.Name))
        return acc.withdraw(amount);
     Console.WriteLine("Withdraw operation is not
     allowed");
     return acc.Balance;
  }
```

This weaving rule enables the following functionality. In the target application, there are supposed to be class(es) whose name(s) end with *BankAccount*. In that class(es) there should be the *withdraw* static method with one argument of the *float* type. According to this rule, all such calls of *withdraw* will be replaced by calls of the new *WithdrawWrapper* method (aspect action) implementing some extra checks performed before the banking *withdraw* operation.

The *args*(..) restriction denotes that all arguments of the target *withdraw* method will be captured and processed as the arguments of the aspect action. In accordance with this restriction, the *WithdrawWrapper* aspect action also has exactly one argument of the *float* type. The *args* functionality is similar to that of AspectJ.

Examples of Method Filtering   The functionality of filtering methods by their signatures is very important and powerful. Here are some examples of method filtering:

```
public static float *BankAccount.withdraw(float)
float *BankAccount.withdraw(..)
    // any arguments
private * *BankAccount.withdraw(float)
private * *BankAccount.withdraw(float, ..)
    // the first argument of type float,
    // the rest of the arguments can be arbitrary
```

Semantics   Weaving rules define how Aspect.NET *weaves* (injects) calls of aspect actions before, after, or instead of a *join point*, a point in the code of the target application that the weaver finds according to the weaving rule condition. In Aspect.NET 2.1, only the *call* kind of join point is implemented. It means that the weaver can inject aspect actions before, after, or instead of any call in the target application. In future releases, we also plan to implement two other kinds of join points: *assign* (assignment to a named entity) and *use* (using a named entity).

The *condition* of a weaving rule, generally speaking, can be a *disjunction* of condition clauses $c1 \| \ldots \| cn$. Such a condition is satisfied if any of the component clauses are satisfied. For example,

> *%before %call *Set* \| *%before %call *Get* -

before any call of a method whose name ends with *Set* or *Get*.

In the simplest and most common case, a condition clause is a method name wild card (e.g., *, which as usual denotes any method). If the target application's method to be located belongs to the target application's class *C*, the *C.* * wild card should be used; and so on.

When using the *%instead* join point, please indicate the target application's static methods only, since the action is also a static method. Otherwise, the weaver issues an error message and weaving will be impossible. A condition clause can also include *restrictions* separated from the method wild card by *&&*. It means that the method wild-card pattern satisfying the condition and its restriction are considered to be a *conjunction*.

The *%arg* types of restriction specify what number and which arguments of the target application's method will be captured by the aspect's action. The *IntLiteral* specifies the number of the target application's method argument (starting from 0) to be captured. For example, if we indicate the *%arg(args[1])* kind of restriction, the aspect's action should have one argument whose type is the same as the type of the first (starting from 0) argument of the target app's method. When the aspect's action call is inserted, its argument will be the first argument of the target application's method. If we indicate the *%arg(args[0],args[1])* kind of restriction, the oncoming aspect's action should have two arguments, whose types should be the same as those of the zeros and the first argument of the target application method.

- The *%arg(..)* kind of restriction means that the oncoming aspect's action should have the same number of arguments as the target application's method. So, in general, *%arg* types of restrictions make possible one method of interaction of the aspect with the context of its join points.
- The *%within(T)* kind of restriction means that the target application's method will be searched only within the definition of the type *T*.
- *%!within(T)* denotes that the target application's methods will be searched everywhere *except* the definition of the type *T*.
- The *%withincode(M)* type of restriction means that the target application's method will be searched only within the code of the method whose name satisfies to the wild card *M*.
- *%!withincode(M)* denotes that the target application's methods will be searched everywhere *except* the code of the method whose name satisfies the wild card *M*. For example, *%!withincode(.ctor)* denotes that the target application's method will be searched everywhere except the code of constructors.

The method filters described were implemented following the tradition of AspectJ.

Capturing Information from the Join Point's Context   Aspect.NET 2.1 provides a number of ways for an aspect to communicate to the context of its join points. The first, the *%arg* functionality, is described in Section A.2. It provides access to the target application's method arguments and is similar to AspectJ. The second is a set of Aspect.NET.ML primitive constructs that can be used anywhere in the aspect definition code and provide access to the target application's name, the line of the source code where the join point is located, and so on.

Syntax

> TargetAppContextItem =
>> **%TargetObject |**
>> **%TargetMemberInfo |**
>> **%This |**
>> **%RetValue |** // Addition implemented in Aspect.NET 2.1
>> **%WithinType |**
>> **%WithinMethod |**
>> **%SourceFilePath |**
>> **%SourceFileLine.**

Semantics   The primitive Aspect.NET.ML constructs listed above can be used in the Aspect.NET.ML aspect definition in any context where a C# primary expression can be used, except for the discarded parts of assignments (i.e., these entities cannot be modified by the aspect). They provide basic ways for the aspect to communicate to the context of its join point.

- *%TargetObject* (of type *System.Object*) is a reference to the object in the target application to which the join point's target method is applied. For example, if the target method at the join point is *p.M()*, the *%TargetObject* denotes a reference to the *p* object. If the target method from the join point is static, *%TargetObject* is *null*.

- *%TargetMemberInfo* (of type *System.Reflection.MemberInfo*) is a reference to the object representing the target method from the join point in a conventional .NET reflection style. It allows us to get a lot of information on the target method from the aspect: in particular, *%TargetMemberInfo.Name* is the public property that contains the name of the target method.

- *%This* is a reference to the object representing the aspect itself.

- *%RetValue* (of type *System.object*) is the value returned by the target application's method subject to aspect weaving (See the *RetValue* sample for the aspect code using this feature).

- *%WithinType* (of type *System.Type*) is a reference to the type definition where the target method call is located.

- *%WithinMethod* (of type *System.Reflection.MethodBase*) is a reference to the object representing the method where the target method call is located.

- *%SourceFilePath* is a string representing the path to the source file where the target method call is located.

- *%SourceFileLine* is a string representing the source code line number where the target method call is located.

According to the current implementation in Aspect 2.1, an aspect is represented by a child class of the abstract class *Aspect* predefined in the *Aspect-DotNet* namespace, part of Aspect.NET implementation. You can notice the relationship between the aspect class and *Aspect* from the *.an.cs* file generated by the Aspect.NET converter. All the other Aspect.NET.ML keywords described in this section are implemented as public static properties of the aspect implementation class.

Self-Documenting Aspects: AspectDescription   You can self-document the source code of your aspects by //-style comments. Aspect.NET provides conversion of these comments to the *AspectDescription* custom attribute. In more detail, if you put a //-style (trailing) comment before the header of the aspect, and (or) trailing comments before the action of the aspect, the Aspect. NET.ML converter will convert them as shown in the example below.

Aspect.NET.ML code:

```
// This is my aspect
%aspect MyAspect
{
// This is my aspect's action
%before %call * %action
public static void A()
{ Console.WriteLine("Action A"); }
 ...
```

The corresponding C# code after conversion:

```
[AspectDescription("This is my aspect")]
    public class Aspect1 : Aspect {
[AspectDescription("This is my aspect's action")]
[AspectAction("%before %call *")]
public static void A()
{ Console.WriteLine("Action A"); }
 ...
```

Aspect descriptions are displayed by the Aspect.NET framework when displaying the open aspect in the Aspect.NET window, which helps the user to make the aspects in Aspect.NET more understandable.

Using Aspect.NET Custom Attributes Directly   As mentioned earlier, Aspect.NET makes it possible to avoid using Aspect.NET.ML metalanguage for representing aspects by using C# code directly with AOP custom attribute definitions (see the *.an.cs* file example above). There are two AOP custom attributes for representing aspects: *AspectDescription* and *AspectAction*. *AspectDescription* provides a user-defined string to describe (annotate) the aspect class itself or its actions. It is displayed by the Aspect.NET framework when displaying information about the aspect. This custom attribute is not mandatory. An aspect definition may or may not have aspect descriptions.

AspectAction marks any aspect action and contains (in the form of a string) the corresponding weaving condition. This is a mandatory custom attribute for Aspect.NET aspects. If the methods implementing the aspect actions are not marked by this attribute, Aspect.NET will not "understand" the aspect structure and the Aspect.NET framework will refuse to load the assembly as aspect.

Use of the foregoing attributes is self-evident from the following sample C# code:

```
namespace BankManagement
{
    [AspectDescription
        ("Design By Contract aspect for verifying
        BankAccount logic")
    ]
    public class BankAccountContractAspect: Aspect
    {
        [AspectDescription("Invariant: this.Balance >=
        0")]
        [AspectAction
            ("%before %call *BankAccount.*(..) || " +
            "%after %call *BankAccount.*(..) ")]
        static public void CheckInvariant()
        {
            if (((BankAccount)TargetObject).Balance <
            0)
                Console.WriteLine
                    ("ERROR INVARIANT: Balance should
                    not be " +
                    "negative at {0} line {1}",
                SourceFilePath, SourceFileLine);
        }
    }
}
```

When using AOP custom attributes directly, don't forget to add the explicit inheritance from the *Aspect* class, as in the example above. Otherwise the Aspect.NET framework will not "understand" your code as an aspect definition.

3.8.7   Samples Included in the Aspect.NET 2.1 Release

The following samples of aspect definitions and target applications used to weave the aspects are included in Aspect.NET 2.1.

1. *Aspect2:*   a very simple aspect definition that demonstrates the basics of aspects and weaving and the use of the *%TargetMemberInfo* functionality. It is similar to the *ConsoleApplication1/Aspect1* example considered in this document. The sample consists of the target application named *ConsoleApplication1* and the aspect *Aspect2* to be woven into it.

2. *TestArgs:* an aspect that demonstrates the target method filters and target method arguments capturing functionality. The sample consists of the target application *TestArgs* and the aspect *TestArgsAspect.*

3. *BankManagement:*   a simple application to manage a bank account and a pair of aspects to extend the target application by some extra security and license checks related to managing the account: The balance should be greater or equal to zero, and so on. This sample can be also regarded as a demonstration of the *design-by-contract* programming style that makes applications more trustworthy. The sample consists of the target application, *BankManagement,* class *BankAccount* used in the application, and two aspects: *BankAccount-ContractAspect* and *UsageLicensingAspect.* For demonstration purposes, the sample aspects are written directly in C# code using AOP custom attributes (the conversion phase is skipped). Note that you can load both aspects into the Aspect.NET framework during one call of Visual Studio, and perform the *"Find Join Points/Weave Aspects"* cycle once, by one call of the Aspect.NET weaver.

4. *MAddNopCounter:* a modest gift from the Aspect.NET team to the Phoenix team. The target application in this sample is the *addnop-tool* application from the samples shipped with Phoenix [7], provided in the *src/samples/AddNop-tool/csharp* subdirectory of the Phoenix RDK (March 2007) installation. That Phoenix-based application inserts the MSIL *nop* instruction after each instruction of the original MSIL code of a given .NET assembly file. But that Phoenix example is pretty silent. Our sample, the *MAddNopCounter* aspect to be woven into the *addnop-tool* application, extends its functionality by "instrumenting" the application's code by some extra outputs (e.g., outputs the number of *nop*'s actually inserted). Note that the application should be called with two command-line arguments: the name of the initial assembly file, and the name of the resulting file after *nop* insertion.

5. *RetTest* and *RetTest2* samples: demonstrate a new Aspect.NET 2.1 *%RetValue* functionality that allows us to get access to the value returned by the target method the subject to weaving. They also demonstrate *WithinType/WithinMethod* functionality (see above). Each sample consists of the aspect definitions and the target application where to weave them. Aspects are self-documented by the comments in the sources and by the *AspectDescription* attribute where necessary.

Visual Studio 2005 solutions for the samples and their target applications are located in the subdirectories whose names are the same as the names of the samples.

3.8.8 Experience of Aspect.NET Use and User Feedback

While working on Aspect.NET and its four releases, we have received a lot of feedback from users from 16 countries: Australia, Brazil, Canada, Colombia, Denmark, Egypt, Germany, Indonesia, Italy, Kasakhstan, Korea, the Netherlands, Russia, Spain, UK, and the United States. We are very grateful to all our users for their suggestions, the bugs they found in Aspect.NET, and their positive feedback. We now understand much better what is lacking in Aspect.NET and are working hard to improve it. Since the first release of Aspect.NET in 2005, we have been doing our best to answer users' questions and fix bugs promptly, following the discipline of *business integrity*, one of the keystones of trustworthy computing described in Chapter 2.

3.9 SUMMARY

This section is a summary of the experience and perspectives of AOP in general and Aspect.NET in particular. The positive effect of AOP tools is discussed and directions for future research and development are outlined.

3.9.1 AOP

Due to AOP, software developers are now paying much more attention to more systematic processes and methods of fixing bugs, software enhancement, and reuse. They realize that even powerful features of modern integrated development environments may not be enough for appropriate handling of cross-cutting concerns they work with all the time, and that a special systematic approach to AOP and its support by tools is needed to do that. AOP, I should say, has made the software developers' level of thinking and level of abstraction higher than it has been using more traditional languages and platforms. Due to AOP, programmers now understand much better that they are to implement in each large software system a "classical" set of cross-cutting concerns: *logging* (to trace the system during its work), *security* (to make proper checks to protect their program and data), and *MT safety* (to make their application workable in a multithreaded environment). AOP provides adequate tools for that. More briefly: *AOP helps make software more trustworthy.*

Next, based on the analysis of AOP in this section, let's outline perspectives of AOP.

1. *Increasing use of AOP in industry.* At present, AOP is used primarily by academic researchers and developers: undergraduate and graduate students,

professors, and research scientists. Their spirit of creativity and experimentation helps them to develop and try new, more efficient, and general approaches to AOP. The industry is still very careful about applying AOP and, moreover, is somewhat reluctant and skeptical about it. Due to AOP enthusiasts and the progress in AOP tools, industrial software companies and developers are just starting to use AOP. But recalling the history of IT, the same situation took place 20 to 25 years ago with OOP. C++ was in the cradle, Borland was just starting to implement its first version of Turbo Pascal, and Smalltalk was known only to a small group of people in Palo Alto. Then, in a few years, the situation with industrial application of OOP changed radically, for two reasons: financial and organizational support by leading IT companies (AT&T, Borland, then Microsoft), and shipping industrial-quality tools and integrated development environments to support OOP (Turbo Pascal, Turbo C, Turbo C++, Visual C++, Visual Basic, etc.). These two factors are still lacking for AOP. Currently, of major software companies, AOP is supported by Sun and IBM. This is very important, but those companies only support AOP implementations for Java, which is not enough, since C and C++ are still widely used, and the .NET user community is growing. AOP for .NET is not so well supported by industry. Although Microsoft Research grants have been very supportive, it would be appropriate for Microsoft to pay more attention and provide more support to industrial applications of AOP, given the fact that .NET is the most convenient platform for implementing AOP in its most general and unified multilanguage form. The way to do that would be to integrate AOP mechanisms and tools with the .NET framework and Visual Studio.NET. Aspect.NET appears to be the best candidate for integration with Microsoft.NET development tools and for shipment with their future releases.

2. *Ubiquitous use of AOP.* We hold as one of the main principles of our approach to AOP that AOP should soon grow out of the "cradle state" of "risky experiments." AOP should not be isolated from the common tools and IDE we are using now but should become just one of many day-to-day technologies, such as OOP, modularity, refactoring, using debuggers, test generators, and test harnesses. The way to do that is to develop a comfortable GUI for AOP tools and integrate it in common-use development environments. Another thing that should be done is to enhance popular operating systems and libraries using AOP engines (weavers, aspects, and pointcut specification languages). Perhaps a general-use AOP specification language will be developed, accepted, and adopted by all major software development companies and communities. This would create the basis for general-purpose reusable aspects for all platforms.

3. *Integration of AOP with knowledge engineering.* As discussed in Section 3.7, modern knowledge engineering and its techniques, concepts, and tools, especially ontologies, rule sets, frames, and semantic nets, could be used to develop hybrid knowledge bases that contain specifications of problem domains, descriptions of their concepts, typical algorithms to solve domain-

specific tasks, and *aspects* to implement typical domain-specific cross-cutting concerns. Conceptually, as already noted, the nature of aspects is relative to knowledge engineering. A knowledge engineering tool that could be used for this purpose is *Knowledge.NET* [36], a knowledge engineering environment for Microsoft.NET integrated as an add-in to Visual Studio in the same way that Aspect.NET is. In Knowledge.NET, all the types of knowledge noted above are implemented. In the future we plan to integrate Aspect.NET and Knowledge.NET to develop and use "AOP knowledge bases."

3.9.2 Aspect.NET

Aspect.NET is evolving rapidly. We have a number of plans yet to be implemented. Not all of our original ideas (see Section 3.7) are implemented in the current version, and we have proposed many new ideas. Aspect.NET users, Microsoft, and AOP experts have provided many valuable recommendations to implement. In addition, the two Microsoft products on which Aspect.NET is dependent—Visual Studio.NET and Phoenix—are changing and being enhanced continuously, and we track these and issue new versions of Aspect. NET compatible with new versions of Visual Studio and Phoenix.

The most important of our prospective plans for development of the Aspect. NET framework are listed below. By the publication date of this book, some of the new features described below may be implemented in new releases of Aspect.NET.

1. *Aspect.NET "productization."* We have already looked at the need to make Aspect.NET a commercial product. The users would like to make this happen, and this is one of our strategic goals. Since our "policy" regarding Aspect.NET is deep integration with the latest Microsoft technologies, we would like to make Aspect.NET a real Microsoft product to be shipped with Visual Studio and Phoenix. Software companies are more accustomed to using commercial software than to using research prototypes. Our experience in international software projects allows us to make Aspect.NET a good commercial product, with testing, maintaining, and documenting as appropriate.

2. *Join point filters using attributes to mark classes or methods.* Taking into account .NET specifics and its intensive use of attributes, it would be useful to include in join point filters attributes to mark the classes and method to capture. For example, the filter

```
%after %call [Serializable]*.*
```

will capture any method of any class marked by the *Serializable* attribute. The filter

```
%after %call *Class1.[STAThread]*
```

will capture any *Class1* method marked by the *STAThread* attribute. The filter

```
%after %call * && %!within([Serializable]*)
```

will capture any method whose call is encountered within nonserializable classes.

3. *Aspect script actions.* This new functionality will make it possible to perform on the classes and methods of the target application scriptlike transformations not related to executable actions: adding fields and methods to the existing classes (similarly to intertype declarations in AspectJ), and marking a class, method, or field with some attribute. For example, the new Aspect. NET.ML construct

```
%mark *Class1 %with [Serializable]
```

will result in marking the captured classes by the *Serializable* attribute. Such functionality will be in the spirit of .NET and can be used, for example, to inject security attributes, thus improving the trustworthiness of the target application.

4. *Implementing the %assign and %use types of join points.* In the current release, join point filters can only include the *%call* keyword to indicate that the target application's code fragment is a method call. In future releases we plan to implement two other types of join points, as described in Section 3.7: *%assign*, assigning to a field or variable, and *%use*, accessing a field or variable.

5. *Generic aspects.* In Section 3.7 I we described the initial idea of generic aspects in Aspect.NET. This idea has not yet been implemented and needs to be accomplished in future releases of Aspect.NET.

6. *Aspect debugger.* We have discussed the fact that debugging in terms of aspects is still an issue for most AOP tools. In the near future, we plan to add to the common-use Visual Studio debugger an add-in for debugging Aspect.NET applications in terms of aspects. Users will then be able not only to detect bugs in the aspect code, but also to trace and watch step by step the behavior of the resulting target application in terms of the aspects woven.

7. *Rule sets.* In Section 3.7 I we described the initial version of the AOP metalanguage, which included a named pointcut-like construct—a *rule set*, a named set of join point filters that need not be tied to some concrete aspect. The usefulness of such a construct is obvious: Many aspects can refer to the same suitable rule set defined only once.

8. *Displaying changes in the source code.* We plan to provide users with an opportunity to "finger" how his or her source code has been changed after aspect weaving made by Aspect.NET. This feature will be implemented by

visualizing appropriate fragments of decompiled code of the modified target assembly.

9. *Aspectizer.* The aspectizer for Aspect.NET (Section 3.7) is now being developed. It will allow us to extract the source code of aspects from non-aspect-oriented programs and to add Aspect.NET.ML annotations or AOP attributes to that code, to mark it appropriately as aspect.

10. *Aspect repository.* To enable enterprise-level aspect reuse, an aspect repository could be created and maintained. Aspect.NET Framework could perform searches in this repository, based on the problem domain and other parameters. When finding a suitable aspect, Aspect.NET Framework could weave it into the target project. Such aspect repositories could be developed for each problem domain. This will enable wider use of Aspect.NET in different problem domains.

4

Principles and Applications of AOP in TWC

This is the core chapter of the book. In it we describe how to implement various approaches to trustworthy software development using the Aspect. NET framework considered in Chapter 3. Appropriate Aspect.NET aspects for TWC are described and critiqued. Readers are warned against possible nontrustworthy use of aspects through concrete examples. Full source code of some other TWC aspects not discussed in this chapter is given in the Appendix. Of special importance are Sections 4.10 to 4.12, which are devoted to analysis on how our approach to AOP for TWC can improve productivity and how it influences software performance. A quantitative analysis and comparison to other popular software process approaches are provided. The focus of the entire chapter is to convince readers using facts and figures (practical examples, quality and efficiency estimates) that AOP with Aspect.NET is an appropriate tool for TWC.

4.1 AOP AND TWC: COOPERATION RATHER THAN VIOLATION

When used properly, AOP is a suitable technology for TWC purposes. In particular, security, one of the four pillars of TWC, has been named as one of the areas most suitable for the use of AOP. This is emphasized in both classical

Using Aspect-Oriented Programming for Trustworthy Software Development,
By Vladimir O. Safonov
Copyright © 2008 John Wiley & Sons, Inc.

publications on AOP [13] and in more recent ones [122]. AOP has what appears to be a generic relation to TWC because most of the trustworthy software development features listed below are cross-cutting concerns by nature. AOP should then be applicable for TWC, since the essence of AOP is to separate, design, implement, and weave implementations of cross-cutting concerns. Speaking more practically, in terms of the changes to be made with the target applications, the effect of AOP is to inject or activate some tangled fragments of code (*advices*, or, in our terms, *actions*) into some appropriate join points of the target application. What type of functionality can the aspect's actions provide? One of the first ideas that comes to mind is that the woven actions of aspects should not only enrich an application's business logic, but should make it more reliable, secure, and understandable; that is, aspects should implement checks or tracings to improve the trustworthiness of applications as follows:

- Security checks (e.g., calls of security API to check permissions of the code; see Section 4.2)
- *Error handling:* processing exceptions or error codes (see Section 4.3)
- Synchronization calls to various types of synchronization of threads or processes (see Section 4.4)
- Multithreading safety code to enable safe execution of the code by multiple concurrent threads (see Section 4.5)
- Design-by-contract checks that the preconditions, postconditions, and invariants hold (see Section 4.9)
- *Logging:* tracing in a log file of key points in the control flow of the application, especially method calls and returns (see Section 4.7)
- *Privacy:* encryption and decryption of sensitive private information in appropriate points of the program; checking permissions to use private information (see Section 4.6)
- *Business integrity:* bug fixes and implementation of customers' requests for enhancement of the product in the form of aspects or aspect libraries (see Section 4.8)
- Other types of checks to improve reliability of applications: in particular, checks for nonnull pointers and checks of appropriate ranges of numerical arguments (see Section 4.7)

In this chapter we present many cases that demonstrate use of AOP for the purposes listed above using Aspect.NET. All the code examples in this chapter are based on Aspect.NET, so they are written in C# and in Aspect.NET.ML metalanguage and are intended for use in an .NET environment with Visual Studio.NET 2005. Hopefully, some of the recommendations and ideas considered in this chapter are sufficiently general in nature to be helpful to AOP users under other platforms.

When applying AOP for TWC purposes, one should be very careful. As discussed in Chapter 3, the results of "blind" weaving of aspects can be unclear or even destructive rather than trustworthy. We should remember that AOP is a very powerful "weapon" and use it with care. Weaving a small aspect can update the target application's behavior so that it becomes difficult to understand, maintain, and debug the resulting application and can worsen its efficiency because of executing a lot of newly injected but redundant code.

Let's formulate some *recipes for trustworthy use of AOP for TWC*: a set of heuristic recommendations that will be helpful in making AOP really trustworthy.

1. *Make the weaving conditions as concrete and narrow as possible.* For example, the weaving rule

```
%before %call * .Set*
%action
%public static void MySecurityCheck() { ... }
```

may appear to be dangerous to apply, since it injects the call of *MySecurity-Check* into the code of *every* class, before *every* call of *every* method whose name starts with *Set*. Suppose that you only need to insert such calls in the class *MyClass* before calls of the method *SetMyResource*, which changes some global resource. Then you should formulate the weaving condition more precisely, to be as narrow as needed:

```
%before %call MyClass.SetMyResource
```

A similar recommendation is usually given for using rule-based knowledge engineering languages: The more specific and concrete the rule conditions is, the greater the chance that the rule will be applicable as appropriate. Beyond the reasonable limits of applicability (expressed by weaving conditions), applying aspects can be unpredictable.

2. *Browse the potential join points found by the weaver; "unselect" them if not appropriate.* In Section 3.8 we described the functionality of the Aspect.NET framework. One of its most important features is an option, prior to actual weaving, to browse all potential join points in terms of the source of the target application and to unselect those that are not appropriate. This feature is lacking in all other AOP frameworks of which I am aware. For example, even if you provided in your aspect a too general weaving condition for some action, you can correct this situation using the option to unselect join points. The AOP tools (including the current version of Aspect.NET) are not "smart" enough to "understand" the semantics of your application or to warn you on inappropriate join points. Only you can prevent redundant join point weavings, and Aspect.NET provides you with an option to do that and thus to make the process of weaving and the resulting code more trustworthy.

3. *Avoid including intersecting weaving conditions within one aspect.* This is an issue of trustworthy aspect-oriented design. In designing your aspect, which in general can be represented as

$$WeavingCondition_1 \rightarrow Action_1; \ldots ; WeavingCondition_n \rightarrow Action_n$$

there might arise a situation when the scope of applicability of two weaving conditions is identical or intersects. For example:

```
%after %call C.My*
%action
public static void Action1() { . . . }
%after %call C.*Method
%action
public static void Action2() { . . . }
```

The question is: What will be the result of weaving at the join point after calls of the method *C.MyMethod?* The result is implementation dependent. We don't offer any rules of aspect domination in Aspect.NET, to make the AOP metalanguage simpler. To make your aspect code and its weavings more trustworthy, don't allow such situations in your aspect design. Avoid combinations of aspects with ambiguous combinations of weaving rules and make your code simpler and thus your life less difficult. Aspect.NET does not analyze different weaving conditions in one aspect for "logical independence" and mutual consistency. Neither, I suppose, does any other AOP tool. In general, it is not possible to do such analysis prior to execution. As for *C.MyMethod*, add to your aspect a separate weaving rule for it that will explain to the weaver what to do in this case. If you really need to define in one aspect several weaving rules with the weaving conditions to intersect, you can either unite them into one weaving rule (if they are related semantically), or better, split the aspect into two aspects such that each of the intersecting weaving conditions will be located in different aspects, since the weaving rules are likely to be different semantically.

4. *Make the aspects code more reusable, adaptable, and reliable by capturing information from the join point context.* Aspect.NET allows us to analyze information from the context of the join point: Extract the reference to the target object to which the target method is applied; capture the target method name, its arguments, and the result; and get the reference to the type definition and the method where the target method call is located (for more details, see Section 3.8.6). Those features are helpful in making aspects more generally reusable, adaptable, and reliable. Using this functionality, the aspect's action code can analyze the context of the target join point at runtime and tune itself to the correct behavior.

As a simplest example of this type, suppose that we need to develop an aspect to log the target method calls. The simplest decision for the weaving rule to be applied before each call would be as follows:

```
%before %call *
%action
public static void HelloAction () {
    System.Console.WriteLine("Hello");
}
```

But surely, such an aspect wouldn't be very useful, as it logs the *same* message, "*Hello*", before the call of *any* method. Much more valuable is the following modification of the weaving rule above using the *%TargetMember-Info* functionality—access to the reference to information on the target method:

```
%before %call *
%action
public static void HelloAction () {
    System.Console.WriteLine("Hello " +
    %TargetMemberInfo.Name);
}
```

This variant logs much more informative messages of the type: "*Hello M*", where *M* is the actual name of the target method.

Using a similar functionality, a TWC aspect can check at runtime for particular target method names (e.g., *SetColor* or *MyMethod*, discussed above) and make a final decision at runtime as to what kind of action (or no action at all) should be performed at the join point executed, thus finally resolving the "*SetColor* issue" at execution time.

We have considered some recommendations on how to reasonably balance the power of weaving conditions and the weaver, on the one hand, and the flexibility of analyzing join point context at runtime, on the other hand, to achieve trustworthy use of AOP for trustworthy software development.

4.2 AOP FOR SECURITY

As described in Section 2.5.2, the specifics of .NET security are as follows. In application code, security settings and checks can be expressed either in *imperative* form, by executable statements calling *security API methods*, or in *declarative* form, by defining appropriate *security attributes*. We don't consider the third form of security settings in .NET, security configuration files in XML format, since AOP mechanisms have no influence on updating those files.

The topic of AOP for security is discussed actively in research papers and Web forums. For Java, there has been a lot of progress in developing security solutions: libraries and frameworks based on AOP. Examples are: *Security Annotation Framework* (SAF) [123], targeted for use in Spring Framework [104]; *Java Security Aspect Library* (JSAL) [124], based on using AspectJ; and *Acegi Security* [125], a solution for Spring Framework.

For .NET, applying AOP for security is mostly at the experimental stage. An example of a security aspect in C# written for use with PostSharp Laos [108] is given in Section 3.6. Typical security functionality is related to various types of *security checks: permission checks* to perform certain kinds of actions, user *authentication checks*, and so on. Software developers often forget or even don't plan any security actions until the software debugging and maintenance stage, when security vulnerabilities become visible. So a typical task related to security functionality is to inject into the existing code various types of security checks through all the application code or its major parts. AOP is perfectly suitable for performing this task. A typical solution of this problem by means of AOP is to develop an aspect or aspect library implementing the security functionality required, and then to weave those aspects into the target application.

Next, let's consider a simple example of a security aspect written in Aspect. NET. Recall the example of DNS permission checking code from Section 2.4 (see Figure 2.3). The code depicted in the figure, although very simple, combines two quite different concerns: *business logic* (getting the host IP address) and *security* (checking the permission to perform DNS related actions). The purpose of AOP is to separate cross-cutting concerns. So let's first develop the code of the application that prints to the console the IP address of the host with the given domain name. The code does not care about security at all (or, speaking more precisely, uses the default security settings):

```
using System.Net;
public class Utilities
{
    public static void PrintHostIP(string hostName)
    {
        Console.WriteLine
            ("IP address of the host=" +
                Dns.GetHostEntry(hostName).AddressList[0]);
        Console.WriteLine("Press ENTER to exit");
        Console.ReadLine();
    }
    static void Main(string[] args)
    {
        PrintHostIP(Dns.GetHostName());
    }
}
```

In the code above, the main functionality is implemented in the static method *PrintHostIP*. The *System.Net* namespace contains a variety of features to develop network applications. In particular, its *Dns* class used in this code supports DNS-related actions (e.g., looking for IP addresses of the host). The static method *GetHostEntry* of the class *Dns* returns the reference to the container object (of the type *IPHostEntry*) for Internet host address information. Note that, in general, several IP addresses may be associated with the host. The *AddressList* property of the *IPHostEntry* class returns the array of all such IP addresses (of type *IPAddress*). The *Main* method of the code just tests the *PrintHostIP* method by calling it once with the local host name returned by calling the *Dns.HostName()* method.

The output of the sample code is as follows:

IP address of the host = 192.168.205.13
Press ENTER to exit

Now let's enhance the functionality of this application by injecting security checking of DNS actions permission. It can be done using the following aspect (written in Aspect.NET.ML metalanguage and C#). In addition to injecting the security checks, the aspect also captures the actual string argument of each target call (the host name) and prints it on the console:

```
%aspect Aspect1
using System;
using System.Net;
using System.Security.Permissions;
class Aspect1
{
    %modules
    private static void DemandDnsPermission() {
        DnsPermission p
            = new DnsPermission(PermissionState.
            Unrestricted);
        p.Demand();
    }
    %rules
    %before %call * .PrintHostIP(string) && args(..)
    %action
    public static void GetHostAction(string hostname) {
        Console.WriteLine("Hostname="+ hostname);
        Console.WriteLine("Demand DNS permission");
        DemandDnsPermission();
        Console.WriteLine("Demand DNS permission
        finished");
    } // GetHostAction
} // Aspect1
```

To build the application and the aspect in Visual Studio.NET and to weave the aspect using the Aspect.NET framework, follow the instructions given in Section 3.8.4, followed by appropriate screenshots of Aspect.NET usage. In the Aspect.NET window, use the *Aspects* tab to open the aspect DLL; then the aspect with its weaving rule will be visualized within the *Joinpoints* tab. Next, press the *Find join points* button in that tab and check that the weaver has found the only join point: the call of *PrintHostIP* from the *Main* method. Then visualize the join point in the source code by clicking at the only red line in the *Joinpoints* tab. Next, press the *Weave aspects* button. On weaving, the Aspect.NET framework will offer to start the updated application code with the aspect woven (the updated code name is *~ConsoleApplication1.exe*). The output of the updated application, with the security aspect woven, will be more verbose than the original one:

> *Hostname = Aphrodite*
> *Demand DNS permission*
> *Demand DNS permission finished*
> *IP address of the host = 192.168.205.13*
> *Press ENTER to exit*

The functionality of the aspect should be clear. We'll comment only on the most tricky fragment of its source code:

```
%before %call * .PrintHostIP(string) && args(..)
```

This weaving condition means that the aspect will capture all calls of the *PrintHostIP* method with one-string arguments and will pass all its arguments to the corresponding argument, *hostname*, of the aspect's action, *GetHostAction*.

Note that the aspect calls the *Demand* method (to check the DNS security permission) in the correct point and context since the *GetHostAction* is called on the current stack with the same state as the subsequent call of *PrintHostIP*. The action call will be part of the same target assembly as *PrintHostIP* and will precede the latter call directly, so it will have the same security permissions.

As explained in Section 2.4, the *Demand* method will perform a security stack walk to check whether *each* method, rather than only the latest one called on the stack in the call chain

> *Main → GetHostAction → DemandDnsPermission*

has DNS permission.

Also note that the code of the aspect's action (or, better, the code of the aspect's private *DemandDnsPermission* method) is easy to refactor by adding a *try/catch* block to handle possible *SecurityException* generated by CLR in case the code or the current principal does not have the permissions demanded. In this case it is quite logical to issue an informative message, with the actual source code line indicated for the interrupted target method call, and to return to the OS by calling *Environment.Exit* with some nonzero *errorCode* to terminate the application:

```
public static void DemandDnsPermission() {
        DnsPermission p
            = new DnsPermission(PermissionState.
            Unrestricted);
        try { p.Demand(); }
        catch (SecurityException e) {
            Console.WriteLine("No DNS permissions, line:
            " + %SourceFileLine);
            Environment.Exit(1);
        }
}
```

Note the use of *%SourceFileLine* in the updated version of the aspect to issue the line number in the target code (see Section 3.8). So at present, our aspect captures all calls of the target method, checks its permissions to perform DNS actions immediately prior to its actual call, and if the security permissions are denied reports the actual source code line where it happened. This is how to make the code really trustworthy using Aspect.NET. The security aspect's code is much simpler and much more self-evident than in security aspects in the other AOP tools for .NET that we considered.

As explained in Section 2.4, there is another, *declarative* form of security check using *security attributes*. The current version, Aspect.NET 2.1, does not allow injecting attributes into the target code, nor does any other AOP tool for .NET as far as I know. In Aspect.NET 3.0, using *aspect action scripts* of the kind

    %mark Entity %with [Attribute]

we'll make it possible (see Section 3.9.2).

4.3 AOP FOR ERROR HANDLING

In this section we use AOP to detect and process two types of errors: *exception handling* and *error handling codes*. Other types of reliability checks (e.g., detecting an incorrect range of a numerical argument, or null pointer) are described in Sections 4.7 and 4.9. It is well known that exceptions are now the most common technique for error indication and handling. However, some software engineers probably don't remember that a mechanism similar to exceptions (*signals*) first appeared in CLU language [20] in 1974. In common-use languages before C++-C, Pascal, FORTRAN, COBOL, and so on, there were no exception mechanisms. So in those languages abnormal results of functions or subroutines had to be indicated by integer *error codes* returned as the result of the routine.

As for exceptions, specific features for their handling are implemented in AspectJ (the *exception* type of join points). Although Aspect.NET up to version 2.1 doesn't have such specific features yet, it is quite possible to handle exceptions with Aspect.NET using the *%instead* type of weaving conditions (see Section 3.8). Those conditions make it possible to replace the captured calls within the target application code by some *wrappers*, aspect actions executed instead of the original calls. Those wrappers can include any type of error handling: notably, handling exceptions that remain unhandled in the original code. It is especially important for software systems (e.g., server side, or real time) whose work should be "permanent" and whose status should not allow exceptions or any other abnormal results. Surely such exception-handling functionality can be, without using AOP, included directly in the code of the application by means of IDE: by hand in text editor, or with the help of refactoring features. But such global changes would require full recompilation and repeatable testing and are therefore very time consuming, which is undesirable when development or maintenance time is critical. AOP can help in this situation as a powerful tool to quickly make the appropriate changes and to continue using the updated code, without its dramatic analysis and refurbishing.

Let's consider an example of how to inject exception-handling functionality without explicit modification of the target code, using Aspect.NET. Here is the application code:

```
using System;
namespace ExceptionHandling
{
    public class BreakerTester
    {
        public static void Breaker(int n) {
            Console.WriteLine("Breaker call number " +
            n);
            switch (n) {
                case 1: throw new ArgumentException();
                case 2: throw new
                NullReferenceException();
                case 3: throw new
                IndexOutOfRangeException ();
```

```
                default:
                    throw new
                    InvalidOperationException();
            }
        }
        static void Main(string[] args)
        {
            Breaker(1);
            Breaker(3);
            Breaker(10);
            Console.WriteLine("Press ENTER to exit";
            Console.ReadLine();
        }
    }
}
```

In this example, the *Breaker* method always yields an exception. The actual type of exception depends on the value of the method's argument. So when the *Main* method calls *Breaker* the first time, the message

>   *Breaker call number 1*

appears on the console, followed by throwing an *ArgumentException*.

Let's improve this demonstration code using the aspect shown below. The idea of the aspect is to use the *%instead* weaving condition for replacing the buggy calls of *Breaker* by their *wrappers*: improved versions that call *Breaker*, perform exception handling for it, issue reasonable-length messages on the types of exceptions handled, and continue normal execution of the program:

```
%aspect Aspect1
using System;
using ExceptionHandling;
class Aspect1
{
    %modules
    %rules
    %instead %call *BreakerTester.Breaker(int) &&
    args(..)
    %action
    public static void WrapperAction (int n)
    {
        try { BreakerTester.Breaker(n); }
        catch (Exception e) {
            string s = e.ToString();
```

```
            Console.WriteLine ("Breaker call number " +
            n + " finished " +
                            "Exception handled: ");
            Console.WriteLine(s.Substring(0, s.
            IndexOf(":")));
        }
    }
}
```

When weaving, the actual argument *n* of the *Breaker* method is captured and used to call the *Breaker* method "safely" from inside the *try/catch* block handling possible exceptions. The type of exception actually handled can be detected by users from the message containing the exception's name (e.g., *System.ArgumentException*).

This very simple demonstrational example illustrates the idea of developing exception-handling wrapper aspects in Aspect.NET. Development of exception-handling interceptors or wrappers is possible using many AOP tools for .NET (see Section 3.6). However, the advantage of our approach, as applicable not only to exception handling, is an explicit, simple, and self-explanatory format of aspect definition, with convenient support by the Aspect.NET framework GUI integrated to Visual Studio. The aspect code can be used as a template for many more complicated programs where using AOP to handle exceptions is often convenient.

The output of the resulting updated application after weaving shows that all undesirable exceptions are handled and the information on their handling is logged:

> *Breaker call number 1*
> *Breaker call number 1 finished. Exception handled:*
> *System.ArgumentException*
> *Breaker call number 3*
> *Breaker call number 3 finished. Exception handled:*
> *System.IndexOutOfRangeException*
> *Breaker call number 10*
> *Breaker call number 10 finished. Exception handled:*
> *System.InvalidOperationException*
> *Press ENTER to exit*

Handling error codes is yet another task suitable for the use of AOP. A typical scenario is as follows. There is a domain-specific or system library of functions or methods. Each can terminate either normally, by performing the desirable operations on its input data, or abnormally, if the operation cannot be performed because of inconsistent input data. Suppose that in the implementation language of the library there is no exception-handling mechanism. Most common examples are C, Pascal, Modula, and FORTRAN. For that reason, each function is organized as follows. Where to store the output data is passed as arguments in the input data and references. The result of the function is an integer *error code*. The result, equal to zero, denotes normal termination; otherwise, the result denotes a specific error code. Although such a technique is quite common in many libraries, it is *not quite trustworthy* compared to exception-handling. The reason is obvious: Programmers often forget to check whether the resulting error code is zero. Only the following coding style looks trustworthy:

```
int resCode = f(in1, in2, out);
if (resCode == 0) {
    DoSomeAction(out);
} else {
    ProcessErrorCode(resCode);
}
```

But a quite common bug, very difficult to detect, is just to forget to check the result code and perform the absurd *DoSomeAction(out)* on probably undefined or absurd output data. The way to fix such bugs using AOP and Aspect.NET is as follows. An aspect can be developed that provides a wrapper method for each library method. The wrapper method calls the library method and analyzes its return code. To replace the library method call by the wrapper call, the aspect can use the *%instead* type of join point condition. There is a subtle semantic restriction which it is strongly recommended be followed when writing such aspects. Since each library function returns a value (error code), it is not recommended that the *%after* type of the join point condition be used here. In terms of implementation, it can be explained as follows: When weaving an action using the *%after* type condition, the weaver injects code that cleans the expression stack.

Suppose that C# does not have exceptions, and let's use integer return codes to indicate abnormal termination of the method. The target application for the aspect is an intentionally simplified version of a mathematical library. Each library function is implemented as a public static method. The actual output is passed as an *out* argument:

```
using System;
    public class MathLibrary
    {
        public const int Ok = 0;
        public const int NegativeArg = 1;
        public const int ZeroDivide = 2;
        public static int Remainder (int a, int b, out
        int res)
        {
```

```
            res = 0;
            if (a < 0 || b < 0)
            {
                return NegativeArg;
            }
            else if (b == 0)
            {
                return ZeroDivide;
            }
            else
            {
                res = a % b;
                return Ok;
            }
        }
        static void Main(string[] args)
        {
            int code;
            int res;
            code = Remainder(2, 1, out res);
            code = Remainder(-1, 1, out res);
            code = Remainder(1, 0, out res);
            Console.WriteLine("Press ENTER to exit");
            Console.ReadLine();
        }
    }
```

If there are no explicit checks of the return code, the implementer may not notice that only in the first case does the result of the *Remainder* method make sense, and may attempt to use the garbage *res* value in the second and third cases. To correct the situation and to make the code trustworthy, the following aspect can be used:

```
%aspect Aspect1
using System;
class Aspect1
{
    %modules
    private static void ProcessResultCode (int code) {
        switch (code) {
            case MathLibrary.Ok:
                Console.WriteLine("Operation finished
                normally");
                break;
            case MathLibrary.NegativeArg:
```

```
                Console.WriteLine("Invalid argument");
                break;
            case MathLibrary.ZeroDivide:
                Console.WriteLine("Division by zero");
                break;
        }
    }
}
%rules
%instead %call *MathLibrary.Remainder(int, int, out
int)
            && %args(arg[0], arg[1], arg[2])
%action
public static int RemainderWrapper (int a, int b, out
int res) {
    int code = MathLibrary.Remainder(a, b, out res);
    ProcessResultCode(code);
    return code;
    }
}
```

The auxiliary *ProcessResultCode* method used in this aspect analyzes the result code and prints out the corresponding message to the console. The *RemainderWrapper* action woven into the target application instead of the original *Remainder* calls uses *ProcessResultCode* and guarantees that the user will be informed of all normal and abnormal results of the method. Use of the *args* clause in the weaving condition is similar to its use in the previous example: It is necessary to capture the arguments of the target method. The example is intentionally simplified to serve better as an illustration of AOP methods used to make return codes trustworthy in applications.

4.4 AOP FOR SYNCHRONIZATION

More than 40 years since Dijkstra's classical paper [126], synchronization of processes and threads is still one of the most important issues in programming. Concurrent processes or threads can use shared resources or communicate via global events. Attempts to use or update the same global resources or events concurrently without special synchronization measures may lead to a *race condition*, an erroneous situation in which one thread updates the resource and the other retrieves the resource at the same moment, so that the second thread gets an out-of-date value of the resource. Synchronization is targeted to *mutual exclusion* of executing *critical sections* in concurrent threads. Examples of critical sections are the code that accesses or updates the common shared resource and the code that generates or processes a global event.

Accordingly, there are two basic types of synchronization: *resource-type* and *event-type*.

A typical bug that occurs when developing concurrently executed code is to omit (forget) resource- or event-type synchronization actions. Common-use development tools—compilers and debuggers—don't detect such bugs. Especially dangerous is the use of semaphores: When coding by hand it is very easy, for example, to use the *P* (close) operation on a semaphore before a critical section, but to forget its pairing *V* (open) operation after a critical section. In terms of code, a correct fragment would look like this:

```
P(Semaphore); CriticalSection(); V(Semaphore);
```

and an incorrect fragment like this:

```
P(Semaphore); CriticalSection(); // the V operation
call forgotten
```

The consequence of the bug is likely to be a deadlock. To detect such bugs, a static deadlock analyzer tool should be used which performs global analysis of the application's control flow graph. Another type of synchronization bug when using two or more semaphores is to swap the order of their operations: for example, if one thread executes the code

```
P(Semaphore1); P(Semaphore2);
```

and the other thread the code

```
P(Semaphore2); P(Semaphore1);
```

In the latter code fragment, the order of calls is swapped, which may also be the reason for a deadlock (the first thread is waiting for the second thread to open *Semaphore2*, but the second thread cannot do that because it is waiting for the first thread to open *Semaphore1*).

To avoid such synchronization bugs, the use of AOP is the best decision. Correct pairing of *P* and *V* operation calls will be guaranteed if they are the result of weaving the same synchronization aspect. Recall the *Synchronization* aspect example from Section 3.7. Let's update it to be usable with the current version of Aspect.NET (2.1). To guarantee the correctness and consistency of weaving semaphore-based synchronization actions, let's require that all critical sections of a target application's code that are to be synchronized be represented as *CriticalSection()* static method calls.

First, let's write a simple but nontrustworthy multithreaded application containing a classical race condition. Two threads are attempting concurrently to update the integer *counter*:

```
using System;
using System.Threading;
namespace ConsoleApplication1
{
    class Program
    {
        private static int counter = 0;
        public static void CriticalSection(string name)
        {
            counter++;
            Console.WriteLine("Thread: " + name + "
            counter updated= " + counter);
        } // CriticalSection
        static void Thread1() {
            for (int i = 1; i < 10; i++)
            {
                CriticalSection("thread1");
            }
        } // Thread1
        static void Thread2() {
            for (int i = 1; i < 10; i++)
            {
                CriticalSection("thread2");
            }
        } // Thread2
        static void Main(string[] args)
        {
            new Thread(new ThreadStart(Thread1)).
            Start();
            new Thread(new ThreadStart(Thread2)).
            Start();
            Console.WriteLine("Press ENTER to exit");
            Console.ReadLine();
        } // Main
    }
}
```

The output of this application illustrates the chaos with the updating *counter*. Its values are not output in the order of their update, and their order may vary from one application run to another. Note that the *Critical-Section* method contains an argument—the actual name of the thread executing it.

Now let's develop a simple synchronization aspect that injects calls of semaphore-type *P and V* operations before and after each call of *CriticalSection*:

```
%aspect Synchronization
using System;
public class Synchronization
{
%modules
%data
    public class Semaphore {
    }
    private static Semaphore s = new Semaphore();
%rules
      %before %call CriticalSection
      %action
        public static void P() {
            System.Threading.Monitor.Enter(s);
        }
      %after %call CriticalSection
      %action
        public static void V() {
            System.Threading.Monitor.Exit(s);
        }
} // Synchronization
```

Weaving such an aspect instead of "hand coding" calls of "synchronization brackets" guarantees that, first, no call or *P* or *V* will be forgotten, and second, the order of calls will never be swapped. It resolves both issues described above and helps to avoid typical bugs. Thus, due to applying AOP and Aspect. NET, using semaphore-like synchronization becomes trustworthy.

Note that the *%before* and *%after* weaving conditions in the aspect above can capture the calls of *CriticalSection* either with or without arguments. Capturing arguments of the method is not used in this example. The output of the synchronized version of the application, with the aspect woven, is quite regular: The order of *counter* values corresponds to the order of their update. Both outputs are omitted here because of their large size.

4.5 AOP FOR TRUSTWORTHY MULTITHREADING- AND MULTICORE-BASED APPLICATIONS

Multithreading and multicore applications comprise a hot research topic that is very important for industry, due to a lot of new multicore processors by Intel, Sun, and other hardware vendors [127–131]. A lot of legacy code should now be ported to the new, highly parallel hardware. But the problem is that most legacy code, especially that written in C and C++, is not multithreaded-safe (i.e., will probably fail in a multithreaded environment). Multithreading and multicore computation experts recommend the following methods to make the code MT-safe:

- All operations that access or update shared static variables and fields should be taken to mutual exclusion "brackets": calls of synchronization primitives (*mutex_lock*/*mutex_unlock*, etc.). Thus, all race conditions should be excluded, and all code should be made reentrant by multiple threads.
- Deadlocks should be avoided. Deadlocks arise when there is a loop dependency between several threads waiting for each other, such that each of them is waiting for some other thread to release some resource that it needs. Deadlocks are likely to be either the result of incorrect use of synchronization brackets (some thread locked a mutex but forgot to unlock it) or the result of incorrect use of suspend or stop operations applied to a thread that has entered its critical section.
- Using atomic synchronization operations is recommended, including test_and_set(x): atomically increment x and return its old value; and swap(x, y): atomically replaces the value of x by y and returns the old value of x.

In all these typical cases of making the code MT-safe, AOP can be very helpful, as we have seen in Section 4.4. Calls of synchronization brackets can be added very comfortably and safely by weaving appropriate aspects without entering bugs such as a forgotten paired synchronization call. Replacement of method calls to their trustworthy or atomic wrappers can also be accomplished by weaving aspects with *%instead* conditions, as demonstrated in a number of examples in this chapter. In particular, the unsafe calls of *stop(t)* can be replaced by calls of a wrapper routine that analyzes whether it is safe or not to call *stop(t)* prior to doing that.

As an example of this section, let's consider the classical task of synchronizing producers and consumers of the shared limited buffer. A producer thread adds a new informational item to the buffer at the free element at the *outPtr* pointer and waits, until a free element appears, to see if the buffer has overflowed. A consumer thread retrieves an informational item from the buffer at the *inPtr* pointer, frees the corresponding buffer element, and waits while the buffer is empty. First, let's develop a partial solution without explicit use of synchronization primitives, as may actually happen in an application ported from C or C++:

```
using System;
using System.Threading;
namespace ProducerConsumer
{
```

```
public class Program
{
    private const int BUFSIZE = 10;
    private static int[] buf = new int[BUFSIZE];
    private static int inPtr = 0;
    private static int outPtr = 0;
    private static int count = 0;
    public static void Put(int x) // put an item
    to the buffer
    {
        while (count == BUFSIZE) { }
        buf[inPtr] = x;
        inPtr = (inPtr + 1) % BUFSIZE;
        count++;
        Console.WriteLine
            ("Put: x = " + x + " inPtr = " + inPtr
            + " count=" + count);
    }
    public static int Get() // get an item from
    the buffer
    {
        int res;
        while (count == 0) { }
        res = buf[outPtr];
        outPtr = (outPtr + 1) % BUFSIZE;
        count - -;
        Console.WriteLine
            ("Get: res = " + res + " outPtr = " +
            outPtr + " count=" + count);
        return res;
    }
    static void Consumer() // the consumer thread
    {
        for (int i = 0; i < 20; i++)
        {
            int x = Get();
        }
    }
    static void Producer() // the produced thread
    {
        for (int i = 0; i < 20; i++)
        {
            Put(i);
        }
    }
```

```
static void Main(string[] args)
{ // let's start two producers and two
consumers in parallel
    new Thread(new ThreadStart(Consumer)).
    Start();
    new Thread(new ThreadStart(Producer)).
    Start();
    new Thread(new ThreadStart(Consumer)).
    Start();
    new Thread(new ThreadStart(Producer)).
    Start();
    Console.WriteLine("Press ENTER to exit");
    Console.ReadLine();
}
    }
}
```

Note that if there is one producer and one consumer thread only, the application will work correctly, since the *Get* and *Put* operations are synchronized due to initial waiting while the boundary condition on the buffer holds (the buffer is empty or overflowed). But such an application is not really multi-threaded safe because if we use several consumer threads and several producer threads, two producers or two consumers will experience a race condition.

To make the code MT-safe and trustworthy, let's implement a simple aspect that replaces the calls of *Get* and *Set* by their synchronized wrappers. However, we should avoid a common mistake here. If we try to use the *same* lock to synchronize the producers and consumers, we'll introduce a deadlock: If a consumer acquires the lock initially, it will then wait in a loop until at least one item appears in the buffer; but this item cannot appear because the producer will be blocked by the same lock! So we'll have to use two different locks, one for mutual exclusion of *Get* operations and another for *Put* operations:

```
%aspect ProducerConsumerSync
using System;
using ProducerConsumer;
public class ProducerConsumerSync
{
    %data
    private class Lock { }
    private static Lock pLock = new Lock();
    private static Lock cLock = new Lock();
    %rules
    %instead %call Program.Get() %% %args(..)
```

```
%action
public static int GetWrapper() {
    int res;
     System.Threading.Monitor.Enter(cLock);
     res = Program.Get();
     System.Threading.Monitor.Exit(cLock);
     return res;
}
%instead %call Program.Put(int) %% %args(arg[0])
%action
public static void PutWrapper(int x) {
     System.Threading.Monitor.Enter(pLock);
     Program.Put(x);
     System.Threading.Monitor.Exit(pLock);
}
}
```

In the *ProducerConsumerSync* aspect above, we use two static reference fields as locks, one for synchronizing the producers and the other for synchronizing the consumers. The aspect replaces all calls of *Get* by calls of *GetWrapper* with appropriate synchronization of consumers, and replaces all calls of *Put* by calls of *PutWrapper* with appropriate synchronization of producers.

Note that no matter how helpful AOP is in injecting synchronization and doing typical injections or corrections to make applications multithreaded safe, AOP does not solve all issues that may arise, since the nature of MT safety is very complicated and depends on a deep understanding of program semantics. If a deadlock occurs, it should, generally speaking, be detected by a static code analyzer or in debugging. Developing and using "smart" aspects that could understand program semantics is a matter for future development, and integration of AOP and knowledge engineering techniques could be helpful in solving this intellectual challenge.

4.6 AOP FOR PRIVACY

Privacy as an IT concept (see Section 2.3.2) relates to methods of protecting private information such as bank accounts, family data, or any other information that should be kept confidential. AOP can be very helpful in enabling and checking privacy. If an application uses or processes some private information, AOP can be applied for developing and weaving aspects to perform various types of actions that may be associated with privacy—in particular:

- Checking whether the application is permitted to use or update sensitive information

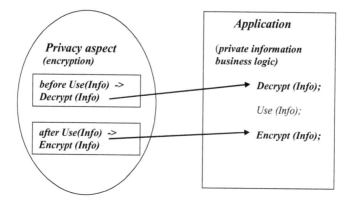

Figure 4.1 Using privacy aspects.

- Issuing warning messages to users asking for such permissions
- Encrypting private information before it is passed via the Internet or an intranet, and its decryption afterward
- Checking for various forms of intrusions of malicious software and users into private information, and for attempts to corrupt it (e.g., checking for spam in the mail client after it downloads new messages from the mail server; an anti-phishing filter in the browser activated on rendering a newly loaded Web page)
- License checking: in particular, for Web applications [131]
- Software tampering detection when a given code is executed on a non-trusted host [132]
- Database encryption [133]

Algorithms to protect private information—in particular, encryption algorithms and anti-phishing filters—can be complicated. So using AOP is beneficial because it helps to separate the concerns of processing and protecting private information, as shown in Figure 4.1. As an example, let's consider an application that may be used for malicious purposes; it inputs the path to a text file and outputs its contents to the console:

```
using System;
using System.IO;
namespace ConsoleApplication1
{
    class Program
    {
        static void Main(string[] args)
        {
            string path;
```

```
        string s;
        StreamReader sr;
        Console.WriteLine("*** FileReader: Enter
        the path to the input file");
        path = Console.ReadLine();
        Console.WriteLine("Contents of the file " +
        path);
        sr = File.OpenText(path);
        while ((s = sr.ReadLine()) != null)
        {
            Console.WriteLine(s);
        }
        Console.WriteLine("*** FileReader: Press
        ENTER to finish");
        Console.ReadLine();
        }
    }
}
```

Even such a simple application can be used for malicious purposes, as when it is used for reading a file containing confidential information. To inject a check for nonconfidentiality of an input text file, it is quite easy to develop an aspect that performs such a check and to weave it if needed. To illustrate the idea in simplified form, suppose it is considered to be a confidentiality violation if there is an attempt to open and read a text file that contains the text "*Microsoft confidential.*" Suppose that the hacker has entered the path *c:\private.txt* to a file containing confidential information. Here is a possible output of the application, with the private information disclosed on the hacker's machine:

*** *FileReader: Enter the path to the input file*
c:\private.txt
Contents of the file c:\private.txt
Microsoft Confidential
Secret 1
Secret 2
Secret 3
*** *FileReader: Press ENTER to finish*

The aspect below, referred to as *PrivacyGuard*, will perform the task of confidentiality checking. If an attempt to access confidential information is detected by the aspect, an exception is thrown and the appropriate text message is issued:

```
%aspect Privacyguard
using System;
using System.IO;
class PrivacyGuard
{
    %data
    public class PrivacyException: SystemException {
        public PrivacyException(string mes): base(mes)
        {}
    }
    %modules
    private static void CheckPrivacy(string path) {
        StreamReader sr;
        string s;
        sr = File.OpenText(path);
        while ((s = sr.ReadLine()) != null) {
            if (s.Contains("Microsoft confidential")) {
                throw new PrivacyException
                    ("Access to Microsoft confidential
                    information denied");
            }
        }
    }
    %rules
    %before %call System.IO.File.OpenText(string) &&
    %args(..)
    %action
    public static void CheckPrivacyAction (string path)
    {
        CheckPrivacy(path);
    }
}
```

If, after weaving the aspect to the application above, one tries to enter the same file path in the same environment, the program will terminate by a *PrivacyException* (this exception type is defined in the aspect) with the error message

Access to Microsoft confidential information denied

To weave the privacy check and to capture the argument of the *OpenText* method, the path to the file, the aspect uses the following weaving condition:

```
%before %call System.IO.File.OpenText(string) &&
%args(..)
```

Although this example is simply educational, the aspect can be a template for the code of aspects that can be helpful to protect information privacy in a realistic situation.

4.7 AOP FOR RELIABILITY

Reliability (see Section 2.3.3) is a key issue related to TWC and one of the most suitable fields for applying AOP. As noted in Section 2.3.3, software reliability goals can be achieved using the following techniques or their combinations: *using reliable design and implementation methods, software testing, and formal methods of software specification and verification.* AOP is applicable in any of those techniques, as explained below.

4.7.1 Using AOP to Make Implementation Reliable

To make a software module reliable, the module should, in the ideal case, check its applicability in the given environment in which it is called, check the consistency of its arguments, and explicitly react to any type of abnormal conditions by issuing understandable error messages, throwing appropriate exceptions, or returning appropriate error codes. But the problem is that most legacy code, for various reasons (e.g., evolution, bugs, and lack of testing because of project time limitations), does not contain such checks. So the task of AOP is to activate or inject reliability checks where needed. In Section 4.3 we considered how to use AOP for exception-handling and processing return codes.

As for *argument consistency checking*, not all checks actually needed in practice are supported by the implementation language and the compiler. In most languages, the argument types (e.g., *int, double[], Pointer,* or *Budget*) specify a possible (very large) set of its values but do not automatically support more subtle checks for specific values, their ranges, and the relations required by the semantics of the method: for example, the *int* argument should be positive or should be in the range 1 to 100; the elements of the *double[]* array should be sorted in ascending order of their values; the *Pointer* argument shouldn't be *null*; and the *Budget* argument should be non-negative and should not exceed a predefined budget limit. The task of AOP is to implement such checks by separately developed aspects and then to inject the argument checks into the resulting code without changing its sources (which, by the way, may be inaccessible for confidentiality reasons), as shown in Figure 4.2.

As an example, consider an application with a method that has a complicated set of arguments: *MinMax* to find the minimal and maximal elements in a given index range of the given array. Its arguments are:

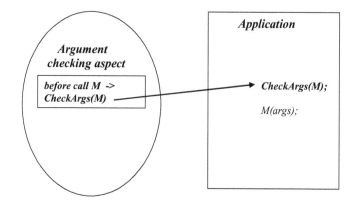

Figure 4.2 *Using reliability aspects for argument consistency checking.*

- *int[] a:* the input array
- *int from, to:* the starting and ending indexes that describe a range of *a*
- *res:* an output object type argument with two fields, *min* and *max*, to store the results

The following "contract" on the method arguments is implied, although not checked explicitly, by the body of the *MinMax* method:

- *from* should not be greater than *to*; both *from* and *to* should be nonnegative and should not exceed *a.Length – 1*.
- *res* should be a nonnull object reference.

```
using System;
namespace MinMaxTest
{
    public class Program
    {
        public class Res
        {
            public int min;
            public int max;
        }
        public static void MinMax(int[] a, int from,
        int to, Res res)
        {
            int min = Int32.MaxValue;
            int max = Int32.MinValue;
            for (int i = from; i <= to; i++)
            {
```

```
                    if (a[i] < min)
                    {
                        min = a[i];
                    }
                    if (a[i] > max)
                    {
                        max = a[i];
                    }
                }
            res.min = min;
            res.max = max;
            Console.WriteLine("MinMax finished");
        }
        static void Main(string[] args)
        {
            Res r = new Res();
            int [] a = new int[] {2, 3, 5, 4};
            MinMax(a, 4, 3, r);
            MinMax(a, 0, 3, null);
            MinMax(a, 0, 5, r);
            Console.WriteLine("Press ENTER to continue");
            Console.ReadLine();
        }
    }
}
```

On running the application, the first call of *MinMax* does not make any sense because the *from* argument is invalid. However, the method is called, although its output object fields have not been assigned any values. Such semantically incorrect calls are quite dangerous, since this bug is not easily detected without applying AOP. The second call crashes with *NullReference-Exception*. But there is actually no attempt to check the arguments for their consistence before the main loop of the method starts working. This is an example of nontrustworthy code.

To make the code trustworthy (it does not matter that arguments in *all* calls of *MinMax* are incorrect), let's capture and diagnose below all argument inconsistencies by an aspect. The aspect tries to detect *all* argument inconsistencies during one incorrect call of the *MinMax* method. For example, if *from*, *to*, and *res* arguments are all (or in part) invalid, the aspect will issue a message on each of the incorrect arguments and then a clear message that the *MinMax* method call was canceled:

```
%aspect MinMaxArgAspect
using System;
using MinMaxTest;
```

```
class MinMaxArgAspect
{
    %rules
    %instead %call MinMax(..)
    %action
    public static void MinMaxArgCheckAction
        (int[] a, int from, int to, MinMaxTest.Program.
        Res res)
{
    bool proceed = true;
    if (from < 0 || from >= a.Length) {
        Console.WriteLine("MinMax: invalid first
        argument: from = " + from);
        proceed = false;
    }
    if (to < 0 || to >= a.Length) {
        Console.WriteLine("MinMax: invalid second
        argument: to = " + to);
        proceed = false;
    }
    if (from > to) {
        Console.WriteLine("MinMax: from > to: from = "
        + from + " to = " + to);
        proceed = false;
    }
    if (res == null) {
        Console.WriteLine("MinMax: res = null");
        proceed = false;
    }
    if (proceed) {
        Program.MinMax(a, from, to, res);
    } else {
        Console.WriteLine
            ("--- MinMax call terminated because of
            invalid arguments");
    }
    } // MinMaxArgCheckAction
}
```

As the result of weaving *MinMaxArgAspect*, all three incorrect calls of *MinMax* will be performed, for the purpose of capturing all argument bugs in one application run. Instead of *MinMax*, its wrapper, with full argument consistency checking, will work. As a result, the author of the application will be able to analyze and correct all three calls of *MinMax* after one run of the updated application. If the *MinMax* wrapper detects that all arguments are correct, it just executes the original version of *MinMax*.

4.7.2   Using AOP for Software Testing

In this section, and in the book in general, testing is considered in the broad sense of this term, not only as running the given test suites to check some definite features of the program and/or all the bug fixes made. To test programs that way, more traditional methods and tools are used, which originated long before AOP: test harnesses, unit test generators, and others. AOP is more useful for other types of testing, for thorough analysis of the runtime behavior of the program not only for the purpose of detecting and fixing bugs, but also for the purpose of improving the efficiency and performance of the software.

One traditional AOP application is *logging*, injecting or activating in the target code various types of log prints helpful when debugging or for any other type of analysis of application behavior. Often, instead of many hours or days spent with the debugger in attempts to understand an application's behavior, it would be more helpful to get a complete log file of, say, all method calls and returns, with the values of all actual arguments and results. It is very easy to do that automatically using AOP, as a result of applying separately developed aspects, without the need to insert the logging prints directly into the application's source code, which can be very large. In this sense, logging can be regarded as one of inherent parts of dynamic testing. We considered a simple example of a logging aspect in Section 3.8.4. In this section we consider a more interesting example. As we have seen, AOP mechanisms are helpful to capture all dynamic behavior elements of an application: method calls, updating or accessing data, and so on.

Another important type of dynamic testing is *profiling*, recording and analyzing the statistics of the dynamic behavior of the program: how many times some methods were called, how much memory was used, how many exceptions were thrown; how many threads created, and so on. For the purpose of profiling, AOP is also very helpful, since it allows us easily to inject profiling actions into target applications. We'll see an interesting example in the next section.

Logging Aspect   Now let's proceed with the logging aspect. At first we should clarify our requirements for it. Let's try to develop a method call *logging aspect*, which should be as universal and reusable as possible, applicable to any method (i.e., a static or instance method), returning or not returning a value. The aspect will be capturing and logging any method call and return. At each method call, the aspect will issue the name of the method to be called, whether or not the method is static, the number of its arguments, and log information on the names and types of each argument. At each method return, the aspect will be logging the method name and the return type. The aspect should be able to turn the logging mode on or off: whatever the user chooses by his or her input. In addition, to collect only really useful information in our log, we'd like to log only the target application method's calls rather than calls of system utilities such as *Console.WriteLine*. To enable us to turn logging on and off, we need to suppose that the target application utilizes the *Init* method, which initializes its data: Attempts to weave aspects before call of the entry *Main* method will fail, since *Main* is called by the CLR host when starting the application in a .NET environment rather than explicitly by our application. Another thing we suppose for the target application is that it should be a namespace called *MyApp*. To capture information on target methods, our aspect will use reflection (provided by .NET framework *System.Reflection* namespace) and Aspect.NET's *%TargetMemberInfo* feature to capture information on target methods.

The code for the *Logging* aspect is shown below. This example is written "in attributes" (see Section 3.8.6)—directly in C#, without explicit use of Aspect.NET.ML metalanguage. Belonging to the aspect for each method is marked by the *AspectAction* custom attribute predefined in *AspectDotNet* namespace. To develop such projects, the user should choose the "Aspect.NET project" type of project in Visual Studio, augmented by the Aspect.NET add-in. The *AspectDescription* attribute is used to insert comments in the aspect source. It can also used be with any aspect's method.

```
using System;
using System.Reflection;
using AspectDotNet;
namespace LoggingAspect
{
    [AspectDescription("Logging aspect")]
    public class LoggingAspect : Aspect
    {
        private static bool LoggingOn = false;
        [AspectAction("%before %call Program.Init")]
        public static void LogInitAction()
        {
            string s;
            Console.Write("Turn on logging?(Y,N)");
            s = Console.ReadLine();
            if (s.StartsWith("Y") || s.
            StartsWith("y"))
            {
                LoggingOn = true;
                Console.WriteLine("Logging turned on");
            }
            else
            {
```

```
            LoggingOn = false;
            Console.WriteLine("Logging turned
            off");
        }
    }
    [AspectAction("%before %call MyApp.*")]
    public static void CallLogAction()
    {
        if (LoggingOn)
        {
            MethodInfo m =
            (MethodInfo)TargetMemberInfo;
            ParameterInfo[] pars = m.
            GetParameters();
            Object to = TargetObject;
            Console.WriteLine
                ("--- Call method: " + m.Name + "
                 number of arguments: " +
                 pars.Length);
            if (to == null)
            {
                Console.WriteLine(" Method is
                static");
            } else {
                Console.WriteLine
                    (" Target object: type=" + to.
                     GetType() +
                    " value=" + to.ToString());
            }
            foreach (ParameterInfo p in pars) {
                    Console.WriteLine
                        (" argument: name: " + p.
                        Name +
                        " type: " + p.
                        ParameterType);
            }
        }
    }
    [AspectAction("%after %call MyApp.*")]
    public static void ReturnLogAction()
    {
        if (LoggingOn)
        {
            MethodInfo m = (MethodInfo)
            TargetMemberInfo;
```

```
                Console.WriteLine(" Returned value
                type: " + m.ReturnType);
                Console.WriteLine("+++ Return from
                method: " + m.Name);
            }
        }
    }
}
```

Next is the target application that we'll use to test our *LoggingAspect*.
It satisfies both requirements of the aspect: It is developed as the
MyApp namespace, and it has the *Init* method (which is empty) to weave
the dialog to initialize or switch off the logging mode. The application has
both class and instance methods, both returning and not returning a
result.

```
using System;
namespace MyApp
{
    public class MyClass
    {
        public int Field = 1;
        public void SetField(int n)
        { Field = n; }
    }
    public class Program
    {
        public static void Init() { }
        public static void M1(int x) {
            int y = M2(x);
        }
        public static int M2(int y) {
            return (y + 1);
        }
        static void Main(string[] args) {
            MyClass p = new MyClass();
            Init();
            M1(0);
            p.SetField(0);
            Console.WriteLine("Press Enter to exit");
            Console.ReadLine();
        }
    }
}
```

On weaving our aspect to this application, we get the following output (provided that we have answered *Y* to switch on the logging mode):

> *Turn on logging?(Y,N)y*
> *Logging turned on*
> *— Call method: Init number of arguments: 0*
>   *Method is static*
>   *Returned value type: System.Void*
> *+++ Return from method: Ini*
> *— Call method: M1 number of arguments: 1*
>   *Method is static*
>   *argument: name: x type: System.Int32*
> *— Call method: M2 number of arguments: 1*
>   *Method is static*
>   *argument: name: y type: System.Int32*
>   *Returned value type: System.Int32*
> *+++ Return from method: M2*
>   *Returned value type: System.Void*
> *+++ Return from method: M1*
> *— Call method: SetField number of arguments: 1*
>   *Target object: type=MyApp.MyClass value=MyApp.MyClass*
>   *argument: name: n type: System.Int32*
>   *Returned value type: System.Void*
> *+++ Return from method: SetField*
> *Press Enter to exit*

The output looks informative enough and can be helpful for testing. The aspect provided in this section can be used in real applications and can be enhanced by any other types of analysis of target methods supported by *System.Reflection*.

Profiling Aspect   As an example of a profiling aspect applied to real software products, let's consider an aspect, *AddNopTool*, developed by Dmitry Grigoriev to enhance one of the samples shipped with Phoenix [7], Microsoft's compiler back-end infrastructure.

Phoenix provides a lot of features: optimization, various types of internal representations of the program, and an extensible set of target platforms, including .NET–PE files and MSIL. The Visual Studio.NET 2005 solution for the Phoenix sample we have enhanced with *AddNopTool* is available in the *c:\Program Files\Phoenix RDK March 2007\src\samples\AddNop-tool\csharp* subdirectory, where *C* is the logical drive where Phoenix is installed. The

AddNopTool application operates with an input PE file and inserts a *nop* (no-operation instruction) after each MSIL code instruction. *AddNopTool* uses Phoenix API, which is very large and located in the *Phx* namespace. In addition, Phoenix is not shipped with its source code, so this is just the kind of realistic situation mentioned earlier when the source code of the target application is inaccessible for confidentiality reasons. Both *AddNopTool* and Phoenix do this job well, using comfortable and self-explanatory API, but they are pretty silent.

AddNopTool provides the following profiling functionality:

- Measures and outputs the time needed for Phoenix initialization
- Counts and outputs the actual number of *nop*'s inserted by *AddNopTool*

```
%aspect AddNopCounter
using System;
// MAddNopCounter aspect extends the AddNop-Tool
sample from Phoenix RDK
// with some tracing information
class AddNopCounter {
    %data
        public static int NopCounts = 0;
        public static DateTime StartTime;
        public static DateTime EndTime;
    %modules
    %rules
        // BeforePhoenixInitialization greets you some
        way
        %before %call AddNopTool.InitializePhx
        %action
        public static void BeforePhoenixInitialization()
        {
            StartTime = DateTime.Now;
            Console.WriteLine("Performing Phoenix
            Initialization...");
        }
        // AfterPhoenixInitialization reports about
        Phoenix configuration state
        %after %call Phx.Initialize.BeginInitialization
        %action
        public static void AfterPhoenixInitialization()
        {
            EndTime = DateTime.Now;
            Console.WriteLine("Phoenix Initialization
            completed ...");
```

```
        if (StartTime.Ticks != 0)
        {
            TimeSpan tsp = EndTime.
            Subtract(StartTime);
            System.Console.WriteLine
                ("Initializing time: {0}
                milliseconds", tsp.Ticks / 10000);
        }
    }
    // BeforeNopInstrumentation action notifies you
    // about starting the nop instrumentation
    %before %call *DoAddNop
    %action
    public static void BeforeNopInstrumentation()
    {
        Console.WriteLine
            ("Performing {0} Instrumentation ...",
            TargetMemberInfo.ToString());
    }
    // AfterNopInstrumentation action prints number
    of inserted nops
    %after %call *DoAddNop
    %action
    public static void AfterNopInstrumentation()
    {
        Console.WriteLine("Total {0} nops added!",
        NopCounts);
    }
    // AfterNopInsert action increments NopCounts
    %after %call *Instruction.InsertBefore
    %action
    public static void AfterNopInsert()
    {
        NopCounts++;
    }
  }
}
```

The *AddNopCounter* aspect has five weaving rules and five actions. Of those actions, two, *AfterPhoenixInitialization* and *AfterNopInsert*, operate directly with Phoenix code accessible in binary form only. Nevertheless, they are quite useful and enhance the functionality of a very large commercial API without modifying or even looking at its source code. So this example is practical proof that AOP and Aspect.NET are usable even with a large confidential code.

On weaving our aspect, the *AddNopTool* sample, which should be launched in a console with two arguments, the input PE file and the output PE file, provides the following output on a laptop with an Intel Pentium M processor and 1 GB of memory:

>*>~addnop-tool addnop-tool.exe new_addnop_tool.exe*
> *Performing Phoenix Initialization...*
> *Phoenix Initialization completed...*
> *Initializing time: 2687 milliseconds*
> *Performing Void DoAddNop(Phx.PEModuleUnit) Instrumentation ...*
> *Total 381 nops added!*

4.7.3   Using AOP to Support Formal Specification and Verification Methods

Current AOP tools, including Aspect.NET 2.1, do not yet directly support formal specification and verification. However, it looks like the time has come to support it by AOP, since, on the one hand, formal methods are beneficial for developing trustworthy software, but on the other hand, are not yet widely used and need appropriate tools suitable not only for development of new, formally specified and verified applications, but also for adding them into legacy code. Here is a possible scheme for applying AOP to support formal methods in a .NET environment using Aspect.NET (see Figure 4.3):

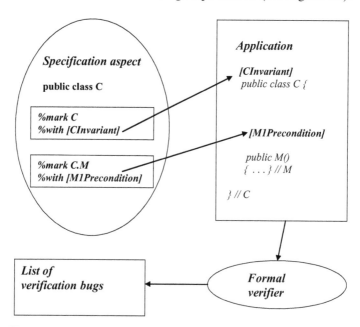

Figure 4.3   *Using aspects to support formal specification and verification.*

- A formal specification language and verifier based on that language is chosen or developed. For example, for C# applications, it can be Spec# [64] with its verifier.
- Aspect.NET is enhanced by aspect *action scripts* (see Section 3.9.2) that allow us to mark the captured classes and methods with the custom attributes given. The attributes will be used to annotate the code with its formal specifications. This enhancement is exactly what we plan to do for Aspect.NET 3.0.
- *Specification aspects* are developed for the application of a related family of applications. They consist of custom attribute–based annotations to be woven into target applications.
- The specification aspects are used (woven), and the resulting target application is checked against the formal verifier.

Hopefully, this approach will be prospective, but to prove it in practice, years of research and development are needed.

4.8 AOP FOR BUSINESS INTEGRITY

Business integrity, the fourth pillar of trustworthy computing (see Section 2.3.4), is closely related to the efficiency and reliability of software maintenance techniques. The more efficient and reliable maintenance techniques are, the faster and more trustworthy all bug and RFE fixes will be, so the more satisfied customers will be and the more trust they will feel toward both the maintenance team and the software developer company as a whole. This is one of the final goals of the business integrity approach.

As noted in Section 2.3.4, in the everyday maintenance of software, two types of tasks should be solved relevant to the use of AOP techniques:

1. *Aspect mining* [29]: locating the functionality to be fixed in the existing code as an aspect or set of aspects. A related technique is *aspectizing* [134], automated refactoring of code to aspects.
2. *Developing and weaving the fix* (or patch) as *an aspect* or *set of aspects*, so as not to break the existing code, and to be able to roll the fix back easily if it is not appropriate in the release, is not needed, or is considered too risky by product management.

The terms *aspect mining* and *aspectizing* as used in this book have a similar meaning: detecting aspects in the existing code and code refactoring to aspects, with the goal of further code reuse. Although there are a lot of research papers in this area, industrial-level aspect mining tools or aspectizers have not yet been developed. This is because aspect mining and aspect-oriented refactoring techniques are complicated and require deep human interaction. If those responsible for software product maintenance are not perfectly familiar with the code for which they are responsible, they cannot really help the AOP mining tool. At present, a more practical approach seems to be use of *concern graphs* and a *FEAT* tool [91] that make it possible to visualize the concerns in the source code. It is very helpful for program maintenance, to make the process of learning the source code easier.

Developing and applying bug and RFE fixes as aspects is quite logical and in the spirit of trustworthy software development. If the software product team has got a set of aspects, each implementing a bug or RFE fix, the team can better understand what happened to the code in the process of its evolution. Otherwise, adding each bug fix to the source code may cause what Myers calls *temporal cohesion* [19]: A new code fragment (say, some initially forgotten *M* method call) is added to the code of some other method *T*, based only on the principle that the call of *M* to be added is to be executed at the same moment as the call of *T* is executed. Figure 4.4 illustrates this situation.

Introducing temporal cohesions in bug fixing is a typical software process evolution flaw. It may jeopardize business integrity because the "fix in a hurry" produced by the maintenance team may cause further problems in the product maintenance process and can lengthen the maintenance team's reaction time from the customer's viewpoint.

The underlying reason for such a situation is that in terms of AOP, a call of *M* is needed because the concern whose part *T* is, should be cross-cut by another concern, whose part is *M*. AOP can help us to cope with situations of this kind. To make the process of bug fixing more systematic, at least those *bug and RFE fixes* that require many tangled insertions of code *should be designed and implemented as aspects*. This approach not only helps to track the code changes, but also helps the maintenance team to *reach a higher conceptual level of reasoning, due to thinking in terms of cross-cutting concerns and aspects* when updating the code, rather than using a "rush" style of work such as the following: "It looks like the call of *M* should be inserted into the

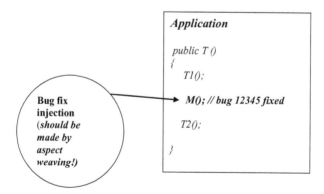

Figure 4.4   *Introducing temporal cohesion through a bug fix.*

implementation of *T*—let's try to do that and use the debugger to test how it works."

As an example, let's assume that the .NET application to be maintained, implemented as the *MyGUIApp* namespace, works with GUI and that customers report that in some cases, after adding new subcomponents to a GUI component, the component is not repainted automatically. Suppose that in our application a GUI component is represented by an object of the class *MyGUI-Component*, adding a subcomponent is implemented by a method call such as *component.AddComponent* (*newSubcomponent*, …), and repainting the component is performed by the method call *component.Repaint*(). The customer is not sure if the buggy situation takes place in all cases. It is the task of the maintenance team to find it quickly and to make a trustworthy bug fix. Common-use development tools don't help a lot to fix the bug. But AOP and Aspect.NET appear to be quite suitable for solving this task. Let's develop the following simple aspect to insert the fix and try to weave it using our Aspect.NET framework:

```
%aspect AddRepaint
using System;
using MyGUIApp;
public class AddRepaint {
%rules
%after %call AddComponent
%action
    public static void AddRepaintAction () {
        MyGUIComponent comp = (MyGUIComponent)
        %TargetObject;
        comp.Repaint();
    }
}
```

The convenience of this solution implemented by Aspect.NET is not only in the functionality to insert the *Repaint* call after all calls of *AddComponent*, but also in the ability of Aspect.NET to visualize potential join points and have the user deselect part of them if not appropriate. Using the Aspect.NET framework, the maintenance engineer can first find the join points and use the *Visualization* tab to browse all of them. If he or she detects, say, that a call of *Repaint* is already present after some of the *AddComponent* calls found by Aspect.NET, the engineer can deselect the corresponding join point and thus avoid a redundant *Repaint* call. Then, on limiting the set of join points really needed, the engineer can weave the aspect and test how the updated application works. The code of the application itself is not changed. If the aspect is no longer needed (say, after testing the fix by the aspect, the engineer actually updated the application source), it can be ignored, but it should be kept as part of the working documentation on the project.

I think an ideal solution would be if each bug or RFE fix were designed, developed, and tested as an aspect woven to the target application. It would help the maintenance team to save a lot of working time afterward. If, for example, the product is passed to another engineer for maintenance (which very often happens in practice), the new engineer will have full information on fixing bugs, due to the bug fix aspect library kept in the product working directories.

Another case in which such a technique would be very helpful is when the source code of the application is inaccessible. Let's say the maintenance team has only been given product documentation describing the API implemented. As we've seen in Section 4.7.2, the Aspect.NET approach allows us to maintain such an application in this case also. In our discussion above of the *AddRepaint* aspect, we didn't use the application sources. We relied solely on our knowledge of which method should be used to add or repaint a GUI component, and how it should be called. So, if for some proprietary reason, a product vendor cannot provide the sources to the maintenance team, the job can still be done (at least, tentatively, as a maintenance experiment) using Aspect.NET and the binary code (assembly code .exe or .dll) of the application only.

So in both this section and Section 4.7.2, we have confirmed that AOP and Aspect.NET can be used by industry in maintaining real software products, which is an inherent part of business integrity.

4.9 AOP FOR DESIGN BY CONTRACT

Finally, as past of the series samples using AOP and Aspect.NET in this chapter, let's consider using AOP for design by contract [66], a worldly known approach to design and implementation of reliable and verifiable bug-free object-oriented applications developed by Bertrand Meyer. AOP appears to be one of the most suitable techniques to use for design-by-contract purposes.

The design-by-contract approach is based on the central notion of a *contract*. Establishing a contract should be the initial stage of developing each software module. A contract for a software module, as well as a contract between a client and a supplier, can be considered as an initial *obligation* of the client: the *preconditions required* that the client fulfill before using a service; and the final *benefits: postconditions* promised by the supplier that must be *ensured* as a result of using the service. The third component of the module contract is the class *invariant*, the assertion that should hold on all instances of the class. The author of the design-by-contract approach developed the Eiffel language [135] for ease of use of this approach. Eiffel contains the *require (precondition), ensure (postcondition),* and *invariant* statements as parts of the language. Nevertheless, it is quite clear that the principles of design by contract can be followed using any language with some kind of *assertion* mechanism, now included as a built-in feature in all contemporary languages:

notably, Java and C#. Even if the implementation language (e.g., C) is lacking built-in assertions, they can be modeled by issuing messages and terminating the program if any of the assertions is violated, so design-by-contract methodology is applicable to any implementation language. We omit Eiffel examples here because there are a plenty of them in the design-by-contract literature and at the Web site [136]. A very important extension of C# by design-by-contract style specifications, Spec# [64], is reviewed in Section 2.5.4.

Even from this initial exposure to design-by-contract basics, it is clear that AOP will work exceptionally well to support this approach. Checking the preconditions (*require*) and postconditions (*ensure*) for each method, before its call and on its return, accordingly, and checking the class invariant before and after calling each method of the class, can be implemented by design-by-contract aspects that can be developed separately from the class (or, most properly, *before* implementing the class) and then woven into the class by AOP mechanisms.

To illustrate these principles of applying AOP for design by contract using Aspect.NET, let's consider several examples developed by members of the Aspect.NET team.

Bank Management Example   In our first example, developed by Dmitry Grigoriev, we need to implement a simple bank management system to support *deposit* and *withdraw* operations on bank accounts. We'll develop it according to the design-by-contract style, but first, let's develop contracts for the classes as comments to the class source and methods; later, we'll see how aspects can be applied to implement and check these contracts.

The basic class of our banking system will be *BankAccount*, with one property, *Balance* (allows us to read the current balance only), and two operations (methods), *withdraw* and *deposit*:

```
using System;
namespace BankManagement
{
    /**Invariant: this.Balance >= 0*/
    public class BankAccount
    {
        float account=0;
        public float Balance
        { get { return account; } }
        /**Pre: amount>=0*/
        public float deposit(float amount) {
            account += amount; return account;
        }
        /**Post:
            this.Balance == old(this.Balance) + amount
            && return == this.Balance
```

```
        */
        /**Pre: amount>=0 && this.Balance-amount>=0*/
        public float withdraw(float amount) {
            account -= amount; return account;
        }
        /**Post:
            this.Balance == old(this.Balance) - amount
            && return == this.Balance
        */
    }
}
```

At this point the code itself is not trustworthy enough, since we haven't added any design-by-contract checks. We'll do that later using aspects.

The principal application that uses the banking system will look as follows:

```
using System;
namespace BankManagement
{
    public class BankManagementProgram
    {
        static void Main(string[] args)
        {
            BankAccount acc1 = new BankAccount();
            acc1.deposit(20); acc1.withdraw(20);
            Console.WriteLine("Final balance is {0}",
            acc1.Balance);
        }
    }
}
```

The output of the initial version of the principal application is:

Final balance is 0

Now let's enhance our banking system by the new functionality using AOP. Implement design-by-contract checks in *BankAccount* (by *BankAccountContractAspect*) and licensing checks (by *UsageLicensingAspect*). That will be yet another demonstration of using AOP custom attributes instead of using Aspect. NET.ML metalanguage. In the *BankAccountContractAspect* code below, for self-documening purposes, comments on the semantics of the checked assertions are kept as *AspectDescription*. The aspect checks the invariant (balance should be nonnegative) before and after call of each method, and checks the preconditions and postconditions for each method. Note how the post-

conditions are checked in *CheckPostDeposit* and *CheckPostWithdraw* actions
where the old and new values of the balance are used: First, the old value of
the target balance is saved in the *oldAccount* local variable, then the operation
is actually performed and the new value of the *target.Balance* is used in the
postcondition check alongside *oldAccount*. Those two actions are implemented
as *%instead* wrappers to perform all checks, and if they hold, to actually
execute the operations. If any violation is detected, the aspect's action issues
a self-explanatory error message, with the source file path and line number
included, to indicate where in the target application it has actually
happened.

```
using System;
using System.Reflection;
using AspectDotNet;
namespace BankManagement
{
    [AspectDescription
        ("Design By Contract aspect for verifying
        BankAccount logic")
    ]
    public class BankAccountContractAspect: Aspect
    {
        [AspectDescription("Invariant: this.Balance >=
        0")]
        [AspectAction
            ("%before %call *BankAccount.*(..) || %after
            %call *BankAccount.*(..)")
        ]
        static public void CheckInvariant()
        {
            if (((BankAccount)TargetObject).Balance < 0)
                Console.WriteLine
                ("ERROR INVARIANT: Balance should not
                be negative at {0} line {1}",
                SourceFilePath, SourceFileLine);
        }
        [AspectDescription("Pre: amount>=0")]
        [AspectAction("%before %call *BankAccount.
        deposit(float) && %args(arg[0])")]
        static public void CheckPreDeposit(float amount)
        {
            if (amount < 0) {
                Console.WriteLine
                    ("ERROR PRE: Amount is {0}. It
                    should not be " +
```

```
                    "negative at {1} line {2}",
            amount, SourceFilePath,
            SourceFileLine);
    }
}
[AspectDescription
    ("Post: this.Balance == old(this.Balance) +
    amount" +
    "&& return == this.Balance")
]
[AspectAction("%instead %call *BankAccount.
deposit(float)" +
" && %args(arg[0])")
]
static public float CheckPostDeposit(float
amount)
{
    if (amount < 0)
        Console.WriteLine
            ("ERROR POST: Amount is {0}. It
            should not " +
            "be negative at {1} line {2}",
            amount, SourceFilePath,
            SourceFileLine);
    BankAccount target = (BankAccount)
    TargetObject;
    float oldAccount = target.Balance;
    float resAccount = target.deposit(amount);
    if (target.Balance != resAccount)
        Console.WriteLine
            ("ERROR POST: BankAccount.
            deposit({0}) returns " +
            "incorrect balance at {1} line
            {2}",
            amount, SourceFilePath,
            SourceFileLine);
    if (target.Balance != oldAccount + amount)
        Console.WriteLine
            ("ERROR POST: BankAccount.
            deposit({0}) logic is not " +
            "correct at {1} line {2}",
            amount, SourceFilePath,
            SourceFileLine);
    return target.Balance;
}
```

```
[AspectDescription("Pre: amount>=0 && this.
Balance-amount>=0")]
[AspectAction
    ("%before %call *BankAccount.withdraw(float)
     && %args(arg[0])")
]
static public void CheckPreWithdraw(float
amount)
{
    if (amount < 0)
    Console.WriteLine
        ("ERROR PRE: Amount is {0}. It should
         not be "+
         "negative at {1} line {2}",
         amount, SourceFilePath,
         SourceFileLine);
    BankAccount target = (BankAccount)TargetObject;
    if (target.Balance - amount < 0)
        Console.WriteLine
            ("ERROR PRE: Withdrawn amount {0}
             should not exceed " +
             "overall balance {1} at {2} line {3}",
             amount, target,SourceFilePath,
             SourceFileLine);
}
[AspectDescription
    ("Post: this.Balance == old(this.Balance) -
     amount " +
     " && return == this.Balance")
]
[AspectAction
    ("%instead %call *BankAccount.withdraw(float)
     && %args(arg[0])")
]
static public float CheckPostWithdraw(float amount)
{
    if (amount < 0)
        Console.WriteLine
            ("ERROR POST: Amount is {0}. " +
             "It should not be negative at {1}
             line {2}",
             amount, SourceFilePath,
             SourceFileLine);
    BankAccount target = (BankAccount)TargetObject;
    float oldAccount = target.Balance;
```

```
        float resAccount = target.withdraw(amount);
        if (target.Balance != resAccount)
            Console.WriteLine
                ("ERROR POST: BankAccount.withdraw({0})
                 returns " +
                 "incorrect balance at {1} line {2}",
                 amount, SourceFilePath,
                 SourceFileLine);
            if (target.Balance != oldAccount - amount)
                Console.WriteLine
                    ("ERROR POST: BankAccount.
                     withdraw({0}) logic " +
                     "is not correct at {1} line {2}",
                     amount, SourceFilePath,
                     SourceFileLine);
            return target.Balance;
        }
    }
}
```

Another aspect to be applied to the target bank management application is *UsageLicensingAspect*. The semantics of the aspect are intentionally simplified for demonstration purposes: Actually, the license check is implemented in this example as a check that the *withdraw* operation is not allowed in this context. The actions of the aspect below are implemented as *%instead* wrappers for banking operations which actually perform the operation if the license condition holds. Here is the aspect code:

```
using System;
using AspectDotNet;
namespace BankManagement
{
    [AspectDescription
        ("Aspect checks the current machine license "
         +
         "and authorizes BankAccount.deposit() and
         BankAccount.withdraw()")
    ]
    public class UsageLicensingAspect: Aspect
    {
        static bool isLicenceValid(string operation)
        {
            return (operation.Contains("withdraw");
        }
        [AspectDescription
```

```
    ("Authorization action that wraps
     BankAccount.deposit(float) " +
     " and captures its argument")
]
[AspectAction("%instead %call *BankAccount.
deposit(float) && %args(..)")]
static public float DepositWrapper(float amount)
{
    BankAccount acc = (BankAccount)
    TargetObject;
    if (isLicenceValid(TargetMemberInfo.Name))
        return acc.deposit(amount);
    Console.WriteLine("Deposit operation is not
    allowed");
    return acc.Balance;
}
[AspectDescription
    ("Authorization action that wraps
     BankAccount.withdraw(float) " +
     "and captures its argument")
]
[AspectAction("%instead %call *BankAccount.
withdraw(float) && %args(..)")]
static public float WithdrawWrapper(float amount)
{
    BankAccount acc =
    (BankAccount)TargetObject;
    if (isLicenceValid(TargetMemberInfo.Name))
        return acc.withdraw(amount);
    Console.WriteLine("Withdraw operation is
    not allowed");
    return acc.Balance;
}
    }
}
```

The output of the updated banking application, with both aspects woven, is changed, since the licensing check by *UsageLicensingAspect* works. Since design-by-contract conditions hold, execution of *BankAccountContractAspect* has to track on the console:

Withdraw operation is not allowed
Final balance is 20

The class diagram is shown in Figure 4.5.

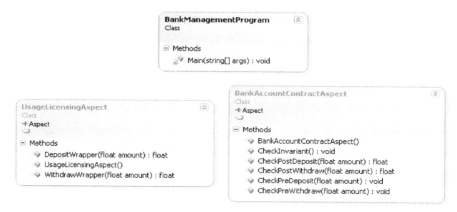

Figure 4.5 *Bank management system classes and aspects.*

This example illustrates both the advantages of using AOP to implement design-by-contract checks and the related difficulties: Developing the design-by-contract checking aspect is much more difficult than developing a class without condition checks. The initial version of the bank account class can be developed by a beginner in OOP and C#. The design-by-contract aspect can only be developed by an experienced software engineer—but this is the price of trustworthy programming.

Stack Example A second, more classical example, developed by Anna Kogay, considers the implementation of a stack according to design-by-contract principles. As in our other examples, the design-by-contract conditions are provided in the source of the *Stack* class as comments. The version of *Stack* implemented in this example allows us to indicate the maximum capacity of a stack and in addition to traditional *Push* and *Pop* operations, has such operations as *count*, the actual number of stack elements; *IsFull* and *isEmpty*, flags to determine whether a stack is full or empty; and *indexer*, which allows us to retrieve any existing stack element as an array element:

```
public class Stack {
        private int capacity; // max number of stack
        elements
        private int count; // current number of stack
        elements
        private int[] representationArray; // stack
        representation
        // class invariant:
        //    0 <= count <= capacity;
        //    representationArray != null
        //    representationArray.Length == capacity;
```

```
public int Capacity
{ return capacity; }
public int Count
{ return count; }
public int[] RepresentationArray
{ return representationArray }
// require: 0 <= index <= capacity-1
public int this[int index]
{ return representationArray[index]; }
// require: capacity >= 0;
public Stack(int capacity)
{// Allocate stack for a maximum of 'capacity'
elements
  this.capacity = capacity;
  this.representationArray = new int[capacity];
}
// ensure:
//    capacity is set: this.capacity ==
     capacity;
//    array is allocated: this.
     representationArray.Length != null
//    stack is empty: this.IsEmpty()

public bool IsEmpty() {
    return (count == 0);
}
// ensure: return == (count == 0)

public bool IsFull() {
    return (count == capacity);
}
// ensure: return == (count == capacity)
// require:
//    stack is not full: !IsFull()
public void Push(int element) { // Add element
on top
    count++;
    representationArray[count - 1] = element;
}
// ensure:
//    stack is not empty: !IsEmpty();
//    count == old_count + 1;
//    representationArray[count-1] == element;
// require:
//    stack is not empty: !IsEmpty()
```

```
public int Pop() {  // Get the top element
    int element = representationArray[count -
    1];
    count - -;
    return element;
}
// ensure:
//    stack is not full: !IsFull();
//    count == old_count - 1;
//    result == representationArray[old_count-1]
} // Stack
```

Here is a stack contract aspect written using AOP attributes without using Aspect.NET.ML metalanguage. Note that the *Stack* class constructor has its own precondition, and the call of the constructor is captured by the following weaving condition:

```
%before %call *Stack..ctor(int)
```

The aspect issues self-explanatory messages if any of the conditions checked do not hold:

```
[AspectDescription("Stack contract aspect")]
    public class StackContract : Aspect {
        [AspectDescription("Push precondition")]
        [AspectAction("%before %call *Stack.Push")]
        public static void CheckPushPrecondition()
        {
            Stack targetStack = (Stack)TargetObject;
            if (targetStack.IsFull()) {
                Console.WriteLine("ERROR Push
                precondition: " +
                                 "stack is full");
            } else {
                Console.WriteLine("--- Push
                precondition succeeded");
            }
        }

        [AspectDescription("Push postcondition")]
        [AspectAction
            ("%instead %call *Stack.Push(int) &&
            %args(arg[0])")]
        public static void CheckPushPostcondition(int
        element)
        {
```

```
    Stack targetStack = (Stack)TargetObject;
    int oldCount = targetStack.Count;
    targetStack.Push(element);
    int newCount = targetStack.Count;
    bool isCorrect = true;
    if (targetStack.IsEmpty()) {
        Console.WriteLine("ERROR Push
        postcondition: " +
                            "stack is empty");
        isCorrect = false;
    }
    if (newCount != oldCount + 1) (
        Console.WriteLine
            ("ERROR Push postcondition: 'count'
            has wrong value");
        isCorrect = false;
    }
    if (targetStack[newCount - 1] != element) {
        Console.WriteLine
            ("ERROR Push postcondition: " +
             "element is not on the top");
        isCorrect = false;
    }
    if (isCorrect) {
        Console.WriteLine("--- Push
        postcondition succeeded");
    }
}

[AspectDescription("Pop precondition")]
[AspectAction("%before %call *Stack.Pop")]
public static void CheckPopPrecondition()
{
    Stack targetStack = (Stack)TargetObject;
    if (targetStack.IsEmpty()) {
        Console.WriteLine
            ("ERROR Pop precondition: stack is
             empty");
    } else {
        Console.WriteLine("--- Pop precondition
        succeeded");
    }
}

[AspectDescription("Pop postcondition")]
[AspectAction("%instead %call *Stack.Pop")]
```

```
public static int CheckPopPostcondition()
{
    Stack targetStack = (Stack)TargetObject;
    int oldCount = targetStack.Count;
    int element = targetStack.Pop();
    int newCount = targetStack.Count;
    bool isCorrect = true;
    if (targetStack.IsFull()) {
        Console.WriteLine
            ("ERROR Pop postcondition: stack is
             full");
        isCorrect = false;
    }
    if (newCount != oldCount - 1) {
        Console.WriteLine
            ("ERROR Pop postcondition: 'count'
             has wrong value");
        isCorrect = false;
    }
    if (element != targetStack[oldCount - 1])
    {
        Console.WriteLine
           ("ERROR Pop postcondition: returned
            element " +
            "is not from the top");
        isCorrect = false;
    }
    if (isCorrect) {
        Console.WriteLine("--- Pop
        postcondition succeeded");
    }
    return element;
}

[AspectDescription("Constructor precondition")]
[AspectAction("%before %call *Stack..ctor(int)
&& %args(arg[0])")]
public static void CheckCtorPrecondition(int
capacity)
{
    if (capacity < 0) {
        Console.WriteLine("ERROR Ctor
        precondition: " +
                        "capacity is < 0");
    } else {
```

```
            Console.WriteLine("--- Ctor
            precondition succeeded");
    }
}

[AspectDescription("Indexer precondition")]
[AspectAction
    ("%before %call *Stack.get_Item &&
     %args(arg[0]) || " +
     " %before %call *Stack.set_Item &&
     %args(arg[0])")
]
public static void CheckIndexerPrecondition(int
index)
{
    Stack targetStack = (Stack)TargetObject;
    int capacity = targetStack.Capacity;
    if (index < 0 || index > capacity-1) {
        Console.WriteLine("ERROR Indexer
        precondition");
    } else {
        Console.WriteLine("--- Indexer
        precondition succeeded");
    }
}

[AspectDescription("Stack invariant")]
[AspectAction("%before %call *Stack.* || %after
%call *Stack.*"]
public static void CheckStackInvariant()
{
    try {
        Stack targetStack =
        (Stack)TargetObject;
        int count = targetStack.Count;
        int capacity = targetStack.Capacity;
        int[] representationArray =
            targetStack.RepresentationArray;
        bool isCorrect = true;
        if (count < 0 || count > capacity) {
            Console.WriteLine
              ("ERROR Stack invariant: '0 <=
               count <= capacity' " +
               "is not true");
            isCorrect = false;
```

```
            }
            if (representationArray == null) {
                Console.WriteLine
                    ("ERROR Stack invariant: " +
                     "representation array is
                     null");
                isCorrect = false;
            }
            if (representationArray.Length !=
            capacity) {
                Console.WriteLine
                    ("ERROR Stack invariant:
                     representation array " +
                     " length != stack capacity");
                isCorrect = false;
            }
            if (isCorrect) {
                Console.WriteLine("--- Stack
                invariant succeeded");
            }
        }
    catch (NullReferenceException)
    {
    }
}


    [AspectDescription("IsFull postcondition")]
    [AspectAction("%after %call *Stack.IsFull")]
    public static void CheckIsFullPostcondition()
    {
        Stack targetStack = (Stack)TargetObject;
        int count = targetStack.Count;
        int capacity = targetStack.Capacity;
        if ((bool)RetValue != (count == capacity))
        {
            Console.WriteLine
            ("ERROR IsFull postcondition: " +
             "returned value is incorrect");
        } else {
            Console.WriteLine("--- IsFull
            postcondition succeeded");
        }
    }


    [AspectDescription("IsEmpty postcondition")]
```

```
[AspectAction("%after %call *Stack.IsEmpty")]
public static void CheckIsEmptyPostcondition()
{
    Stack targetStack = (Stack)TargetObject;
    int count = targetStack.Count;
    if ((bool)RetValue != (count == 0)) {
        Console.WriteLine
            ("ERROR IsEmpty postcondition: " +
            "returned value is incorrect");
    } else {
        Console.WriteLine("--- IsEmpty
        postcondition succeeded");
    }
}
}
```

Summary The two detailed examples demonstrated in this section show clearly how meticulous the work of developing design-by-contract aspects must be. Many more examples of design-by-contract aspects developed using Aspect.NET are given in the Appendix.

To conclude this section, note that use of AOP for design-by-contract purposes is right in the spirit of the design-by-contract paradigm: According to its principles, the method should not check its precondition, postcondition, or the class invariant itself. Checks of those conditions, once specified, should be enabled by the design-by-contract programming framework. Thus, when implementing the method, its author can rely on the fact than its precondition holds and so not attempt to check it explicitly. Due to that fact, the logic of the method implementation becomes simpler: The concern of the method's business logic is separated from the cross-cutting concern on performing design-by-contract checks. On the other hand, if the method implementation calls another method, it can rely on the fact that the callee's method postcondition holds on returning from it. So as you can see from the *BankAccount* and *Stack* class code in the two examples, their logic is not overwhelmed with checks for various conditions. The classes just do their business. The complicated checks are isolated into aspects. So design by contract and AOP demonstrate productive teamwork using Aspect.NET.

4.10 USING AOP VIA Aspect.NET TO IMPROVE PRODUCTIVITY AND RELIABILITY

Now that we've seen through practical examples the advantages of applying AOP to trustworthy software development using Aspect.NET, it's time to analyze the costs using common quantitative assessment techniques and to compare AOP to other approaches. The following basic questions arise, whose answers are given in this section and in Sections 4.11 and 4.12:

- Does AOP really increase programmer productivity?
- Does applying AOP to trustworthy software development really increase software reliability?
- How can the points above be proved using quantitative assessment techniques?
- Isn't the use of AOP too expensive in terms of application performance? Is AOP implementation really efficient enough to be used in commercial software projects?

Answers to all these questions are necessary before AOP can be used for commercial software development.

4.10.1   Effort Estimation Using the COCOMO Model

First, let's estimate the effort and number of person-months involved in developing code using the COCOMO model [137]. Consider a typical task of developing or updating a program that software developers come across in relation to trustworthy computing: injecting some code before and after all calls of the method P. As we have seen earlier in the chapter, many typical enhancements of the application code related to making the code more trustworthy (secure, synchronized, MT-safe, etc.) using the AOP and Aspect.NET approach, can be reduced to injecting some code before and after the calls of some given method or methods, or injecting code before method calls only, or after method calls only, or replacing the code of the method by the code of its wrapper. The code to be inserted for TWC purposes can be synchronization brackets (%*before* and %*after* types of weaving actions should be used), or security checks (%*before*), or argument checks (%*instead*), or exception or return code processing (%*instead*), and so on.

Let's make our estimates for the most typical case of using %*before* and %*after* weaving actions. According to the COCOMO model, we should first estimate the size of the code ($KLOC$) to be developed. We'll estimate the total size of the code, with all the necessary code insertions made "by hand," without applying AOP. Then we'll make the same estimate for the updated code as the result of applying AOP. There can be quite different approaches to AOP with different joint point models and different ways of weaving, but the advantage of our approach to AOP is that we perform weaving at the binary (MSIL) code level after the target program and the aspect are built rather than at the source code level. As the result of weaving, we get the resulting binary assembly but the source code remains unchanged. So, actually, using our approach, *the total size of the source code of the enhanced program equals the sum of the size of its original source plus the size of the aspect source code.*

Let's denote by s the total size of the original application source code. Let's assume that what we should do to make the application trustworthy is to inject some pieces of code before and after all calls of the method P throughout the entire application. Let a be the size of the code to be injected *after* calls of P and b be the size of the code to be injected *before* calls of P. Let c be the number of calls of P in the entire application code. If we perform the required changes manually, without using Aspect.NET, the total size of the enhanced code will be calculated as follows:

$$s^* = s + (a+b)*c$$

If we make the required changes using Aspect.NET, the total size of the enhanced code will be calculated by another formula:

$$s^* = s + a + b$$

since the total size of the aspect that will make the changes is $a + b$.

So, in case we don't apply Aspect.NET, the resulting application code will be larger than the enhanced application code in case we do apply Aspect.NET, by the following amount:

$$\Delta_s = [s + (a+b)c] - (s+a+b) = (a+b)(c-1)$$

For example, suppose that the number of calls of P equals 100 (which may be the case in large software systems). Even if the size of a and b is minimal, just one line of code, Δ_s, will equal 198 lines.

Next, according to the basic COCOMO model, the summary effort E in person-months in case we don't apply Aspect.NET will be calculated as follows:

$$E_{\text{plain}} = a_b \left[\frac{s + (a+b)c}{1000} \right]_b^b$$

and in case we apply Aspect.NET, E will be calculated as

$$E_{\text{Aspect.NET}} = a_b \left(\frac{s+a+b}{1000} \right)_b^b$$

In terms of COCOMO, in the "worst" case, for *embedded software projects* (projects that must be developed under tight hardware, software, and operational constraints), the formulas, with the appropriate values of the coefficients substituted, will look like this:

$$E_{\text{plain}} = 3.6 \left[\frac{s + (a+b)c}{1000} \right]^{1.2}$$

$$E_{\text{Aspect.NET}} = 3.6 \left(\frac{s+a+b}{1000} \right)^{1.2}$$

To take a more concrete example, let's assume that our project is not so large: $s = 1000$ lines of code, $a = 1$ and $b = 1$ (the size of the code insertions is the smallest possible), and $c = 100$. Even in this case, approximately, $E_{\text{plain}} = 4.48$ person-months and $E_{\text{Aspect.NET}} = 3.6$ person-months (i.e., applying Aspect. NET helps project management save about one person-month, one-fourth of the project effort).

Skeptics may argue that developing the aspect requires more effort than developing the ordinary code. Actually, when applying our Aspect.NET with very simple AOP metalanguage, it is *not* so: It is really not difficult to learn that injection of the code C before call of P is coded in the aspect as *%before %call P %action C*. It can be learned in 5 minutes using a suitable aspect code template. Minimal adaptation time is needed to start using Aspect.NET. I can teach users the basics of AOP and the use of Aspect.NET in 1 or 2 hours. It is very important from a psychological viewpoint that to start using Aspect. NET, the users need not leave the comfortable Visual Studio IDE they are accustomed to; they just need to learn how to use the new Aspect.NET framework window, which is also very simple.

An estimate made using the COCOMO model does not take into account another quantitative and qualitative difference: the complexity of the process of searching and modifying all calls of P in the application source code without using Aspect.NET, and the simplicity of performing the same actions using Aspect.NET. If the project team uses Visual Studio but does not use Aspect. NET, it will have to search manually all the required calls in the code, or use UNIX-like tools like *sed* to make "blind" group insertions into the source code. This process is not completely reliable; it is easy to forget some method call or some code insertion. If the team uses Aspect.NET as a Visual Studio add-in, it will use our *Find join points* functionality, which will find all join points (calls of P) automatically and reliably, show all of them in the Aspect.NET window, allow us to visualize and deselect any of them if necessary, and produce the result—the updated assembly binary—in a few seconds instead of spending hours to update the application sources manually.

Since COCOMO is not intended specifically for reliability assessment, here are some concluding qualitative remarks about the reliability of applying Aspect.NET and the resulting updated program. Software reliability depends on its source code size. If the source code is subject to transformations targeted to insert similar scattered pieces of code in many points of the program, then when we are doing it manually, the more insertions we made, the less reliable the code is. There is a risk of missing or corrupting a code injection, proportional to the size of the code inserted ($a + b$, in our terms) and to the number of insertions (c, in our terms). The advantages of AOP and Aspect.NET in this relation are as follows: If we develop a reliable aspect's code once, and apply a reliable, automated, visualizable, and undoable process of code injections, controlled by Aspect.NET and the aspect developed, the resulting code will remain as reliable as the original code.

4.10.2 Assessment of Aspect.NET Using the ICED-T Model

The ICED-T model [138] is intended to assess and test subjective software qualities in a quantitative way by a simple-to-use set of concepts important for users of a software product. The subjective qualities of the product estimated by the ICED-T model are:

- *Intuitive*—Does the use of the product make sense?
- *Consistent*—Does the product operate in a uniform manner?
- *Efficient*—Is the product quick and swift to use?
- *Durable*—Is the product solid and reliable?
- *Thoughtful*—Does the product anticipate the users' needs?

As the result of applying ICED-T to some product, each of the foregoing qualities should be measured using the following quantitative scale:

1	the worst I've ever seen
2	worse than average
3	about the same as other applications I've used
4	better than average
5	the best I've ever seen

The resulting set of quantitative ICED-T assessments [e.g., (4, 5, 3, 5, 4)], together with some comments that have arisen during the ICED-T process, is passed to product management and discussed at a special ICED-T meeting to take concrete measures on improving the product. Although this technique is intended primarily for assessment of the product by its testers and users, we'll attempt to make such an assessment of Aspect.NET, its current state, and our approach to AOP from a user's and tester's viewpoint, relying on extra suggestions on the five ICED-T items provided by Roth [138].

1. *Intuitive.* This product quality means that the product (functioning and user interface) meets user's intuitions in the following respects: whether the GUI is comfortable and intuitive, and whether the result and reaction from the product the user gets meet expectations. In this relation, based on the user's opinion (see Section 3.8.8), we can give ourselves a mark of at least a 4, or hopefully, a 5. Refer to Section 3.8.4 and its illustrations for a review of the process of using Aspect.NET while reading this item. The Aspect.NET framework GUI is designed to be both very simple and intuitive. Its main window, launched automatically as part of Visual Studio.NET GUI, has three tabs: *Aspects, Join points*, and *Visualization*. Logically and simply, Aspect.NET

leads the user to their goal: to weave the aspects to the application and to try the results—updated code. The main buttons—*Find join points* and *Weave Aspects*—are logically enabled or disabled, depending on the status of the user's work. When the join points are found, the user can either visualize them in the source and deselect some of them if needed, or press another button, *Weave aspects*, which becomes enabled. Finally, when the aspects are woven, the user can launch the updated code without exiting from Aspect.NET and Visual Studio and see how the code behavior changed due to aspect weaving. Each stage, including the initial one—choosing an aspect assembly or assemblies—can be rolled back. In particular, it is possible to undo loading one aspect into Aspect.NET and to load the other one using the *Remove selected Aspect.NET assembly* and *Add existing Aspect.NET assemblies* buttons. Moreover, Aspect.NET foresees the user's intuition to get into the same aspect environment during the next launch of the same Visual Studio solution. Aspect. NET saves the aspect configuration in the XML in the *.sln.anf* file in XML format and opens the same aspects automatically when the same Visual Studio solution is opened again.

2. *Consistent.* The ICED-T model offers three levels of assessment of this product quality: *the first, consistency with itself* (calling the same function each time leads to the same results); *the second, consistency with itself throughout the user interface* (all the elements of the product's GUI should follow the same standard); and *the third, consistency with other applications* (compliance to the other related products and with the operating system). I think Aspect. NET is consistent at the highest (i.e., third) level and deserves a rating of 5 for this quality. Here are the justifications. Aspect.NET pursues the traditions and standards of Windows XP and Visual Studio.NET. It uses traditional icons (e.g., aspect opening icon) in a traditional meaning and the actions tied to it. It also supports drag-and-drop of aspect assemblies from the Windows Explorer directly to the *Aspects* tab: Instead of opening an aspect using the appropriate button, the user can drag the aspect assembly (a *.dll* file, located usually in the *bin\debug* subdirectory of the aspect solution) onto the *Aspects* tab of the Aspect.NET main window. Aspect.NET is quite consistent with Visual Studio. NET: It is integrated to Visual Studio as an add-in using a standard mechanism for add-ins. It is started simultaneously to Visual Studio automatically. The Aspect.NET user can create two additional types of Visual Studio projects: *Aspect.NET.ML project* (aspect definition in AOP metalanguage) or *Aspect. NET project* (aspect definition in C# with AOP custom attributes). Both types of projects are supported by code templates. For Aspect.NET.ML projects, the converter from AOP metalanguage to C# is called automatically and implicitly as part of the aspect solution building process. Aspect.NET (unlike AspectJ) uses the common Visual Studio C# compiler rather than its own specific compiler. The resulting assembly after weaving can be used with the help of ordinary .NET framework and Visual Studio tools and features, such as debugging and verifying. All these Aspect.NET consistency qualities allow us to give our

product the highest rating, 5. No other AOP tool for .NET provides the same level of consistency. Although this opinion is subjective, it is based on analyzing a lot of AOP tools for .NET (see Section 3.6). The ICED-T approach is intended for quantifying subjective opinions on software products.

3. *Efficient.* Assessment of this quality is subdivided into *GUI efficiency* and *code efficiency.* GUI efficiency, in its turn, is subdivided into the following parts: *efficiency of using shortcuts and hotkeys, absence of GUI redundancies that could be eliminated,* and a *minimal amount of action and time to navigate.* I think Aspect.NET GUI satisfies all three criteria and deserves the maximal rating of 5. As for hotkeys, to open an aspect, for example, the user can use the traditional combination *Ctrl+O.* There are no redundancies in the Aspect. NET GUI, which is maximally self-explanatory and user-friendly, as can be seen from previous justifications. As for *code efficiency,* to make a proper assessment of Aspect.NET against this criterion, it should be subdivided into two parts: the *efficiency of the code of Aspect.NET itself* and its components: the *weaver,* the converter and *Aspect.NET* framework, and the *efficiency of the code injected by Aspect.NET into the target application.* The efficiency of the Aspect.NET code is acceptable and can be rated as 4, not as 5, since the efficiency of the weaver is not ideal because for handling assemblies and for code injections it uses Phoenix, a very large API that requires substantial time to deploy. But using Phoenix is quite justifiable for implementation reasons; Phoenix provides a comfortable API and a high-level internal representation of the program suitable to implement weaving. An alternative (probably more efficient but surely more limited) could be to "reinvent the wheel" by implementing our own API to handle .NET assemblies, only for the purpose of making the weaver faster. We don't think that would be a proper approach, since one of our principles is maximal integration with the existing Microsoft technologies and tools. The second part of efficiency (most important for users), the efficiency of the resulting assembly after weaving, is one of the key points in our approach and its implementation: We generate *no redundant or slow instrumentation code; the cost of executing each aspect's action is the ordinary cost of a static method call* (see Section 4.11 for more details). So, as compared to AOP tools for .NET, the efficiency of the resulting code after weaving can be rated as 5.

4. *Durable.* Assessment of this quality means a subjective estimate of the product reliability. There are three parts in durability assessment: and *first, how often the product crashes; second, if it happens, how catastrophic are the crashes* (can the user lose data?); and *third, can the product serve for nonordinary use* (like using a hammer to put in screws)? Right now I can estimate Aspect.NET durability by a rating of 4, since there are cases when Aspect.NET crashes (because some types of features are not implemented completely). We are doing our best to improve Aspect.NET in this respect. As for the second durability criterion, it is certainly satisfied. Crashes of weaver due to under-implemented features are not catastrophic. All exceptions are processed by

.NET, and explanatory messages are issued; no crash can force a user to restart the system. As for the third criterion of durability, I think it is just not applicable for Aspect.NET, since it is integrated to Visual Studio and as opposed to aspect weaving, cannot be used for any other functions.

5. *Thoughtful.* This quality means that the product provides users with all they need. This quality of Aspect.NET can be rated as 4 (rather than 5), since we do not yet provide debugging in terms of aspects nor support the relationship between the aspect definition and its UML diagram. There are also a number of other features that we plan to implement (see Section 3.9).

To summarize our self-assessment of Aspect.NET using ICED-T, we can realistically estimate its current status (Aspect.NET 2.1, August 2007) by the following ICED-T rating: (5, 5, 4, 4, 4). We thus have a lot of perspectives for further growth. The ICED-T approach appears to be very helpful.

4.10.3 Assessment of Requirements of Aspect.NET Using the SQFD Model

Software quality function deployment (SQFD) [139] is a prospective requirements engineering model used by many software companies at early stages of the software life cycle. The purpose of SQFD is to obtain quantitative assessment for technical requirements of the product, based on the *voice of the customer*, the customer's major input and deep participation in the assessment process, including subjective quantitative ratings for technical requirements. The scheme of the SQFD model is shown in Figure 4.6.

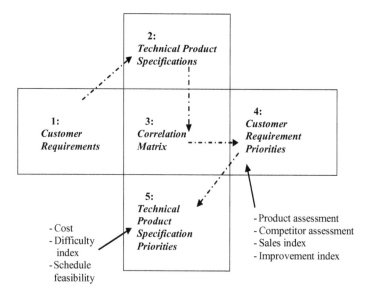

Figure 4.6 *SQFD model.*

The SQFD process consists of five steps:

- *Step 1.* Customers' requirements are formulated and placed on the left *y*-axis of the scheme. Typically, customer requirements are qualitative rather than quantitative, such as "simple GUI."
- *Step 2.* Customer requirements are converted into measurable technical requirements. This step is accomplished by the project team in coordination with the customers. Any customer's requirements can be converted into several technical requirements; for example, the *"simple GUI"* requirement can be converted to the following technical requirements: *"number of icons," "number of tabs,"* and so on.
- *Step 3.* A *correlation matrix* is completed by the customers. It provides a rating (typically, an integer from 0 to 10) to characterize the correlation between each customer requirement obtained at step 1 and each technical requirement obtained at step 2. For example, the *simple GUI* customer requirement will probably get a correlation rating of zero with the technical requirement *mean time between failures*. At this step, many customers may participate, so they should agree on some consensus in their ratings.
- *Step 4. Customer requirement priorities*, numerical values based on customer survey, are determined and placed on the right *y*-axis of the scheme. At this step, customer opinions on the competitive products can be taken into account.
- *Step 5.* Now that all necessary figures are ready, finally, *technical product specification priorities* are calculated. Each of them (let's denote it by *TechPrioj*) is calculated by the following formula:

$$TechPrio_i = CorrCustTech_{1,j} * CustPrio_{1,j} + \cdots + CorrCustTech_{n,j}$$
$$* CustPrio_{n,j}$$

where *CorrCustTech* represent correlation ratings obtained at step 3, and *CustPrio* represents customer requirement priorities determined at step 4.

Finally, the technical product specification priorities are converted into percentage ratings of the importance of each technical requirement.

Using the SQFD technique, we'll make a "postfactum" quantitative assessment of technical requirements to Aspect.NET, although the product has already passed the requirements phase and we don't yet have a real SQFD assessment from customers. So, I will act as both a customer and a developer at the same time.

SQFD Step 1: Customer Requirements   Here is a possible set of customer requirements, based on e-mail correspondence with real customers of Aspect. NET:

- *C1:* use of the new AOP tool for .NET in Visual Studio
- *C2:* simple to learn
- *C3:* similar to AspectJ at least in basic functionality (aspects, join points, advices, weaving)
- *C4:* simple and comfortable GUI
- *C5:* simple language to specify aspects
- *C6:* transparent weaving process
- *C7:* easy to launch the resulting target application
- *C8:* no dramatic application performance decrease as the result of weaving

SQFD Step 2: Converting Customer Requirements into Technical Requirements

- *T1:* There should be integration with Visual Studio (follows directly from C1).
- *T2:* A detailed user's guide should be shipped with the product (from C2).
- *T3:* A set of working samples should be shipped with the product (from C2).
- *T4:* Aspects, join points, advices, and weaving should be implemented (from C3).
- *T5:* GUI should follow the style of Visual Studio (from C4).
- *T6:* GUI should have one window and the minimum possible number of tabs, icons, and buttons (from C4).
- *T7:* The aspect specification language constructs should be simpler than in AspectJ: preferably, looking like annotations (from C5).
- *T8:* There should be visualization of components of the aspect (from C6).
- *T9:* There should be visualization of join points attached to the source of the target application (from C6).
- *T10:* The resulting target application should be launched or offered the user to launch as the next step after weaving (from C7).
- *T11:* Join points model should not be dynamic (from C8).
- *T12:* No redundant "instrumentation" code should be woven to the target application (from C9).

SQFD Steps 3, 4, and 5: Correlation Matrix, Customer Requirement Priorities, and Resulting Technical Requirement Assessment The correlation matrix, together with the customer requirement priorities based on e-mail correspondence with users, is given in Table 4.1, where CP denotes the column with customer requirement priorities and TP denotes the row containing the resulting technical requirement priorities.

TABLE 4.1   SQFD: Correlation Matrix and the Resulting Quantitative Assessment of Requirements

	T1	T2	T3	T4	T5	T6	T7	T8	T9	T10	T11	T12	CP
C1	10	0	0	0	5	0	0	0	0	3	0	0	7
C2	5	10	10	5	6	6	8	8	8	6	5	1	8
C3	0	0	0	10	0	0	5	5	5	0	2	0	7
C4	5	0	0	0	8	9	0	8	8	8	0	0	8
C5	0	0	0	6	0	0	9	0	0	0	2	0	7
C6	3	0	0	0	3	3	4	10	10	4	2	6	6
C7	4	0	0	0	0	0	0	0	0	10	0	0	4
C8	0	0	0	0	0	0	0	0	0	0	8	8	8
TP	184	80	80	152	163	138	186	223	223	197	144	108	

Let's look at the most important figures presented in the table. A correlation value of 10 is given to the technical requirements following directly from customer requirements: T1 from C1; T2 and T3 from C2; T4 from C3; and so on. However, in other situations, the correlation is high enough: for example, T5 and T6, which relate to GUI, correlate highly to C2—simplicity to learn Aspect.NET, since GUI is a tool for everyday use, and its simplicity and following Visual Studio traditions is very important for customers.

All the customer requirement priorities (the CP column) are very important. They were selected using this principle, so it would be difficult to rank their priorities. For users, C2, C3, and C4 are equally important, since the principal requirements for a framework that supports new a programming paradigm should be its simplicity for the use (in all respects) and efficiency of the resulting applications. Nobody will use an awkward and complicated tool that generates very slow code, so we rated C2, C3, and C4 as 8.

As can be seen from the table, the most important technical requirements appeared to be T8, visualization of components of the aspect; T9, visualization of join points attached to the application source (the priority of both is 223); and T10, launching the resulting target application. It may seem surprising, but these concrete requirements appear to be very important for customers. All 12 technical requirements are implemented in Aspect.NET, so it satisfies the SQFD model.

4.11   APPLICATION EFFICIENCY AND PERFORMANCE USING AOP

Poor application efficiency and performance when applying AOP is still a counterarguments that one hears. But is it really so? In general, using AOP can in some cases worsen the application performance, but it depends on the join point model and on the implementation. When investigating how to implement AOP in Aspect.NET, we analyzed many different approaches. Of all techniques of AOP implementation (see Section 3.2), what can really cause dramatic performance decrease is dynamic debugger-style weaving such as runtime checking of all possible weaving conditions before each executable statement. Any of the other approaches to AOP implementation (weaving at the source code level, the intermediate code level, the object code level, at class loading time, and during JIT compilation) can be applied efficiently. Users should pay only for AOP features that they use. For example, if the aspect does not use the join point context functionality (see Section 3.8.6), it should be executed faster than the aspect that uses such a functionality. In general, no redundant instructions of code should be executed for the purpose of using AOP. That was our principle when implementing Aspect. NET.

Subsequent material in this section is organized according to the following plan. We look first at application performance when using Aspect.NET from the outside from the user's viewpoint: Measure the application performance with and without using AOP, and compare the results. Then we'll introspect Aspect.NET: overview the details of weaving implementation in Aspect.NET and analyze why our implementation is really efficient and why using Aspect. NET will not lead to a dramatic performance decrease.

4.11.1   Performance Measurement

By a simple measurement example, let's find out whether or not aspect weaving with Aspect.NET decreases the application execution time (runtime performance). A simple console application that we'll use for time measurements calls a static method 1 million times and outputs the total execution time:

```
using System;
namespace ConsoleApplication1
{
    class Program
    {
      public static void P()
      { }
      static void Main(string[] args)
      {
            DateTime StartTime;
            DateTime EndTime;
            StartTime = DateTime.Now;
            for (int i = 1; i <= 1000000; i++) {
                P();
            }
            EndTime = DateTime.Now;
            if (StartTime.Ticks != 0)
            {
                TimeSpan tsp = EndTime.
                Subtract(StartTime);
```

```
                  Console.WriteLine
                       ("Execution time: {0}
                        milliseconds", tsp.Ticks / 10000);
               }
               Console.WriteLine("Press Enter to exit");
               Console.ReadLine();
           }
       }
}
```

The output of this application on a 1300-GHz 1-GB RAM laptop is as follows:

Execution time: 15 milliseconds

Suppose that we need to enhance this application by calling other static methods: Q before each call of P and R after each call of P. Let's do that using two methods: first, create the resulting application by hand using Visual Studio:

```
using System;
namespace ConsoleApplication2
{
    class Program
    {
        public static void P()
        { }
        public static void Q()
        { }
        public static void R()
        { }
        static void Main(string[] args)
        {
            DateTime StartTime;
            DateTime EndTime;
            StartTime = DateTime.Now;
            for (int i = 1; i <= 1000000; i++)
            {
                Q();
                P();
                R();
            }
            EndTime = DateTime.Now;
            if (StartTime.Ticks != 0)
            {
```

```
              TimeSpan tsp = EndTime.
              Subtract(StartTime);
              Console.WriteLine
                  ("Execution time: {0} milliseconds",
                    tsp.Ticks / 10000);
              }
              Console.WriteLine("Press Enter to exit");
              Console.ReadLine();
        }
      }
}
```

The output of the application will change:

Execution time: 46 milliseconds

Now let's do the same transformation of *ConsoleApplication1* (inject calls of *Q* and *R*) by the aspect *Aspect1* below and see if the execution time of the resulting application after weaving will be longer than the execution time of *ConsoleApplication2*:

```
%aspect Aspect1
using System;
class Aspect1
{
    %rules
    %before %call P
    %action
    public static void Q()
    { }
    %after %call P
    %action
    public static void R()
    { }
}
```

The output of *ConsoleApplication1* after weaving *Aspect1* will be the same as for *ConsoleApplication2*:

Execution time: 46 milliseconds

So we come to a very important conclusion: ***AOP using Aspect.NET costs us nothing at execution time. No redundant instrumentation code is generated by Aspect.NET.***

Execution time after manual insertion of calls of *Q* and *P* and after their injection using Aspect.NET is the same. This is a proof in practice that using Aspect.NET does *not* decrease performance.

4.11.2   Implementation Details and the Woven IL Code

To analyze the resulting MSIL code of *ConsoleApplication1* after weaving and to compare it to the MSIL code of *ConsoleApplication2*, we'll use the *ildasm* utility, part of Microsoft Visual Studio.NET 2005 SDK. The full path to the code (*ildasm.exe*) of this utility is as follows:

```
C:\Program Files\Microsoft Visual Studio 8\SDK\v2.0\Bin
```

where *C:* is the partition where Visual Studio is installed.

Here is the fragment of the MSIL code of the *Main* method of *Console-Application2* implementing the main loop:

```
IL_0007:  ldc.i4.1
IL_0008:  stloc.2
IL_0009:  br.s      IL_0023
IL_000b:  nop
IL_000c:  call      void ConsoleApplication2.Program::Q()
IL_0011:  nop
IL_0012:  call      void ConsoleApplication2.Program::P()
IL_0017:  nop
IL_0018:  call      void ConsoleApplication2.Program::R()
IL_001d:  nop
IL_001e:  nop
IL_001f:  ldloc.2
IL_0020:  ldc.i4.1
IL_0021:  add
IL_0022:  stloc.2
IL_0023:  ldloc.2
IL_0024:  ldc.i4    0xf4240
IL_0029:  cgt
IL_002b:  ldc.i4.0
IL_002c:  ceq
IL_002e:  stloc.s   CS.4.0000
IL_0030:  ldloc.s   CS.4.0000
IL_0032:  brtrue.s  IL_000b
```

The MSIL code corresponding to the sequence of calls of static methods *Q*, *P*, and *R* is shown in bold.

Here is the same fragment of MSIL code of *ConsoleApplication1* after weaving our aspect:

```
IL_0007:  ldc.i4.1
IL_0008:  stloc.2
IL_0009:  br          IL_0024
IL_000e:  nop
IL_000f:  call        void [Aspect1]Aspect1.Aspect1::Q()
IL_0014:  call        void ConsoleApplication1.Program::P()
IL_0019:  call        void [Aspect1]Aspect1.Aspect1::R()
IL_001e:  nop
IL_001f:  nop
IL_0020:  ldloc.2
IL_0021:  ldc.i4.1
IL_0022:  add
IL_0023:  stloc.2
IL_0024:  ldloc.2
IL_0025:  ldc.i4      0xf4240
IL_002a:  cgt
IL_002c:  ldc.i4.0
IL_002d:  ceq
IL_002f:  stloc.s     V_4
IL_0031:  ldloc.s     V_4
IL_0033:  brtrue      IL_000e
```

There is only one difference between these two MSIL code fragments: Instead of calls of static methods *ConsoleApplication2.Program.Q* and *ConsoleApplication2.Program.R*, in the code of ~*ConsoleApplication1* (*Console-Application1* after weaving Aspect1) there are calls of the same methods but included in the *Aspect1* aspect assembly: *Aspect1.Aspect1.Q* and *Aspect1. Aspect1.R*. Their execution time is the same. Note that the latter fragment of MSIL code is generated by Phoenix [7], and because of that fact, its size is even less than the original one: The number of *nop*'s decreased. You already know from Chapter 3 that the Aspect.NET weaver uses Phoenix for all weaving operations. Actually, it means that the weaver uses the *Phoenix PE reader* component that converts the PE files of the target assembly and the aspect assembly into *Phoenix HIR*: high-level intermediate representation. Then, weaving is made at the Phoenix HIR level, and the resulting MSIL code is generated by Phoenix using the HIR of the target assembly.

4.11.3 Another Performance Measurement Example

Now let's make the time measurement example above a bit more complicated. Suppose that we need to add a simple logging functionality, so that the *Q* and *R* methods, to be called before and after the *P* method calls, should issue the messages *"Hello P"* and *"Bye P"* accordingly. Let's reduce the number of iterations to 1000 and add an argument to *P*. Here is the updated fragment of the source of *ConsoleApplication1*:

```
public static void P(int x)
{ }
static void Main(string[] args)
{
      ...
      for (int i = 1; i <= 1000; i++)
      {
          P(1);
      }
  ...
}
```

and here is the updated fragment of the source of *ConsoleApplication2*:

```
public static void Q()
{
    Console.WriteLine("Hello P");
}
public static void R()
{
    Console.WriteLine("Bye P");
}
static void Main(string[] args)
{
      ...
      StartTime = DateTime.Now;
      for (int i = 1; i <= 1000; i++)
      {
          Q();
          P(1);
          R();
      }
  ...
}
```

You will have noticed that *Q* and *R* are printing out their messages in a straightforward way, and the name of *P* is included in their message strings.

As for the *Aspect1* aspect, let's make it more general. Let's use the *%TargetMemberInfo* functionality (see Section 3.8.6) to extract the name of *P*. Here is the full source of the updated *Aspect1*:

```
%aspect Aspect1
using System;
using System.Reflection;
```

```
class Aspect1
{
    %rules
    %before %call P
    %action
    public static void Q()
    {
        Console.WriteLine("Hello " + %TargetMemberInfo.
        Name);
    }
    %after %call P
    %action
    public static void R()
    {
        Console.WriteLine("Bye " + %TargetMemberInfo.
        Name);
    }
}
```

Thus, we would like to determine the execution time cost of using an aspect with *%TargetMemberInfo* (based on reflection) for extracting the name of the target method in the aspect actions woven before and after the call of *P*, as compared to straightforward insertion of logging without using reflection.

Surprising as it may seem, we got the following results: The execution time of *ConsoleApplication2* appeared to be 484 milliseconds, whereas the execution time of *~ConsoleApplication1* (*ConsoleApplication1* after weaving our aspect) is 421 milliseconds! So the performance of an Aspect.NET aspect using reflection and *%TargetMemberInfo* is better than the performance of nonreflective, less general, straightforward application doing the same.

To be more specific about implementation, let's examine the cost of an aspect using target join point analysis functionality such as *%TargetMember-Info*, as compared to the aspect that does not use it. To understand it, we'll check some more details of our implementation using MSIL code fragments obtained by *ildasm*. Here is the MSIL code fragment of *ConsoleApplication2* implementing the sequence of calls *Q, P(1)*, and *R*:

```
IL_000c: call     void ConsoleApplication2.Program::Q()
IL_0011: nop
IL_0012: ldc.i4.1
IL_0013: call     void ConsoleApplication2.Program::
P(int32)
IL_0018: nop
IL_0019: call     void ConsoleApplication2.Program::R()
IL_001e: nop
```

and here is the corresponding fragment of ~*ConsoleApplication1* (after weaving the aspect):

```
IL_000f: ldtoken  method void ConsoleApplication1.
Program::P(int32)
IL_0014: call void
         [AspectDotNet]AspectDotNet.Aspect::
         InternalSetTargetMethodHandle
         (valuetype [mscorlib]System.
         RuntimeMethodHandle)
IL_0019: call     void [Aspect1]Aspect1.Aspect1::Q()
IL_001e: ldc.i4.1
IL_001f: call     void ConsoleApplication1.Program::
P(int32)
IL_0024: ldtoken  method void ConsoleApplication1.
Program::P(int32)
IL_0029: call void
         [AspectDotNet]AspectDotNet.Aspect::
         InternalSetTargetMethodHandle
         (valuetype [mscorlib]System.
         RuntimeMethodHandle)
IL_002e: call     void [Aspect1]Aspect1.Aspect1::R()
```

This MSIL code fragment needs some comment. The *ldtoken* instruction loads onto the stack the *metadata token* of *P*: the reference to *P*'s metadata, used by the aspect's *InternalSetTargetMethodHandle* static method to extract the reflective information about *P* of type *System.Reflection.MethodInfo*. The fragments in bold illustrate the cost of using *%TargetMemberInfo*. They are added to the aspect's woven code, in contrast to the simpler version without logging. They precede the calls of aspects's actions *Q* and *R*. As you know from Section 3.8, the source code of the aspect is converted from Aspect.NET. ML into the pure C# source code of a class that inherits from Aspect.NET's service class *AspectDotNet.Aspect*. The *Aspect* class contains a number of static fields used for passing information about the context of the join point from the target application code to the aspect code. The *InternalSetTargetMethod-Handle* static method of the *Aspect* class is called to store reflective information on *P* in a static property of the *Aspect* class, which is extracted by the aspect's actions. Such an approach saves a lot of execution time, since Aspect. NET does not create a separate object for each join point. The scheme of passing information from the target application to the aspect's actions is shown in Figure 4.7.

If the application obtained as the result of weaving such an aspect is intended for use in a multithreaded environment, it is easy to add to aspect's actions some synchronization calls, such as *System.Threading.Monitor.Enter* and *Exit*

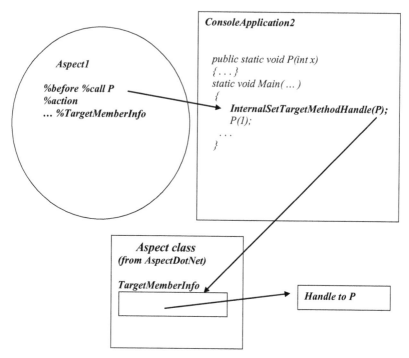

Figure 4.7 *Passing information on join point context from target application to aspect's actions.*

before and after using join point analysis features such as *%TargetMember-Info*. That will guarantee MT safety of the updated application.

To summarize this section, we have proven the efficiency of application runtime performance due to using Aspect.NET and analyzed some important details of aspect implementation in Aspect.NET.

4.12   AOP AND AGILE PROGRAMMING APPROACHES

AOP has a lot of similarity to *agile software development methods* [140]: in particular, *Extreme Programming (XP)* [141] and *Scrum* [142]. The basic idea of agile methods is to develop software in short *iterations* (one or several weeks each), each of them resulting in software delivery. The main purposes of agile methods are *adaptation* to changing requirements to the product, and *quick delivery*, as opposed to using a traditional waterfall method (with its longer phases of requirements, specification, design, implementation, and testing). In a sense, from the viewpoint of a software process organization, using AOP can also be considered as one of the agile techniques. I'll show how AOP can be used to satisfy both purposes.

Let's illustrate the point by an example. Suppose that in view of the current popularity of the TWC approach, or as a forced measure to struggle with security attacks, the customers and management of an existing large software project, in the middle or at the end of its long waterfall-based development, decided to implement security features in the product. A similar situation is described by Howard and LeBlanc [27]: Microsoft had to make a "security push" in the newly developed version of Windows. How can it be done? Traditional waterfall-based techniques prescribe doing that as a long sequence of the five phases mentioned above. However, customers press project management because they experience security flaws, and management presses the development team. Both require quick implementation of at least basic security functionality (e.g., role-based security). If during the initial phase of implementing security it is decided to elicit *all* security requirements and subject them to *all* five phases of the waterfall life cycle, it would be too long. The development team is forced to make the development process "agile." So the most suitable decision in such a situation is to apply *iterative, agile* techniques. The security requirements should be prioritized, and an *iterative* security implementation plan (or *backlog*, in terms of Scrum) should be made. According to this plan, each security feature will be implemented in the product in the decreasing order of priorities. Each iteration implementing one security feature will last one or several weeks and can be organized as *scrum* and *sprint*, speaking in Scrum terms.

But we do remember that implementation of any security feature, as a cross-cutting concern, is scattered through the source code of the application. So a lot of questions arise in relation to the quantitative assessment of the results of each iteration: *How many lines of code are developed in this iteration? How many software components are developed? Can I take a look at the source code the team has developed? Show me the concrete result for this week! How can I estimate funding the iteration effort?* Those questions are difficult to answer if no special technique is used to modularize the result of each iteration. If the project lead answers the manager by saying: "please take a look into the following 156 classes, track the latest security code insertions after calls of the following 50 methods, and sum the total number of lines developed," the reaction may be very negative.

A possible solution to the problem, as you can guess, is to use AOP. Each iteration is targeted to developing an *aspect* or *aspect library* implementing the required (security) feature in the product code. According to agile tradition, an iteration starts with a meeting to discuss the implementation. Then the microphases of requirements, specification, design, implementation, and testing of the aspect to implement the functionality selected are "sprinted" during one or several weeks. The result the customer and the management can see is a new modular component—aspect. It can be "fingered" (without the need of looking for any scattered code fragments in 156 modules) as some definite working result of the iteration submitted to the customer, and can be measured easily in terms of KLOC, cyclomatic complexity, and so on, so the effort to develop the aspect can be estimated quickly. Due to AOP weaving mechanisms that enable automatic aspect code injection to the product, testing the aspect can proceed in the real environment of the entire workable software product. Let's refer to such software process technique as *AOP-based agile development*.

The specifics and advantages of *AOP-based agile development using Aspect. NET* (in its integration with Visual Studio) are as follows:

- At the specification and design miniphases of the aspect development, the development team can use the simple Aspect.NET.ML language to design an appropriate *aspect stub* implementation in the following style:

```
%aspect RoleBasedSecurity
using System;
using System.Security;
public class RoleBasedSecurity {
%data
// delayed up to the coding mini-phase
%rules
%before %call M1
%action
    public static void SecurityCheck()
    { Console.WriteLine("Security check before M");
    }
// stub: implementation is delayed up to coding
mini-phase
. . .
}
```

The aspect stub can be built and woven, to test the correctness of all its action injections. Later, at the coding miniphase, the action stubs will be replaced by real implementations.
- All aspect actions and the weaving rule are visualized when opening the aspect in Aspect.NET.
- All join points can be visualized and deselected prior to weaving if needed, using Aspect.NET framework features (see Section 3.8).
- All Visual Studio features (highlighting, refactoring, debugging, automatic generation of unit tests, etc.) can be used at all microphases.

Thus, the entire task of adding some complicated cross-cutting functionality such as security can be solved incrementally using AOP-based agile development and Aspect.NET, as described. Using AOP, due to delivering "fingerable" and tested modular results at each iteration, can further increase customers' and higher management's trust of agile techniques in general. On the other hand, using AOP for agile development will also make the development team disciplined and thinking systematically about product updates.

As for further possible product adaptation after big changes have been made such as adding more or correcting some of the existing security checks, they will be much more comfortably, reliably, and quickly expressed in terms of aspects (e.g., make one change in the code of one action of one aspect—it takes just a few minutes) than when applying agile techniques without AOP (e.g., make the same change in the scattered code fragments located in 156 methods—that would take hours or days of working time).

AOP can be used with *Extreme Programming* (*XP*) [141]. The basic principles of XP are:

- *Communication* of system requirements to all developers of the system; *collective code ownership; paired programming*
- *Simplicity* of the initial design and implementation (with subsequent *refactoring* to enhance the functionality if needed)
- *Feedback* from the system, the customers, and the developers; *test-driven development*
- *Courage* to refactor the code when necessary
- *Respect* for each other by team members, making safe nonbreaking changes only

1. *Communication and respect.* AOP can be used with XP as follows. Each developer (or pair of developers, if pair programming is used) is responsible for some cross-cutting functionality to be implemented as an aspect. The team leader and the team discuss the AOP structure of the system and the manner of weaving the aspects to get an entire working system. System requirements can be distributed throughout the team as aspect stubs that at the initial stage or at any other moment, can be discussed, criticized by anybody, and updated upon mutual agreement. As for aspect implementation, according to the respect principle, nobody can modify an aspect developed by another programmer without prior discussion with the aspect developer. That will enable really safe and modular implementation of the collective code ownership principle. If developer A remembers, say, that the developer B is the best expert on the security *aspect*, A will consult B before changing security functionality in B's aspect, or, better, suggest the changes to B, and it will be B's final decision whether or not to include the changes.

2. *Simplicity and courage.* Incremental development is quite suitable for applying AOP. The simplest version of the new feature implementation can be developed as an aspect. It will help us to correctly determine the join points at which to inject fragments of the new feature implementation. If there is a need to enhance the feature implementation, it is likely to be done only by modifying the aspect's actions only. The scheme of weaving the aspect will remain the same; it means that the XP team will not have to do big group

changes in the entire code of the product, and all changes will be localized in the aspect.

3. *Feedback and test-driven development.* If a new functionality is designed, a new aspect should be developed. Prior to that, *acceptance tests* are developed for the functionality aspect. Implementation of the aspect is driven by its acceptance tests. Customers who are participating in the development process, according to XP principles, will also think about system development and enhancement in terms of aspects.

All the principles of using AOP with agile programming approaches suggested above need to be proved in the practice of real projects.

4.13 SUMMARY

Our aim in this chapter has been to demonstrate to readers that AOP with Aspect.NET is an adequate, suitable, comfortable, and reliable tool for developing trustworthy software or to make the existing legacy code more trustworthy. We've considered the *pillars of TWC—security, privacy, reliability,* and *business integrity*—and many of the typical tasks and uses related to these categories where trustworthy programming is especially valuable. Using AOP with Aspect.NET helps us to solve the task in a modular, comfortable, and efficient way. Based on the examples and assessments, we can now really feel that aspect-oriented programming was "born" for trustworthy software development and that the two approaches have a generic relationship.

In this chapter, *Aspect.NET is* proven to be *efficient* in the following respects:

- Applying AOP with Aspect.NET improves the productivity of software developers based on an estimate using the COCOMO model.
- The runtime performance of applications after aspect weaving by Aspect. NET is *not worse*, and in some examples it is even *better* than the performance of the same application updated by hand; no byte of redundant "instrumentation code" is woven or executed.
- Aspect.NET design and implementation are highly rated in terms of the popular ICED-T and SQFD models.
- Aspect.NET can be used effectively with popular software design and development techniques: *design by contract* and *agile programming* (in particular, *extreme programming* and *scrum*).
- Aspect.NET has proven to be usable for enhancement of large commercial code whose sources are, for confidentiality reasons, not accessible.

Let's again summarize *the convenience features of Aspect.NET.* They are difficult to measure but can really save a lot of working time for product development teams:

- Integration to Visual Studio.NET 2005 as an add-in
- Using special types of AOP projects: *Aspect.NET.ML project* and *Aspect. NET project*
- Simplicity of the metalanguage of AOP annotations: Aspect.NET.ML
- Visualization of aspects and their components: weaving conditions, actions, and user-defined descriptions (comments) to the aspect and each of its actions.
- Visualization of possible join points before actual weaving.
- The ability for users to control the process of weaving: visualizing possible join points in the application source, and deselecting any of them if not appropriate
- The ability to launch the updated target application right after weaving by just pressing a button
- Saving and restoring the context of open aspects for the target application on re-starting the same solution
- The ability to delete aspects from the working configuration and to load or reload all or selected aspects

So, based on the principles, results, practical examples, and estimates of the approach provided in Chapter 3 and this chapter, and on positive experience with Aspect.NET use, it appears to be time to start using Aspect.NET as the basis for wider application of AOP for .NET for a variety of commercial software projects. This process has just begun. We appreciate that our AOP framework is used in 16 countries. But we'd like its commercial use to be much wider. We are working to implement what is lacking in Aspect.NET to be even more convenient for users: new types of join points, debugging in terms of aspects, aspect libraries for various problem domains, aspect modeling features using UML, and so on. But even in the current state, Aspect.NET is already a quite usable and efficient industrial-level AOP framework.

Successful use of Aspect.NET in commercial projects will be one more proof of the commercial applicability of AOP for trustworthy software development. Using Aspect.NET as an inherent part of Visual Studio.NET should allow users to make AOP a ubiquitous technology and to confirm its usability for TWC and for other tasks.

5

Teaching TWC and AOP

This chapter deviates from preceding chapters in being devoted to teaching TWC, AOP, and related IT disciplines. I have included a teaching chapter in a research book because both TWC and AOP are popular new approaches to software development, and to widen their industrial use, it is necessary to develop principles and courses for university students. Currently, teaching of TWC and AOP is not as widespread as, for example, teaching operating systems or networking, although elements of TWC and AOP are included into many university courses. This chapter covers my *ERATO* teaching paradigm [9] and its enhancement for trustworthy computing, *T-ERATO* [8]. Next, we look at two teaching projects: *SPBU.NET* [9], development of curricula for teaching .NET, compilers, software engineering, and OS; and *TrustSPBU.NET* [8], enhancement of SPBU.NET curricula by trustworthy computing content. Both projects have been supported by Microsoft Research, and their results (materials for university courses and seminars [143–149] are available at the Microsoft Research Academic Web site. Next, we consider in more detail the principles of teaching IT disciplines related to TWC and AOP that I teach at St. Petersburg University: *trustworthy software engineering (including AOP), .NET and C#, Java technology, operating systems and networking, and compilers.* When considering each course or seminar, I emphasize its relation to TWC, students' reactions, opinions, and activity, and the subjects most interesting and most difficult for students to understand. The chapter summary analyzes pervasive trustworthy programming principles that now penetrate any IT discipline and

Using Aspect-Oriented Programming for Trustworthy Software Development,
By Vladimir O. Safonov
Copyright © 2008 John Wiley & Sons, Inc.

its teaching. Although the material of this chapter is closely related to that of earlier chapters, it can also be used separately, as an educational aid for both IT students and IT teachers.

In this chapter I mention a number of classical academic papers. Although these papers and their authors deserve our deepest respect, I omit explicit reference to them so as not to overload the book's list of references. Readers can find those references in my course curricula [143–149], which should be considered an inherent part of this chapter.

5.1 THE ERATO TEACHING PARADIGM AND THE SPBU.NET PROJECT

This section is devoted to my SPBU.NET educational project, supported by Microsoft Research and carried out in 2004–2005. The goal of the project was to develop a complex of educational materials on Microsoft.NET, compilers, and software engineering and operating systems, based on my teaching, research, and development experience at St. Petersburg University. The results of the project, course and seminar curricula [143–148] are uploaded to the Microsoft Developer's Network Academic Alliance Curriculum Repository (MSDNAA CR) Web site in the form of presentations and lecture notes on four courses (in English) and presentations to two seminars. The results have attracted wide attention and I have received a lot of invaluable feedback from many countries.

In this section I describe the ERATO teaching paradigm I've been using in my university teaching work, the contents of the courses and seminars included into the SPBU.NET project, and the experience gained from teaching these courses and seminars (especially, what was most interesting and most difficult for students). Most current tutorials and other curricula on various domains of IT tend to represent new techniques developed by commercial companies. My viewpoint regarding software engineering today is that we are now in a period of *commercialization* of fundamental ideas (OOP, modular and component programming, exception handling, etc.), implemented by commercial systems and used by millions of customers, whose foundations were laid down in the 1960s and 1970s.

5.1.1 The ERATO Teaching Paradigm

ERATO is an acronym for *experience–retrospective–analysis–theory–oncoming perspectives*. Erato is also the name of the muse of romantic poetry in antique Greek mythology. Her sculpture, erected in a beautiful park in Pavlovsk near St. Petersburg, is shown in Figure 5.1.

Experience   As an inherent part of my courses, I describe my long-term commercial and research software development experience. From 1977 to

Figure 5.1   *Erato, the antique muse of romantic poetry.*

1990, I was the project leader of a team that developed eight compilers and interpreters for Elbrus computers [11], used in many Soviet and Russian companies. From 1992 to 2002 I was the manager and technical leader of Sun projects performed at St. Petersburg University in the areas of compilers, tools, and Java technology. Since 2002, I have worked with Microsoft Research on the Aspect.NET project described in Chapters 3 and 4. In 2003 my team and I became the first academic users of Microsoft Phoenix [7] within the framework of the Phoenix Academic Program. Since 2006 we have been working for Sun on a research agreement related to developing the NetBeans C/C++ Pack open-source project. From 2003 to 2006 we have worked with the Panasonic Princeton Research Laboratory on implementing Java API for instant messaging and presence.

Such activities attract a lot of student interest. Some students participate in these projects under my supervision, and experience helps to better understand concepts and principles being taught. Another important factor is the *practical experience acquired by students* themselves in parallel to their studies. Students should feel not only that they are learning new software technologies but should also feel themselves to be part of a worldwide team creating these technologies. This *factor of personal participation* gives students more courage and even more desire to learn new technologies well and to attempt them in practice. That is why personal participation of undergraduate and graduate students in projects such as Aspect.NET is so important.

Retrospective   As an important part of my classes, I consider the historical background of each topic being taught since its origin, for a deeper understanding of fundamental concepts by students. For example, I consider the concepts of *concurrency* and *multithreading* since Dijkstra's pioneering works on semaphores in the 1960s and Hoare's fundamental papers on monitors in the 1970s. As another example, I consider the concept of *exception* since the invention of the signal construct by Liskov in the CLU language in the early 1970s. It is important to emphasize that as a result of such a retrospective approach, students themselves (even without the teacher's recommendations) start an analytic overview of historical background of the topic as part of their seminar presentations. This is very helpful for students in acquiring more thorough understanding of the material as compared simply to "surfing" the latest achievements in the area.

Analysis   In my courses I present critical and comparative analyses of the most important concepts and technologies while teaching them. For example, I analyze the Microsoft.NET platform compared to the competitive Java platform, and explain the fundamental reasons why .NET is more general, open-style, and prospective. I explain to students that the authors of .NET have taken the best of Java, since .NET was developed about five years later. On the other hand, I show students that .NET technologies have a lot of backward influence on Java. In particular, I analyze the decision by Java technology authors to introduce *boxing, unboxing*, and *annotations* (or *metadata*) to Java 1.5, and C# style *properties* to the developing Java 1.7 language. In this way students can better understand the dialectic nature of software engineering progress.

Theory   In my classes I provide theoretical definitions, justifications, basic theorems, and known theoretical issues relevant to the topic being taught. In particular, when teaching the concept of data type, I review the techniques of formal specification of abstract data types: Hoare's theoretical papers on data types published in the 1960s and 1970s; Scott's papers on type theory based on lattices; and papers of the 1970s on initial and final algebra semantics of abstract data types by the ADJ group, resulting in algebraic data type specification languages OBJ, CafeOBJ, and SDL. Adding analysis of theoretical results to pragmatic courses and their relation to practice leads to deeper learning.

Oncoming Perspectives   In the summary part of my classes, I explain my and my academic colleagues' vision of future progress in the topic area. For example, I explain to students the use of Microsoft.NET as a scalable and trustworthy software development platform in coming years, I emphasize the growing role of AOP and its industrial potential, and I highlight the growing role of knowledge engineering technologies and their integration to software engineering technologies.

5.1.2 The SPBU.NET Project

This section covers the principles and specifics of the curriculum structure provided as the result of the SPBU.NET project and the specific details and issues related to each item. For each result of the SPBU.NET project [143–148] uploaded to the MSDNAA CR Web site, I provide a README file explaining the structure of the corresponding course (or seminar) archive. For each course [143–146] I provide *lecture presentations* and *lecture notes*. Each set of lecture notes is related to slides of the corresponding lecture presentation. The lecture notes can be used as the basis for teaching the lecture. Also, a practical home task (e.g., "implement this method/algorithm in C#") is provided for each lecture based on the lecture notes.

Each seminar [147,148] curriculum includes the best student presentations made at a seminar on the subject in recent years. To get credit at my seminar, each student gives a talk (one or two academic hours long) on one topic I offered or on any related topic selected and offered by the student. For any student's talk, I require the use of a PowerPoint presentation (preferably in English) which includes not only theoretical results and definitions, but also a set of understandable and workable code examples that the student develops and debugs before the seminar. Thus, students learn to make good presentations and to catch quickly the essence of a new topic that is both interesting and complicated.

Next, we provide a brief overview of the four courses and two seminars included in the SPBU.NET projects. More details are provided in Sections 5.3 to 5.7.

Microsoft.NET Architecture and C# Language Course   This is an undergraduate course [143] for fourth-year students that I started teaching in 2003 as one of the first in Russia on this new subject. According to my teaching principles, in this course I consider .NET not just per se, but from a historical perspective. In the history of computing, long before .NET there have appeared a number of approaches to supporting multilanguage programming whose foundations were somewhat similar to .NET, although they supported an older, procedural paradigm. For example, the legendary Burroughs 5000/6700/7700 series of computers of the 1960s and 1970s, and the Russian Elbrus family of computers [11], were based on principles of hardware support of basic mechanisms of programming languages and their implementation. They used postfix notation as their instruction set. But in Elbrus these postfix instructions were compiled "on the fly" by hardware in ordinary three-address code. Speaking in modern terms, it was a kind of hardware-supported just-in-time compilation (implemented in the 1970s). There was also an analog of metadata in Elbrus, referred to as object code file extension: actually, program structure and type-related information in some treelike common language-agnostic format, used by the common runtime of that system.

Other elements of .NET are also considered in the course from a general, analytical, and retrospective viewpoint. For example, when teaching the .NET Common Type System (CTS), I thoroughly review the most widely known type systems and approaches in classical languages, such as Pascal, C, C++, Simula 67, and others. I show students that CTS is a reasonable generalization of most of the well-known type systems known long before .NET. The course covers all main topics of Microsoft.NET: CLI, CTS, CLS, CLR, assemblies and strong names, .NET languages and tools, security, Web services, remoting, and so on (see Section 5.4 for more details).

It is interesting to analyze the most difficult .NET topics for student to understand, and which .NET topics attract the most student attention. The most difficult themes for students are metadata and security. Students do not always realize the role of metadata in .NET as language-agnostic information on the types defined and used in an assembly. To explain it more clearly, historical analogies and the role of types on all stages of computation, including runtime are used. As for security, students don't always understand various types of .NET security, especially role-based security, evidence-based security, and security stack walks. To better explain these concepts, historical analogies and practical examples are used.

The topics most interesting to students appear to be the XML Web Services and security. Students understand their importance and are happy to provide examples and to participate in deep analytical discussion of these subjects.

Compiler Development Course This is a course [144] for graduate (in Russian practice, fifth-year) students. The specifics of this compiler course, compared to many others, are as follows. I teach my own efficient compiler development techniques developed and implemented in commercial compilers (in particular, in the Sun Pascal compiler for SPARC architecture in 1990s). Some of them were presented in four U.S. patents [150–153] in the 1990s. The preparation, filing, and issuing of these patents was supported by Sun Microsystems. Most of the methods relate to semantic analysis: efficient lookup and semantic attributes (in particular, type) evaluation. Although in the course I refer to classical compiler textbooks by Gries, Aho, Sethi, and Ullman, I show students that in some cases it is quite possible to offer much more efficient techniques than those described in classical books. For example, I explain how my principle of storing and updating the reference to the *current effective definition(s)* for an identifier from the hashed identifiers table helps to make semantic analysis much more efficient and to avoid linear search in most cases. Another very important topic in the course is the concept of data type and related efficient algorithms of type checking for languages with name identity and structural identity of types. As one of the first users of Microsoft Phoenix, I also teach students the basics of Phoenix, an API for developing optimizing and multitargeting compiler back ends [7] by Microsoft. Based on my extensive experience with .NET and Java, in the course I explain to students both the specifics of compiler development for .NET and the principles of Java implementation.

In the course, students learn both classical and modern concepts of compiling, including lexical analysis, top-down and bottom-up parsing, semantic analysis, optimization, code generation, runtime and its relation to OS, and just-in-time and ahead-of-time compilation. Students' growing interest in the subject of compiler development appears due to the spread of .NET, with its fundamentals of multilanguage programming and interoperability. The topics most interesting to students appear to be parsing, optimization, and code generation for RISC, VLIW, EPIC, and multicore hardware architectures. For more details, see Section 5.7.

Software Engineering Course   This is a course [145] for graduate (fifth-year) students. A major part of the course is devoted to a detailed review of *programming paradigms*: both the classical ones, such as structured programming, modular programming, abstract data types (including the CLU language, which laid the foundation for many modern ideas), object-oriented programming, and modern paradigms, especially aspect-oriented programming (AOP). In this course, I explain to students major concepts of software engineering, from Dijkstra's structured programming and Brooks' chief programmer's team, to the modern paradigm of AOP: in particular, principles of the Aspect.NET project and framework described in Chapters 3 and 4. Another major part of the course is concerned with detailed analysis of approaches and techniques used at various stages of the *software life cycle*: requirements, specifications, design, implementation, testing, and maintenance. The material is based on my experience in leading commercial and research software projects for major companies, including Microsoft and Sun. The topics most interesting to students appear to be abstract data types, aspect-oriented programming, and software testing.

Operating Systems and Networking Course   This is a course [146] for undergraduate (second-year) students. It explains basic ideas, principles, and algorithms used for resource allocation, synchronization, networking protocols, and so on. The material is based on my experience using a lot of operating systems for mainframe (IBM 360 and Russian BESM-6) computers, minicomputers (PDP-11 and its Russian clones), supercomputers (Russian Elbrus [11]), personal computers (MS-DOS, all versions of Windows, and Linux), and SPARC workstations (Solaris). Special attention is paid to such fundamentals as multithreading. In particular, it is interesting to note that a kind of multithreading with semaphore-based synchronization was implemented and used in Elbrus in the late 1970s and early 1980s. The concept of process in Elbrus corresponds semantically to the newer concept of lightweight processes found in many contemporary operating systems. A lot of material in the course is illustrated by examples from Windows 2000/XP/Embedded and Solaris. As for networking technologies, both fundamental concepts (e.g., ISO/OSI network layers model) and new ones (e.g., IEEE 802.11x wireless networking, instant messaging, and presence, GPRS) are considered. A review of computer and networking hardware and its parts is included. The topics most interesting to students appear to be multithreading, synchronization, semaphores and monitors, memory management, and paging.

Programming for the Microsoft.NET Seminar This is an undergraduate seminar [147] for fourth-year students. Many of them have provided good presentations with working code examples that initiated agile discussions during the seminar. Some students made presentations on commercial projects based on .NET because in Russia at present, most students have to work beginning with their first year at the university, in parallel with their education, to support themselves and their families. This is very helpful from the viewpoint of software engineering practice. Some students even present their own tools for .NET, such as an experimental tool to check automatically for an assembly's compliance with CLS.

Compiler Development Seminar This is a seminar [148] for graduate (fifth-year) students. Most of them have shown a deep understanding of compiler topics and good practical experience in the compiler area. One of the most popular topics at the seminar appeared to be ANTLR (Another Tool for Language Recognition), a widely used compiler development tool used as the basis for a lot of research and development compiler projects, including Sun's NetBeans project. Very interesting contributions were also made on optimization, code generation, and on compiling for VLIW and EPIC architectures.

5.2 THE T-ERATO TEACHING PARADIGM AND THE TrustSPBU.NET PROJECT

In this section I describe the trustworthy ERATO (T-ERATO) teaching paradigm [8], an updated version of the ERATO paradigm [9] used as the basis of the SPBU.NET project. Then I discuss my experience and the results of the TrustSPBU.NET [8] project, and outline perspectives of their application, enhancement, and use.

5.2.1 The T-ERATO Teaching Paradigm

The main idea behind the T-ERATO teaching paradigm is similar that of Microsoft's trustworthy computing initiative (see Section 2.2), which inspired my project: *trustworthy computing considerations should be pervasive*, always taken into account at each stage and item of software design, development, use, and teaching. According to the T-ERATO paradigm, when teaching according to the ERATO paradigm (see Section 5.1.1) I consider the TWC issues related to the subject being taught. Below I refer to the parts of the

T-ERATO paradigm as *T-experience, T-retrospective, T-analysis, T-theory*, and *T-oncoming perspectives*.

T-Experience   I consider the experience of using the subject from the TWC viewpoint: what type of security, reliability, privacy, and business integrity issues software developers come across, how to avoid them, how to enhance the product to mitigate attacks, how to make product use more reliable, and how to ensure the privacy of the data it uses. A common example I use in my teaching is *e-mail*, which is the source of many TWC issues. I explain the history of e-mail use and development since the 1970s; remind students of the types of actions that can be dangerous and should be avoided (e.g., opening some attachments and how network worms are spread via e-mail by scanning address books; consider Microsoft's security patches for Outlook; make a critical review of spam filters (which often filter out important e-mails instead of spam); and provide recommendations on reasonable and secure e-mail content and use.

T-Retrospective   I overview the history of the subject, starting with the origin and papers by classicists in the field, and consider the evolution of TWC vision, approaches, and implementations in the area. For example, when teaching the concept of types and typing, as related to .NET and OS courses, I emphasize that John von Neumann's computer architecture model of the 1940s was not quite type-safe, then explain how the principles of tagged architecture (hardware-implemented dynamic typing) of the 1960s and 1970s implemented by Burroughs machines and their analogs worked to protect data and memory and to make computations more secure, and finally, consider the modern software development platforms: .NET and Java and their type-safe computational models as new cross-platform and software-implemented "incarnations" of safe dynamic typing ideas of the past.

T-Analysis   When doing comparative analysis of contemporary operating systems and application development platforms, I compare their security, privacy, and reliability foundations. In particular, I compare different security approaches in classical UNIX (tied to user accounts and the concept of "user/user-group/rest-of-the-world" subdivision) and in .NET (tied to assemblies, evidence about them, with an opportunity to configure security policy, based on an extensible set of user roles, XML security configuration files, and security attributes). Thus, students can deduce which model is more flexible but will be able to use both models in appropriate environments in the correct way when needed.

T-Theory   I consider theoretical models and justifications for software engineering techniques related to security, privacy, and reliability. I also consider the evolution of those theoretical concepts. A good example is the concept of software *module*, which plays a fundamental role in TWC, since all security checks, design-by-contract assertions, and so on, can be tied to modules and their calls. First, I explain the classical approach to modularity by Myers and the concepts of module coupling and cohesion. Next, I emphasize that the complexity of software is growing and there is an everyday need for systematic cross-cutting software updates (e.g., adding security checks or MT safety features to legacy code) For that reason, the classical approach to modularity should be extended to cover novel concepts and technologies, such as aspect-oriented programming (AOP), that implement *cross-cutting concerns*. This is a bridge to teaching AOP concepts, principles, and tools: in entire chapter in my secure software engineering course [149]. I teach AOP on the basis of Aspect.NET. I show in my secure software engineering course that AOP (when used appropriately) is an important basis for developing trustworthy software. Hopefully, this book can be used as a textbook in my secure software engineering course.

T-Oncoming Perspectives Modern trends in software evolution related to TWC should always be emphasized in university courses. One of the examples is the evolution of security in operating systems: levels of security in new versions of Windows, new types of file system architecture with automatic encryption and decryption in Solaris, and so on. Another important trend is extensible use of *knowledge management* and integration of knowledge engineering with software engineering: Using knowledge bases and inference engines integrated with traditional programming features helps to make software solutions more intelligent, in particular as far as TWC issues are concerned. For example, a network traffic-handling system can use an extensible knowledge base to "learn" more about different types of attacks and attackers, based on its analysis of network traffic and functioning. One system that can help to develop integrated and secure intelligent solutions based on modern software platforms is our Knowledge.NET toolkit [36], an extension of C# by knowledge representation features (ontologies, frames, and rule sets) implemented as an add-in to Visual Studio.NET 2005.

5.2.2 The TrustSPBU.NET Project

As mentioned before, the goal of the TrustSPBU.NET project is to enhance by TWC content the curricula developed during the SPBU.NET project. Specifics of the project curricula structure are explained in Section 5.1.2. The TrustSPBU.NET project consists of four courses, enhancements of the corresponding SPBU.NET courses:

1. *Trustworthy computing using Microsoft.NET and C#:* TWC enhancement of the undergraduate .NET course [143]
2. *Secure software engineering* [149]: TWC enhancement of the graduate software engineering course [145]

3. *Trustworthy compiler development:* TWC enhancement of the graduate compiler course [144]

4. *Trustworthy operating systems and networking:* TWC enhancement of the undergraduate OS course [146]

My present secure software engineering course curriculum [149] is available on the Microsoft Academic Web site; the others will be uploaded by finishing the 2007–2008 educational year according to the project plan. Parts of the TWC curricula are the program and the presentation slides for the course [149].

When preparing the TWC-enhanced courses, I relied on parts of the existing materials from their original versions, already related to TWC. My approach was similar to Microsoft's: When they were developing the principles of their TWC initiative, they relied on all previous 40+ years of experience in developing security, reliability, and privacy concepts. The main things that Microsoft added are a pervasive approach to TWC at all stages of software development, a security development life-cycle scheme, and principles and practice of business integrity. Following Microsoft, I added such material to my secure software engineering course.

The concepts of *structured programming, modular programming, abstract data types,* and *object-oriented programming*—classical foundations of any modern programming language and software development platform—were developed in the 1960s and 1970s. They were aimed at software reliability, one of the pillars of the modern TWC approach. In particular, principles of encapsulating concrete representation of data structure and exporting the set of abstract operations (methods or functions) to handle the data reliably and securely were developed by classicists of computer science: Hoare, Parnas, and Liskov. Those principles then became the basis of .NET and Java developed 30 to 35 years later and help to make these modern platforms trustworthy. It seems very important that students understand it and don't think that TWC is related only to cryptography and methods of mitigating network attacks (although the two disciplines mentioned are so important that they deserve to be taught by separate courses and hands-on labs). As for object orientation, I show not only its importance for TWC (tying security checks to classes and methods), but also the known "pitfalls" of OOP prevented by TWC, such as *conceptual explosion*, indirect inheritance of hundreds of entities developed by other software engineers whose semantics may not be well documented and not quite understandable by their user. Such an approach helps students to realize how to design modern complicated software to make it trustworthy.

In my TWC-enhanced courses I also emphasize the importance of *formal methods*: formal *specification* and formal *verification* of software. The latter term is now used in quite a different meaning, as applicable to .NET and Java: Verification of dynamically loaded Java classes and .NET assemblies refers to their type checking and checking those complicated binary file structures for consistency (e.g., using correct numbers of local variables, correct stack size, and branches to correct relative addresses). Such verification is definitely very important for TWC. But verification in its initial, much broader meaning (considered in Hoare's and Goguen's papers of the 1970s) refers to the process of formal proof that the implementation of any module, and the software system as a whole, satisfies its formal specification. Unfortunately, for years, software practitioners have become more and more skeptical of formal methods. I think that happened mostly because of a lack of adequate tools comfortable to use. Now we can say that such tools, which combine modern programming with practical-to-use formal specification and verification methods, are appearing. The first to be mentioned and studied by software engineering students is Spec# [64] by Microsoft Research, an extension of C# by formal specification and formal verification features, implemented as an add-in to Visual Studio. NET 2005 (a more detailed description of Spec# is given in Section 2.5.4). This tool can be used to develop really trustworthy software whose correctness is verified by the theorem prover. It is close to Hoare's idea of a *verifying compiler* [65]. I think students (who will probably become the developers of newer and more convenient trustworthy software development tools in the near future) should understand and appreciate formal specification and verification techniques and tools such as Spec#. In my course I teach the best known specification and verification techniques: the *Floyd–Hoare method*, based on $P\{S\}Q$ triples; *denotational semantics; algebraic specification* (implemented in industrial SDL language used for telecommunication, and in the family of OBJ specification languages by Goguen); and *design by contract* (implemented in Meyer's Eiffel language and system).

As for TWC tools, special attention should be paid to tools such as Microsoft's FxCop [39] (see Section 2.5.4). Students should appreciate the variety of security and other checks performed by FxCop and understand how important they are to improving TWC characteristics of the code. Students should also know classical tools (e.g., the *lint* static code checker) and their role in improving the security and reliability of code. That can be very well realized by a student who is given a large piece of C code and the task to "get the *lint* quiet" (i.e., get rid of all *lint* warnings), and in the course of that, analyze the reason for each warning.

Whereas the subjects of the .NET, software engineering, and OS seem to be tied closely to TWC, the compiler course may be considered as totally unrelated to TWC. However, it is not really so. One of the goals of the trustworthy compiler course is to analyze all aspects of a *trustworthy compiler*. Such a compiler should be seen as one whose behavior and operation at each compilation phase (including the quality of error messages, error recovery, and the code generated) are comfortable, transparent, and dependable for the user. In this regard, I agree with Hoare's challenge of a verifying compiler [65]. For example, a trustworthy compiler should be able to catch logical bugs such as: *if* $(x == 0 \ \&\& \ x == 1)$ using AND instead of OR, should detect and diagnose possible deadlocks when using semaphores, and so on.

A great advantage of the TWC domain for teachers is that it is very attractive for students to learn. Students are eager to learn, for example, the meaning of a distributed denial of service (DDoS) attack, and how to configure .NET security using attributes or XML configuration files. On finishing our autumn semester in December 2006, my secure software engineering course exam was passed by 126 students, about half of the total number of students who study at our university department of mathematics and mechanics each year (including majories).

In the near future, I will upload the curricula of three other courses, on trustworthy .NET, compilers, and operating systems. I also plan to organize seminars and hands-on labs on TWC, following requests by many students, since I think it is really important to teach TWC on the basis of practical experience. I also give my doctoral students a number of themes related to TWC which, in the near term, can result in developing new, practically useful TWC tools: for example, *an algebraic specification and verification system for C#, a trustworthy programming tool for C# integrated to Visual Studio, and a library of reusable TWC aspects for Aspect.NET.*

Readers are invited to provide critiques, comments, and suggestions on this chapter and on my TWC curricula, to strengthen teaching students modern TWC principles and tools, with the goal of making software products more trustworthy.

5.3 TEACHING TRUSTWORTHY SOFTWARE ENGINEERING, INCLUDING AOP

In this section we consider in detail the secure software engineering course [149] and all related specifics. The general principles of preparing the course are described in Section 5.2.2. The structure of the section is tied to the program of the course. For each topic, its name and contents are explained, and necessary comments are provided. The course was taken by 126 students during the 2006–2007 educational year. All in all, I have been teaching software engineering courses for students and engineers (as their postgraduate education) for more than 20 years. The course is updated and enhanced each educational year, according to new trends in software engineering, I have been teaching the version of the course enhanced with trustworthy content since the 2005–2006 educational year.

5.3.1 Structure of the Secure Software Engineering Course

This section covers in detail the structure and the program of the secure software engineering course. Comments on course topics are provided when necessary. Readers may consult the course curricula [149] for more details and related references.

Topic 1. *Evolution of software and its development methods. The trust-worthy computing (TWC) initiative by Microsoft. Modern types of applications, specifics of modern software. Qualities and properties of software products, elements of programming technologies.*

Lecture notes for topic 1. The concept of software evolution is central in software engineering courses today. But students should understand immediately that TWC principles are pervasive and are now of special attention, due to Microsoft's TWC initiative, begun in 2002. So the preliminary set of software qualities and properties should be augmented by TWC principles. In particular, security, reliability, and privacy should be the main principles of software development, together with its usability, efficiency, portability, and other qualities.

Topic 2. *Classical (waterfall) software life cycle and its stages. Rapid proto-typing. Software life cycle, as treated by TWC [trustworthy computing security development life cycle (SDLC)]. The basic principles of TWC: SD³C, STRIDE, and DREAD.*

Lecture notes for topic 2. Traditionally, as for any software engineering course, my course begins with a waterfall software life-cycle model overview, with its five successive phases: requirements, specification, design, implementation, and testing. I also overview the rapid application development (RAD) model, based on iterative improvement in the software prototype, and compare it to the waterfall model. Of special importance in this part of the course is an overview of the Microsoft security development life cycle (SDLC) (see Section 2.3). I explain to students that the SDLC model adds security concerns to each waterfall phase. Next, SD³C, STRIDE, and DREAD principles are reviewed (see Section 2.3).

Topic 3. *Structured programming and stepwise refinement: the first technique of secure software engineering.*

Lecture notes for topic 3. The scheme of teaching structured programming as part of the secure software engineering course is a very suitable example to demonstrate all elements of the T-ERATO paradigm. First, a *retrospective* of "bowl-of-spaghetti" (BS) software development is exposed, as a negative *experience* of misuse of GOTO, resulting in totally *nontrustworthy* software. *Analysis* for the reasons for BS software is provided: The main reason is the need to quickly patch a code written in low-level language or directly in machine instructions. Then the *theory* of structured programming is considered: Boehm and Jacopini's theoretical result on the possibility of transforming any program into a functionally equivalent one written using only the primitives of structured programming—succession of statements, *if* statement, *while* statement, and *call*, without GOTO. Dijkstra's *"GOTO statement considered harmful"* and *"Notes on structured programming"* papers are overviewed, and their influence on improving *trustworthiness* of software is *analyzed*. Then a historical *retrospective* of programming languages and tools for structured programming is provided, starting with Pascal and structured programming support tools for assembler-level languages and FORTRAN. The importance of structured programming as one of the keystones of the trustworthy programming culture is emphasized. Examples of trustworthy and nontrustworthy use of GOTO are provided. Next, the current status and *oncoming perspectives* of structured programming are outlined—exception handling with a try/catch/finally block into the set of structured programming constructs is now considered a part of structured programming. As a result of applying the T-ERATO scheme, students should understand, on the basis of theory, analysis, and experience, that structured programming is not only the first systematic programming technique but also the *first trustworthy programming technique.*

> *Topic 4.* *Modular programming: methodology of secure software design and development. Module: its interface and implementation. Coupling and cohesion of modules. Modular constructs and tools in programming languages. Typical bugs of "nonmodularity" and recommendations to improve the modularity of programs.*

Lecture notes for topic 4. Modular programming is another keystone of TWC. The theory of modularity of Myers and Parnas is considered: the concepts of a module, its specification, its interface and implementation, and coupling and cohesion of modules. Special emphasis is put on methods of trustworthy module design and implementation: design by contract and defensive programming. The interface of any model includes not only its arguments and results, but also its possible exceptions, the side effects (the set of global entities modified by the module), and the primary description of *semantics* (*functionality*) of the module. The structure of the interface of a module is shown in Figure 5.2. Together with classic papers on modularity from the United States, I describe Russian papers on modular programming by Gregory Tseytin and his view on modules and units of knowledge. Modularity in programming languages is overviewed. Practical recommendations on how to achieve modularity and how to avoid nonmodular style of programming are considered. Then a bridge is built from classical modularity to aspects as new kinds of modules; traditional modularity appeared not to be enough to cover cross-cutting concerns.

> *Topic 5.* *Abstract data types (ADT): methodology of trustworthy manipulation of data structures. Theoretical models of ADT. ADT languages. The CLU language and its role in programming.*

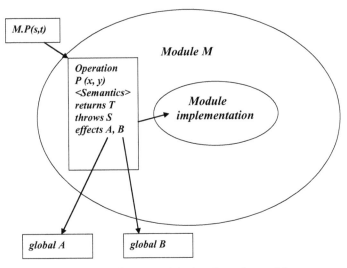

Figure 5.2   Structure of the interface of a module.

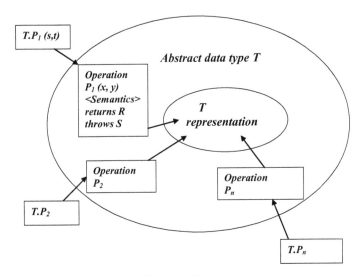

Figure 5.3   Architecture of an abstract data type.

Lecture notes for topic 5. The architecture of ADT is shown in Figure 5.3. ADT consists of an interface a set of *abstract operations* visible to its user; opaque implementation of ADT, *concrete* representation of ADT in terms of other types; and *implementations of* its abstract *operations*. The importance of ADT for trustworthy programming and for progress in programming languages is emphasized. The pioneering paper by Hoare, "*Proof of correctness of data representations*," is considered. Next, the CLU language by Liskov and her approach to ADT is described in detail using examples. My team and I developed the first implementation of CLU in the Soviet Union in 1985 and communicated to Liskov on CLU in the early 1980s. ADT and CLU really made an impressive effect on the entire programming world. ADT extensions were implemented for many languages, including Pascal, FORTRAN, and assembler. I show students how the pioneering concepts of *cluster* (ADT), *signal* (exception), *iterator*, and *parametrized* (generic) *type*, originated in CLU in 1974, influenced all later programming approaches and languages, including Java and C#. They became an inherent part of contemporary trustworthy programming basis. Also, part of this topic is the theory of ADT, especially the algebraic approach to ADT proposed in the mid-1970s by the ADJ group: Goguen, Thatcher, Wagner, and Wright. In general, an important part of the ADT model is the *formal specification* of the ADT, its *input and output conditions* for each abstract operation, the *abstract invariant* of the ADT (a condition to hold the abstract elements of the ADT structure), and the *concrete invariant* of the ADT (a condition to hold the elements of concrete representation). CLU is compared to another ADT project of the 1970s: ALPHARD [154], developed by Shaw (Carnegie-Mellon University) and her group. ALPHARD was similar to CLU but included formal specifications of abstract data types, as described above, and a built-in verifier to prove their correctness. APLHARD did not become as popular because of its more complicated structure and the need to formally prove the correctness of each module. However, the ALPHARD system can be considered one of the world's first trustworthy programming systems. The ideas of CLU and ALPHARD became the basis of modern trustworthy programming systems such as Spec# (see Section 2.5.4).

> ***Topic 6.*** *Object-oriented programming (OOP). Basic concepts of OOP. The SIMULA-67 programming language. The C++ language and its history. The languages Smalltalk and Eiffel. Pitfalls of OOP, issues of security and reliability with OOP.*

Lecture notes for topic 6. OOP is considered to be well known by students by their fourth year, when they take this course. Most students acquire commercial experience of object-oriented software development in their first year at the university. By the fourth year students have had enough practice in programming in Java and C#, so the OOP topic in this course should be analytical, to retain student interest. As a result, students find a lot of new and interesting information in the OOP topic. OOP originated in 1960s, due to the SIMULA and SIMULA 67 programming languages developed by Nugoord and Dahl in Norway for the purpose of modeling discrete event–based systems. Many students and even some software engineering professionals don't know that. I explain the foundations of SIMULA 67 and emphasize what kind of pioneering ideas its authors brought to programming—objects, classes, inheritance, and virtual functions—everything that even now, 40 years later, forms the basis of OOP. If it were not for SIMULA, there wouldn't be C++, the classic commercial OOP, the language its author Bjarne Stroustrup initially named "C with classes" and positioned as an extension of C by SIMULA-like classes. On the other hand, another, quite different approach to OOP was developed by the Smalltalk team at Xerox PARC in the 1970s. They considered the object model to be based on the concepts of message passing between objects, and of *methods*, reactions by an object to each type of message such that the set of object's methods is determined at runtime. All these hints of OOP history are of deep interest to students. Another subject of special interest to students is my analysis of OOP model trustworthiness and its "pitfalls," in the spirit of Website's book [22]. Students need to understand both the power of OOP mechanisms and that applying OOP can lead to a conceptual explosion, that implementation inheritance used in OOP is not quite reliable and secure, and that OOP is not enough to cover all types of concerns in software development; in particular, OOP is not quite suitable for implementing cross-cutting concerns. This is another bridge to teaching the basics of AOP in this course.

> *Topic 7. Aspect-oriented programming (AOP). Basic concepts of AOP. Cross-cutting concerns, aspects, pointcuts, join points, weaving. Advantages and pitfalls of AOP for trustworthy software development. Overview of AOP tools. AspectJ. Aspect.NET.*

Lecture notes for topic 7. AOP is one of the central topics in this course as well as in this book. Two bridges to teaching AOP, as you already know, lead from topic 5 (modularity) and topic 6 (OOP). Topic 7 covered in two or three lectures. However, my book can be the basis of a one-semester course on AOP. My approach to teaching AOP as part of the course is to help students feel its generality, power, and perspectives. Another thing to emphasize in this topic is the generic relation of AOP and TWC and applicability of AOP for making software more trustworthy. I make an overview of AspectJ and some other AOP tools and pay a lot of attention to Aspect.NET: its principles, architecture, and features. Actually, the contents of this topic may be based on a brief version of Chapters 3 and 4 of this book. AOP appeared to be one of the most interesting topics for students in this course.

> *Topic 8. Requirements and specification phases. Overview of specification methods and languages. Algebraic specification. The OBJ3 specification language. Other approaches to specification. The Spec# toolkit: secure software engineering in C# using formal specifications. Specifications and requirements. Issues of using formal specifications and their importance for improving software trustworthiness. The SQFD model and its use to elicit software requirements.*

Lecture notes for topic 8. In this topic requirements and specifications phases are overviewed, with an accent on their importance on software trustworthiness. As a common-use requirement eliciting and prioritizing technique, the SQFD model is described (see Section 4.10.3). In particular, the SQFD model can include assessment of TWC requirements to the product. As for specifications, the following formal specification techniques are considered: decision tables, HIPO diagrams, Floyd–Hoare program calculus, the Vienna definition method (VDM), and the denotational semantics and algebraic specification methods. I emphasize that algebraic specifications are the most practical, since properties of data types can be specified completely and comfortably in algebraic form. A type is considered as a multisorted algebra whose signature is the set of type operation (method) headers.

The semantics of operations is expressed in a clear and simple form of algebraic equation containing calls of the type's operations. The algebraic approach can be used to specify abnormal conditions by extending the operation result set by *error values*. The latest algebraic specification languages used in practice are *SDL* (used in telecommunication software) and *OBJ3* by Goguen. The Spec# language and its design-by-contract specification features for C# source codes are also considered a prospective approach. We analyze why formal methods have not yet widely been used in most of software projects (see Section 2.3.3).

Topic 9. *Software design. Architectural design. System modeling and structuring. UML and its use in software requirements, design, and subsequent phases.*

Topic 10. *Design strategies. Top-down design. Stepwise refinement. M. Jackson's method.*

Topic 11. *Bottom-up design. Abstraction levels and vertical cuts. Kernel extension method. TIP technology [153]. Cross-cutting concerns and AOP. GUI design. The MVC paradigm. Design patterns.*

Lecture notes for topics 9, 10, and 11. The most widely used software design strategies are top-down design (stepwise refinement and Jackson's method), bottom-up design (based on abstraction levels), and kernel extension design: representation of the software system as a set of the kernel and extension functions that enhance its functionality. The latter strategy looks most suitable for applying AOP and other technologies to handle cross-cutting concerns. TIP technology [11,153] is considered as an approach using design patterns for abstraction levels and groups of operations on data structures. Specifics of GUI design are analyzed, and the model–view–controller (MVC) paradigm is described as the most widely used for GUI design.

Topic 12. *Implementation (coding). Principles of choosing the implementation language. Recommendations on coding style and source code presentation. The Hungarian notation. Code reusability. Code refactoring. Using code patterns. Principles of developing secure code. Open- and shared-source code.*

Lecture notes for topic 12. The implementation stage actually determines the quality of the product, since the actual working code is the result of the implementation stage. For this reason, coding should be made by highly skilled software engineers rather than newbies, as often happens. The approach of "smart designers and dumb coders" is nontrustworthy. Here are the main issues to be solved during the coding stage:

- Choosing the implementation language (or languages)
- Using a proper set of coding templates to make the process of coding easier
- Using some definite coding style to make programs more readable and maintainable
- Self-documenting of the code to make it clearer to its own authors of to engineers who come later to maintain and enhance the code

The *choice of implementation language* is determined by a number of factors. The first factor, as Wirth noticed in his Pascal user manual, is *the first language* a person learned. The first programming language that a person learns has a great influence on his or her way of thinking as a programmer. Sometimes the first language learned remains the only one. That's why there are various types of software systems (from application packages to compilers and expert systems) written in FORTRAN. Choosing and learning a new language is often considered to be too risky and too time consuming. Many people intuitively resist starting to use a new language. This is a well-known psychological phenomenon in IT.

The next factor is *the customer.* Very often, customers strictly determine (or even order) the implementation language. An example is the Ada language created by order of the U.S. Department of Defense as a result of a language project competition. However, Ada appeared to be too complicated. Sometimes, for the purpose of program portability, an implementation language is chosen that has an international standard. For example, most Sun compilers were written in ANSI C.

Finally, there is the phenomenon of *proprietary languages.* A proprietary language (most often, a specific dialect of BASIC) is a language developed by a company, intended for internal use within that company only for developing all its software. I know a number of such examples but cannot disclose them, since those languages are still confidential. A proprietary language has its proprietary implementation and its proprietary core API: for example, wrapping the use of specific hardware instructions. The software developed in a proprietary language is not portable and is unusable outside the host company.

The need for *coding templates* arose because of the growing complexity of software. For example, to implement a Web service for Microsoft.NET, it is necessary to create several related code and XML files, to set up the appropriate attributes correctly, and so on. Without the development environment's support for coding templates, creating all of that by hand might cause a number of bugs. Visual Studio.NET 2005 provides such coding templates for any type of project, including Web services. In general, almost no software is now being developed from scratch; coding templates ate used everywhere, and their support is included in many integration development environments (IDEs). From a TWC viewpoint, using code templates is preferable, since the probability of a bug is much lower. *Using code templates is a good secure software engineering practice.*

Coding style is a primary influence on software maintenance. During the entire period that the product source exists, it has been developing and maintained by many people, and is sometimes passed from one company to another. Moreover, a specific coding style is characteristic of each person, and code maintained by different people often looks almost unreadable. To avoid this issue, coding style guides were developed for C, C++, Java, and C#. In particular, the coding style guide for C prescribes having two files (*MyModule.c* and *MyModule.h*), where *.c* is the implementation file and *.h* is the interface file; to place define and extern declarations only into .h files; to use capital letters only for constant names; and so on. Important issues of coding style are the system of *naming the entities* in the program code, making proper *indentations*, and *self-documenting* the code. The most widely used naming system is *Hungarian notation*, denoting the type and the semantics of the identifier by lowercase letters (e.g., *szLoginName*, where *sz* means "string, zero terminated") starting the identifier. A unified coding style is an important factor in code trustworthiness, since it lowers the probability of a bug and makes the code more understandable and self-explanatory.

Self-documenting is supported in Java and .NET by special *documentation comments* of specific formats, automatically converted by the development environment to HTML or XML documentation on the API implemented.

Part of this topic is an overview of *principles of developing secure code*, in the spirit of Howard and LeBlanc's classical book [27] on the subject: in particular, minimizing the attack surface of the application; avoiding typical bugs such as buffer overrun, null pointer checks, and testing the application with the least privilege (see Section 2.3).

> **Topic 13.** *Software testing. Types and methods of testing. Black box and white box strategies. Static and dynamic testing. Code inspection. The lint utility and other source code static analyzers (verifiers).*
>
> **Topic 14.** *Testing commercial software products. Test base, test, test case, test harness, test coverage, and measuring tools.*

Lecture notes for topics 13 and 14. Testing is one of the most important parts of implementing the TWC paradigm. Testing is the stage of the software life cycle following the design and coding stages or performed parallel to coding. Extreme programming (XP) even prescribes *test-driven development,* which means that the code is developed when the tests are ready. It is very important to understand that testing and debugging are not the same. Testing in general may include not only searching bugs but also checking various characteristics of the program, such as the amount of resources it takes, its performance, and compatibility to appropriate standards. Dijkstra formulated a classical aphorism on testing: that it can prove the presence of bugs but cannot prove their absence. In this relation, an alternative to testing could be full formal verification of the program, using its specification. But such a verification practice is not yet common (Section 2.3).

Testing should be made in a systematic way and should require planning separate time and human resources to be spent. There are several *types of testing* that should be performed and always taken into account for any product:

1. *Regression testing* is *testing all the bug fixes*. A separate test suite should be run after each bug fix to make sure that all previous bug fixes work after the new one. There should be *no regressions*; the new bug fix or functionality entered should not break old bug fixes.

2. *Compatibility testing* is testing a product against a known set of specifications. The product should be developed in accordance with specifications: For example, a compiler should implement the language dialect to comply with its international standard; and a third-party implementation of .NET or Java should comply with the appropriate set of standards. A well-known example is JCK (the Java compatibility kit), a set of more than 30,000 tests used for compatibility testing of any third-party Java implementation to comply with Java language, JVM, and Java API standard specifications.

3. *Performance testing*, or *benchmarking*, is testing the performance of an application: its execution time and the amount of other resources used, such as virtual and external memory. A classical example of a benchmarking test suite is SPEC, a set of former realistic big applications used to measure the performance of new hardware platforms and language implementations.

4. *Stress testing* is testing an application against "critical values," requests to the server, objects created, and so on. The application should demonstrate stable behavior, ever when subjected to such stress overloads. This type of testing is like testing an astronaut against critical overloads and situations using training tools and simulators.

5. *Security testing*—in particular, *penetration testing* and *fuzzing* (see Section 2.3.1), are parts of the security development life cycle. These types of testing are intended to check the resistance of the application to various types of security attacks.

Main *testing strategies* are subdivided into *black box testing* (with the source code of the application unknown) and *white box testing* (with various types of test coverage of the source code). The goal of white box testing is to achieve maximum possible *test coverage* (i.e., to execute at least once all the code fragments of the application as the result of running of a given test suite). Test coverage is typically measured in *basic blocks*, as *block coverage*. Basic block is a fragment of the source code executed in a purely linear way: no branches, no calls, no exceptions. *Branch coverage* is the percentage of coverage of the source in terms of *branches*: GOTO statements, switches, and so on. *Condition coverage* is the percentage of the coverage of all conditions: For example, for an *if* statement, the condition coverage will be full in case both of the alternatives are executed, the one corresponding to the "true" value of the condition, and one corresponding to the "false" value. *Method coverage* is probably the simplest type of coverage. It is the percentage of methods (or functions) being called as the result of running the test suite.

Testing techniques to be used, as defined by Myers, are *boundary value testing, equivalence class partitioning,* and *cause–effect graphing* [45]. According to the other criteria to separate the types of testing, testing can be *static* and *dynamic*. In general, *static testing* is testing without running (or before running) the program to be tested. According to statistics, static testing can catch about 70% of bugs. A popular method of static testing is *individual through code review* or *group through code review*. Usually, it is performed by another programmer or group of programmers who didn't develop the code (i.e., *mutual code review* is the most valuable).

An alternative way of static testing is *code inspection*, taking into account *typical bugs* that can occur. According to statistics, the most typical bugs are *using noninitialized values of variables; an array index out of bounds; pointer bugs*, including no check for a null pointer value; and *module interface bugs* (i.e., calling a module with the same set of argument values somewhat swapped).

The main principle of the testing process in major software companies is *systematic testing on a regular basis*. This principle is often ignored by small companies which claim to have no resources for testing. The result is inevitable: poor quality of their products. Testing of each product should be made on a *nightly, weekly, and monthly basis*, and after each build of the product. Quite common is the term *heartbeat tests*, tests that should run each night on changed versions of the product.

There should be *special kinds of testing engineers (testers), SQE and SQA*, managed by a separate manager and funded from a separate budget. *SQEs (software quality engineers)* are software engineers who develop tests and testing tools. Unlike what many young programmers think, SQ engineering is a very creative type of software engineering work. Sometimes SQEs actually have to implement not only the tests and testing tools for testing a library, but also implement the same library functionality, although probably in a less efficient way, to compare the results obtained by different algorithms.

SQA (software quality assurance) engineers are "pure testers," those who run ready-to-use test suites (press buttons), or test GUI or other applications manually (working as "robots"). That is certainly a much less creative type of activity.

To perform systematic testing of a product, a *test plan* should be developed by the SQE manager and coordinated for the entire team.

The following *testing tools* are used in commercial testing.

1. *A test harness* is a testing tool used to run tests and analyze their results in a given environment. In the simplest case, this is just a command script (sometimes a *make* utility and make files are used as the driving forces for testing). In more complicated cases, this is a separate complicated testing application. For Java applications, for example, *JavaTest* and *JUnit* test harnesses are the most common.

2. *A test base* is a directory structure (or database) containing all information for the tests to run, including the tests themselves. Usually a test base consists of several *test suites*: groups of related tests. For a compiler, for example, a typical set of test suites is as follows: *a regression test suite, a language standard compatibility test suite, test suites for testing various implemented dialects of the language, and benchmarking test suites.*

Each test suite consists of *tests*. In their turn, tests consist of *test cases*. Intuitively, a test may correspond to all examples used for testing a given method, and test cases correspond to concrete input sets of values of its arguments. For each test and test case, there should be a proper *configuration files* to enable testing in a proper environment.

In most cases, *golden files* (expected output files) are used to analyze the results of testing. But if random testing is required (i.e., the sets of argument values are pseudorandom numbers), it does not make sense to keep any golden files. In this case, the *check correct functions* are used; the testing tools should evaluate the result of the method being tested (probably by some less efficient algorithm) and compare it to the actual result that the method produces.

A helpful technique used in the JavaTest harness for test reconfiguration is the method of *exclude lists*, lists of tests *not to run* for some reasons (e.g., if some methods of the API are not yet implemented and there is no need yet to try testing them), to avoid testing results that do not make sense. Among testing tools, there are also *testing workspaces* that should be stored separately from the test base. A testing workspace is a directory structure or database to keep the results of testing, usually in some engineer's "sandbox," for an experimental version of the product.

Topic 15. *Software maintenance. Maintenance costs. Analyzing and fixing bugs. Bug-tracking database. Issuing patches. Roles of software engineers participating in bug fixing.*

Lecture notes for topic 15. *Maintenance*, or *sustaining*, is the stage of the software life cycle that follows shipment of the product to the customer. This is the most resource-consuming part of software development. This fact (as well as the importance of testing noted above) is often ignored by project managers, who often assign as many as "0.25 engineer" of human resources to maintaining a product.

It should be kept in mind that when a product is stopped for maintenance, it dies. No customer will use a product whose team wouldn't fix any bugs found, or wouldn't answer any customer questions. In other words, during product maintenance, the *business integrity* principles should be followed. See Section 2.3.4, where business integrity is overviewed, and principles of successful maintenance are formulated. Maintenance includes *installing the product, training users, answering users' questions, fixing bugs, and enhancing the product according to the user's requests and needs.*

Maintenance is often especially difficult, since it is usually performed not by the authors of the original version of the product but by other engineers assigned to this task. Maintenance engineers often have to learn and fix the code written by some other programmers, often not well self-documented, representing a mixture of different coding styles developed by several companies over a few years.

There is a crucial software technology issue related to maintenance. In their everyday work, software maintenance engineers have to *locate and update aspects* (speaking in terms of AOP). In other words, a typical type of activity for a software maintenance engineer is *to find in the code all the parts responsible for implementing some functionality*, and *to update that functionality*. This activity is very difficult to perform, since none of the commonly used software development tools enable adequate support for solving this task. The code of the functionality can be tangled within the code of the product. AOP helps to do this. But, in general, this task is now very far from satisfactory solution using current AOP tools.

One of the most common types of software maintenance activity is *bug fixing*. To support this activity, a *bug-tracking database* is used. This is a database containing information on all *bug reports submitted*. For understandable reasons, a bug-tracking database is proprietary and confidential. Only for open- and shared-source products is a bug-tracking database publicly available (e.g., *Bugzilla*).

Next, let's consider typical information for each bug report stored in a bug-tracking database.

- *Bug id* is the ordering number of the bug. In several bug-tracking databases, the number of digits in the bug id can be five to seven.
- *Synopsis* is a brief description of the bug, including appropriate *keywords*, to make any search in the bug-tracking database easier.
- *Description* is a more detailed description of the bug—the more detailed, the better.

- *Priority* is the urgency of the bug according to the customer's opinion. The priority can vary, for example, from 1 to 5, the priority 1 being the highest. Unfortunately, a common practice for product managers is to decrease the priorities of known bugs, to avoid a rush to fix them. A priority 1 bug typically means that the maintenance engineer should concentrate immediately on fixing the bug first and should fix it at most a week. It is recommended that customers prioritize *security bugs* by the highest priority, to promptly receive security patches that fix them.

When processed by the maintenance team, a bug passes through the following stages:

1. **Submitted.** The bug report is submitted by a customer technical escalations (CTE) engineer responsible for contacts to product customers in some region of the world (or city).
2. **Accepted.** The bug report is looked through by the product's *responsible manager*, who appoints the *responsible engineer* to fix the bug.
3. **Evaluated.** The responsible engineer has investigated the problem, localized it, and found a way to fix it—a *suggested fix*. He or she puts into the bug report an evaluation of the bug and the fix suggested: a collection of the source code updates.
4. **Fixed.** The bug fix is tested in the responsible engineer's sandbox, and all tests were passed. Note that in addition to the bug fix, a regression test or tests should be developed and added to the regression test suite.
5. **Integrated.** The bug fix is integrated into the master source code workspace and tested. For priority 1 and 2 bugs, for each bug fix, a *patch* should be shipped to the user. The patch is the fixed version of the product distribution, containing the urgent bug fix and probably some other recent fixes.

As a result of processing the bug, the following outcomes are possible:

1. The bug can be *fixed and verified.* Verification means that the fix has been tested by a special independent tester, the *release engineer.*
2. The bug can be *closed* (note that in this case the bug report is *preserved* in the bug-tracking database), for one of the following reasons:
   a. Closed because fixed and verified. The processing of the bug has been finished successfully.
   b. Closed because it is a duplicate. This is one of the most common cases. Since many customers use the same version of the product, they are very likely to find the same bugs. These bugs are stored in the database with different bug ids. It is the job of the project lead responsible for

maintenance to determine whether the bug had already been found and fixed and this is only a duplicate of a known bug. This type of analysis cannot be automated in any way.

c. Closed because it is not reproducible. The bug can appear once only, in a specific hardware and software environment used by the customer. The maintainers sometimes are unable to reproduce the bug, and this effect is stable.

d. Closed because it will not be fixed. This type of outcome is undesirable for any customer. It means that the maintenance team does not have the resources to fix the bug. I don't recommend closing any bugs, so as not to undermine the business integrity principle. See Section 2.3.4 for more recommendations.

Topic 16. *Team work and maintenance tools. SCCS, TeamWare/CodeManager, CVS. Manufacturing of software product and its milestones. Releases and their numbering.*

Lecture notes for topic 16. There are several important details related to *manufacturing the product*.

1. Versions and version numbers. There are two types of product versions: those containing major new features, and those containing bug fixes only. The former are referred to as *dot releases* and are identified by a two-number version id, such as 2.0 or 3.1. The latter are referred to as *dot-dot releases* and are identified by a three-number version id, such as 1.4.1.

2. The intermediate and final stages of shipping the product. Usually, there are three stages of shipping any version of a product: *alpha version, beta version*, and the *first customer shipment (FCS) version*. The alpha and beta versions are intermediate versions that can be characterized in terms of the absence of urgent bugs: In the alpha version, there should not be any priority 1 (the most urgent) bugs; in the beta version, there should not be any priority 1 or 2 bugs. Alpha and beta versions are shipped to volunteers only—those organizations (usually, universities or individual volunteers) that agree to get and test the version of the product in a limited time (usually, one to two months) and to produce an alpha (or beta) testing report. An FCS version is the first version to be shipped to all customers. It should not have priority 1, 2, or 3 bugs. Before each stage (alpha, beta, and FCS) of the release, a quality assurance (QA) cycle should be performed. This means that the product should be tested carefully using ready-to-use test suites.

3. *Documentation* is a very important part of each release. Documentation typically includes an *installation guide*, a *user guide*, a *system administrator's guide*, and (for compilers) a *language reference guide*. It includes *product notes*: a specific "last minute" document that contains an overview of the specifics of the current version, and usually contains brief information as

to which bugs have been fixed in the release and which known bugs have not.

4. *Source code control systems* [e.g., SCCS, TeamWare (a product of Sun), RCS, CVS, Microsoft Visual SourceSafe] play an important role in software maintenance and manufacturing, since they allow the team to share the same code, to develop and maintain it safely in parallel. The following basic principles of such systems are very similar. There is an *integration workspace for* integrating changes. Also, there is a *sandbox* (a copy of the integration workspace) for each developer. If a change made in a sandbox needs to be integrated, changes from different developers should be coordinated. For example, in SCCS, each version of each source code is referred to as *delta*. The following SCCS commands are most often used: *info* (information on the files being modified), *edit* (open a file for modification); *get* (retrieve a given version of the file), and *delta* (add a new delta with comments). Each delta corresponds to a bug fix or an RFE fix (or part of a fix). It is not recommended that the file permissions be changed manually; instead, anyone should use the *sccs edit* and *sccs delta* pair of commands.

5. *The TeamWare CodeManager* is the product I used for 10 years of Sun projects. It is based on *copy–modify–merge paradigm*. Each developer can create his or her own sandbox (by the *bringover* command). When changes are made and tested in the sandbox, they can be integrated by the *putback* command. If there is a conflict with anybody else's changes, the developer should resolve it (using the interactive *FileMerge* utility) in the integration workspace before actually doing *putback*. The team and the project manager are notified automatically by e-mail on each putback.

Topic 17. *Software development process organization. Chief programmer's team (F. P. Books). Organization of software process in computer companies. Software process measurement. Capability maturity model (CMM / CMMI), a method of certifying the maturity of a software process. Other software process schemes. The COCOMO model for estimating the effort in a software process. The ICED-T software process and product assessment model.*

Lecture notes for topic 17. A *software process* is a set of organizational principles, standards, documents, and tools to regulate the entire process of software development. There are several well-known types of software process organization.

One of the earliest types, invented by Frederick Brooks in the 1970s, is referred to as a *chief programmer's team*. Actually, this is a breakdown of *roles* in software development for a small team of people. Only five of them are programmers. The team should consist of a *chief programmer*, the leader and most experienced programmer; a *second pilot*, his backup and assistant; an *administrator* with a *secretary*; a *programming language expert*; a *tester* (an

SQE engineer, speaking in modern terms); a *toolmaster*, the person responsible for all the software tools used; a *project archive keeper*; and an *editor* (the person who edits documentation developed by the chief programmer) with a *secretary*: a total of 10 persons. These organizational principles are still useful, although some of the terms have been changed—for example, the *tester* is now called an *SQ* or *SQA engineer* and the *editor* is now called a *technical writer*; but the essence of these roles remained the same.

A more recent, highly developed, and automated type of software process organization, developed by Carnegie-Mellon University's Software Engineering Institute (CMU SEI) in the 1990s, is referred to as the *capability maturity model* (CMM). It has five levels of "maturity" of software process organization: *initial, repeated, documented, supported by tools,* and *optimizing*. Very few companies are certified by CMU SEI as working at level five of the CMM.

Another, very unusual kind of software process organization is referred to as *eXtreme Programming* (XP). It is very popular now, especially between young software developers. Its main principles are *paired coding, implementing test suites before implementing the functionality, refactoring,* and *collective code ownership*. XP is the most popular type of *agile software process organization*, targeted to delivering the software product step by step by small iterations, each one or a few weeks long. See Section 4.12 for an overview of the agile software process.

Microsoft offers its own approach to *software project organization*, to be used *for critical projects* [155]. One of its important principles is using *tiger teams*, small teams of very experienced and smart software engineers to save projects that are far behind schedule. Another, newer type of software process modification by Microsoft is the *security development life cycle*, targeted to the development of secure software products (see Section 2.3.1).

In addition to any type of software process issues, in any human team, including a software development team, there can appear a lot of psychological and moral issues. Among them are too optimistic an assessment of the time required to perform the project, over-self-estimation by some of the youngest members of the team, and many others. See Section 4.10 for an overview of the COCOMO, ICED-T, and SQFD quantitative methods of software process assessment.

Topic 18. *Using e-mail as a trustworthy software process organization tool.*

Lecture notes for topic 18. This topic may seem too specific or even exotic in a software engineering course. Nevertheless, based on my own experience of remote working with Sun and later with Microsoft Research, and based on the current popularity of outsourcing projects, I pay a lot of attention to *e-mail as a software process tool*. In our own practice of software development, e-mail has played an outstanding role. On the other hand, many young programmers have almost no experience on the proper use of technical e-mails and do not understand even basic issues, so I need to provide explanations. Here are my recommendations on using e-mail as a software process tool.

1. All important design decisions should be discussed by e-mail. E-mails are *documents* that remain on everyone's computer and can be used as an important part of working documentation.

2. Each technical e-mail should be addressed to the concrete engineer but copied to the entire product engineering team and to the product manager.

3. The subject of each e-mail should be very concrete. It is poor practice to send an e-mail to someone and include in it *everything* on *various subjects* that you'd like to tell him. Split that e-mail into several, each directed to a concrete person on an explicit subject.

4. A friendly reminder should be repeated when writing to a person who does not answer your very important e-mail for a long time. The friendly reminder heuristic can be formulated as follows: *send 10 friendly reminders and you are likely to get an answer from the eleventh attempt.*

5. To be promptly responsive by e-mail is an inherent part of business integrity. Each software developer should be responsive by e-mail. Practically, it means that if a project is developed by a remote team and the time difference with the customer is 8 to 11 hours, each e-mail from the customer side should be answered at least the next calendar day—and in the most urgent cases in one or two hours maximum (it does make sense to appoint an "on duty" developer engineer who reads and answers urgent e-mails at night). Not replying by e-mail within 24 hours should be considered abnormal and should be avoided as an action jeopardizing business integrity.

6. E-mail should be used for technical discussions, event notifications, bug report notifications, source code workspace notifications (automated), forwarding working documentation, and shipping updates on the product (automated; most important for remote outsourcing projects).

7. E-mail should be polite. One shouldn't forget that each e-mail is a type of letter and therefore should have the initial *salutation* (e.g., *Dear Bob*), the body of the message, and the *final part* (e.g., *Best regards, John*). E-mails in one line, without greetings, signature, commas, and capital letters, often look very impolite, as if they were generated by a robot rather than by an intelligent person. I also don't recommend using greetings such as "Hi" when writing to people such as bosses who are much older. Instead, I recommend that they use "Dear. . . . "

8. Follow a policy of no rudeness and no spam. Negative emotions, rudeness, or spam shouldn't appear in e-mails at all. This is one of the main principles of the entire Internet community.

9. Don't use automatic e-mail answers or e-mail forwarding for any purpose. This is a heuristic that follows from my practice and the practice of my teams. Because of e-mail attacks, of spam, and of other unpredictable things that happen with e-mails, *any e-mail "machine" inevitably breaks.* If for example,

you have set up automatic forwarding of technical e-mails to your other e-mail address (e.g., home), the machine may break, for example, because of overflow of your home directory or file system during your vacation. As a result, the incoming e-mails will bounce to your correspondents, which may cause an unpredictable negative reaction from them, including firing you (I am quite serious). So instead of setting up automatic answers such as "I am on vacation," look through your e-mail inbox remotely at least once a day, even if you are on vacation.

10. Follow the empty inbox principle. The e-mail inbox should be empty when the e-mail is processed. Each e-mail should be moved to the appropriate mailbox, according to subject or sender. Otherwise, the software developer will inevitably be behind in e-mail, and thousand of unanswered e-mails will occupy the inbox.

To summarize the experience of teaching trustworthy software engineering: Many students, teachers, and engineers attend my course with keen interest. I don't include in my course such typical security topics as cryptography, since separate classes on such subjects are already available at our university. Some students have asked for hands-on labs related to this course, which I will organize together with my team in the near future.

5.4   TEACHING TRUSTWORTHY .NET AND C# PROGRAMMING

I have been teaching .NET and C# at our university since 2003, after I received my first Microsoft Research grant award on Aspect.NET. Thanks to the kind invitation from Microsoft Research to the .NET crash course in Cambridge in March 2002, I got very interested in .NET. As I have already mentioned, for me, the .NET approach looks very similar to earlier approaches to multilanguage programming support (in Burroughs and Elbrus machines), which also used a postfix format of the object code and a type of metadata to represent types. When I got acquainted with .NET in 2002, my first impression was that .NET was what I had already been doing for 25 years.

My .NET classes at our university consist of a one-semester *course* and a one-semester *seminar*, both for fourth-year students. The interest of our students in .NET is deep. Many of them already use .NET for commercial projects at software companies where they work in parallel to their education. More than 100 students have taken and passed my .NET course and my .NET seminar. But compared to teaching Java, I should say that currently (2007) the interest of students in Java (on average, 150 students take and pass my Java course) is greater than their interest in .NET. It somewhat reflects the general situation in Russia (and I suppose not only in Russia): Java appeared five years before .NET and still dominates commercial and educational markets. But I suspect in a few years the situation may change in favor of .NET, because since

2003 the number of students who take my .NET classes has increased two- to threefold. I always emphasize to my students that both platforms, .NET and Java, be studied thoroughly, in vast detail, as the most advanced and trustworthy software development platforms right now. Knowledge of .NET and practical experience with it, as well as with Java, is currently one of the most important criteria that software managers use when selecting and hiring people. More details on teaching Java are provided in Section 5.5.

5.4.1 Structure of the Trustworthy .NET and C# Programming Course

This course is based on my .NET and C# course [143], whose specifics are described in Section 5.1.2. The course has been taken and passed by more than 100 students at our university. The course has received much more feedback from many countries than any other of my curricula [143–149] published at the MSDNAA Web site. In 2005 my .NET course was recommended for teaching at Columbia University by Microsoft, and the same year I received an invitation to teach .NET at the University of Hawaii. I am a permanent author of *.NET Developer's Journal.*

The essence of my approach to teaching .NET is, of course, using the T-ERATO paradigm. I don't teach "surfing .NET" or "digging into .NET" only. I show the inheritance of ideas between earlier approaches and .NET, and between Java and .NET. I compare .NET to other technologies, I always let the students know about the latest achievements in .NET, and I demonstrate to the students the results of my team in the .NET area. Hopefully, this is beneficial for deeper student understanding of .NET.

I have included into this section a few characteristic fragments of my .NET lectures, since teaching .NET is not the main theme of the book. I am ready to publish my full .NET course as a separate book.

> **Topic 1.** *Types of modern applications. Features of modern software systems. Basic concepts and principles of .NET. Comparison to the Java platform.*

Lecture notes for topic 1. Among contemporary tasks in the area of software engineering, client–server systems of all types have played an important part for a number of years. As a specific type of such a system, Internet, and in particular *Web applications*, have probably become the most common. These are Web client and Web server applications. They are part of our everyday activities: stock price tracking with technical analysis, Internet shops, and so on.

Developing *integrated solutions* is one of the most important goals of most companies, both major and minor, that would like to automate the process of their production and development. Typical solutions include authentication and authorization, networking, DBMS, and specialized business logic.

Embedded systems to control a variety of devices and processes have always played an important role. Unlike solutions, they are used on devices with much more limited resources.

During the past 10 to 15 years, mobile devices (cell phones, Web phones, smart phones, etc.) have been used more and more extensively. The task of *developing software for mobile devices* is related, on the one hand, to balancing within the range of the most limited resources. On the other hand, such devices should be able to plug temporarily into the Internet and intranet to get information from servers.

A modern example of an embedded system is a *wearable computer* embedded into human clothes, for the purpose of checking personal health status and providing day-to-day recommendations on health care, behavior, and navigation. This wide spectrum of software development tasks is required for a software platform to provide a general, scalable, and portable approach. That's why .NET is so important: because it is the platform that provides the best approach to all current software platforms.

Here are several important features of modern software systems:

1. Most systems are *Internet and intranet aware.* Any proprietary solution uses the intranet of an enterprise to distribute resources and to optimize their use.
2. Most worldwide use informational services are now implemented as *Web services* or *portals.*
3. As for development techniques and tools, the requirements and design stages for many applications are now based on a de facto standard: *UML* (*unified modeling language*). Its graphical diagrams are clear and understandable, and in many areas typical solutions are constructed by automated generation of the source code and test suites from UML specifications.

The *format of data* transferred via Internet and intranet between applications now *also has a de facto standard: XML.* It enables us to represent any type of hierarchical structure of data, including not only data itself but also configuration information for customizing applications.

Other important requirements for modern applications are *security* and *reliability.* In network-oriented solutions, security is especially important, both for user authentication and authorization and for protection against viruses and worms. Enhanced reliability should be based on type safety and various kinds of runtime checks. Now that an application is actually assembled, linked, and extended at runtime, and its components may arrive from anywhere on the network, it is especially important to be able to integrate these components and to check their security and reliability on the basis of a common approach to typing.

For the same reason, it is very important for modern software development platforms to provide a way to integrate various useful components across a complicated *heterogeneous network*. The components may be written in different languages and work on different platforms.

Finally, modern software is *component-oriented*. Monolithic applications are no longer developed from scratch. Since the 1980s, software developers have attempted to provide an adequate approach to rapid application development on the basis of well-defined ready-to-use reusable components. The following approaches prior to .NET should be mentioned: CORBA (common object request broker architecture), COM (component object model), and JavaBeans.

Only one development platform satisfies all of the foregoing requirements: Microsoft.NET (announced in 2000). It is a multilanguage software development platform based on a common intermediate language (CIL) which is just-in-time compiled to native code. Data representation for transfer across the network, and configuration files in .NET, are both in XML format. Microsoft.NET provides various types of security policies and models. What is especially important is that Microsoft.NET features are defined as a set of international (ISO/ECMA) standards. So, from this viewpoint, .NET can be regarded as a set of international standards, and Microsoft.NET as one implementation of these standards (there are already several others, including SSCLI and Mono).

C# is a new programming language developed specifically for .NET. But it is not the only one that can be used in a .NET environment and it is not "mandatory."

An earlier software development platform that can be considered as a predecessor of Microsoft.NET is Java (announced in 1995). Java is a platform for developing software in Java programming language. It also uses intermediate code (referred to as *bytecode*), but everything in this platform is Java-oriented. Those who would like to use other languages for some of the modules of their applications would have to define them as "native methods," preferably in C or C++. So, unlike .NET, these modules will have a subordinate status relative to a Java application, unlike the more general .NET approach, which enables peer-to-peer multilanguage interoperability. In addition, Java language, API, and Java Virtual Machine (JVM, including bytecode) don't yet have an international standard. The specifications of these three parts of Java technology are still proprietary standards of Sun Microsystems, the company that developed Java. The specifics of Java are substantial limitations on this technology, regardless of the fact that it is used widely around the world. The Microsoft.NET approach is much more general, more open-style, and more prospective. An overview of basic principles and concepts of .NET is given in Section 2.5.1.

Topic 2. Overview of common language runtime.

Topic 3. Overview of Windows forms, web forms, and ADO.NET.

Lecture notes for topics 2 and 3. The lower layer of .NET architecture is the common language runtime (CLR). This is the execution engine of .NET

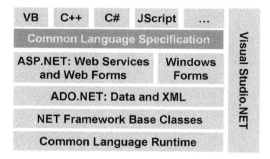

Figure 5.4   .NET framework and Visual Studio.NET.

applications, represented as assemblies or groups of assemblies. CLR implements what we call *managed execution*. It performs all necessary runtime checks, including type checks and security checks, using metadata of the assemblies being executed. It calls the JIT compiler and may throw exceptions. It also performs memory management, including garbage collection and finalization of objects. The architecture of .NET framework and Visual Studio.NET is shown in Figure 5.4.

CLR uses the framework's basic class library (BCL), organized as a set of namespaces. The root namespace is *System*. It is used in all applications. Another namespace, *System.Reflection.Emit*, contains classes and methods for generating new assemblies at runtime.

ADO.NET is a subsystem of .NET to manipulate data provided by relational database servers such as the Microsoft SQL server. The data are accessible via a set of classes, without user knowledge of the underlying data sources. It is integrated with Web programming tools of .NET. Data exchange with Web servers is performed in XML format.

Windows Forms is a set of classes to support enhanced GUI. It is used by all other parts of the .NET framework, including ADO.NET.

ASP.NET is a part of .NET responsible for Web programming. Its main parts support Web servers and Web forms. Web servers are based on the XML format of data and XML descriptions of server functionality. Web forms are quite similar to Windows forms and provide GUI for Web services to clients.

The .NET class hierarchy scheme is depicted in Figure 5.5. All the names are sufficiently self-explanatory, so we'll comment on the most important only.

- *System.IO* and *System.Net* provide input–output features and networking protocol support. In Java technology the corresponding packages are referred to as *java.io* and *java.net*.
- *System.Xml* namespace and its subspaces *System.Xml.XSLT, System. Xml.XPath*, and *System.Xml.Serialization* provide all kinds of XML support necessary for modern applications, including XSLT transforma-

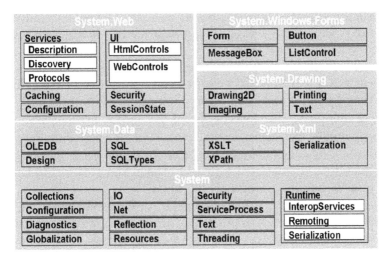

Figure 5.5 *.NET framework basic class library.*

tions of XML files, XPath navigation in XML files, and serialization of data in XML format.

- *System.Runtime.Remoting* is a namespace to support .NET remoting API used for communications between *application domains* (*AppDomains*), a kind of logical process in .NET that has its own resources and types attached, to be loaded and unloaded together with the host domain. There is nothing similar in Java technology.

- *System.Runtime.InteropServices* classes provide interaction between components developed in various CLS-compliant languages on .NET. Java technology provides no multilanguage interoperability, except for very limited master–slave functionality of "native" methods.

- *System.Web* and its subspaces support client- and server-side Web programming, *System.Data* supports ADO.NET functionality, *System. Drawing* provides the API for graphics, imaging, and printing, and *System. Windows.Forms* supports the Windows forms GUI.

Topic 4. *.NET common type system* (*CTS*).

Lecture notes for topic 4. I include a detailed version of my lecture notes on the .NET common type system since types and typing models play an especially important part in the trustworthiness of the software development platform as whole.

First, we present a very brief history of types. The concept of type is an extremely important one in programming.

- Each program can be considered as a definition and use of types and operations on these types.

- Each programming language has its own set of types, and studying this set of types is highly recommended when starting to learn any language and to better understand it.
- Even in FORTRAN, the first programming language developed in 1957, there was a relatively simple set of types: consisting of numeric types, integer and float, and array types.
- Since those times, the concept of type has evolved dramatically.
- Programming languages treat the concept of type very differently.
- Most languages (e.g., Pascal, Java, C#) are *strictly typed*, meaning that a definite type is associated with each named entity of such a language: a variable, a formal parameter, and so on.
- Some languages (e.g., LISP or SNOBOL, string manipulation languages) are *typeless*. No type is strictly tied to any variable or parameter in these languages. A variable can take the value of any type. In other words, in such languages, types are associated with values rather than with variables. It is clear that typeless languages require a lot of runtime checks and transformations of values.

Now let's consider evolution of the concept of type. In the user manual for the first version of Pascal (1970), Wirth wrote: "Type is a set of values that a variable can take." This is a typical approach to earlier, strictly typed languages. The type of any variable is fixed (e.g., an array or a record). The set of operations on the type is implied. It is the "standard" set of operations provided by the language: for an array—indexing, for a record—selecting a field with a given name, and so on.

Later in the 1970s there was great progress in clarifying the common view as to what a type is. This development was so important that had a dramatic influence on all later programming languages and platforms, up to .NET and C#.

"Types are not sets" was the title of a later article by Morris. It was realized that the type was not just a set of values, but also a set of operations defined on those values.

In 1972, Hoare formulated the concept of *abstract data type* (ADT) as the *concrete representation* of the type (in terms of the other types that are considered to be already defined, either primitive or abstract), plus a *set of abstract operations* on this type defined as procedures. Hoare proved that a program preserves its semantics and functionality if it is rewritten in terms of abstract operations and their calls.

Based on this idea, in the mid-1970s Barbara Liskov and Mary Shaw launched two competitive projects on abstract data type languages: CLU and ALPHARD (see Section 5.3.1 for a more detailed description of ADT). In perspective, the CLU project survived its time for many years and became the basis of the main ideas for many languages and tools. It's unbelievable, but only now, 30 years later, have such constructs and concepts of CLU as iterators and parametrized (or generic) types been reborn in the state-of-the-art commercial language C# 2.0.

The object-oriented approach has made its corrections to the concept of type. This approach distinguishes between *type* (or *class*) as a common definition of data and operations (or methods) on all instances of some type, and *object*, an instance of the type inheriting from the type its common properties: data (fields) and operations (methods).

In addition, classes may have a hierarchical structure, and any *descendant class* can inherit part of its data and operations from another class (defined as its *ancestor class*). Each language has its own specific type system. Moreover, on different platforms the implementations of language types can actually be different because of different sizes of numbers or different representations of symbolic information.

So, given a variety of different language type systems, to achieve multilanguage interoperability, a common, unified type system is required. Only a common type system can provide a single common view as to how to treat a language-specific type in terms of common types.

Now let's consider the concept of type identity in CTS. As we've already seen, a type in OOP is characterized by a set of values and a set of operations defined on a type (or methods). In CTS, *types are considered to be different if they have different representations.* In other words, they have a different set of fields.

Types implement the same interface if they respond to the same set of messages. This means that *interfaces* in CTS (groups of method headers) are used as descriptions of *protocols* (i.e., *sets of message formats*: the name of the message, its arguments and their types, possible exceptions, and the type of result).

Types are identical if they have the same representation and they respond to the same set of messages. In other words, types are identical if they have the same set of fields and implement the same set of methods.

Another fundamental concept of CTS and of programming as a whole is that of *location*. The history of the location concept takes its origin from papers in the 1940s by von Neumann on principles of hardware architecture. In von Neumann's architecture, a key concepts is the *cell*, an elementary part of memory. Each cell has its *address* expressed by an integer number.

The concept of an addressed cell whose contents may be changed laid the foundation of the concept of a *variable* in programming. Note that the concept of variable in mathematics and in programming is fundamentally different. In programming, a variable is a cell, with its address denoted by a symbolic name, or identifier. In mathematics, a variable is just a denotation for an arbitrary quantity, but its value cannot be changed by an assignment. This treatment is close to functional languages and to production (or rule-based) languages, whose semantics are close to those of mathematics.

So, in CTS, a *location* is a named and typed memory area that can keep one value only at each moment. The type determines the set of values to be stored at a location and the ways to use the values (or, in other words, a *signature of available operations*). The value should be *assignment compatible* to the type of the location. Examples of locations are local variables and parameters.

In modern programming, and in CTS in particular, one of the most important concepts is a *contract*. In everyday practice and in business it's a widely used term. In CTS, contracts relate to *signatures* (in terms of C language: *prototypes*). But let's recall the other important treatment of a contract used in Meyer's *design-by-contract* methodology: contracts are assertions used as a basis to correct program design; there are two types of contracts: *require* is a precondition for a method; *ensure* is its postcondition. Design-by-contract methodology is supported in Eiffel language implemented for .NET by Eiffel Software (see Section 4.9).

A contract in CTS is a specification of requirements to an implementation of a type. More clearly, the specification defines a set of methods that it should implement. A type determines its supported set of contracts. Contracts are publicly available requirements to signatures. Signatures determine restrictions to types, addresses, parameters, methods, and exceptions. They determine which values can be stored in parameters. They also list the set of available operations. Signatures are parts of contracts that can be checked, mostly at compile time and, if necessary, at runtime, due to metadata.

The implementation of a type can be verified. Verification is performed during the load of the assembly hosting the type definition. Ideally, contracts should be not only sets of signatures, but also formal specifications of semantics of the type and its operations. This can be achieved using special custom attributes to represent formal specifications, and developing a "formal verifier" tool that checks the type implementation satisfies the requirements of the specifications.

Coercion is another basic notion of CTS. Coercion is a transformation of a value to another value with another relative type, usually for the purpose of fitting the assignment compatibility condition. Coercions have appeared in each programming language since FORTRAN, primarily for numerical type. When, for example, an integer value is assigned to a double variable, the coercion of that value to double is performed implicitly. Interesting coercions were introduced in PL/1 (1965): it was possible in PL/1, for example, to implicitly coerce a single bit to an array of bits of length 1. Later, in ALGOL 68, an entire very complicated system of coercions and related *positions* of the constructs subject to coercion was developed. Probably it is for this reason that ALGOL 68 was not so widely used and was too complicated for learning.

Later, the authors of C and C++ took a reasonably simplified approach. They introduced just two concepts: L-value and R-value. The idea is illustrated by a general form of assignment:

L_value = R_value;

CTS distinguishes between two types of coercions: *coercion with extension* and *coercion with truncation*. Coercions with extension (e.g., conversion of a float to a double) don't cause any information loss. They are usually implemented as implicit conversions. The compiler just inserts appropriate conversion instructions for intermediate or native code to enable such conversions.

Coercions with truncation (e.g., conversion of a double to a float) may cause information loss. The lower bits of mantissa that don't fit into a smaller format are truncated. Such coercions are usually implemented as explicit conversions:

float f = (float) double_value;

In any case, coercions update the value.

Casting is another kind of type conversions that, unlike coercion, does not change the value. The value has the same type as its address (except for *ref* or "*"). Casting allows us to consider the value as if it were of another type. In the history of casting, C and C++ provide the most unsafe method of casting, which may be called "arbitrary": If *p* is a pointer to a structure, than any casting such as *(T) p* is possible, where *T* is a type of pointer to any other structure, regardless of its size.

Such casting may lead to incorrect memory access, segmentation violation, and so on. In the worst case, it is not checked at all and allows the user to intrude into a "foreign" area of memory. Usually, casting is a compile-time operation, if the exact type is known at compile time. In CTS, due to metadata, casting is a completely safe operation. The types of the value to cast and the resulting type are compared at compile time, if possible, or at runtime. Runtime type checking can lead to throwing an exception.

In OOP, a typical example of casting is as follows:

(AncestorType) descendant

where *AncestorType* is the type of the superclass, and *descendant* is a managed pointer to an object of the subclass. On the contrary, an attempt to convert an ancestor pointer to a descendant is considered unsafe and leads to throwing an exception.

To compare all of this to Java technology, in Java the situation is almost the same. All castings are completely safe, and an attempt at unsafe casting leads to throwing a *ClassCastException*.

CLS is a specific set of rules (or restrictions) to support multilanguage interoperability. If a language and its implementation are CLS-compliant, or at least in a component written in a .NET language, non-CLS compliant features are not used. The component can then be interoperable to CLS-compliant components written in other languages. All in all, there are 48 CLS rules in the ECMA 335 standard (dated 2006).

CLS requirements are a subset of common type system requirements. On the one hand, they are wide and expressive enough; on the other hand, they are narrow enough to be applicable to all languages. Only verifiable constructs are included in CLS. This means that CLS compliance can be checked at compile time or at runtime.

CLS rules are applicable only to types accessible from outside an assembly. In this case, assemblies are considered as subjects of multilanguage interoperability. Here are examples of CLS rules with some comments:

- *Example 1:* Case sensitivity for identifiers; identifiers differing only in the case of letters are considered to be different. In earlier languages such as ALGOL or Pascal, this was not so. That's why compliance to this rule is very important.

- *Example 2:* An identifier cannot be the same as a keyword in any language. Earlier languages solved this problem in the other way: keywords were made graphically different from identifiers by putting them into quotes, putting a dot before the keyword, and so on. Since Pascal, that practice has gone, so there should be no confusion related, for example, to using (in some exotic language) identifiers such as DO or BEGIN.

- *Example 3:* CTS allows for a method and a field to have the same name; CLS does *not*. In different languages there are different rules as to whether or not the same names of entities of different natures are allowed. So, in CLS, a "maximal" restriction is taken as the rule.

The common type system distinguished between *value types* and *reference types*. As mentioned before, in the history of programming languages, two approaches to the concept of object and variable were developed: the *container approach* and the *object reference approach*. The container approach was used in earlier languages such as ALGOL and Pascal. The same approach was taken in C++ to "struggle" with the potential inefficiency of the object reference approach. This approach means that a variable is treated as the name of a container (structure, array, etc.). The container should be allocated as efficiently as possible, preferably on the stack, to avoid extra indirect addressing operators when accessing components of the variable. Creating a container is performed implicitly by declaring the variable. In addition, if heap allocation is necessary for dynamic structures, it is necessary to define an explicit type of pointer to the structure, and to use an explicit *global generator* or *constructor* such as *new* or *allocate*.

On the contrary, the essence of an *object reference approach* is that all variables are implicit pointers to structures or objects, and all structures and objects themselves are allocated on the heap only. Such an approach was first taken in SIMULA 67, one of the first OOP languages, and many earlier ADT and OOP languages, such as CLU and Java, followed this model.

So now it should be clear why the designers of CTS decided to combine the two approaches. As a result, both *reference types* (which follow the *object reference model*) and *value types* (which follow the *container model*) coexist in CTS, and it does not lead to any confusions. Moreover, value types and reference types can be converted to each other.

Value types are represented by a *sequence of bits stored at some location*. Value types are primitive types (e.g., integer and float). But what is very important is that *structures* are also *value types* (as opposed to classes).

Reference types are represented by a *location* and by a *sequence of bits stored at the location*. Examples of reference types are *objects (classes), interfaces, managed pointers*, and *delegates*. In Java, all types are reference types, except for primitive types.

So as not to make the chapter too monotonic, I have omitted the rest of the lecture notes on CTS, as well as the lecture notes to all subsequent .NET course topics. An overview of .NET and its security model is provided in Section 2.5. I believe that the lecture notes included here are enough to get a feeling for the style of the course. The full list of .NET course topics starting with topic 5 is given below. The readers can find the full version of the lecture notes in my undergraduate .NET course [143].

Topic 5. *Attributes, metadata, and reflection.*

Topic 6. *Assemblies and PE files. Versioning.*

Topic 7. *Compilation and just-in-time compilation in .NET.*

Topic 8. *The C# language: differences from C++, data types, interfaces, classes, access modifiers, namespaces.*

Topic 9. *The C# language: control statements, memory management and garbage collection, generics, partial classes.*

Topic 10. *.NET tools: .NET Framework SDK, Visual Studio .NET.*

Topic 11. *Web programming and Web services in .NET.*

Topic 12. *Application domains and .NET remoting.*

Topic 13. *.NET security.*

Topic 14. *Multithreading in .NET.*

As the result of taking and passing this .NET course and the .NET seminar (see Section 5.4.2), students acquire fundamental knowledge of all major .NET parts and functionality.

5.4.2 Structure of the .NET and C# Programming Seminar

The .NET seminar under my supervision at St. Petersburg University gives students more detailed information on a variety of .NET features, including .NET tools such as FxCop and Spec#, which is especially important for trustworthy programming. That and my other seminars consist of student presentations on selected topics, followed by my comments and critiques if necessary, and by discussions on the topics being considered. It is especially important for students to demonstrate their practical commercial development experience in .NET. In general, in this seminar as well as my other seminars, interesting presentations are illustrated by understandable code examples. Topics 1 to 7 are basic in nature; they cover the principal concepts of .NET, so the presentations on those topics are recommended in the order indicated, at several starting classes of the seminar. The order of the rest of the topics can vary. Topics 8 to 13 are related to *SSCLI (Rotor)*, the academic shared-source version of .NET. Their importance and usability is strengthened by the fact that the sources of all Rotor parts are available, and the task of the speaker is not only to expose general principles, but also to study the appropriate part of the Rotor sources and refer to them during the presentation. References to and reviews of the working code are the most difficult for students, but there are good examples of students managing to do it appropriately. Topics 14 to 16 are devoted to trustworthy programming principles, recommendations, and tools. I was very pleased when the student who made a presentation on FxCop related that at the company where she works, using FxCop is mandatory for all software product code under development. Topics 17 to 19 are concerned with Web programming for .NET, a favorite topic for students. They are very proud to demonstrate the "code behind" their Web services and to explain to their classmates what AJAX is and how it is supported in the latest version of ASP.NET for AJAX. All topics are of interest to students, even those usually considered mundane, such as Windows forms. You can find the best student presentations in the undergraduate .NET seminar [147]. Most of them are in Russian, since I don't require presenting the topics in English; but some students do that, to improve their professional English.

Here is the list of all the topics presented at the .NET seminar.

Topic 1. *Overview of .NET architecture and features.*

Topic 2. *.NET common language infrastructure (CLI).*

Topic 3. *.NET common type system (CTS).*

Topic 4. *.NET common language runtime (CLR).*

Topic 5. *.NET common intermediate language (CIL, MSIL).*

Topic 6. *Metadata, attributes, and reflection in .NET.*

Topic 7. *Assemblies, versioning, strong names, portable executable (PE) files.*

Topic 8. *Overview of academic noncommercial shared-source version of .NET (shared-source CLI, Rotor 2.0).*

Topic 9. *C# compiler in Rotor 2.0.*

Topic 10. *JScript compiler in Rotor 2.0.*

Topic 11. *Just-in-time compilation in .NET. Just-in-time compiler (FJIT) in Rotor 2.0.*

Topic 12. *Memory management and garbage collection in .NET and in Rotor 2.0.*

Topic 13. *Platform adaptation layer (PAL) in Rotor 2.0.*

Topic 14. *.NET security.*

Topic 15. *.NET security tools. The FxCop utility.*

Topic 16. *Trustworthy programming for .NET in C#, VB.NET, and Managed C++.NET: principles and recommendations.*

Topic 17. *Web programming for .NET: ASP.NET.*

Topic 18. *Web programming for .NET: XML Web services.*

Topic 19. *The AJAX technology and its support in ASP.NET.*

Topic 20. *Application domains. Remoting.*

Topic 21. *ADO.NET: database connectivity in .NET.*

Topic 22. *Asynchronous programming, multithreading, and synchronization in .NET.*

Topic 23. *Debugging and logging in .NET.*

Topic 24. *GUI support in .NET. Windows forms. Web forms.*

Topic 25. *C# 2.0: generics and partial classes.*

Topic 26. *New features of .NET framework 3.0. Visual Studio.NET for .NET 3.0. .NET 3.0 and Windows Vista.*

Topic 27. *.NET compact framework.*

Topic 28. *The indigo (WCF) technology for creating service-oriented applications.*

Topic 29. *Comparative analysis of .NET and Java performance.*

Topic 30. *Spec#: program specification, verification, and trustworthy programming in C#.*

Topic 31. *Mono: a shared-source version of .NET.*

Topic 32. *Aspect-oriented programming for .NET. Aspect.NET, Weave. NET, Wicca, LOOM.NET, and so on.*

Topic 33. *Knowledge management tools for .NET. Knowledge.NET.*

5.5 TEACHING TRUSTWORTHY JAVA TECHNOLOGY

Java technology is a subject I started teaching at our university in 1996 with our Sun Java projects. During 11 years of teaching Java, the course and seminar on Java technology have become more and more popular. In 2006, my Java course was taken and passed by about 150 students. Based on my experience of teaching Java and of our Sun Java projects, in 2002 I published a book [70] which was recommended by our Ministry of Higher Education as the basic textbook on Java. Now the book is used by many thousands of Russian students in Moscow, St. Petersburg, Nizhny Novgorod, Novosibirsk, and other major scientific and educational centers in Russia. My principle in my Java book was different from many others. I made my book very compact (186 pages only), used the ERATO paradigm (see Section 5.1.1) to make the knowledge of Java acquired by the readers more fundamental and deep, and included many small but self-explanatory Java code examples of my own. As a result, my Java book became very popular among university students and teachers who are eager to learn Java. Many of our students and even some our teachers reported that to reading my book is enough to capture the Java basics and to start one's own Java programming practice, based on the accompanying Java API documentation only.

No matter how popular my book is, I renew the content of my Java classes each year, since the Java technology is moving forward by giant steps, and plenty of new features are now part of Java technology, compared to the first release, Java 1.0, shipped in 1995. When teaching Java, I follow the principles of trustworthy computing. Although programming in Java seems to imply automatically that the resulting code is trustworthy and bug-free, in practice, it is not. See Section 2.6.3 for an analysis of Java reliability issues. I analyze all of them in detail in my Java course. Especially important is the "*string1 == string2*" issue. More complicated are Java multithreading and synchronization issues and methods to avoid deadlocks. Such problems arise in any language and software development platform that supports multithreading. Also, trustworthy class design issues such as the well-known example by Gosling (*Circle* class incorrectly designed as a descendant of the *Point* class), and trustworthy use of exceptions (*StackUnderflow* as a trustworthy use and *EndOfFile* as nontrustworthy use), are considered.

5.5.1 Structure of the Java Course

Next we look at the topics I teach in my Java course. They cover the basics of Java technology. Where really necessary, I provide a brief version of the lecture notes for some of the topics. The full version of the course curriculum (in Russian) is published at the Sun Russia Web site [156], based on the teaching grant award I received from Sun in 2006. I didn't upload English versions of my Java presentations, but I am ready and interested in teaching Java in English in case there is an interest in it at foreign universities.

> **Topic 1.** *Java history, domains of application of Java technology. Differences from C++. The Java and .NET platforms. Java community process. Overview of new features of Java 1.5, Java 1.6, and Java 1.7.*

Lecture notes for topic 1. Students should feel the range and spectrum of Java evolution, understand how popular is Java all over the world, and understand how important is for them to study Java technology and participate in its development. As a way of doing that, the Java community process (JCP) is considered. Everyone can become a member of JCP for free and participate in Java development and discussions. Also, I emphasize that right now it is quite possible for everyone to participate in the Java development kit (JDK) development process using its sources, since Sun assigned shared-source status to the JDK.

Topic 2. *Basic concepts of Java. The first Java application, its compile and execution. Types of Java applications.*

Topic 3. *Objects, object references, classes, fields, methods, inheritance. Access modifiers of fields, methods, classes, and packages.*

Topic 4. *The Object class. Interfaces and their use. Interfaces and annotations.*

Topic 5. *Packages. Structure of Java projects. The CLASSPATH environment variable, property, and option. Overview of Java core API predefined packages.*

Topic 6. *Nested classes and interfaces. Static initializers.*

Lecture notes for topic 6. Nested classes are somewhat difficult for students to understand. I think such difficulties are consequences of the early C and early FORTRAN style of programming, with no use of nested methods. I provide simple practical examples to show why nested classes are important: in particular, using nested anonymous classes for event listeners. To compare Java to other platforms, I emphasize that Wirth in 1977 included nested modules in the first version of his *Modula* language, due to their special importance.

Topic 7. *Runtime type analysis features: java.lang.Class, reflection API.*

Lecture notes for topic 7. Reflection is, on the one hand, a very interesting topic for students, but on the other hand, they don't always understand its features and are unable to compare reflection in Java and .NET. My description of reflection features is based on practical examples, such as using reflection to develop a test harness that needs to call different methods without using the source code of their headers. When comparing reflection features in Java and .NET, I emphasize that in .NET it is quite possible not only to *analyze* types using reflection, but also to *generate* new assemblies using *Reflection.Emit*. In Java it is still only possible to analyze types rather than to construct new class files. This limitation discovers the generic difference in Java's and .NET's approach to using bytecode: In Java, unlike .NET, programmers are not welcome to use "Java assembler" to write applications directly in bytecode.

Topic 8. *Primitive types int, double, Boolean, etc. Integer and floating-point arithmetic. Wrapper classes. Boxing and unboxing in Java 1.5.*

Lecture notes for topic 8. The simplicity of this topic is misleading. In reality, there are a lot of TWC pitfalls when using arithmetic operations in Java. In particular, it is surprising for Java beginners that

```
Double.NaN == Double.NaN
```

returns *false*. See Section 2.5.1 for more detailed analysis of TWC issues of Java arithmetic. As for boxing and unboxing introduced in Java 1.5, this is a good example of the backward influence of .NET to Java: Compared to .NET-style boxing and unboxing, explicit use of wrapper classes in Java before 1.5 looks awkward.

Topic 9. *Initialization of fields and variables. Strings and arrays.*

Lecture notes for topic 9. Speaking of Java strings, it is necessary to warn students about the string equality issue (see Section 2.5.1): For trustworthy comparison of two strings, the *equals* method should be used. Also, the *StringBuffer* class that implements variable-length string buffer should be overviewed as a realistic way to achieve efficient memory use.

Topic 10. *Java control statements.*

Lecture notes for topic 10. Teaching Java statements should refer to C and C++, since Java syntax is inherited from those languages.

Topic 11. *Exceptions in Java, their taxonomy, throwing and catching. Assertions.*

Lecture notes for topic 11. Exception handling is one of the most interesting topics for students in Java, and one of the most difficult. Surprising as it may seem, not all students learn from the first attempt what kind of Java entity (a class, rather than an object, or field, or any other entity kind) is denoted by the *NullPointerException* identifier. I provide detailed analysis of the exception concept and its historical retrospective, including the origin of the *signal* concept in CLU in the mid-1970s, and introducing exceptions as objects into C++ in 1993. I consider Java exceptions taxonomy, checked and unchecked exceptions, and practical recommendations on how to use exceptions appropriately (e.g., bad practice is to throw an exception when the input stream finishes; instead, the *break* statement should be used, to terminate the loop).

Topic 12. *Threads and multithreading in Java. New threading features in Java 1.5.*

Lecture notes for topic 12. Multithreading is another interesting but difficult topic for students. I consider the origin and history of multithreading, the lightweight process concept, classical ways and types of synchronization, and practical recommendations on deadlock prevention. Of special important is the discussion on why the *stop* and *suspend* methods acquired their *deprecated* status since Java 1.1. An evident example of nontrustworthy use of *t.stop*() is at the moment when thread *t* has entered into its critical section. Trustworthy versions of implementing *suspend* and *stop* actions are considered. I emphasize that Java was the first language to introduce the concept of thread directly at the language and core API level.

Topic 13. *Applets: architecture, security, event processing, output, resource handling.*

Lecture notes for topic 13. This is one of the most demonstrative topics in teaching the principles of Java security and their evolution. I consider the concept of the applet, the basic methods of the applet, and its communication with its Web server and other applets. I trace the entire process of the evolution of applet security in Java 1.0 (sandbox), Java 1.1 (trusted and signed applets), and the latest versions of Java (configurable security policies). See Section 2.6.2 for more details.

Topic 14. *Serialization and deserialization.*

Lecture notes for topic 14. The topic is simple and can be taught by a couple of practical examples of serializing and deserializing Java objects. I emphasize the trustworthiness of Java serialization and deserialization, due to the fact that types are also serialized and can be checked at runtime during deserialization.

Topic 15. *The JavaBeans technology.*

Lecture notes for topic 15. This is one of the central topics in teaching Java. I overview the retrospective of component approaches to programming and emphasize the importance of JavaBeans in this respect. All JavaBeans basic elements are considered in detail: simple and indexed properties, bound properties, and constrained properties. I emphasize that initially, in Java 1.1, shipped in 1996, JavaBeans had to be introduced without Java language support, as a discipline of naming and designing methods to form the *get/set* "property pair." I show how, using reflection, the introspector and Java builder tools analyze the structure of a JavaBean. I pay attention to the fact that in Java 1.7, Sun plans to implement properties in Java at the language syntax level in C#-like style. This is another proof of the backward influence of .NET to Java technology.

Topic 16. *Abstract windowing toolkit (AWT).*

Lecture notes for topic 16. As a historical retrospective, I overview all major stages of GUI evolution: Apple MacOS, XWindow, ActiveX, OpenLook, Motif, and so on. The historical role of AWT is the first platform-independent GUI supporting API. I overview its main concepts and class hierarchy, consider a number of practical examples, and analyze AWT shortcomings, such heavy-weight implementation of GUI components, all related to their native peers.

Topic 17. *Swing. New Swing features in Java 1.5 and 1.6.*

Lecture notes for topic 17. Compared to AWT, Swing components are lightweight, written in Java, more efficient, and more flexible. Swing provides much more control, such as *JTree* for handling tree-structured information. The model–view–controller (MVC) GUI design paradigm is considered, and its use in Swing basic classes' hierarchy design is emphasized. As one of the most important features, I describe *Pluggable Look-and-Feel* (*PLAF*), an API that allows us easily to change the style of visualization of all Swing components drawn by an application at runtime (e.g., change *Motif* to *Ocean*).

Topic 18. *Networking in Java. The java.net package. New networking features in Java 1.5.*

Lecture notes for topic 18. Due to extensive networking support in Java, we can refer to Java as a *universal language for network application development*. Java allows us easily to develop a network application to implement any type of common-use network protocol (e.g., *ftp* or *telnet*) and to develop various kinds of Web applications. I consider the support in Java of basic networking concepts such as *INetAddess, ClientSocket, ServerSocket*, and IP multicasting.

Topic 19. *Enumerations.*

Lecture notes for topic 19. Java enumerations were introduced in version 1.5 only. To my mind, Java enumerations are overly complicated, since a Java enumeration, contrary to all Pascal and C traditions, is a class, with the enumeration values being the objects of the class. However, I show by examples that such an approach provides more opportunities: for example, allows us to bind a set of values to each enumeration member and to define methods to operate the members of an enumeration. In C#, enumerations are much simpler and semantically relative to Pascal enumerations.

Topic 20. *Parametrized types and methods* (*generics*).

Lecture notes for topic 20. Generics were also introduced in Java 1.5 only, after five years of discussion and trial use of their experimental implementation. This concept is of fundamental importance, both for trustworthy programming and for software reusability. In my course I analyze the Java approach to generics and their implementation. It appears to be quite trustworthy and efficient. In particular (unlike C++ templates), instantiating a template class does not lead to any code duplication: All instances of generic with different parameters share the same class file. In addition, the approach to formulating *restrictions* to the type parameter is right in the spirit of Java; they are specified as a set of interfaces that the type parameter is required to implement. Quite comfortable are *wildcards* in generic instantiation constructs; they allow us to develop general-purpose methods, such as printing any collection. Unlike C++ templates, Java generics are type-safe. To my mind, there is only one drawback: no *constant parameters* in Java generics (e.g., a stack parametrized by its maximal depth, as in CLU in 1974).

Topic 21. *Annotations.*

Lecture notes for topic 21. Annotations were implemented in Java 1.5 as a backward influence of .NET attributes. The importance of annotations, in particular, for implementing AOP is discussed in Section 3.5. The use of annotations in Java is quite trustworthy. Moreover, since Java 1.6 it is possible to develop user-defined annotation processors, which is especially important for trustworthy programming, since it allows us to implement formal verification and other types of program analysis and transformations.

Topic 22. *Java Micro Edition.*

Lecture notes for topic 22. This topic is a one-lecture overview of JME, the basic concepts and profiles (MIDP, CLDC, CDC, midlets). I allow students to give more detailed presentations on JME (as one of the most interesting subjects for students) at our Java seminar. I emphasize the importance of JME for oncoming perspectives of Java technology, since all the leading mobile phone vendor companies support Java.

Topic 23. *Java Enterprise Edition.*

Lecture notes for topic 23. In my lecture course, as well as for JME, I provide only a one-lecture overview of the basic concepts of JEE. I allow students to give more presentations on JEE and Enterprise JavaBeans at our seminar.

Note that there is no special lecture on Java security in this course program. I overview security issues when talking about applets. I allow students to make detailed presentations on Java security themselves during our Java seminar, since security is traditionally a very interesting topic for students. The same educational principle is used for Java Web programming and Web services.

5.5.2 Structure of the Java Seminar

My Java seminar [157], as well as my Java course described in Section 5.5.1, are parts of the Java technology educational program I organized at

St. Petersburg university in 1996, the year we started working for Sun. The Java seminar, as well as the Java course, was awarded Sun's teaching grants in 2006.

The seminar curricula [157] uploaded to the Sun Russia Web site contains the best presentations made by our students at our seminar. The principles of the seminar organization are similar to the principles of my .NET seminar (see Section 5.4.2): Any student's talk should be based on a *PowerPoint presentation*; it is necessary to include *working Java code examples* in addition to principles and concepts; *students can offer their own topics* for their talks, related to the commercial Java projects they participate in; much attention is paid to *trustworthy computing*.

Compared to the .NET seminar (Section 5.4.2) and compiler seminar (Section 5.7.2), the Java seminar is intended for third-year students, so they are not yet experienced in making public presentations and need additional guidance. Their presentations are subject to one or more "iterations" of understanding my remarks and correcting a presentation before it is used in class. When a student experiences any problems during public presentation (e.g., is too shy or cannot demonstrate good professional speech), I always recommend writing down the full text of the presentation and repeating it several times to family or friends to better get ready for the class presentation.

The Java technology topics the students are mostly interested in are *Java Micro Edition* (topic 5), *Java Enterprise Edition* (topic 6), *Java security* (topic 9), *Java and XML* (topic 10), *AJAX technology and its support in Java* (topic 12), *Java Web programming* (topics 13 and 14), *Java decompilers and obfuscators* (topic 20), and *Java generics* (topic 22). The topics most difficult for students to understand are *Java Enterprise Edition, Java security, Java Web programming*, and *Java generics*.

In the seminar program listed in detail below, there are different groups of topics. Topics 1 to 3 can be referred to as "mundane but need-to-know." In my Java course I have no time to consider these topics in detail, although I refer to them in my Java code examples. Topics 7, 8, and 19 are devoted to important but more internal elements of Java technology, which nevertheless, students majoring in system programming should learn. Topics 4, 26, and 27 are related to the most widely use Java integrated development environments, so presentations on those topics should be followed by a demonstration of their functioning. In particular, topic 26 (NetBeans and its C/C++ pack) is closely related to the themes of our joint projects with Sun. Note that in topics 22, 26, 28, and 31 to 33 we require from students good knowledge of *new* Java features. I consider it especially important that students learn and start to use new features quickly, so that they follow the same traditions during all of their professional work after graduation; software technologies are evolving rapidly. In particular, Java 1.6 and the coming Java 1.7 are much more complicated and much less conceptually clear than both Java 1.0 and 1.1. But in the latest releases of Java, a lot of commercially important features are implemented, and students should understand them correctly and evolve in their use of Java to avoid remaining "early Java fans" throughout their professional lives. In particular, they should understand the importance of Java generics, know them in detail based on practical code examples, use them in their own projects, and understand why Java generics are much more trustworthy than C++ templates.

Topic 1. *Java input and output. The java.io and java.nio packages.*

Topic 2. *Java data structures and utilities. The java.util package.*

Topic 3. *Java and databases. JDBC.*

Topic 4. *Overview of Java development tools: JDK, NetBeans, Borland JBuilder, IBM WebSphere, IntelliJ IDEA, and so on.*

Topic 5. *Java Micro Edition: MIDP, CLDC, CDC, midlets, Sun J2ME Wireless Toolkit.*

Topic 6. *Java Enterprise Edition. Enterprise JavaBeans.*

Topic 7. *Java virtual machine (JVM). The structure of Java class files.*

Topic 8. *Runtime class loading in Java. Class verification.*

Topic 9. *Java security.*

Topic 10. *Java and XML.*

Topic 11. *Servlets in Java. Java servlet API.*

Topic 12. *The AJAX technology and its support in Java.*

Topic 13. *Java Web programming. Java Web services.*

Topic 14. *Developing Java Web applications using Jakarta Struts framework.*

Topic 15. *Native methods in Java. Java Native Interface (JNI).*

Topic 16. *Remote Method Invocations (RMI) in Java.*

Topic 17. *Java and .NET platforms: comparative analysis of features and performance.*

Topic 18. *Overview of Java virtual machines: Classic VM, HotSpot, CDC Virtual Machine, KVM, IBM DK, Jikes RVM, and other shared-source Java virtual machines.*

Topic 19. *Just-in-time compilation in Java.*

Topic 20. *Decompilers and obfuscators for Java.*

Topic 21. *Overview of memory management and garbage collection techniques in Java.*

Topic 22. *Generics in Java 1.5 and Java 1.6. Generic collections, their examples and use cases.*

Topic 23. *Java Card technology for smart card application development.*

Topic 24. *Jini technology.*

Topic 25. *Sun Java Studio Creator toolkit.*

Topic 26. *NetBeans IDE and open-source project. NetBeans C/C++ pack.*

Topic 27. *Developing Java technology by the community of its developers and users. Java Community Process (JCP), Java Specification Requests (JSR).*

Topic 28. *New multithreading features in Java 1.5: thread-local storage, new ways of synchronization, atomic operations.*

Topic 29. *Aspect-oriented programming (AOP) in Java: AspectJ, Aspect-Werks, HyperJ, and so on.*

Topic 30. *Java application servers and their use.*

Topic 31. *Annotations in Java 1.5 and Java 1.6 and their use cases. Implementing user-defined annotation processors.*

Topic 32. *Overview of the shared-source version of JDK 1.6.*

Topic 33. *New features in Java 1.6.*

5.6 TEACHING TRUSTWORTHY OPERATING SYSTEMS AND NETWORKING

Operating systems and networking constitute a synthetic and complicated discipline which requires learning many theoretical and practical elements, and which is closely related to principles, concepts, and mechanisms of trustworthy computing. Teaching OS begins formally at our university in the second year of IT students' education. I teach the OS and networking course for second-year students in the spring semester, two "pairs" of educational hours a week, so actually the size of the course (64 academic hours) is equivalent to that of a normal course taught two hours a week for the entire educational year. In my OS and networking course [146] I rely on excellent contemporary OS textbooks [158,159], although I do think the classical OS textbook [160], written more than 30 years ago, looks quite contemporary and covers many subjects (especially scheduling and synchronization) very well, so I refer to it also. A novel feature of my OS course is my analysis of principles and usage experience of Russian operating systems of the past: *OS DISPAK* [161] for Russian *BESM-6* mainframe computers (used intensively in the 1970s) and *OS Elbrus* [11] (used in the 1980s). This experience may be interesting to American readers. Some readers may not know, in particular, that in the Elbrus operating system in the late 1970s there was a working implementation of multithreading and lightweight processes (speaking in modern terms). You can find this information in the OS course curricula [146].

For professional and other reasons, operating systems and compilers became IT areas in which thousands of talented American and Russian programmers had to work independently, on similar problems, without any knowledge of each other's results; sometimes this way of working resulted in real masterpieces, such as OS DISPAK. When Sun, an outsourcing pioneer, came to

Russia to hire software engineering teams in the early 1990s, Sun managers were pleasantly surprised to find experienced and highly skilled "ready-to-use" groups on operating systems and compilers at Russian institutes. The reason was clear: We had to develop our own inventions for use in operating systems and compilers for the specific architecture computers available in Russia only.

The structure and organization of my OS and networking course are determined primarily by the factor of teaching beginners such a difficult subject as OS. So in the course, a lot of attention is paid not only to OS basics, but also to software engineering basics in general (e.g., processing lists and queues) since it is used widely in OS. When students begin the OS course, some even need detailed explanations of the difference between the FAT and UNIX file systems, and why executing a command such as *rm –rf* * in UNIX is fatal, unlike executing the *delete* command in MS-DOS.

When teaching the OS course, I refer to my extensive Sun experience (10 years of working on Solaris), which helps to illustrate many topics, such as network file systems and mounting (in particular, I consider Sun's NFS and my own experience of its use in detail). In teaching OS, current open- and shared-source OS projects by major software companies are of great help, and I rely on the *Microsoft Windows Shared Source Academic Program, Sun's OpenSolaris project*, and some of the *Linux* distributions available with their sources. So IT students of the early twenty-first century have a unique opportunity to study operating systems using their shared sources (30 years ago when we were students we couldn't even dream of that). The first operating system we learned using its sources was OS Elbrus in the 1980s. It was shipped together with its source code, which was quite positive for skilled system programmers. However, instead of learning the complicated OS better, some software engineering groups using Elbrus tried to build their own simplified version of an OS using its sources without appropriate education on operating systems. I had to explain in the 1980s that it is not appropriate to use such "brute force" as a lower-level physical memory handling primitives directly while working with an OS based on very subtle, mixed type paging and segmentation virtual memory mechanisms. Such examples are very interesting for students and may be of interest for the readers of my OS curriculum.

A separate part of the OS course is devoted to security. I consider OS security basics and overview Microsoft's TWC initiative. Everything related to security is of special interest to students.

I also track the latest advances in networking and explain them to students. In the course, students learn not only the basics of networking and LAN but also GPRS, Wi-Fi, instant messaging, Cingular WWAN, and so on. From my OS course students learn how to organize a LAN properly, what types of servers should be available on the LAN, remote mounting and how it is organized in Solaris and how to make network settings on a workstation or a server.

5.6.1 Structure of the Trustworthy Operating Systems and Networking Course

The full curriculum for this course is available at the MSDNAA CR Web site [146].

Topic 1. *The concept of operating system (OS), its goals. Classification of computer systems.*

Topic 2. *History of OSs. Russian OSs. UNIX dialects. Batch mode, multi-programming mode, time-sharing mode.*

Topic 3. *Specifics of OSs for various types of computer systems (multiprocessor and distributed systems, desktop, laptop, handheld computers). Real-time OSs.*

Topic 4. *Computer system architecture basics. Interrupt, memory, and I/O control. Memory hierarchy. Caching. Memory protection. Hardware support of memory protection in computer systems with tagged architecture.*

Topic 5. *LAN and WAN basics. OS architecture basics. Process management basic concepts. Semaphores and monitors.*

Topic 6. *Overview of OS functions: memory management, file management, process management, network management, command interpreter support, OS services, system calls. Levels of abstraction in OS architecture. UNIX and MS-DOS architecture overview.*

Topic 7. *OS with microkernel architecture. Virtual machine approach. OS design and implementation. OS generation.*

Topic 8. *Process management, scheduling, and dispatching.*

Topic 9. *Interprocess communication. Bounded buffer scheme. Producer–consumer scheme. Direct and indirect interprocess communication. Client–server relationship. Socket communication. Remote procedure call (RPC) and remote management invocation (RMI). Marshaling (serializing) the arguments.*

Topic 10. *Threads and multithreading. Threading models. User threads and kernel threads. Lightweight processes. Threading overview in Elbrus OS, Solaris, Linux, Windows 2000/XP, Java.*

Topic 11. *CPU scheduling and dispatching. Scheduling and dispatching criteria. Dispatching strategies (FCFS, SJF, RR). Multilevel queues.*

Topic 12. *Process synchronization. Critical sections. Algorithms to solve the problem of mutual exclusion of critical sections.*

Topic 13. *Binary and counting semaphores. Solution of the problems "bounded buffer," "readers and writers," and "dining philosophers" using semaphores. Monitors. Synchronization in Solaris and Windows 2000/XP.*

Topic 14. *Deadlocks. The model of the system. The resource allocation graph and the wait-for graph. Methods of deadlock handling and prevention. The banker's algorithm. Algorithms of deadlock detection.*

Topic 15. *Memory management. Memory management unit (MMU). Logical and physical address spaces. Dynamic linking. Overlay program structure.*

Topic 16. *Swapping. Swapping-in and swapping-out. Dynamic memory allocation strategies. Fragmentation. Paging. Page table. Caching. Two-level, hierarchical, hashed, and inverted architecture of page table. Shared pages.*

Topic 17. *Segmenation. Segment-paging memory organization (MULTICS, Elbrus, Intel x86).*

Topic 18. *Virtual memory. Virtual memory paging. Page faults and their handling. On-demand paging. Sharing pages by multiple processes. Memory-mapped files. Page replacement strategies. FIFO and LRU algorithms. The "second chance" algorithm. Counter-based algorithms. Frame allocation: fixed and priority-based. Thrashing. Paging in Windows NT/2000/XP and Solaris.*

Topic 19. *Interface to file system. File structure and operations. File types. Differences of file systems in MULTICS and Elbrus from file systems in OS for PC. Sequential and direct access files. Directories and ways of organizing directory structure. File system mounting. File protection. File control block (FCB).*

Topic 20. *Virtual file systems (VFSs). File representation using FAT (Windows) and index blocks (UNIX). External memory management. Caching. Transaction log–based file systems. The NFS file system.*

Topic 21. *Networking and network structures. Distributed and networking systems. Topologies and types of networks. Communication on the network. Routing. Naming and name resolution.*

Topic 22. *Communication protocols. Network layering by the ISO/OSI model. TCP/IP protocols. GPRS protocols. Wireless networking and IEEE 802.11x (Wi-Fi) protocols. Instant messaging and presence. Error detection in networks and network reconfiguration. Network design.*

Topic 23. *Security. Network and system threats and attacks. Threat mitigation. Networking system auditing. Firewalls. Detection of intrusion attempts. Cryptography. Secure Socket Layer (SSL). Security levels of computers. Security problems decision in Windows NT/2000/XP and in Microsoft. NET. Security policies. The Microsoft trustworthy computing initiative.*

Topic 24. *Overview of Linux operating systems.*

Topic 25. *Overview of Windows 2000, Windows XP, Windows 2003, Windows Vista operating systems.*

5.7 TEACHING TRUSTWORTHY COMPILER DEVELOPMENT

Due to the fact that compiler development started in the 1950s, some people may think that the compiler development area is too old and that nothing new has appeared in that area since the times of early FORTRAN and ALGOL 60. In reality, compiler development is now one of the most actively evolving fields of computer science and software engineering. The following main factors activated research and development in the compiler area:

- *Developing new hardware architectures:* in particular, VLIW, EPIC, and multicore architectures that require much more nontrivial work on static parallelizing of computations from the compilers than before.
- *.NET development.* One of the main .NET programming paradigms is *peer-to-peer multilanguage programming.* So, .NET stimulates the development of more and more compilers for all widely used languages. It can be considered the *.NET compiler boom.*
- *Wide use of just-in-time (JIT) compilation.* In modern software development platforms such as Java and .NET, JIT compilation is one of the principal techniques of runtime performance increase. However, as compared to "ordinary" compiler techniques, JIT compilation techniques are far from ideal.
- *Wide use of languages with elements of dynamic typing (JavaScript, Ruby, Python, etc.).* Those languages are used more and more widely for Web programming. However, some key features of those languages require new efficient compilation and JIT compilation techniques. For example, the structure of an *object type* (*class*), in general, is finally determined in these languages at runtime, since there can appear a statement such as $p.X = V$, where X is a *new* field of the object p belonging to some class C such that in the initial definition of C there was *no* field X. Such features require efficient implementation to avoid unnecessary linear searching at runtime.

My compiler development experience is rich and intensive. My team and I developed a lot of compilers for Elbrus and the IBM PC and participated in Sun's project on compiler development and maintenance. So, in teaching compilers, I rely not only on such classical textbooks as *Dragon Book* by Aho et al. and *Compiler Construction* by Gries, but also teach my own efficient compiling techniques developed, implemented, and applied to industrial compilers [11,150–153]. The compiler teaching program I organized at St. Petersburg University consists of a compiler course [144] and a compiler seminar [148]. In my compiler classes I rely on my Sun compiler experience and my more recent experience of using Microsoft Phoenix. Special parts of my compiler course are devoted to overview and analysis of Sun Studio compilers and the Phoenix compiler optimizing back-end development toolkit by Microsoft. Special importance is paid to Hoare's concept of *trustworthy compiler* and to trustworthy organization and functioning of modern compilers. In each part of the course, for example, when considering parsing and semantic analysis, I especially emphasize what types of features and behavior a compiler should have to be considered trustworthy. It means, above all, that the compiler should enable good *error recovery* techniques and good *error diagnostics* for users.

5.7.1 Structure of the Trustworthy Compiler Development Course

The full curriculum for this course is available at the MSDNAA CR Web site [144].

Topic 1. *The concept of the trustworthy compiler. Types of compilers. Phases of compilation. Specifics of Java implementation. Compilation in NET.*

Topic 2. *Compiler architecture principles. Front end and back end. Boot-strapping. Compiler design systems (CDSs).*

Topic 3. *Lexical analysis. Token classes. Processing identifiers and keywords. Identifier table (id_tab) and its hashing.*

Topic 4. *Lexical analyzer: architecture and implementation principles. The lex utility.*

Topic 5. *Parsing. Derivation (parse) trees and abstract syntax trees (AST). Recursive descent technique. Implementation of lookahead for recursive descent parser.*

Topic 6. *Syntax error recovery techniques. Error recovery for recursive descent parser: the "panic mode" and "intelligent panic mode" strategies.*

Topic 7. *Bottom-up parsing. Shift-reduce parsers. The $LL(k)$ and $LR(k)$ language classes. $SLR(0)$ parsing. $LR(0)$ items. The closure (I) and $goto(I,X)$ functions. Canonical collection of sets of $LR(0)$ items.*

Topic 8. *Non-SLR(0) languages. $LR(1)$ items. $LR(1)$ parser. Overview of LALR(1) parser. Error recovery in LR parsing.*

Topic 9. *The yacc utility and its clones (bison, etc.). The ANTLR parser generator.*

Topic 10. *Semantic analysis. Attributed grammars. Synthesized and inherited attributes and their evaluation schemes.*

Topic 11. *L-attributed grammars. Semantic attributes of types, variables, and expressions. Principles and techniques of efficient semantic attribute evaluation.*

Topic 12. *Semantic analysis of definitions and declarations. Lookup. The definition (namelist) table (NL). Efficient lookup algorithms.*

Topic 13. *Semantic analysis of types and type definitions. Type denotation table (Types). Type identity. Type compatibility and assignment compatibility. Type checking.*

Topic 14. *Forms of intermediate representation of the programs in compilers: postfix notation, triples, PCC trees.*

Topic 15. *Program optimizations. Overview of optimization techniques. The concept of mixed (staged) computations.*

Topic 16. *Program optimization: Static single assignment (SSA) intermediate representation. Control and data dependencies. Antidependencies. Data structures used in optimizations. Overview of optimization techniques in Microsoft Phoenix and in Sun Studio compilers.*

Topic 17. *Overview of code generation techniques and tasks. Specifics of code generation for Microsoft.NET. The general architecture of a compiler for the SPARC/Solaris platform. The role of the code generator.*

Topic 18. *Representation of types and variables. Simple types. Records (structures). Variant records and unions. Arrays. Pointers (unmanaged and managed).*

Topic 19. *Procedures, functions, methods, procedural arguments, and their implementation. Organizing stack for procedure calls. Static and dynamic chains on the stack. Display. Addressing local variables. Uplvel addressing. Address pairs. Implementation of display for RISC architectures.*

Topic 20. *Basics of RISC and SPARC architecture. Register windows. Application binary interface (ABI) for the SPARC/Solaris platform. ELF files of object code, their structure and sections. Code generation for SPARC (example).*

Topic 21. *Debugging information and its role in the entire programming system. Generation of debugging information for Microsoft.NET and the SPARC platform. STABS—the format of debugging information on SPARC.*

Topic 22. *Code generation techniques for declarations (definitions), expressions and statements.*

Topic 23. *Runtime and its functions. Relation of runtime and the operating system.*

Topic 24. *Overview of Microsoft Phoenix.*

5.7.2   Structure of the Compiler Development Seminar

The materials of the compiler seminars [the best selected students' presentations (in Russian or English)] are available on the MSDNAA CR Web site [148].

Organizational and teaching principles of this seminar are the same as those of my other seminars on .NET (Section 5.4.2) and on Java (Section 5.5.2). Unlike them, the compiler seminar is intended for graduate (fifth-year) students, already experienced in making public presentations. Many of the students bring to this seminar their own commercial compiler project presentations, which is especially important. Compared to my compiler course, where I overview classical methods, explain my efficient compiling techniques, and consider Sun Studio and Phoenix (Section 5.7.1), in my seminar I try to consider a maximally wide spectrum of topics, from advanced techniques and tools for parsing, to compilation for EPIC architecture and for mobile phones.

Topics 1 to 7 are related to .NET and have some intersection to my .NET seminar program (Section 5.4.2). But the accents of student presentations at this seminar should be different. They should consider .NET from the viewpoint of a compiler developer whose task is to make a compiler for .NET for a new language.

Topics 8 to 12 are devoted to various types of compilers which are only overviewed in my compiler course. Students should get interested not only in JIT and AOT compilers characteristic of .NET, but also understand the nature and architecture of a cross-compiler and a binary compiler. Some of the topics are concerned with compilation techniques for new hardware architectures for Java and for .NET.

Topics 17 to 20 are intended to provide thorough knowledge of Microsoft Phoenix. Students should comprehend the unique architecture of Phoenix and its powerful features for organizing phases of the compiler, for optimization, and for multitargeted code generation. Students should also understand the shared ideas among Phoenix, Sun Studio, and earlier compilers—everything is better learned by comparison. Some students choose to use Phoenix to develop interesting tools as the subject of graduate and doctoral projects.

Topics 23 and 24 are devoted to ANTLR and CoCo/R, two widely used modern parser generators.

Topic 1. *.NET 2.0 and .NET 3.0 architecture overview. Rotor 2.0 overview.*

Topic 2. *Common type system (CTS) in .NET 2.0, .NET 3.0, and Rotor 2.0.*

Topic 3. *Common language infrastructure (CLI) in .NET 2.0, .NET 3.0, and Rotor 2.0.*

Topic 4. *Common intermediate language (CIL) in .NET 2.0, .NET 3.0, and Rotor 2.0.*

Topic 5. *Metadata and attributes in .NET 2.0, .NET 3.0, and Rotor 2.0.*

Topic 6. *C# compiler in Rotor 2.0.*

Topic 7. *JScript compiler in Rotor 2.0.*

Topic 8. *Just-in-time (JIT) compilation. JIT compilers for Java and .NET.*

Topic 9. *Ahead-of-time (AOT) compilation. AOT compilers for Java and .NET.*

Topic 10. *Cross-compilers: research projects and industrial products.*

Topic 11. *Interpreters: their architecture and applications in classic and modern development projects.*

Topic 12. *Binary compilers: their architecture and use cases.*

Topic 13. *Analysis of optimization techniques in classical and modern compilers.*

Topic 14. *Compilers for VLIW, EPIC, and multicore hardware architectures. Methods of static parallelizing of applications.*

Topic 15. *Comparative analysis of Java implementations.*

Topic 16. *Comparative analysis of .NET ISO/ECMA standards implementation (Microsoft.NET, Rotor, Mono, DotGNU, etc.).*

Topic 17. *Overview of Phoenix architecture.*

Topic 18. *Type system and intermediate representations of programs in Phoenix (High-Level IR, Low-Level IR, tables).*

Topic 19. *Optimizations and target platforms in Phoenix.*

Topic 20. *Phoenix tools. Sample C++ compiler back-end (c2) based on Phoenix.*

Topic 21. *Mono's shared-source noncommercial implementation of .NET standards: C# compiler, VM, libraries.*

Topic 22. *Microsoft JLCA: a toolkit for porting applications from Java and .NET.*

Topic 23. *Coco/R: a compiler development toolkit for .NET.*

Topic 24. *ANTLR: a compiler development toolkit.*

5.8 SUMMARY

Trustworthy computing is now *pervasive* not only in commercial and research software projects but also in teaching. Modern IT students should understand how to make an operating system trustworthy and how to protect it from attack; how to organize a trustworthy compiler using efficient compilation techniques; proper use of powerful trustworthy computing features and mechanisms implemented in Java and .NET—modern software development platforms; and how, in general, to use a flexible combination of classical trustworthy computing paradigms (modular programming, abstract data types, and object-oriented programming) and postobject trustworthy computing paradigms such as aspect-oriented programming. As a result of IT education, students should become TWC-oriented and TWC-educated professionals. They should be able to use modern TWC tools (e.g., FxCop), and it should become their everyday practice to do so. Students should also be stimulated to enhance TWC theory, tools, and technologies more and more, for the purpose of developing trustworthy software. In particular, they should be able to use AOP and understand how important it is to make software more trustworthy.

Worldwide TWC education is only at its starting point. This chapter, my book in general, and my SPBU.NET and TrustSPBU.NET teaching projects are my modest contribution to the global challenge of making software and its developers more TWC-oriented.

6

Conclusions

We conclude the book with a summary of the results achieved, and outline perspectives of TWC, AOP, their relationship, and their integration to formal methods and knowledge management techniques to make software technologies more trustworthy and smart.

6.1 SUMMARY OF THE BOOK

Throughout the book I followed several key principles, ideas, and methods formulated at the start or in the core of the book. Hopefully, I managed to prove that they are consistent and applicable, by my analysis, examples, practical experience, and where appropriate, by quantitative assessments:

1. *Trustworthy computing* (*TWC*), whose foundations were formulated and investigated step by step by computer science and software engineering classicists in the 1960s to 1980s, and whose principles were summarized and shed by Microsoft in 2002 through their TWC initiative, is playing a more and more important part in software development, including not only software design and development itself, but organizational and business issues. TWC principles have become pervasive. Following those principles means not only developing new code the right way, but also making a giant piece of legacy code more trustworthy. The latest software development platform, Java and .NET, provide

Using Aspect-Oriented Programming for Trustworthy Software Development,
By Vladimir O. Safonov
Copyright © 2008 John Wiley & Sons, Inc.

many important TWC mechanisms, type-safe managed code execution and flexible models of security. But even using Java and .NET does not guarantee trustworthiness of software. New approaches, technologies, and tools are needed to support TWC on its troublesome way. Typical TWC functionality to be added to the existing software includes security, MT safety, logging, reliability checks, error handling, synchronization, privacy, and others. This functionality has a generic *cross-cutting* nature (i.e., its implementation looks like a set of tangled code fragments to be added to existing code).

2. *Aspect-oriented programming (AOP)* is one such technology. Its essence is absolutely relevant to the needs of TWC: to design some cross-cutting functionality as a new type of module, *aspect,* and to provide tools to *weave* this functionality to existing code. Thus, AOP has a generic relation to TWC. AOP originated in the mid-1990s and is on its way from research experiments and projects to wide industrial use. The main reason for that, I think, is the relevance of AOP for TWC tasks. Detailed analytical overview of the existing AOP approaches and tools is made. One of the most appropriate platforms of implementing AOP appears to be .NET, since it allows us to use custom attributes to represent aspects, and to make aspects language-independent.

3. Our approach to implementation of AOP for .NET is described and implemented in the *Aspect.NET framework.* The approach is based on using simple AOP metalanguage and its converter to custom attributes, integration of Aspect.NET to Visual Studio.NET, a comfortable user interface that allows to visualize aspects and join points, and for deselection of undesirable join points before weaving. Weaving is implemented at the level of assembly's binary code using Microsoft Phoenix as a tool to handle .NET assemblies. Due to that we managed to implement weaving efficiently without instrumentation code and without runtime efficiency loss, as proven by practical examples with time measurement. Following our approach, it is shown to be possible to enhance a large industrial code without using its sources, based on Aspect. NET. Our approach has been proven to increase the productivity of software engineers. Features and use cases of Aspect.NET are described and positive feedback from users in 16 countries is reviewed. Quantitative and qualitative assessment of Aspect.NET is given using the COCOMO, ICED-T, and SQFD models. Aspect.NET and its documentation are available for downloading at the Microsoft Academic Alliance Curriculum Repository Web site. Desirable perspectives of Aspect.NET are its *productizing* (to be shipped with Visual Studio.NET and Phoenix), further enhancements, and wider industrial and academic use.

4. A variety of *TWC tasks* is considered, appropriate ways and examples of solving these tasks using Aspect.NET are described, and working Aspect. NET TWC aspects are presented. This is a practical proof of applicability and adequacy of our approach and the Aspect.NET framework for solving TWC tasks and improving the trustworthiness of programs.

5. To improve software trustworthiness and for TWC orientation of software developers—in particular, for the purpose of wider use of AOP for TWC—consistent and systematic worldwide *TWC education system* is necessary. My contributions to this challenge are the *ERATO* (*experience, retrospective, analysis, theory, oncoming perspectives*) and *T-ERATO* (*trustworthy ERATO*) teaching paradigms, and *SPBU.NET* and *TrustSPBU.NET* resulted in the development and successful use at St. Petersburg University of a number of courses and seminars on *secure software engineering, .NET and C#, Java technology, compilers, operating systems,* and *networking.* The resulting curriculum is disseminated through the Microsoft Academic Alliance Curriculum Repository Web site and (in Java technology) through the Sun Russia Web site.

6.2   PERSPECTIVES: INTEGRATION OF TWC, AOP, FORMAL METHODS, AND KNOWLEDGE MANAGEMENT

This book describes trustworthy computing. We know that the current status of TWC and AOP provides techniques and tools to develop trustworthy software or to make the existing software more trustworthy. These tools, like our Aspect.NET, are comfortable to use.

However, in the near term, keeping in mind further grow of software complexity, this is not enough. Several very important features are lacking in most existing TWC, AOP, and AOP for TWC tools:

1. AOP and TWC tools lack *simple-to-use and practically applicable formal methods to support development of applications whose correctness is proved formally using verifiers.* In particular, it is needed to apply AOP properly for TWC purposes. Future users would not only like to have a powerful *verifying compiler* in use, in terms of Hoare's paper [65], but also a *verifying AOP framework* which not only proves correctness of traditional modules and their parts, but also proves *correctness of aspect-oriented transformations.* For details, see Section 6.2.1.

2. AOP and TWC tools are *not yet smart enough, not adaptive or self-trainable,* since they *lack knowledge* in the traditional meaning of this terms used in knowledge management. Users who develop trustworthy software—in particular, aspects to make software trustworthy—would like the framework they use to suggest methods of trustworthy programming and to protect them from nontrustworthy programming. The current integrated development environments provide *code completion* and *code refactoring* mechanisms only. They are powerful—but it is not enough. Users educated in TWC basics would expect *trustworthy programming suggestions, templates, and schemes*—more than just code completion. What is needed is a tool that *would not allow nontrustworthy code to be developed at all,* or *it should not allow any nontrustworthy use of aspects.* Such tools should be self-trainable as to both positive

and negative experience of trustworthy software development. In other words, trustworthy programming tools—in particular, trustworthy AOP tools—should not totally trust the user's code; instead, they should check it, verify it formally, and suggest how the code should be improved to be trustworthy. For details, see in Section 6.2.2.

3. AOP tools need more specification and design features to suggest the most complicated parts of aspects (weaving rules) to be designed and implemented. For details, see Section 6.2.3.

4. AOP and TWC need relevant *reverse engineering tools* to *extract trustworthy aspects from legacy code* and the *trustworthy (formally verified) reuse of the aspects found* in further trustworthy software development. Also, AOP frameworks need special aspect-oriented refactoring tools. For details, see Section 6.2.4.

5. AOP tools need aspect modeling support, in terms of UML extended by aspect-oriented concepts. For details, see Section 6.2.5.

6.2.1 Application of Formal Methods to Trustworthy AOP

Currently, as mentioned in Section 2.3.3, formal methods are only beginning to enter the phase of worldwide industrial application, although most of the methods were suggested 30–40 years ago. To put it simply, formal methods appeared to be too complicated for most programmers to use. In other words, tools to support formal methods are lacking or inadequate at present, or still have research status, such as the Spec# extension of C# by design-by-contract style specifications. Formal methods to prove the correctness of AOP transformations are currently either completely lacking or are not available in existing AOP frameworks. The desired formal model can be referred to as *aspect calculus* formalizing the effects of aspect weaving. For example, to formulate it in Hoare's style, such as aspect calculus could contain an inference rule scheme such as

$$P\{S\}Q| = R\{A(S)\}T$$

where P, Q, R, and T are predicates on the set of free (global) variables of the program S; A is an aspect; and $A(S)$ is the result of weaving the aspect A to code S. The semantics (interpretation) of this scheme is as follows: Let the program S satisfy Hoare's triple $P\{S\}Q$ (if the precondition P holds before execution of S, then S completes and the postcondition Q holds after S is finished). Then, on weaving the aspect A to S, the weaving result $A(S)$ satisfies Hoare's triple $R\{A(S)\}T$. This inference rule scheme can be regarded as a specification of the semantics of aspect A. In these terms, pre- and postconditions R and T for the program $A(S)$ to be trustworthy can be formulated. The formal verifier of such a *verifying AOP framework* should verify that the result of AOP transformations satisfies the desirable conditions. Complete research on this subject may take a few years. Nevertheless, only by verifying AOP frameworks can we guarantee that the aspect transforms the application as desired, in a trustworthy way, and that the resulting target application is trustworthy.

6.2.2   Smart Knowledge-Based AOP

Our Aspect.NET provides code templates for aspect definition in the Aspect. NET.ML metalanguage or directly in custom attributes. This is an aid for programmers, but that's not enough. The suggestions to programmers regarding what types of aspects to design and develop should rely on *knowledge bases on the problem domains*. Only in this case will the aid to aspect designers and implementers be smart enough.

The simplest version of such aspect designer may not explicitly use knowledge. Instead, it can be based on the domain- and task-oriented repositories of aspect definition templates. The user can make his or her choice of the available set of tasks and domains. Among them should be repositories of typical trustworthy aspect transformation templates. The initial set of trustworthy AOP transformations could be the set considered in Chapter 4. For example, if a synchronization aspect is needed, the smart AOP designer could offer a number of code templates, such as the aspect defined in Section 4.4.

A more flexible smart aspect designer may start the design with selection of the problem domain and the appropriate knowledge base. Any domain-specific knowledge base should contain knowledge as to each domain entity and its relationship to other entities. It can be represented as ontology, augmented by *aspect knowledge*: a set of typical aspects applicable to domain entities. The user should start the design at the conceptual level by choosing the entities with which the application will deal. When the implementation is started, the smart AOP framework should examine correctness at the conceptual level, recommend appropriate aspects, and reject the nonappropriate. To represent such knowledge bases, the Knowledge.NET toolkit [36] can be used. It provides an extension of C# by knowledge representation features: ontologies, rule sets, and frames. The Knowledge.NET language allows us to implement part of the knowledge base directly in C#. It means that the user can implement, as part of the Knowledge.NET knowledge base, a set of Aspect. NET *aspects* implemented in terms of our AOP custom attributes. We have just started research in the direction of integration Aspect.NET and Knowledge.NET features. But it looks prospective, and it corresponds to modern ideas by other authors [117] of integrating knowledge engineering and software engineering techniques. I think this is a way that trustworthy software designer tools can be made intelligent, flexible, and learnable.

6.2.3   AOP Specification and Design Support Tools

We noted in Chapter 3 that compared with ordinary code development, AOP specifics may appear difficult for some users. In particular, what can be the most complicated is the proper formulation of weaving rules. With respect to Aspect.NET, I think a good addition to the Aspect.NET framework could be functionality for automated simplification of weaving rules or converting them to more readable form. For example, a rule of the type:

```
(%after %call *) || (%after %call MyMethod)
```

can be replaced automatically by a simpler but equivalent rule:

```
%after %call *.
```

If an aspect is being developed for a concrete target application, a functionality to convert its weaving rules based on the specifics of the target application could also be helpful. For example, if the application contains the two methods only, "MyMethod1" and "MyMethod2," the weaving rule

```
(%after %call MyMethod1) || (%after %call MyMethod2)
```

could be converted to a shorter one:

```
(%after %call MyMethod*)
```

or, vice versa, the latter rule could be converted to the former one.

Weaving Rule Reader   To simplify the understanding of weaving rules for the user, a *weaving rule reader* could be developed: a component of the Aspect. NET framework to provide a more readable verbal form for the weaving rules selected. A weaving rule could generate an adequate comment to a weaving rule in English. For example, the weaving rule

```
%call %before (private set*(..,int))
```

could have as a comment the following phrase: "before any call of a private method whose name starts with *set*, defined on any type, and whose last argument is an int."

Logical enhancement of the idea of a weaving rules wizard could be a functionality to support the generation of weaving rules in an interactive mode, based on the existing code of target application: for example, by clicking at the points of the source code of the target application to be affected by the aspect weaving rule being designed. This task requires separate research.

6.2.4 Trustworthy Reverse Engineering and Refactoring Tools for AOP

In Visual Studio.NET 2005, advanced code refactoring functionality is supported: automated renaming members of an application, extracting interfaces from classes, transforming fragments of code into separate methods, and so on. For more enhanced support of Aspect.NET, this set of refactoring transformations could be extended by such actions as "transform a method to an aspect's action" or "convert a data definition in an application into an inter-type declaration." Supporting these two functions would actually be equivalent to a basic built-in aspectizer. Surely the set of refactoring transformations related to AOP can be much wider.

Also, *aspect mining* (or *aspectizing*) research should result in developing an industrial-level aspect mining tool. It could be a great moving force to switch many users to AOP if they, as the beginning of a project to convert large piece of legacy code, could apply the aspect mining tool and get a set of possible aspects and possible set of their join points, extracted from the code. This could be very helpful for understanding the code and making it more readable and reusable. As mentioned in Chapters 3 and 4, generally speaking, the task of aspect mining (as well as our research on developing an aspect mining tool for Aspect.NET) is far from solution. But in the near term, solving this task will be one of the principal reverse engineering challenges of AOP.

6.2.5 Aspect-Oriented Modeling on the Basis of Extended UML

Unified Modeling Language (UML) is now widely used for software modeling at the requirements, specification, and design stages. At later stages of the software life cycle (implementation and testing), the code of the system whose architecture is modeled by UML, and the set of unit tests for testing the system are generated automatically. At any moment of the development cycle, the system can be reverse engineered to its UML-based model, which is quite transparent. As for TWC use of UML, there are interesting research papers on UML extensions for security: in particular, Secure UML [162]. AOP does not yet have its "canonized" set of UML extensions, although in AOP research papers such a problem is analyzed. Aspect-oriented modeling on the basis of AOP extension of UML could make the modeling–design–code generation–test generation life cycle available for AOP.

It is hardly possible to conclude a book devoted to such rapidly evolving and popular areas as trustworthy computing, aspect-oriented programming, and their relationships. My contribution and the contribution of my team is still relatively modest; we can do much more. We have a lot of plans and ideas and need interested customers and sponsors to fund our projects. We are open to proposals. We can educate users in AOP basics and in using our system. We hope that Microsoft and other companies will be interested in industrial uses of Aspect.NET.

Thanks again to the creators of AOP and .NET for the great opportunity to do such advanced research in such a new area. It is very rewarding to know that our work on Aspect.NET is interesting to so many people. We'll do our best to make Aspect.NET an industrial AOP framework for trustworthy software development.

Examples of Aspect.NET Aspects

We present here some examples of Aspect.NET aspects not included in Chapters 3 and 4. We start with simple aspects that illustrate Aspect.NET features, then present more complicated design-by-contract aspects. For each of the aspects, the corresponding target application is included and necessary comments are given. The aspects can be used to study Aspect.NET and as the basis for other aspects developed using Aspect.NET. I thank the authors of the examples, Dmitry Grigoriev (Examples A.1 to A.3) and Anna Kogay (Examples A.4 and A.5).

A.1 TestArgs EXAMPLE

This aspect demonstrates the use of Aspect.NET features to capture arguments of the target application method. The example is included in the set of aspect samples shipped with Aspect.NET 2.1 [6]. The example consists of the Visual Studio solution for the target application, *TestArgs*, and the aspect solution, *TestArgsAspect*.

The code of the target application, *TestArgs*, is given below. The application calls two methods, *Method1* (with two arguments) and *Method2* (with two arguments, delivering an integer result). Both *Method1* and *Method2* are called the first time from the *Program.Main* method, and the second time from the *MainClass.Run* method.

Using Aspect-Oriented Programming for Trustworthy Software Development,
By Vladimir O. Safonov
Copyright © 2008 John Wiley & Sons, Inc.

```
using System;
namespace TestArgs
{
    class MainClass
    {
        static public void Run()
        {
            Program.Method1(1, 0.6);
            Program.Method2(1, 0.6);
        }
    }
    class Program
    {
        static void Main(string[] args)
        {
            Method1(1, 0.6);
            Method2(1, 0.6);
            MainClass.Run();
        }
        public static void Method1(int i, double f)
        {
            Console.WriteLine("Hello 1");
        }
        public static int Method2(int i, double f)
        {
            Console.WriteLine("Hello 2");
            return 0;
        }
    }
}
```

The output of the application is as follows:

Hello 1
Hello 2
Hello 1
Hello 2

Next is the code of the *TestArgsAspect* aspect (its *aspect.an* file). The aspect demonstrates the functionality of capturing the arguments of a method and the functionality of limiting the scope for searching join points. In the aspect below, the action *ActionMethod1* works only when the appropriate join point is located within the class whose name ends with *MainClass*. So this weaving rule captures only the calls of *Method1* and *Method2* from *MainClass.Run*, as can be seen from the output of the application after weaving. Similarly, the second weaving rule, with the action *ActionMethod2*, captures the same join points, since they are located within the code of the *Run* method. The third weaving rule, with the action *ActionMethod3*, captures only the call of *Method2* from *Program.Main*, since, first, the target method filter is targeted to catch a method that returns an integer result (i.e., *Method2*), and second, the extra weaving condition catches only join points located *beyond* the code of *MainClass*.

```
%aspect TestArgsAspect
using System;
class TestArgsAspect
{
    %modules
    %rules
        /*
        * Pass the second argument of target method to
          action.
        * Argument indexes 'arg[i]' should start from
          0.
        * Captures target method only with Method(int,
          float) signature
        */
        %before %call Method*(int, double) &&
        %args(arg[1]) && %within(*MainClass)
        %action
        static public void ActionMethod1(float f)
        {
            Console.WriteLine("ActionMethod1: {0}",f);
        }
        /*
        * Pass the first argument of target method to
          action.
        * Captures target method only with Method(int,
          ...) signature
        */
        %before %call Method*(int, ..) && %args(arg[0])
        && %withincode(*Run)
        %action
        static public void ActionMethod2(int i)
        {
            Console.WriteLine("ActionMethod2: {0}", i);
        }
        /*
```

```
    *  Implicitly passing arguments of target
       method directly to action.
    *  Their signatures must be equal.
    *  Captures target method with the Method name
    and any set of arguments.
    */
%before %call int Method*(..) &&
%!within(*MainClass)
%action
static public void ActionMethod3(int i, float
f)
{
    Console.WriteLine("ActionMethod3: {0},
    {1}",i,f);
}
}
```

Here is the output of the enhanced target application after weaving:

Hello 1

ActionMethod3: 1, 0.6

Hello 2

ActionMethod1: 0.6

ActionMethod2: 1

Hello 1

ActionMethod1: 0.6

ActionMethod2: 1

Hello 2

A.2 RetTest EXAMPLE

The *RetTest* example is shipped with Aspect.NET 2.1 [6]. The example is represented by a single Visual Studio.NET solution containing both the target application *RetTest* and the aspect *RetTestAspect*. The example demonstrates various forms of capturing the result of the target application's method. The results of the methods captured by the *RetTestAspect* aspect are an integer, a structure, and a class. The target application uses boxing and unboxing for testing purposes. Here is the code of the target application *RetTest* located in the *Program.cs* source file:

```
using System;
namespace RetTest
{
    struct Struct
    {
        public int a;
    }
    class Class
    {
        public int a;
    }
    class Program
    {
        static void Main(string[] args)
        {
            Console.WriteLine("Non-boxing tests");
            Console.WriteLine(getStruct().a);
            Console.WriteLine(getInt());
            Console.WriteLine(getClass().a);
            Console.WriteLine("Boxing/Unboxing
            tests");
            object o = getStruct();
            Console.WriteLine(((Struct)o).a);
            object i = getInt();
            Console.WriteLine((int)i);
            object c = getClass();
            Console.WriteLine(((Class)c).a);
        }
        static Struct getStruct()
        {
            Struct s = new Struct();
            s.a = 10;
            return s;
        } // getStruct
        static int getInt()
        {
            return 3;
        } // getInt
        static Class getClass()
        {
            Class s = new Class();
            s.a = 10;
            return s;
        } // getClass
    }
}
```

Here is the output of the target application:

Non-boxing tests
10
3
10
Boxing/Unboxing tests
10
3
10

The aspect *RetTestAspect*, whose code (written in pure C# using AOP attributes, without Aspect.NET.ML) is located in the *Aspect.cs* source file, captures the results of the methods directly after their calls and prints them out to the console:

```
using System;
using System.Reflection;
using AspectDotNet;
namespace RetTestAspect
{
    [AspectDescription("MyAspect description")]
    public class MyAspect : Aspect
    {
        [AspectAction("%after %call *getStruct")]
        public static void PrintStruct()
        {
            Console.WriteLine(RetValue.ToString());
            Console.WriteLine(RetValue.GetType().
            GetField("a").GetValue(RetValue));
        }
        [AspectAction("%after %call *getInt")]
        public static void PrintInt()
        {
            Console.WriteLine(RetValue.ToString());
            Console.WriteLine((int) RetValue);
        }
        [AspectAction("%after %call *getClass")]
        public static void PrintClass()
        {
            Console.WriteLine(RetValue.ToString());
            Console.WriteLine(RetValue.GetType().
            GetField("a").GetValue(RetValue));
        }
    }
}
```

The output of the enhanced target application after weaving is as follows:

> *Non-boxing tests*
> *RetTest.Struct*
> *10*
> *10*
> *3*
> *3*
> *3*
> *RetTest.Class*
> *10*
> *10*
> *Boxing/Unboxing tests*
> *RetTest.Struct*
> *10*
> *10*
> *3*
> *3*
> *3*
> *RetTest.Class*
> *10*
> *10*

Note that the *RetValue.ToString()* construct returns the full name of the actual type of the result: *RetTest.Struct* (structure) or *RetTest.Class* (class). The fields of the structure and of the object are accessed using reflection.

A.3 RetTest2 EXAMPLE

The example demonstrates the Aspect.NET functionality of capturing the information on the target method, *TargetMemberInfo*; on the enclosing target method where the join point is located, *WithinMethod*; and on the enclosing type in whose definition the join point is located, *WithinType*. The example is shipped with Aspect.NET 2.1 [6]. The example unites in one Visual Studio. NET solution the target application, *RetTest2*, and the aspect to be woven, *MyAspect*.

The target application contains two overloads of the method *Method*: without arguments, and with a *string* argument. Here is the code of the target application located in the *Program.cs* source file:

```
using System;
using System.Collections.Generic;
using System.Text;
using System.Reflection;
namespace RetTest2
{
    class Program
    {
        static void Main(string[] args)
        {
            DateTime start = DateTime.Now;
            Method();
            Method("Dima");
            Console.WriteLine(DateTime.Now.Ticks -
            start.Ticks);
        }
        static public void Method()
        { Console.WriteLine("Hello!"); }
        static public void Method(string s)
        { Console.WriteLine("Hello "+s+"!"); }
    }
}
```

The application just calls the two versions of the method *Method* and measures the execution time in CPU clock ticks. The output of the target application is as follows:

> *Hello!*
> *Hello Dima!*
> *0*

The aspect *MyAspect* given below is intended to weave the actions that print the actual signatures of the target methods, the full names of the enclosing method, and the enclosing type definition for each join point:

```
using System;
using System.Collections.Generic;
using System.Text;
using AspectDotNet;
namespace Aspect1
{
    [AspectDescription("MyAspect description")]
    public class MyAspect : Aspect
    {
```

```
[AspectAction("%after %call *Method")]
public static void AfterAction()
{
    Console.WriteLine(TargetMemberInfo.
    ToString());
    Console.WriteLine(WithinMethod.ToString());
    Console.WriteLine(WithinType.ToString());
}
}
}
```

The output of the enhanced target application after aspect weaving is self-explanatory:

> *Hello!*
> *Void Method()*
> *Void Main(System.String[])*
> *RetTest2.Program*
> *Hello Dima!*
> *Void Method(System.String)*
> *Void Main(System.String[])*
> *RetTest2.Program*
> *156250*

Note that as we saw in Sections 4.11.1 and 4.11.3, weaving such an aspect does not inject any redundant instrumentation code. Only internal calls of static methods of the *Aspect* class are injected, to capture the information on the target method used in the aspect actions.

A.4   QuickSort EXAMPLE

This example and the following example (see Section A.5) continue the series of examples on using AOP and Aspect.NET for design by contract (started in Section 4.9 by the *Stack* example). Our next example is an implementation of the QuickSort algorithm in design-by-contract style. First, let's look at some details regarding the implementation.

If A is an input array to be sorted, the sorting of its range, $A[p \, .. \, r]$, proceeds as follows. The elements of A are swapped such that each of the elements $A[q+1], \ldots, A[r]$, where q is a number such that $p \le q < r$. This operation is referred to as *partition*. The sorting algorithm is called recursively for the array ranges $A[p \, .. \, q]$ and $A[q+1 \, .. \, r]$. After that, the array $A[p \, .. \, r]$ is sorted.

Although the idea behind the algorithm is very simple, there is one important detail: The boundary value is taken to be $A[p]$ rather than $A[r]$. Because $A[r]$ may appear to be the largest element in the array, at the end of *Partition*, $i = j = r$ will hold, so to return $q = j$ will not be possible; otherwise, the condition $q < r$ will be violated and the *QuickSort* algorithm falls into an infinite loop. Keeping this in mind, let's represent the functioning of *QuickSort* and *Partition* in terms of pre- and postcondition.

The *QuickSort* algorithm takes as input the indices q and r that determine the range of the array to be sorted. The following preconditions should hold:

$$0 \leq p \leq A.length - 1,$$

$$0 \leq r \leq A.length - 1.$$

Requiring this precondition to hold, *QuickSort* ensures that on returning, the array will be sorted; that is, the following postcondition should hold:

$$\forall i \in [0, \ A.length\text{-}1) \ A[i] \leq A[i+1]$$

The main step of the algorithm, *Partition*, also takes as input the range indexes p and r, assuming that

$$0 \leq p \leq A.length - \text{L}$$

$$0 \leq r \leq A.length - 1$$

In case the precondition holds, *Partition* swaps the elements of A as needed and returns the threshold index q. The postcondition can be formulated as follows:

$$return == q : (p \leq q < r) \,\&\,\&\,(\forall i \in [p, \ q]\forall j \in [q+1, \ r] \ A[i] \leq A[j])$$

The algorithms described are implemented as instance methods of the *Matrix* class. They change the state of the underlying object.

It is important that the method of the design-by-contract aspect should be woven not only directly into the target *.exe* application but also into all the *.dll* libraries used in the application, especially if the library methods themselves contain internal recursive calls. It allows us to perform incremental debugging and capture all bugs before they are passed to the client module.

As for *QuickSort*, it should be noted that the *startIndex < endIndex* check in the main method body is *not* a precondition. The precondition checks are placed into separate aspect actions. The check above is part of the algorithm. Based on *QuickSort* example, we measured how design-by-contract aspects can increase target application reliability. We already noted that the threshold array element should be taken as the first element of the array range but *not* as the last one; otherwise, *partitionIndex == endIndex* will hold, and *QuickSort* will fall into an infinite loop. Let's suppose that this requirement was *not* taken into account in the implementation. To make an experiment, let's fill out the array by random numbers and measure the statistics as to how often the algorithm fails. Our experiment shows that when arrays of length 10 are taken, from each 10,000 runs, about 1000 fail. So the reliability of the application (measured as the MTBF) is

$$R = 1 - \frac{k}{n} = 1 - \frac{1000}{10,000} = 0.9(90\%)$$

When using the design-by-contract aspect below, the reliability of the application becomes 100%; that is, in each fault the aspect issues an understandable error message of the type

> *ERROR detected while checking Partition postcondition:*
> *'startIndex <= partitionIndex < endIndex' is violated at {%SourceFilePath}, line {%SourceFileLine}*

The Aspect.NET %SourceFilePath and %SourceFileLine functionality allows us to indicate explicitly where the condition violates and to make bug detection easier. So **using the design-by-contract aspect increases the reliability of the application by 10%.**

Following is the code for the target application implementing the QuickSort algorithm.

```
public class MyArray
    {
        private int[] array;
        private int length;
        // class invariant:
        //    length >= 0;
        //    array != null;
        //    array.Length == length
        // require: 0 <= index <= length-1
        public int this[int index]
        { return array[index]; }
        public int[] Array
        { return array; }
        public int Length
        { return length; }
        // require: length >= 0
        public MyArray(int length) {
            this.length = length;
            this.array = new int[length];
```

```
}
// ensure:
//   this.length == length
//   this.array != null (.Length == length)
public void SetRandomValues() {
    Random random = new Random();
    int length = this.Length;
    for (int i = 0; i < length; i++)
        this[i] = random.Next(0, 20);
}
public void SetUserValues()
{
    int length = this.Length;
    Console.WriteLine("Enter an array of length
    {0}:", length);
    for (int i = 0; i < length; i++) {
        Console.Write("array[{0}] = ", i);
        this[i] = int.Parse(Console.ReadLine());
    }
}
public void Print()
{
    int length = this.Length;
    for (int i = 0; i < length; i++)
        Console.Write(this[i] + " ");
    Console.WriteLine();
}
// require:
//   0 <= startIndex <= length-1
//   0 <= endIndex <= length-1
public void QuickSort(int startIndex, int
endIndex)
{
    if (startIndex < endIndex)
    {
        int partitionIndex =
        Partition(startIndex, endIndex);
        QuickSort(startIndex, partitionIndex);
        QuickSort(partitionIndex + 1,
        endIndex);
    }
}
// ensure:
//   array segment from startIndex to endIndex
     is sorted accordingly, i.e.
```

```
//    for each i in [startIndex .. endIndex-1]
      array[i] <= array[i+1]
// require:
//    0 <= startIndex <= length-1
//    0 <= endIndex <= length-1
public int Partition(int startIndex, int
endIndex)
{
    int boundary = this[startIndex];
    int i = startIndex - 1;
    int j = endIndex + 1;
    while (true)
    {
        do
            j--;
        while (this[j] > boundary);
        do
            i++;
        while (this[i] < boundary);
        if (i < j) {
            int temp = this[i];
            this[i] = this[j];
            this[j] = temp;
        } else {
          return j;
        }
    }
    // ensure:
    //    return == partitionIndex :
    //    1. startIndex <= partitionIndex <
    //       endIndex;
    //    2. for each i in [startIndex,
    //       partitionIndex],
    //       for each j in [partitionIndex+1,
    //       endIndex]
    //       array[i] <= array[j]
}
}
```

Here is the code of the *MyArray* contract aspect:

```
[AspectDescription("Array contract")]
public class ArrayContractAspect : Aspect
{
```

```
[AspectDescription("MyArray invariant")]
[AspectAction("%before %call *MyArray.* || %after
%call *MyArray.* ")]
public static void CheckInvariant()
{
    try
    {
      MyArray targetObject = (MyArray)
      TargetObject;
      int length = targetObject.Length;
      int[] array = targetObject.Array;
      bool isCorrect = true;
      if (length < 0) {
          Console.WriteLine
              ("ERROR detected while checking
               " +
               "MyArray INVARIANT: 'length' < 0 at
               {0}, line {1}",
               SourceFilePath, SourceFileLine);
          isCorrect = false;
      }
    if (array == null) {
        Console.WriteLine("ERROR MyArray invariant:
        array is null");
        isCorrect = false;
    }
    if (array.Length != length) {
        Console.WriteLine
            ("ERROR detected while checking MyArray
             INVARIANT:" +
             "array.Length != 'length' at {0},
             line {1}",
             SourceFilePath, SourceFileLine);
        isCorrect = false;
    }
    if (isCorrect) {
        Console.WriteLine("--- Array invariant
        succeeded.");
    }
  }
  catch (NullReferenceException)
  { // Error message output can be inserted here
  }
}
```

```
[AspectDescription("QuickSort precondition")]
[AspectAction("%before %call *MyArray.QuickSort(int,
int) && %args(..)")]
public static void CheckQuicksortPrecondition(int
startIndex, int endIndex)
{
    MyArray targetArray = (MyArray)TargetObject;
    int length = targetArray.Length;
    bool isCorrect = true;
    if ((startIndex < 0) || (startIndex > length - 1)) {
        Console.WriteLine
            ("ERROR Quicksort precondition: startIndex
            is invalid");
        isCorrect = false;
    }
    if ((endIndex < 0) || (endIndex > length - 1)) {
        Console.WriteLine
            ("ERROR Quicksort precondition: endIndex is
             invalid");
        isCorrect = false;
    }
    if (isCorrect) {
        Console.WriteLine("--- Quicksort precondition
        succeeded");
    }
}
[AspectDescription("Quicksort postcondition")]
[AspectAction("%instead %call *MyArray.QuickSort(int,
int) && %args(..)")]
public static void CheckQuicksortPostcondition(int
startIndex, int endIndex)
{
    MyArray targetArray = (MyArray)TargetObject;
    int length = targetArray.Length;
    MyArray originalArray = new MyArray(length); //
    copy of target object
    for (int k = 0; k < length; k++)
    {
        originalArray[k] = targetArray[k];
    }
    targetArray.QuickSort(startIndex, endIndex);
    MyArray sortedArray = targetArray;
    //1. Check that set of elements is the same
    int i = startIndex;
    bool elementNotFound = false;
```

```
while ((i <= endIndex) && (!elementNotFound))
{
    int j = startIndex;
    elementNotFound = true; //i element has not
    yet been found
    while ((j <= endIndex) && elementNotFound)
    {
        if (sortedArray[i] == originalArray[j])
        {
            elementNotFound = false;
            originalArray[j] = -1;
        }
        j++;
    }
    if (elementNotFound) {
        Console.WriteLine
            ("ERROR detected while checking
             QuickSort POSTCONDITION: " +
             " the resulting array has a different
             set of items." +
             " QuickSort logic is incorrect at {0}
             line {1}",
             SourceFilePath, SourceFileLine);
    }
        i++;
    }
    //2. Array is sorted indeed
    i = startIndex;
    bool sortedCorrectly = true;
    while ((i <= endIndex - 1) && sortedCorrectly)
    {
        if (!(sortedArray[i] <= sortedArray[i +
        1])) {
            sortedCorrectly = false;
            Console.WriteLine
                ("ERROR detected while checking
                 QuickSort POSTCONDITION:" +
                 " the resulting array is not
                 sorted properly. " +
                 " QuickSort logic is not correct
                 at {0} line {1}",
                 SourceFilePath, SourceFileLine);
        }
        i++;
    }
```

```
      if (!elementNotFound && sortedCorrectly)
      {
         Console.WriteLine("--- QuickSort
         postcondition succeeded.");
      }
}
// should be woven into MyArray.dll
[AspectDescription("Partition precondition")]
[AspectAction("%before %call *MyArray.
Partition(int, int) && %args(..)")]
public static void CheckPartitionPrecondition(int
startIndex, int endIndex)
{
    MyArray targetArray = (MyArray)TargetObject;
    int length = targetArray.Length;
    bool isCorrect = true;
    if ((startIndex < 0) || (startIndex > length -
    1)) {
        Console.WriteLine
           ("ERROR Partition precondition:
            startIndex is invalid");
         isCorrect = false;
    }
    if ((endIndex < 0) || (endIndex > length - 1))
    {
         Console.WriteLine
             ("ERROR Partition precondition:
              endIndex is invalid");
          isCorrect = false;
    }
    if (isCorrect) {
        Console.WriteLine("--- Partition
        precondition succeeded");
    }
}
// relevant for version 2.0
[AspectDescription("Partition postcondition 2.0")]
[AspectAction("%instead %call *MyArray.
Partition(int, int) && %args(..)")]
public static int CheckPartitionPostcondition_old
    (int startIndex, int endIndex)
{
    MyArray targetArray = (MyArray)TargetObject;
    int partitionIndex = targetArray.
    Partition(startIndex, endIndex);
```

```
        MyArray resultArray = targetArray;
        bool indexIsCorrect = true;
        //1. startIndex <= partitionIndex < endIndex
        if (!(startIndex <= partitionIndex) ||
        !(partitionIndex < endIndex)) {
            Console.WriteLine
                ("ERROR detected while checking
                 Partition POSTCONDITION: " +
                 "'startIndex <= partitionIndex <
                 endIndex' " +
                 "is not true at {0} line {1}",
            SourceFilePath, SourceFileLine);
        indexIsCorrect = false;
    }
    //2. For each i in [startIndex, partitionIndex],
    //   for each j in [partitionIndex+1, endIndex]
    //   resultArray[i] <= resultArray[j]
    int i = startIndex;
    int j = partitionIndex + 1;
    bool sortedCorrectly = true;
    while ((i <= partitionIndex) && sortedCorrectly) {
        while ((j <= endIndex) && sortedCorrectly) {
            if (!(resultArray[i] <= resultArray[j])) {
                sortedCorrectly = false;
                Console.WriteLine
                    ("ERROR detected while checking
                     Partition POSTCONDITION"
                     + " the resulting array is not
                     sorted properly. " +
                     "Logic is incorrect at {0} line
                     {1}",
                     SourceFilePath, SourceFileLine);
            }
            j++;
        }
        i++;
    }
    if (indexIsCorrect && sortedCorrectly) {
        Console.WriteLine("--- Partition postcondition
        succeeded.");
    }
    return partitionIndex;
}
//relevant for version 2.1
[AspectDescription("Partition postcondition 2.1")]
```

```
[AspectAction("%after %call *MyArray.Partition(int,
int) && %args(..)")]
public static int CheckPartitionPostcondition_new
 (int startIndex, int endIndex)
{
    MyArray resultArray = (MyArray)TargetObject;
    int partitionIndex = (int)RetValue;
    bool indexIsCorrect = true;
    //1. startIndex <= partitionIndex < endIndex
    if (!(startIndex <= partitionIndex) ||
    !(partitionIndex < endIndex)) {
       Console.WriteLine
          ("ERROR detected while checking Partition" +
           " POSTCONDITION: 'startIndex <=
           partitionIndex < endIndex' " +
           "is not true at {0} line {1}",
           SourceFilePath, SourceFileLine);
       indexIsCorrect = false;
    }
    //2. For each i in [startIndex, partitionIndex],
    //   for each j in [partitionIndex+1, endIndex]
    //   resultArray[i] <= resultArray[j]
    int i = startIndex;
    int j = partitionIndex + 1;
    bool sortedCorrectly = true;
    while ((i <= partitionIndex) && sortedCorrectly) {
        while ((j <= endIndex) && sortedCorrectly) {
            if (!(.resultArray[i] <= resultArray[j])) {
                sortedCorrectly = false;
                Console.WriteLine
                    ("ERROR detected while checking
                     Partition POSTCONDITION"+
                     " the resulting array is not
                     sorted properly. " +
                     "Logic is incorrect at {0} line
                     {1}",
                     SourceFilePath, SourceFileLine);
            }
            j++;
        }
        i++;
    }
    if (indexIsCorrect && sortedCorrectly) {
        Console.WriteLine("--- Partition postcondition
        succeeded.");
    }
```

```
      return partitionIndex;
}
[AspectDescription("Ctor precondition")]
[AspectAction("%before %call *MyArray..ctor(int) &&
%args(arg[0])")]
public static void CheckCtorPrecondition(int length)
{
    if (length < 0) {
        Console.WriteLine("ERROR Ctor precondition:
        length < 0");
    } else {
        Console.WriteLine("--- Ctor precondition
        succeeded");
    }
}
[AspectDescription("Indexer precondition")]
[AspectAction
  ("%before %call *MyArray.get_Item && %args(arg[0]) ||
    " +
    "%before %call *MyArray.set_Item && %args(arg[0])")
]
public static void CheckIndexerPrecondition(int index)
{
    MyArray targetArray = (MyArray)TargetObject;
    int length = targetArray.Length;
    if ((index < 0) || (index > length - 1)) {
        Console.WriteLine("ERROR Indexer precondition:
        index is invalid");
    } else {
        Console.WriteLine("--- Indexer precondition
        succeeded");
        }
    }
}
```

A.5 Matrix EXAMPLE

This example continues the series of examples of applying Aspect.NET for design by contract (see also Sections 4.9 and A.4). The example consists of the target application that implements matrix multiplication, and the aspect implementing the application's contract.

The *MatrixContractAspect* aspect of this example implements design-by-contract checks for the *Matrix* class below. Contract checks for the constructor, indexer, and the class invariant are performed similar to the *Stack* aspect (see Section 4.9). The most interesting are the *Multiply, ChainOrder*, and

ChainMultiply methods of implementing an efficient multiply of several matrices. Let's consider them in more detail.

The static method *Multiply(Matrix first, Matrix second)* takes as input two matrices and multiplies them. It is well known that matrices A and B can be multiplied only if the number of columns of A equals the number of rows of B. If A is a $(p * q)$ matrix and B is a $(q * r)$ matrix, their product, $C = A * B$, is a $(p * r)$ matrix. When using the common algorithm, $p * q * r$ multiplications are to be made.

In terms of our class, these semantic properties are expressed by the precondition

```
first.Length == second.Depth
```

and the postcondition

```
return == result:
result.Depth == first.Depth && result.Length == second.
Length
```

Suppose that we'd like to find the product of n matrices $A_1 \cdot A_2 \cdot ... \cdot A_n$. First, brackets should be positioned to indicate the most efficient order of multiplication. To understand how the right positioning of the brackets can influence the efficiency, let's consider the sequence of three matrices $<A_1, A_2, A_3>$ of dimensions 10×100, 100×5 and 5×50 accordingly. When multiplying them as $((A_1A_2)A_3)$, we need $10 \cdot 100 \cdot 5 = 5000$ multiplications in order to find the 10×5 matrix of A_1A_2, and then $10 \cdot 5 \cdot 50 = 2500$ multiplications, to multiply this matrix by A_3—a total of 7500 multiplications. When the brackets are placed as $(A_1(A_2A_3))$, we perform $100 \cdot 5 \cdot 50 = 25,000$ multiplications to find the 100×50 matrix of A_2A_3, plus $10 \cdot 100 \cdot 50 = 50,000$ more multiplications to perform $A_1 \times (A_2A_3)$, a total of 75,000 multiplications. So the first multiplication method appears to be 10 times more efficient.

The *ChainOrder(int[] dimensions)* method takes as input the dimensions of the matrices to multiply, and returns as the result a two-dimensional array of *effectiveOrder* containing information on efficient placement of brackets. The number k in the element $[i, j]$ of this array denotes that when the brackets are placed the optimal way, in the product of $A_i \cdot A_{i+1} \cdot ... \cdot A_j$, the last multiplication operation is taken to be $A_i \cdot ... \cdot A_k$ by $A_{k+1} \cdot ... \cdot A_j$.

Among the method's preconditions, besides standard mull checks, the following can be emphasized. Taking into account that the input array of *dimensions* is a sequence of the type: $<p_0, p_1, ... , p_n>$, where $(p_{i-1} * p_i)$ is the dimension of the matrix A_i, we should expect as input a minimum of two numbers:

```
dimensions.Length >= 2
```

Moreover, despite the fact that the semantics of our class allows a degenerate matrix case of ((*depth* == 0) || (*length* == 0)) in our case, it is quite logical to suppose that the matrix is nondegenerate:

```
foreach (int size in dimensions) size > 0
```

Let's now consider the structure of the resulting array *effectiveOrder*. At first, it is a square matrix whose size is determined by the number of matrices participating in the multiplication:

```
effectiveOrder.Length == effectiveOrder.Depth ==
dimensions.Length-1
```

The second important property of this matrix is as follows:

$$\forall I, j \ I \leq effectiveOrder[I, j] < j$$

It is important that the value k in the $[i, j]$ cell is lower than j; otherwise, it would mean that in the product of $A_i \cdot \ldots \cdot A_j$ the last multiplication is $A_i \cdot \ldots \cdot A_j$, which does not lead to decomposition of the task into subtasks and excludes the opportunity of recursive use of the algorithm.

The properties of the *effectiveOrder* array described below should also be checked on entering the *ChainMultiply* (*List* <Matrix>*matrixChain, Matrix effectiveOrder, int startIndex, int endIndex*) method. Among the other method's preconditions, there is a check of the dimensions of matrices in the *matrixChain* sequence and a check of the validity of the boundary indexes.

Implementing the contract in Aspect.NET does not cause algorithmic difficulties. The *RetValue* functionality implemented in Aspect.NET 2.1 appeared to be quite useful, as can be seen from the aspect below. Here is the target application class (*Matrix*):

```
public class Matrix {
        private int[,] array;
        private int depth;
        private int length;
        // class invariant:
        //    depth >= 0;
        //    length >= 0;
        //    array.GetLength(0) == depth;
        //    array.GetLength(1) == length;
        public int[,] Array
        { return array; }
        // require:
        //    0 <= i <= depth-1
        //    0 <= j <= length-1
```

```
public int this[int i, int j]
{ return array[i, j]; }
public int Depth
{ return depth; }
public int Length
{ return length; }
// require: depth >=0; length >=0
public Matrix(int depth, int length)
{
    this.depth = depth;
    this.length = length;
    this.array = new int[depth, length];
}
// ensure:
//    this.depth == depth
//    this.length == length
//    array != null
public void SetRandomValues()
{
    Random random = new Random();
    int depth = this.Depth;
    int length = this.Length;
    for (int i = 0; i < depth; i++) {
        for (int j = 0; j < length; j++)
            this[i, j] = random.Next(0, 5);
    }
}
public void Print()
{
    int depth = this.Depth;
    int length = this.Length;
    for (int i = 0; i < depth; i++) {
        for (int j = 0; j < length; j++) {
            Console.Write(this[i, j] + " ");
        }
        Console.WriteLine();
    }
    Console.WriteLine();
}
// require: first.Length == second.Depth
public static Matrix Multiply(Matrix first,
Matrix second)
{
    int firstDepth = first.Depth;
    int firstLength = first.Length;
```

```
    int secondDepth = second.Depth;
    int secondLength = second.Length;
    Matrix result = new Matrix(firstDepth,
    secondLength);
    for (int i = 0; i < firstDepth; i++) {
        for (int j = 0; j < secondLength; j++) {
            result[i, j] = 0;
            for (int k = 0; k < firstLength;
            k++) {
                result[i, j] = result[i, j] +
                first[i, k] * second[k, j];
            }
        }
    }
    return result;
}
// ensure:
//    return == result:
//    result.Depth == first.Depth
//    result.Length == second.Length
// Correct chain order for effective matrix
multiply
// require:
//    dimensions != null
//    dimensions.Length >= 3
//    foreach (int size in dimensions) size > 0
public static Matrix ChainOrder(int[]
dimensions)
// dimensions of matrices being multiplied
{
    int number = dimensions.Length - 1; //
    number of matrices in the chain
    Matrix costs = new Matrix(number, number);
    // matrix of costs
    Matrix effectiveOrder = new Matrix(number,
    number);
    // matrix of effective chain order
    for (int i = 0; i <= number - 1; i++) {
        costs[i, i] = 0;
    }
    for (int l = 2; l <= number; l++) {
        for (int i = 0; i <= number - 1; i++) {
            int j = i + l - 1;
            costs[i, j] = int.MaxValue;
            for (int k = i; k <= j - 1; k++) {
```

```
                    int value =
                        costs[i, k] + costs[k +
                        1, j] +
                        dimensions[i] *
                        dimensions[k+1] *
                        dimensions[j+1];
                    if (value < costs[i, j]) {
                        costs[i, j] = value;
                        effectiveOrder[i, j] = k;
                    }
                }
            }
        }
        return effectiveOrder;
    }
    // ensure:
    //   effectiveOrder != null;
    //   effectiveOrder.Length == effectiveOrder
        Depth == dimensions.Length-1;
    //   foreach (int item in effectiveOrder) 0 <=
        item < dimensions.Length-1
    // require:
    //   valid dimensions of matrices
    //   effectiveOrder.Length == effectiveOrder.
        Depth == matrixChain.Count
    //   foreach (int item in effectiveOrder) 0 <=
        item < matrixChain.Count
    //   0 <= startIndex <= matrixChain.Count-1;
    //   0 <= endIndex <= matrixChain.Count-1
    public static Matrix ChainMultiply
        (List <Matrix>matrixChain, Matrix
        effectiveOrder,
        int startIndex, int endIndex)
    {
        if (startIndex < endIndex) {
            Matrix x =
                ChainMultiply(matrixChain,
                effectiveOrder, startIndex,
                            effectiveOrder[start
                            Index, endIndex]);
            Matrix y =
                ChainMultiply(matrixChain,
                effectiveOrder,
                            effectiveOrder[start
                            Index, endIndex] + 1,
                            endIndex);
```

```
            return Multiply(x, y);
        } else {
            return matrixChain[startIndex];
        }
    }
    // ensure:
    //   return == result:
    //   result.Depth == firstMatrix.Depth;
    //   result.Length == lastMatrix.Length
    // require: the source should be (n x n)
    matrix
    public double GetDeterminant()
    {
        int n = this.Depth;
        // copy of this.Array
        double[,] sourceMatrix = new double[n, n];
        for (int i = 0; i <= n - 1; i++) {
            for (int j = 0; j <= n - 1; j++) {
                sourceMatrix[i, j] = this[i, j];
            }
        }
        int sign = 1;
        for (int k = 0; k <= n - 1; k++) {
            double p = 0;
            int k1 = 0;
            for (int i = k; i <= n - 1; i++) {
                if (Math.Abs(sourceMatrix[i, k])
                  > p) {
                    p = Math.Abs(sourceMatrix[i,
                      k]);
                    k1 = i;
                }
            }
            if (p == 0) {
                return 0;
            }
            if (k1 != k) {
                for (int i = 0; i <= n - 1; i++) {
                    double temp1 =
                    sourceMatrix[k, i];
                    sourceMatrix[k, i] =
                    sourceMatrix[k1, i];
                    sourceMatrix[k1, i] = temp1;
                }
                sign = -sign;
            }
```

```
                for (int i = k + 1; i <= n - 1; i++) {
                    sourceMatrix[i, k] /=
                    sourceMatrix[k, k];
                    for (int j = k + 1; j <= n - 1;
                    j++) {
                        sourceMatrix[i, j] -=
                            sourceMatrix[i, k] *
                            sourceMatrix[k, j];
                    }
                }
            }
        double determinant = 1;
        for (int i = 0; i <= n - 1; i++) {
            determinant *= sourceMatrix[i, i];
        }
        return determinant * sign;
    }
    // require:
    //    sourceMatrix is a non-degenerate square
    //     (n x n) matrix
    public static void LUP_Decomposition
        (Matrix source, out Matrix lowerMatrix,
         out Matrix upperMatrix,
         out int[] pivots)
    {
        int n = source.Depth;
        // copy of source.Array
        double[,] sourceMatrix = new double[n,n];
        for (int i = 0; i <= n - 1; i++) {
            for (int j = 0; j <= n - 1; j++) {
                sourceMatrix[i, j] = source[i, j];
            }
        }
        lowerMatrix = new Matrix(n, n);
        upperMatrix = new Matrix(n, n);
        pivots = new int[n];
        for (int i = 0; i <= n - 1; i++) {
            pivots[i] = i;
        }
        for (int k = 0; k <= n - 1; k++) {
            double p = 0;
            int k1 = 0;
            for (int i = k; i <= n - 1; i++) {
                if (Math.Abs(sourceMatrix[i, k])
                > p) {
```

```
                    p = Math.Abs(sourceMatrix[i,
                    k]);
                    k1 = i;
            }
        }
        if (p == 0) {
            // Error
        }
        if (k1 != k) {
            int temp = pivots[k];
            pivots[k] = pivots[k1];
            pivots[k1] = temp;
            for (int i = 0; i <= n - 1; i++) {
                double temp1 = sourceMatrix[k,
                i];
                sourceMatrix[k, i] =
                sourceMatrix[k1, i];
                sourceMatrix[k1, i] = temp1;
            }
        }
        for (int i = k + 1; i <= n - 1; i++) {
            sourceMatrix[i, k] /=
            sourceMatrix[k, k];
            for (int j = k + 1; j <= n - 1;
            j++) {
                sourceMatrix[i, j] -=
                    sourceMatrix[i, k] *
                    sourceMatrix[k, j];
            }
        }
    }
}
// lowerMatrix
for (int i = 0; i <= n - 1; i++) {
    for (int j = 0; j <= i; j++) {
        if (i == j) {
            lowerMatrix[i, j] = 1;
        } else {
            lowerMatrix[i, j] =
            sourceMatrix[i, j];
        }
    }
}
// upperMatrix
for (int i = 0; i <= n - 1; i++) {
    for (int j = i; j <= n - 1; j++) {
```

```
                    upperMatrix[i, j] =
                    sourceMatrix[i, j];
            }
        }
    }
    // ensure:
    //    1. lowerMatrix - (n x n), lower-diagonal,
            1 on the diagonal
    //    2. upperMatrix - (n x n), upper-diagonal
    //    3. pivots - [n], 0 <= pivots[i] <= n-1
    //    4. pivots*source = lowerMatrix*upperMatrix
    // require:
    //       a is a non-degenerate (n x n) square
            matrix
    //       b is a (n x 1) vector
    public static Matrix Solve(Matrix a, Matrix b)
    // Ax = b
    {
        Matrix lower, upper;
        int[] pivots;
        Matrix.LUP_Decomposition(a, out lower, out
        upper, out pivots);
        int n = a.Depth;
        Matrix x = new Matrix(n, 1);
        Matrix y = new Matrix(n, 1);
        for (int i = 0; i <= n-1; i++) {
            double sum = 0;
            for (int j = 0; j <= i-1; j++) {
                sum += lower[i,j] * y[j,0];
            }
            y[i,0] = b[pivots[i],0] - sum;
        }
        for (int i = n-1; i >= 0; i--) {
            double sum = 0;
            for (int j = i+1; j <= n-1; j++) {
                sum += upper[i,j] * x[j,0];
            }
            x[i,0] = (y[i,0] - sum) / upper[i,i];
        }
        return x;
    }
    // ensure:
    //    return == x: vector (n x 1), ax = b
    //
    public static bool operator ==(Matrix first,
    Matrix second)
```

```
{
    int firstDepth = 0;
    int firstLength = 0;
    int secondDepth = 0;
    int secondLength = 0;
    bool firstIsNull = false;
    bool secondIsNull = false;
    try {
        firstDepth = first.Depth;
        firstLength = first.Length;
    } catch(NullReferenceException) {
        firstIsNull = true;
    }
    try {
        secondDepth = second.Depth;
        secondLength = second.Length;
    } catch(NullReferenceException) {
        secondIsNull = true;
    }
    if (firstIsNull && secondIsNull) {
        return true;
    } else if (firstIsNull || secondIsNull) {
        return false;
    }
    if ((firstDepth != secondDepth) ||
    (firstLength != secondLength)) {
        return false;
    }
    int i = 0;
    while (i <= firstDepth-1) {
        int j = 0;
        while (j <= firstLength-1)
        {
            if (first[i, j] != second[i, j])
            {
                return false;
            }
            j++;
        }
        i++;
    }
    return true;
}
public static bool operator !=(Matrix first,
Matrix second)
{
```

```
int firstDepth = 0;
int firstLength = 0;
int secondDepth = 0;
int secondLength = 0;
bool firstIsNull = false;
bool secondIsNull = false;
try {
    firstDepth = first.Depth;
    firstLength = first.Length;
}
catch (NullReferenceException)
{
    firstIsNull = true;
}
try
{
    secondDepth = second.Depth;
    secondLength = second.Length;
}
catch (NullReferenceException)
{
    secondIsNull = true;
}
if (firstIsNull && secondIsNull)
{
    return false;
}
else if (firstIsNull || secondIsNull)
{
    return true;
}
if ((firstDepth != secondDepth) ||
(firstLength != secondLength))
{
    return true;
}
int i = 0;
while (i <= firstDepth-1) {
    int j = 0;
    while (j <= firstLength-1) {
        if (first[i, j] != second[i, j]) {
            return true;
        }
        j++;
    }
```

```
                i++;
            }
            return false;
        }
}


    Here is the source code of the matrix contract aspect:

[AspectDescription("Matrix contract aspect")]
public class MatrixContract : Aspect
{
    [AspectDescription("Multiply precondition")]
    [AspectAction
        ("%before %call *Matrix.Multiply(Matrix,
        Matrix) && %args(..)")
    ]
    public static void CheckMultiplyPrecondition(Matrix
    first, Matrix second)
    {
        if (first.Length != second.Depth)
        {
            Console.WriteLine
                ("ERROR Multiply precondition: matrices'
                dimensions " +
                "are invalid at {0}, line {1}",
                SourceFilePath, SourceFileLine);
        } else {
            Console.WriteLine("--- Multiply
            precondition succeeded");
        }
    }
    [AspectDescription("Multiply postcondition")]
    [AspectAction("%after %call *Matrix.
    Multiply(Matrix, Matrix) && %args(..)")]
    public static void CheckMultiplyPostcondition(Matri
    x first, Matrix second)
    {
        Matrix resultMatrix = (Matrix)RetValue;
        if ((resultMatrix.Depth != first.Depth) ||
            (resultMatrix.Length != second.Length))
        {
            Console.WriteLine
                ("ERROR Multiply postcondition: result
                matrix' dimensions" +
                "are invalid at {0}, line {1}",
```

```
                  SourceFilePath, SourceFileLine);
    } else {
        Console.WriteLine("--- Multiply
        postcondition succeeded");
    }
}
[AspectDescription("ChainOrder precondition")]
[AspectAction("%before %call *Matrix.ChainOrder &&
%args(arg[0])")]
public static void CheckChainOrderPrecondition(int
[] dimensions)
{
    bool isCorrect = true;
    if (dimensions == null) {
        Console.WriteLine
                ("ERROR ChainOrder precondition:
                dimensions_array is null " +
                "at {0}, line {1}",
                SourceFilePath, SourceFileLine);
        isCorrect = false;
    }
    if (dimensions.Length < 3) {
        Console.WriteLine
            ("ERROR ChainOrder precondition: " +
            "not enough dimensions specified at
            {0}, line {1}",
            SourceFilePath, SourceFileLine);
        isCorrect = false;
    }
    int length = dimensions.Length;
    for (int i = 0; i < length; i++) {
        if (dimensions[i] <= 0)
        {
            Console.WriteLine
                ("ERROR ChainOrder precondition: "
                +
                "non-positive dimension specified at
                position {0}", i);
            isCorrect = false;
        }
    }
    if (isCorrect)
    {
        Console.WriteLine("--- ChainOrder
        precondition succeeded");
```

```
    }
}
[AspectDescription("ChainOrder postcondition")]
[AspectAction("%after %call *Matrix.ChainOrder &&
%args(arg[0])")]
public static void CheckChainOrderPostcondition(int
[] dimensions)
{
    Matrix effectiveOrder = (Matrix)RetValue;
    int depth = effectiveOrder.Depth;
    int length = effectiveOrder.Length;
    bool isCorrect = true;
    if (effectiveOrder == null)
    {
        Console.WriteLine
            ("ERROR ChainOrder postcondition:
             result array is null");
        isCorrect = false;
    }
    if ((depth != dimensions.Length) || (length !=
    dimensions.Length))
    {
        Console.WriteLine
            ("ERROR ChainOrder postcondition: " +
             "result array has invalid
             dimensions");
        isCorrect = false;
    }
    for (int i = 0; i < depth; i++)
    {
        for (int j = 0; j < length; j++)
        {
            int item = effectiveOrder[i, j];
            if ((item < 0) || (item >= length))
            {
                Console.WriteLine
                    ("ERROR ChainOrder
                     postcondition: resultant
                     array" +
                     "contains invalid item at
                     position [{0},{1}]", i, j);
                isCorrect = false;
            }
        }
    }
```

```
    if (isCorrect)
    {
        Console.WriteLine("--- ChainOrder
        postcondition succeeded");
    }
}
[AspectDescription("ChainMultiply precondition")]
[AspectAction("%before %call *ChainMultiply &&
%args(..)")]
public static void CheckChainMultiplyPrecondition
    (List<Matrix>matrixChain, Matrix
     effectiveOrder,
     int startIndex, int endIndex)
{
    bool isCorrect = true;
    //startIndex && endIndex
    int matrixCount = matrixChain.Count;
    if ((startIndex < 0) || (startIndex >
    matrixCount - 1))
    {
        Console.WriteLine
            ("ERROR ChainMultiply precondition:
             invalid startIndex");
        isCorrect = false;
    }
    if ((endIndex < 0) || (endIndex > matrixCount
    - 1))
    {
        Console.WriteLine
            ("ERROR ChainMultiply precondition:
             invalid endIndex");
        isCorrect = false;
    }
    //matrixChain
    for (int i = startIndex; i < endIndex; i++)
    {
        Matrix first = matrixChain[i];
        Matrix second = matrixChain[i + 1];
        if (first.Length != second.Depth)
        {
            Console.WriteLine
                ("ERROR ChainMultiply precondition:
                 " +
                 "impossible to multiply matrices
                 at " +
```

```
                "positions {0} and {1}: invalid
                dimensions", i, i + 1);
            isCorrect = false;
        }
    }
    // effectiveOrder
    int depth = effectiveOrder.Depth;
    int length = effectiveOrder.Length;
    if ((depth != matrixCount) || (length !=
    matrixCount))
    {
        Console.WriteLine
            ("ERROR ChainMultiply precondition: " +
            "effectiveOrder array has invalid
            dimensions");
        isCorrect = false;
    }
    for (int i = 0; i < depth; i++)
    {
        for (int j = 0; j < length; j++)
        {
            int item = effectiveOrder[i, j];
            if ((item < 0) || (item >=
            matrixCount))
            {
                Console.WriteLine
                    ("ERROR ChainMultiply
                    precondition: " +
                    "effectiveOrder array contains
                    invalid item" +
                    "at position [{0},{1}]", i,
                    j);
                isCorrect = false;
            }
        }
    }
    if (isCorrect) {
        Console.WriteLine("--- ChainMultiply
        precondition succeeded");
    }
}


[AspectDescription("ChainMultiply postcondition")]
[AspectAction
```

```
        ("%after %call *Matrix.ChainMultiply(List
        <Matrix>, Matrix, int, int)" +
        " && %args(arg[0], arg[2], arg[3])")
]
public static void CheckChainMultiplyPostcondition
    (List<Matrix> matrixChain, int startIndex, int
    endIndex)
{
    Matrix resultMatrix = (Matrix)RetValue;
    Matrix firstMatrix = matrixChain[startIndex];
    Matrix lastMatrix = matrixChain[endIndex];
    if ((resultMatrix.Depth != firstMatrix.Depth) ||
        (resultMatrix.Length != lastMatrix.Length))
    {
        Console.WriteLine
            ("ERROR ChainMultiply postcondition: "
            +
            "result matrix has invalid
            dimensions");
    } else {
        Console.WriteLine("--- ChainMultiply
        postcondition succeeded");
    }
}


[AspectDescription("Matrix invariant")]
[AspectAction("%before %call *Matrix.* || %after
%call *Matrix.* ")]
public static void CheckMatrixInvariant()
{
    try {
        Matrix targetMatrix = (Matrix)TargetObject;
        int depth = targetMatrix.Depth;
        int length = targetMatrix.Length;
        int[,] array = targetMatrix.Array;
        bool isCorrect = true;
        if ((depth < 0) || (length < 0))
        {
            Console.WriteLine("ERROR Matrix
            invariant: negative dimension");
            isCorrect = false;
        }
        if ((array.GetLength(0) != depth) ||
        (array.GetLength(1) != length))
        {
```

```
                Console.WriteLine
                    ("ERROR Matrix invariant: invalid
                     array dimensions");
                isCorrect = false;
            }
            if (isCorrect)
            {
                Console.WriteLine("--- Matrix invariant
                succeeded");
            }
        }
        catch (NullReferenceException)
        {
        }
    }
    [AspectDescription("Ctor precondition")]
    [AspectAction("%before %call *Matrix..ctor(int,
    int) && %args(..)")]
    public static void CheckCtorPrecondition(int depth,
    int length)
    {
        bool isCorrect = true;
        if (depth < 0)
        {
            Console.WriteLine("ERROR Ctor precondition:
            invalid depth");
            isCorrect = false;
        }
        if (length < 0)
        {
            Console.WriteLine("ERROR Ctor precondition:
            invalid length");
            isCorrect = false;
        }
        if (isCorrect)
        {
            Console.WriteLine("--- Ctor precondition
            succeeded");
        }
    }
    [AspectDescription("Indexer precondition")]
    [AspectAction
        ("%before %call *Matrix.get_Item && %args(..)
        || " +
        "%before %call *Matrix.set_Item &&
        %args(arg[0], arg[1])")
```

```
]
public static void CheckIndexerPrecondition(int
depthIndex, int lengthIndex)
{
    Matrix targetMatrix = (Matrix)TargetObject;
    int depth = targetMatrix.Depth;
    int length = targetMatrix.Length;
    bool isCorrect = true;
    if ((depthIndex < 0) ||
    (depthIndex > depth - 1))
    {
        Console.WriteLine
            ("ERROR Indexer precondition:
             depthIndex is invalid");
        isCorrect = false;
    }
    if ((lengthIndex < 0) || (lengthIndex > length
    - 1))
    {
        Console.WriteLine
            ("ERROR Indexer precondition:
             lengthIndex is invalid");
        isCorrect = false;
    }
    if (isCorrect)
    {
        Console.WriteLine("--- Indexer precondition
        succeeded");
    }
}


[AspectDescription("LUP_Decomposition
precondition")]
[AspectAction("%before %call *Matrix.LUP_
Decomposition && %args(arg[0])")]
public static void CheckLUP_Decomposition
Precondition(Matrix sourceMatrix)
{
    // square matrix
    int depth = sourceMatrix.Depth;
    int length = sourceMatrix.Length;
    if (depth != length)
    {
        Console.WriteLine
```

```
                        ("ERROR LUP_Decomposition precondition:
                         " +
                        "source matrix is not square");
            return;
        }
        // non-degenerate matrix
        if (sourceMatrix.GetDeterminant() == 0)
        {
            Console.WriteLine
                ("ERROR LUP_Decomposition precondition:
                 " +
                "source matrix is degenerate");
        } else {
            Console.WriteLine("--- LUP_Decomposition
            precondition succeeded");
        }
}

[AspectDescription("LUP_Decomposition
postcondition")]
[AspectAction
    ("%after %call *Matrix.LUP_Decomposition" +
     " (Matrix, out Matrix, out Matrix, out
     int[]) && %args(..)")
]
public static void
CheckLUP_DecompositionPostcondition
    (Matrix source, Matrix lower, Matrix upper,
    int[] pivots)
{
    int n = source.Depth;
    // lower
    int lowerDepth = lower.Depth;
    int lowerLength = lower.Length;
    if ((lowerDepth != n) || (lowerLength != n))
    {
        Console.WriteLine
            ("ERROR LUP_Decomposition
             postcondition: " +
            "LowerMatrix has invalid dimensions");
        return;
    }
    bool correctStructure = true;
    int i = 0;
    while ((i <= n - 1) && correctStructure)
```

```
    {
        if (lower[i, i] != 1)
        {
            correctStructure = false;
    }
    int j = i + 1;
    while ((j <= n - 1) && correctStructure)
    {
        if (lower[i, j] != 0)
        {
            correctStructure = false;
        }
        j++;
    }
        i++;
        }
    if (!correctStructure)
    {
        Console.WriteLine
            ("ERROR LUP_Decomposition
             postcondition: " +
             "LowerMatrix has invalid structure");
    }
    // upper
    int upperDepth = upper.Depth;
    int upperLength = upper.Length;
    if ((upperDepth != n) || (upperLength != n))
    {
        Console.WriteLine
            ("ERROR LUP_Decomposition
             postcondition: " +
             "UpperMatrix has invalid dimensions");
        return;
    }
    correctStructure = true;
    i = 0;
    while ((i <= n - 1) && correctStructure)
    {
        int j = 0;
        while ((j <= i - 1) && correctStructure)
        {
            if (upper[i, j] != 0)
            {
                correctStructure = false;
            }
```

```
            j++;
    }
    i++;
}
if (!correctStructure)
{
    Console.WriteLine
        ("ERROR LUP_Decomposition postcondition:
        " +
        "UpperMatrix has invalid structure");
}
// pivots
int pivotsLength = pivots.Length;
if (pivotsLength != n) {
    Console.WriteLine
        ("ERROR LUP_Decomposition
         postcondition: " +
         "Pivots vector has invalid length");
    return;
}
i = 0;
correctStructure = true;
while ((i <= pivotsLength - 1) &&
correctStructure)
{
    if ((pivots[i] < 0) || (pivots[i] >
    pivotsLength - 1))
    {
        correctStructure = false;
        Console.WriteLine
            ("ERROR LUP_Decomposition
             postcondition: " +
             "Pivots vector has invalid
             structure");
    }
}
// PA = LU (pivots * source = lower * upper)
Matrix pivotsMatrix = new Matrix(n, n);
for (int k = 0; k <= n - 1; k++)
{
    pivotsMatrix[k, pivots[k]] = 1;
}
Matrix pa = Matrix.Multiply(pivotsMatrix,
source);
Matrix lu = Matrix.Multiply(lower, upper);
```

```
        if (pa != lu)
        {
            Console.WriteLine
                ("ERROR LUP_Decomposition postcondition:
                 " +
                 "invalid decomposition, logic is
                 incorrect");
            return;
        }
        if (correctStructure)
        {
            Console.WriteLine("--- LUP_Decomposition
            postcondition succeeded");
        }
}

[AspectDescription("Solve precondition")]
[AspectAction("%before %call *Matrix.Solve(Matrix,
Matrix) && %args(..)")]
public static void CheckSolvePrecondition(Matrix a,
Matrix b)
{
    // a should be square (n x n) matrix
    int aDepth = a.Depth;
    int aLength = a.Length;
    if (aDepth != aLength)
    {
        Console.WriteLine
            ("ERROR Solve precondition: source
             matrix is not square");
        return;
    }
    // a should be non-degenerate
    if (a.GetDeterminant() == 0)
    {
        Console.WriteLine
            ("ERROR Solve precondition: source
             matrix is degenerate");
        return;
    }
    // b should be (n x 1) vector
    int bDepth = b.Depth;
    int bLength = b.Length;
    if ((bDepth != aDepth) || (bLength != 1))
    {
```

```
            Console.WriteLine
                ("ERROR Solve precondition: " +
                "source vector has invalid
                dimensions");
        } else {
            Console.WriteLine("--- Solve precondition
            succeeded");
        }
}
[AspectDescription("Solve postcondition")]
[AspectAction("%after %call *Matrix.Solve(Matrix,
Matrix) && %args(..)")]
public static void CheckSolvePostcondition(Matrix
a, Matrix b)
{
    int n = a.Depth;
    // x should be (n x 1) vector
    Matrix x = (Matrix)RetValue;
    int xDepth = x.Depth;
    int xLength = x.Length;
    if ((xDepth != n) || (xLength != 1)) {
        Console.WriteLine
            ("ERROR Solve postcondition: " +
            "result vector has invalid
            dimensions");
        return;
    }
    // x: ax == b
    Matrix ax = Matrix.Multiply(a, x);
    if (ax.Array != b.Array) {
        Console.WriteLine
            ("ERROR Solve postcondition: " +
            "invalid logic, result is incorrect");
        return;
    }
}
[AspectDescription("GetDeterminant precondition")]
[AspectAction("%before %call *Matrix.
GetDeterminant")]
public static void
CheckGetDeterminantPrecondition()
{
    Matrix source = (Matrix)TargetObject;
    if (source.Depth != source.Length)
    {
```

```
            Console.WriteLine
                ("ERROR GetDeterminant precondition: "
                +
                "source matrix is not square");
        } else {
            Console.WriteLine("--- GetDeterminant
            precondition succeeded");
        }
    }
}
```

References

1. Safonov V. Aspect.NET: a new approach to aspect-oriented programming. *.NET Developer's Journal* 2003;(4):36–40.
2. Safonov V. Aspect.NET: concepts and architecture. *.NET Developer's Journal* 2004;(10):44–48.
3. Safonov V, Grigoryev D. Aspect.NET: aspect-oriented programming for Microsoft.NET in practice. *.NET Developer's Journal* 2005;(7):28–33.
4. Safonov V, et al. Aspect.NET: aspect-oriented toolkit for Microsoft.NET based on Phoenix and Whidbey. In: Knoop J, Skala V, Eds. *Proceedings of .NET Technologies 2006*, University of West Bohemia, Campus Bory, Pilsen, Czech Republic, 2006, pp. 19–34.
5. Safonov V, Grigoryev D. Aspect.NET: an aspect-oriented programming tool for Microsoft.NET. In: *Proceedings of the 110th Anniversary of Radio Invention*, St. Petersburg, Russia, 2006, pp. 11–21.
6. Safonov V, et al. Aspect.NET 2.1. Available at http://www.msdnaa.net/curriculum/ ?id=6801. Accessed April 24, 2007.
7. Microsoft Phoenix. Available at http://research.microsoft.com/phoenix.
8. Safonov V. TrustSPBU.NET: extending university courses on .NET, compilers, software engineering and OS by trustworthy computing content. *.NET Developer's Journal* 2007;(3):28–32.
9. Safonov V. SPBU.NET: principles and experience of teaching .NET, compilers, software engineering, and OS. *.NET Developer's Journal* 2006;(2):38–41.

10. AspectJ. Available at http://www.aspectj.org.

11. Safonov V. *Programming Languages and Methods for the Elbrus System*. Science Publishers, Moscow, 1989.

12. Aspect-oriented software development Web site. Available at http://aosd.net.

13. Kiczales G, et al. *Aspect-Oriented Programming*. Xerox Research Center, Palo Alto, CA, 1997.

14. Dijkstra EW. Go to statement considered harmful. *Communications of the ACM* 1968;11(3):147–148.

15. Bohm C, Jacopini G. Flow diagrams, Turing machines and languages with only two formation rules. *Communications of the ACM* 1966;9(5).

16. Dijkstra EW. Notes on structured programming. *EWD 249*. August 1969.

17. Wirth N. Program development by stepwise refinement. *Communications of the ACM* 1971;14(4):221–227.

18. Parnas D. A technique for software module specifications with examples. *Communications of the ACM* 1972;15(5):330–336.

19. Myers G. *Software Reliability: Principles and Practices*. Wiley, New York, 1976.

20. Liskov B, Guttag J. *Abstraction and Specification in Program Development*. MIT Press, Cambridge, MA, 1986.

21. Hoare CAR. Proof of correctness of data representations. *Acta Informatica* 1972;1(4):271–281.

22. Webster B. *Pitfalls of Object-Oriented Development*. M&T Books, New York, 1995.

23. Saltzer JH, Schroeder MD. The protection of information in computer systems. *Proceedings of the IEEE* 1975;63(9):1278–1308.

24. Iliffe JK. *Basic Machine Principles*. American Elsevier, New York, 1968.

25. Turchin VF. *REFAL-5 Programming Guide and Reference Manual*. New England Publishing Co., Holyoke, MA, 1989.

26. Pentkovsky V. *The Programming Language EL-76*. Science, Moscow, 1989 (in Russian).

27. Howard M, LeBlanc DC. *Writing Secure Code*, 2nd ed. Microsoft Press, Redmond, WA, 2002.

28. Elrad T, et al. Discussing aspects of AOP. *Communications of the ACM* 2001;44(10):33–38.

29. Hannemann J, Kiczales G. Overcoming the prevalent decomposition of legacy code. In *Proceedings of the Workshop on Advanced Separation of Concerns*, International Conference on Software Engineering, Toronto, Canada, 2001.

30. Schneider FB, Ed. *Trust in Cyberspace*. Committee on Information Systems Trustworthiness, National Research Council, Washington, DC, 1999.

31. Wikipedia article on trustworthy computing. Available at http://en.wikipedia.org/wiki/Trustworthy_Computing.

32. Mundie C, et al. Trustworthy computing. Microsoft white paper. October 2002. Available at http://www.microsoft.com/mscorp/twc/default.mspx.

33. Gates B. E-mail to Microsoft employees on trustworthy computing. January 17, 2002. Available at http://www.microsoft.com/mscorp/execmail/2002/01-17twc.asp.

34. Gates B. E-mail to Microsoft employees on trustworthy computing. July 18, 2002. Available at http://www.microsoft.com/mscorp/execmail/2002/07-18twc.asp.

35. Materials for Microsoft Academic Days on Trustworthy Computing. Microsoft, Redmond WA, April 7–9, 2006 (published on DVD).

36. Knowledge.NET. Available at http://www.knowledge-net.ru.

37. Wikipedia article on security. Available at http://en.wikipedia.org/wiki/Security.

38. Wikipedia article on computer security. Available at http://en.wikipedia.org/wiki/Computer_Security.

39. Microsoft FxCop Web page. Available at http://www.gotdotnet.com/team/fxcop/.

40. Howard M, Lipner S. *The Security Development Lifecycle*. Microsoft Press, Redmond, WA, 2006.

41. Stoneburner GH, et al. Engineering principles for information technology security (a baseline for achieving security). Revision A. *NIST Special Publication 800–27 Rev A*. June 2004.

42. Payne SC. A guide to security metrics. In *SANS Security Essentials GSEC Practical Assignments Version 1.2e*. SANS Institute, Bethesda, MD, 2007.

43. Swiderski F, Snyder W. *Threat Modeling*. Microsoft Press, Redmond, WA, 2004.

44. Oehlert P. Violating assumptions with fuzzing. *IEEE Security and Privacy* 2005;1(2):58–62.

45. Myers G. *The art of Software Testing*. Wiley-Interscience, New York, 1979.

46. Johnson S. Lint, a C program checker. *Computer Science Technical Report 65*. Bell Laboratories, Murray Hill, NJ, December 1977.

47. Pincus J. Steering the pyramides: tools, technology and process in engineering at Microsoft. Available at http://www.research.microsoft.com/users/jpincus/icsm.ppt.

48. Wikipedia article on privacy. Available at http://en.wikipedia.org/wiki/Privacy.

49. Privacy at Microsoft. March 2005. Available at http://www.microsoft.com/mscorp/twc/privacyatmicrosoft.mspx.

50. Microsoft SmartScreen: spam filtering. Available at http://www.microsoft.com/protect/yourself/email/spam.mspx.

51. Microsoft AuthentiCode reference guide. Available at http://www.microsoft.com/technet/archive/security/topics/secaps/authcode.mspx.

52. Institute of Electrical and Electronics Engineers (IEEE). Available at: http://www.ieee.org.

53. Wikipedia article on mean time between failure (MTBF). Available at http://en.wikipedia.org/wiki/MTBF.

54. Rosenberg L, Hammer T, Shaw J. *Software Metrics and Reliability*. NASA Software Assurance Technology Center, Greenbelt, MD, 1998.

55. Tseytin GS. On the relationship between mathematical and ordinary thinking. *Technicheskaya Kibernetika* 1987(2);193–196 (in Russian).

56. Russian computer whizzes to write Sun programs. *San Francisco Chronicle*, September 2, 1992.

57. ECMA-334: C# language specification, 4th ed. June 2006. Available at http://www.ecma-international.com.

58. ECMA-335: common language infrastructure, partitions 1 to 6, 4th ed. June 2006. Available at http://www.ecma-international.com.

59. Microsoft.NET. Available at http://msdn2.microsoft.com/en-us/netframework/default.aspx.

60. 60. SSCLI/Rotor. Available at http://research.microsoft.com/sscli.

61. Mono. Available at http://www.mono-project.com.

62. Eiffel for .NET. Available at http://archive.eiffel.com/doc/manuals/technology/dotnet/eiffelsharp/.

63. Zonnon for .NET: a language and compiler experiment. Available at http://www.springerlink.com/index/uuhl0rx74tuytm8l.pdf.

64. Spec#. Available at http://research.microsoft.com/specsharp.

65. Hoare CAR. The verifying compiler: a grand challenge for computing research. 2004. Available at http://www.csl.sri.com/users/shankar/GC04/hoare-compiler.pdf.

66. Meyer B. *Object-Oriented Software Construction*. Prentice Hall, Englewood Cliffs, NJ, 1988.

67. Detlefs D, Nelson G, Saxe JB. Simplify: a theorem prover for program checking. *Technical Report HPL-2003-148*. HP Labs, Palo Alto, CA, 2003. Available at http://citeseer.ist.psu.edu/detlefs03simplify.html.

68. Meier JD, Mackman A, Wastell B, Bansode P, Bijwe C. Security guidelines: .NET Framework 2.0. October 2005. Available at https://buildsecurityin.us-cert.gov/daisy/bsi/87/version/15/part/4/data/SwA%.

69. Dr. Dobb's .NET 3.0 RoadShow Web site. Available at http://searchvb.techtarget.com/originalContent/0,289142,sid8_gci1225694,00.html.

70. Safonov V. *Introduction to Java Technology*. Science Publishers, St. Petersburg, Russia, 2002 (in Russian).

71. Java security overview. Available at http://java.sun.com/developer/technicalArticles/Security/whitepaper/index.html.

72. Wasp for Java. Available at http://www.waspsoft.com/waspj.html.

73. Dijkstra EW. The structure of the "THE" multiprogramming system. *Communications of the ACM* 1968;11(5):341–346.

74. Koster CH. *Using the CDL Compiler Compiler*. Lecture Notes in Computer Science, Vol. 21. Springer-Verlag, Berlin, 1977.

75. Tseytin GS. Towards assembly programming. *Programmirovanie* 1990;(1) (in Russian).

76. Fouxman AL. *Technological Aspects of Software Systems Development*. Statistics Publishers, Moscow, 1979 (in Russian).

77. HyperJ. Available at http://www.research.ibm.com/hyperspace/HyperJ/HyperJ.htm.

78. Wikipedia article on aspect. Available at http://en.wikipedia.org/wiki/Aspect.

79. Weave.NET. Available at http://www.dsg.cs.tcd.ie/dynamic/?category_id=-26.

80. Laddad R. AspectJ in action. Practical aspect-oriented programming. Manning Publications, Greenwich, CT, 2003.

81. AspectJ development tools (AJDT) Web site. Available at http://eclipse.org/ajdt.

82. Apache Ant. Available at http://ant.apache.org.

83. AspectWerkz. Available at http://aspectwerkz.copehaus.org/.

84. Dijkstra EW. On the role of scientific thought. EWD 447.1974. Available at http://www.cs.utexas.edu/users/EWD/ewd04xx/EWD447.PDF.

85. IBM multi-dimensional separation of concerns. Available at http://www.research.ibm.com/hyperspace/index.htm.

86. HyperJ home Web page. Available at http://www.alphaworks.ibm.com/tech/hyperj.

87. IBM's subject-oriented programming Web page. Available at http://www.research.ibm.com/sop/.

88. Lieberherr K. *Adaptive Object-Oriented Software: The Demeter Method with Propagation Patterns*. PWS Publishing Company, Boston, MA, 1996.

89. Kroha P. Adaptive programming. Presented at DATACON'2004. Available at http://www.datakon.cz/datakon04/d04_it_kroha.pdf (in Russian).

90. Bergmans L, Aksit M. Composing multiple concerns using composition filters. Available at http://wwwtrese.cs.utwente.nl/.

91. Robillard M, Murphy G. Representing concerns in source code. *ACM Transactions on Software Engineering and Methodology* 2007;16(1).

92. Simonyi C. Intentional programming: innovation in the legacy age. 1996. Available at http://citeseer.ist.psu.edu/simonyi96intentional.html.

93. Czarnetski K, Eisenecker U. *Generative Programming: Methods, Tools and Applications*. Addison-Wesley, Reading, MA, 2000.

94. Wikipedia article on aspect-oriented programming. Available at http://en.wikipedia.org/wiki/Aspect-oriented_programming.

95. JBoss AOP Web site. Available at http://labs.jboss.com/portal/jbossaop.

96. Seasar Web site. Available at http://en.wikipedia.org/wiki/Seasar.

97. CaesarJ Web site. Available at http://www.caesarj.org/.

98. JAC Web site. Available at http://jac.objectweb.org/.

99. Dynaop Web site. Available at http://dynaop.dev.java.net/.

100. Javassist Web page. Available at http://www.csg.is.titech.ac.jp/~chiba/javassist/.

101. LogicAJ Web page. Available at http://roots.iai.uni-bonn.de/research/logicaj.

102. Reflex Web site, Available at http://www.pleiad.doc.tichile.cl/research/software/reflex.

103. JMangler Web site. Available at http://roots.iai.uni-bonn.de/research/jmangler.

104. Spring Framework Web site. Available at http://www.springframework.org/.

105. LOOM.NET Web pages. Available at http://www.rapier-loom.net/.

106. AspectDNG Web pages. Available at http://sourceforge.net/projects/aspectdng/.

107. Aspect# Web pages. Available at http://www.castleproject.org/aspectsharp/.

108. PostSharp Web pages. Available at http://www.postsharp.org/.

109. DotSpect Web pages. Available at http://dotspect.tigris.org/.

110. Encase Web pages. Available at http://theagiledeveloper.com/articles/Encase.aspx.

111. Compose* Web pages. Available at http://composestar.sourceforge.net/.

112. Seasar.NET Web pages. Available at http://www.seasar.org/en/dotnet/.

113. Spring.NET Framework Web pages. Available at http://www.springframework. net/.

114. Puzzle.NET NAspect Web pages. Available at http://www.puzzleframework.com/ forum/forum.aspx?Forum=24.

115. Wicca and Phx.Morph Web site. Available at http://www.cs.columbia. edu/~eaddy/wicca.

116. Microsoft Managed Debugger (mdbg) Web pages. Available at http://msdn. microsoft.com/msdntv/episode.aspx?xml=episodes/en/20060302clrjs/manifest. xml.

117. Zhuk J. *Integration-Ready Architecture and Design*. Cambridge University Press, Cambridge, 2004.

118. Professor Vladimir Safonov's professional biography at Microsoft Faculty Connection Web site. Available at http://www.microsoft.com/education/ facultyconnection/articles/articledetails.aspx?cid=445.

119. IEEE Distinguished Visitor's Program, 2007–2009, Vladimir Safonov. Available at http://www.computer.org/portal/site/ieeecs/menuitem.c5efb9b8ade9096b 8a9ca0108bcd45f3/index.jsp?&pName=ieeecs_level1&path=ieeecs/Communities/ chapter/DVP&file=safonov.xml&xsl=generic.xsl&.

120. Rippamonti A. Integrazióne di meccanismi di contròllo dégli accèssi Single Sign-On in Service-Oriented Architecture con Aspect-Oriented Programming. Graduate thesis, Universita degli Studi di Milano, Milan, Italy, 2007 (in Italian).

121. Barros MB. Programação Orientada a Aspectos com .NET. *.NET Magazine (Brazil)* 2007;(45).

122. Filman RE, Elrad T, Clarke S, Aksit M. *Aspect-Oriented Software Development*. Addison-Wesley, Reading, MA, 2005.

123. Security Annotation Framework Web site. Available at http://safr.sourceforge. net/resources.html.

124. Huang M, Wang C, Zhang L. Towards a reusable and generic security aspect library. Beijing Institute of System Engineering, Beijing, China, 2004. Available at http://www.cs.kuleuven.ac.be/~distrinet/events/aosdsec/AOSDSEC04_Minwell_ Huang.pdf.

125. Acegi Security Web site. Available at http://acegisecurity.org.

126. Dijkstra EW. *Cooperating Sequential Processes*. Technological University, Eindhoven, The Netherlands, September 1965. Reprinted in *Programming Languages*, F. Genuys, Ed. Academic Press, New York, 1968, pp. 43–112.

127. Multi-core computing. Course at Rice University. Fall 2006. Available at http:// www.cs.rice.edu/~johnmc/comp522/info.html.

128. Sun Multithreaded programming guide. Available at http://docsun.cites.uiuc.edu/ sun_docs/C/solaris_9/SUNWdev/MTP/toc.html.

129. Azmi K. Multi-core applications: programming and debugging. Mentor Graphics white paper. Available at http://www.embeddedstar.com/technicalpapers/content/ m/embedded2267.html.

130. Gonzales A. Speculative threading: creating new methods of thread-level parallelization. *Technology@Intel*, December 2005.

131. License management for Java Web applications using aspects. Available at http://manoharviswanathan.com/blog/tech/license-management-for-java-web-applications-using-aspects/.

132. Falcarin P, Baldi M, Mazzocchi D. Software tampering detection using AOP and mobile code. Available at http://www.cs.kuleuven.ac.be/~distrinet/events/aosdsec/AOSDSEC04_Paolo_Falcarin.pdf.

133. Bostroem G. Database encryption as an aspect. Available at http://www.csc.com/aboutus/leadingedgeforum/knowledgelibrary/uploads/SOA%20Security%20Technologies%20-%20AWilson.pdf.

134. Binkley D, Ceccato M, Harman M, Ricca F, Tonella P. Tool-supported refactoring of existing object-oriented code into aspects. *IEEE Transactions on Software Engineering* 2006;32(9):698–717.

135. Meyer B. *Eiffel: The Language*. Prentice Hall, Upper Saddle River, NJ, 1992.

136. Design by contract and Eiffel Web pages. Available at http://www.eiffel.com.

137. Boehm B. *Software Engineering Economics*. Prentice Hall, Englewood Cliffs, NJ, 1981.

138. Roth A. Using the ICED-T model to test subjective software qualities. Presented at the International Conference on Software Testing, Analysis and Review, San Jose, CA, November 1–5, 1999.

139. Haag S, Raja MK, Schkade LL. Quality function deployment usage in software development. *Communications of the ACM* 1996;39(1):42–49.

140. Manifesto for Agile software development. Available at http://www.agilemanifesto.org/.

141. Extreme Programming Web pages. Available at http://www.extremeprogramming.org/.

142. Rising L, Janoff NS. The scrum software development process for small teams. *IEEE Software*, 2000;(4):2–8.

143. Safonov VO. Microsoft.NET architecture and the C# language. Undergraduate university course curriculum. Available at http://www.msdnaa.net/curriculum/?id=5911.

144. Safonov VO. Compiler development. Graduate university course curriculum. Available at http://www.msdnaa.net/curriculum/?id=5938.

145. Safonov VO. Software engineering. Graduate university course curriculum. Available at http://www.msdnaa.net/curriculum/?id=5983.

146. Safonov VO. Operating systems and networking. Undergraduate university course curriculum. Available at http://www.msdnaa.net/curriculum/?id=6006.

147. Safonov VO. Programming for Microsoft.NET. Undergraduate university seminar curriculum. Available at http://www.msdnaa.net/curriculum/?id=6243.

148. Safonov VO. Compiler development. Graduate university seminar curriculum. Available at http://www.msdnaa.net/curriculum/?id=6244.

149. Safonov VO. Secure software engineering. Undergraduate university course curriculum. Available at http://www.msdnaa.net/curriculum/?id=6753. Accessed February 2007.

150. Safonov VO. Method and apparatus for compiler symbol table organization with no lookup in semantic analysis. U.S. patent 5,701,490. December 23, 1997.

151. Safonov VO. Method and apparatus for efficient evaluation of semantic attributes in LALR parsing. U.S. patent 5,892,951. April 6, 1999.

152. Safonov VO. Method and apparatus for record fields usage checking at compile time. U.S. patent 5,758,163. May 26, 1998.

153. Safonov VO. TIP technology and its application to SPARCompiler Pascal. U.S. patent 6,305,011. October 16, 2001.

154. Shaw M, Ed. *ALPHARD: Form and Content.* Springer-Verlag, New York, 1981.

155. McConnell S. *Microsoft Software Product Survival Guide.* Microsoft Press, Redmond, WA, 1997.

156. Safonov VO. The Java programming language. Undergraduate university course curriculum. Available at http://ru.sun.com/research/teachingmaterials.html (in Russian).

157. Safonov VO. Java technology. Undergraduate university seminar curriculum. Available at http://ru.sun.com/research/teachinggrants.html (in Russian).

158. Silbershatz A, Galvin P, Gagne G. *Operating System Concepts*, 6th ed. Wiley, New York, 2001.

159. Tanenbaum A. *Operating Systems. Design and Implementation*, 3rd ed. Prentice Hall, Upper Saddle River, NJ, 2006.

160. Tsichritzis D, Bernstein PA. *Operating Systems.* Wiley, New York, 1974.

161. Developing operating systems for BESM-6. Available at http://www.computer-museum.ru/histsoft/osbesm6.htm (in Russian).

162. Secure UML. Available at http://www.kirya.net/articles/secure-uml-setup-on-debian/.

Index